Knowledge Construction in Late Antiquity

Trends in Classics – Supplementary Volumes

Edited by
Franco Montanari and Antonios Rengakos

Associate Editors
Stavros Frangoulidis · Fausto Montana · Lara Pagani
Serena Perrone · Evina Sistakou · Christos Tsagalis

Scientific Committee
Alberto Bernabé · Margarethe Billerbeck
Claude Calame · Kathleen Coleman · Jonas Grethlein
Philip R. Hardie · Stephen J. Harrison · Stephen Hinds
Richard Hunter · Giuseppe Mastromarco
Gregory Nagy · Theodore D. Papanghelis
Giusto Picone · Alessandro Schiesaro
Tim Whitmarsh · Bernhard Zimmermann

Volume 142

Knowledge Construction in Late Antiquity

Edited by
Monika Amsler

DE GRUYTER

The open access version and prepress of this publication has been funded by the Swiss National Science Foundation.

ISBN 978-3-11-162801-1
e-ISBN (PDF) 978-3-11-101031-1
e-ISBN (EPUB) 978-3-11-101104-2
ISSN 1868-4785
DOI https://doi.org/10.1515/9783111010311

This work is licensed under the Creative Commons Attribution 4.0 International License. For details go to https://creativecommons.org/licenses/by/4.0/.

Creative Commons license terms for re-use do not apply to any content (such as graphs, figures, photos, excerpts, etc.) not original to the Open Access publication and further permission may be required from the rights holder. The obligation to research and clear permission lies solely with the party re-using the material.

Library of Congress Control Number: 2023932368

Bibliographic information published by the Deutsche Nationalbibliothek
The Deutsche Nationalbibliothek lists this publication in the Deutsche Nationalbibliografie; detailed bibliographic data are available on the internet at http://dnb.dnb.de.

© 2024 with the author(s), editing © 2024 Monika Amsler,
published by Walter de Gruyter GmbH, Berlin/Boston.
This volume is text- and page-identical with the hardback published in 2023.
This book is published with open access at www.degruyter.com.

Editorial Office: Alessia Ferreccio and Katerina Zianna
Logo: Christopher Schneider, Laufen

www.degruyter.com

Acknowledgements

This volume is the result of a workshop that was supposed to take place at the University of Maryland in May 2020. As can easily be guessed, the workshop had to be cancelled due to the COVID-19 pandemic. It finally took place online in January 2021. I thank professors Antoine Borrut and Hayim Lapin for their support in the different organization and reorganization processes, and the Meyerhoff Center for Jewish Studies for the financial support. The online workshop was graciously facilitated by Mikol Bailey, who was a graduate student at the University of Maryland at the time. I am grateful to the series editors for accepting the volume as a Trends in Classics—Supplementary Volume, and especially to Antonios Rengakos for his speedy and patient replies to so many questions.

The Swiss National Scientific Foundation is to be thanked for approving the project who allowed me to spend time at the University of Maryland (P2ZHP1_181576), and for funding the open access publication of the present volume.

Finally, I would like my colleagues who contributed to this book — thank you for showing up to the workshop, although it took place online and during a pandemic, and for entrusting me, to most of you a total stranger at this point, with your marvelous work!

Monika Amsler

Contents

Acknowledgements —— V
List of Figures and Tables —— IX

Monika Amsler
Introduction: Knowledge Construction in Late Antiquity —— 1

Daniel Picus
Better Left Unread: Rabbinic Interpretations of Prophetic Scrolls —— 29

Jeremiah Coogan
Tabular Thinking in Late Ancient Palestine: Instrumentality, Work, and the Construction of Knowledge —— 57

Elizabeth Mattingly Conner
Leading Sources of Knowledge at the Monastery: Isidore of Pelusium —— 83

Rebecca Stephens Falcasantos
Fabricating Monstrosity: Archival Manipulation and the Production of Orthodoxy in Socrates of Constantinople's *Ecclesiastical History* —— 105

Nicola Reggiani
Knowledge Construction in Progress: From Paratext to Marginal Annotations in the Greek Medical Papyri —— 133

Courtney A. Roby
Learning from Mistakes: Constructing Knowledge in Late Antique Mathematical Texts —— 155

Monika Amsler
The "Poetic Itch" and Numerical Maxims in the Talmud – An Inquiry into Factors of Knowledge Construction —— 189

Lillian I. Larsen
Re-scaffolding a 'Missing Chapter' —— 219

Robert Edwards
Grammar in the School of Diodore of Tarsus: An Institutional Context for the Transfer of Exegetical Knowledge —— 257

List of Contributors —— 283
General Index —— 285
Index Locorum —— 293

List of Figures and Tables

Fig. 1: BML Plut. 70.7, f. 232v. Chapter title in left column is rubricated. —— **130**
Fig. 2: BML Plut. 70.7, f. 249v. Chapter title in right column is rubricated. —— **131**
Fig. 3: BML Plut. 70.7, f. 263v. —— **132**
Fig. 4: "Granary" diagram from *P. Math.*, problem 01 (after Bagnall/Jones). —— **165**
Fig. 5a-b: Figures 5a and 5b: Two different approaches to diagrammatic problem-solving, author's drawing after van Garderen *et al.* 2013. —— **167**
Fig. 6: Schematic depiction of the features of a torus from Hero *Metrica* II.13. —— **173**
Fig. 7: Stereometrica text and images from Vat. gr. 215, fol. 9r. —— **177**
Fig. 8: Greek Alphabet, Monastery of Epiphanius (O.MMA. 12.180.107). —— **232**
Fig. 9: Writing Exercise, Monastery of Epiphanius (O.MMA.14.1.188). —— **233**
Fig. 10: Alphabets and Syllabary, Beni Hasan (Newberry 1893, Pl. XXV) © Universitätsbibliothek Heidelberg. —— **237**
Fig. 11: Days of the Week, Monastery of Epiphanius (O.MMA. 14.1.214). —— **241**
Fig. 12: *Iliad* 1.1–2 Monastery of Epiphanius (O.MMA 14.1.139). —— **245**
Fig. 13: Sentences of Menander, Monastery of Epiphanius (O.MMA. 14.1.210). —— **246**
Fig. 14a-b: Proverbs and Saying, Monastery of Epiphanius (Cairo 44674.118 verso/recto; Photo Courtesy of K. Brown). —— **247**

Tab. 1: Mixed Alphabets, Thebes AM 21 (C.O. 16). —— **234**
Tab. 2: Mixed Alphabets, Beni Hasan. —— **235**
Tab. 3: Coptic Syllabary, The Fayyum (T.Mich. inv. N. 765). —— **239**

Monika Amsler
Introduction: Knowledge Construction in Late Antiquity

Social studies of the sciences have long analyzed and exposed the constructed nature of knowledge. Pioneering studies of research in laboratories conducted by eminent scholars such as Karin Knorr Cetina, Bruno Latour, and Steve Woolgar have identified many factors that affect the processes by which scientific results are generated and interpreted.[1] The factors they found dictating *what* knowledge is being produced, and *how*, were money, training and curriculum, location and infrastructure, biography-based knowledge and talent, and coincidence.

The method adopted by these groundbreaking studies has since led to the establishment of the "sociology of science."[2] In subsequent years, the field has left the realm of the laboratory to analyze all kinds of spaces in which forms of knowledge are being produced. Yet, unintentionally, the focus shifted from the interactions between nonhuman and human actors, which was a central part of Knorr Cetina's, and Latour and Woolgar's, study of knowledge construction in the laboratory, to an almost exclusive focus on human agency. This led to criticism by said founding scholars, which in turn led to the development of "practice theories" that place a distinct focus on the role played by nonhuman factors in the construction of knowledge.[3] Ultimately, this renewed focus on the object led to a material turn in the humanities, which came to be interested in material culture. As the compound terminology suggests, material culture still focuses predominantly on human culture, yet it does so by positing a distinct relationship between (social) culture and material.[4] Among other things, this interest moved archaeology out of the shadow of text and accorded the field a standing in its own right. Nowadays, however, the term "materiality" is preferred over "cultural studies," in an attempt to "move away from the idea of a separation between material and cultural domains, and to accommodate the material form of things."[5]

We find a good example of materiality thinking in Latour's discussion of the *Berliner Schlüssel*, the Berlin key. Latour depicts this special key as a disciplinarian, since it can only be retrieved by the resident of an apartment building after

---

1 See Latour/Woolgar 1979; Knorr Cetina 1981.
2 See Knorr Cetina/Mulkay 1983.
3 E.g., Knorr Cetina *et al.* 2001; Latour 1999; 2007.
4 Hicks 2010, 26.
5 Hicks 2010, 74.

∂ Open Access. © 2023 Monika Amsler, published by De Gruyter. This work is licensed under the Creative Commons Attribution 4.0 International License.
https://doi.org/10.1515/9783111010311-001

he has locked the door.⁶ As a result, the key forces residents to lock the house and imposes a precaution against burglaries. By way of mass production, the key, although the product of human invention, skill, and ethics, emancipates and, seemingly independently, begins to interfere in and shape the local community. Jennifer Knust has applied these insights to a type of materiality that is somewhat closer to the topic of knowledge construction in late antiquity than is the Berlin key: New Testament manuscripts.⁷ As she points out, the mix and match of works transmitted (or not) in single manuscripts shaped the cognitive resources of individuals and communities. Similarly, the system of rows for numeric cross-referencing that Eusebius adapted for the Gospels has, as a cognitive tool, shaped the reading of these four separate books as a coherent canon.⁸ Knowledge construction and knowledge practice, these studies have shown, cannot be separated from the material with which (or, more precisely, in which) knowledge is conceived and transmitted.

The sheer idea to investigate what factors constructed knowledge in a laboratory, rather than just to assume that laboratories produced some sort of independent and pure knowledge, resulted from the linguistic turn in the Humanities that unearthed the social constructedness of what it means to "know." The linguistic turn ultimately also paved the way for critical theories and New Historicism, which, together with the material turn, merged in theories of thingness that draw from "social theories of emotion and affect."⁹ These theoretical momenta have shaped the historiography of late antiquity, which, as a conceptual chronological framework, is equally recent and has generated research foci such as "knowledge production" or "objects of knowledge."¹⁰

Somewhat parallel to these developments, epistemology has become another field of research in the study of late antiquity. Multiple monographs, collected volumes, and essays have been devoted to topics such as, for example, the social and political impact of the Roman Empire on the formation of knowledge, its order, and its encyclopedic expansion.¹¹ Other issues that have been addressed concern knowledge building and transmission in terms of "finding," "inheriting," or

---

6 Latour 1991.
7 Knust 2017.
8 See Crawford 2019, 96–121; Coogan, this volume.
9 Kotrosits 2020, 3. As she further points out, these theories themselves "emerged out of a kind of frustration or weariness with the linguistic turn, of which these same fields were prime propagators" (3).
10 On the history of the concept of late antiquity, see Martin 2005.
11 E.g., Formisano 2013; König/Whitmarsh 2007; Lehmhaus 2015.

"borrowing";[12] structures and strategies of knowledge;[13] applicability;[14] the development or attribution of authority by way of knowledge production;[15] sociological aspects of knowledge;[16] the practical negotiation of knowledge as "knowing";[17] and the cross-fertilization of knowledge.[18] In his monograph *What Did the Romans Know?*, Daryn Lehoux engages with implicit taxonomies that regulate credibility and incredibility (i.e., Why did the ancients believe that garlic was magnetic?), and Michael Chin has worked on the symmetry between grammar, education, and the cosmic order.[19] Obviously, an unprecedented array of research has been devoted to questions of how knowledge was gathered, weighted, produced, consumed, and distributed.

With a knowledge construction framework, the present volume offers ways of thinking about knowledge that combine insights from material culture and materiality studies with those gained from studies of late-antique epistemology. Knowledge will be presented as attached to and transmitted by objects. But knowledge construction goes even a bit further in that it encompasses the specific task of "knowledge production," the haptic "knowledge manufacture," and the social factors that regulate and weigh forms of knowledge.[20] Indeed, benefiting from the momentum of these issues and theories in the study of late antiquity in recent years, scholars are now able to ask questions about issues including the use of material, economic aspects of availability and access to material, the social incentives for writing, the author's or artist's education, as well as the time, space, and budget that allowed or impeded the production of a certain type of knowledge. All these aspects are prerequisites for the construction of knowledge. They shape a text or another epistemological object not regarding content and genre but also regarding its morphological appearance. Like epistemological factors, material factors can limit or promote the development of knowledge,

---

12 E.g., Althoff *et al.* 2019.
13 E.g., Doody *et al.* 2012; for a bibliographical essay on technical and science literature in Greco-Roman antiquity, see Taub 2017, 149–156.
14 E.g., Formisano/van der Eijk 2017.
15 E.g., Berkovitz/Letteney 2018; König/Woolf 2017; Taub/Doody 2009.
16 E.g., Wissa 2017.
17 E.g., Chin/Vidas 2015.
18 E.g., Burnett/Mantas-Espana 2014.
19 See Lehoux 2012; Chin 2008; 2015; and Stefaniw 2018.
20 On knowledge production, see Stefaniw 2018; on knowledge manufacture, see, e.g., Lundhaug/Lied 2017. They succinctly address the challenges that rise from negotiating templates of redaction criticism as they evolved around texts with ongoing religious reception histories and the actual manufacture of texts.

sometimes also urging creative solutions due to constraint. Coincidence and chance play an indeterminable role in this and point to the importance of the consideration of contingent factors in knowledge construction, such as imagination, projection, misconception, and error, any or all of which may ultimately serve as the basis for innovation.

As this overview has shown, knowledge remains associated with the study of a given text as the intellectual output identified as knowledge. Only a few studies have started to make the transmitting object the center of attention, and not necessarily with respect to how these media help expand, shape, and confine knowledge.[21] The work of Andrew Riggsby, Matthew Crawford, and Jeremiah Coogan has broken ground in that regard by looking at cognitive tools that help bundle disparate data. Riggsby has addressed decisive tools in the construction of knowledge, such as lists, tables, maps, and weights and measures.[22] Crawford has shown how Eusebius's use of tables to organize literary works has impacted a whole religious tradition.[23] Coogan has drawn attention to the innovative and versatile character of certain seemingly simple paratextual features such as the table of contents, the recipe book, or simply the row as it appears in documents or tables.[24] Much work remains to be done in this regard, and many cognitive tools still need to be recognized as such. The focus could still be expanded, for example, to view the materiality of texts itself as epistemic objects rather than reduce them to mere transmitters of knowledge, and to ask about the disciplinary function (remember the Berlin key!) of basic writing materials such as tablets, scraps, styluses and their contribution to the very particular structure of late-antique knowledge.

Indeed, the field seems to move gradually in a direction in which questions become of interest that probably seemed too basic to prior scholars. How, for example, did the habit of writing primarily on wooden tablets, pottery shards (ostraca), or papyrus scraps shape the texts to which we can often access only through much later, polished manuscripts? Can the original shapes of the physical material involved in a text's composition still be detected? How did the meager space on such limiting writing surfaces allow for the production of late antiquity's bulky volumes?[25] Indeed, thinking about knowledge construction in the

---

[21] E.g., Kotrosits 2020; Miller 2009.
[22] Riggsby 2019.
[23] Crawford 2019.
[24] See Coogan 2021a; 2021b; and this volume.
[25] Questions regarding a material surface's influence on a given text's reception have received more consideration; see Kehnel/Panagiotopoulos 2015.

case of bulky volumes means moving beyond contending simply with the fact that the material was collected and arranged. It would imply asking how people collected literary excerpts or information, where and how they acquired the skills to collect them, how they stored and managed their data, and what systems they had implemented for data retrieval. How did the arrangement proceed? How was it planned? Who arranged the material, and who sponsored all this labor? Who was interested in a bulky volume, and was it actually read? How and where did people learn to write or compile books? The answers to these questions must be inferred from material finds and the texts themselves — unfortunately, there is no ancient account that moves beyond collecting and arranging.[26] Drafts, so valuable for this particular purpose, did not survive: the material surfaces of drafts were reused or left to perish because they no longer mattered next to the fair copy.

1 What Makes Knowledge: Data and Information

Knowledge construction obviously has to do with processes of collecting, sorting, arranging, and ultimately using, whether we can describe these processes or not, and whether they are mechanized or not. What is being collected has come to be referred to as "data" in the past century. Data can then be arranged into information, which is then used as knowledge. Knowledge, again, combined with experience, will lead to wisdom. This process has been transferred into a hierarchy, the hierarchy of knowledge. Generally depicted in the form of a triangle, the hierarchy suggests a succession of data, information, knowledge, and wisdom, with data being placed at the large bottom of the triangle and wisdom at the narrow top.[27] There is much to be learned about how we are trained to think about knowledge production through this graphic hierarchization: It assumes a large quantity of data against a much smaller amount of wisdom and an increasing contraction of data through processes of generating information, knowledge, and, finally, wisdom. Alas, the pyramid ultimately devalorizes data and data collection and its arrangement into information. These processes may indeed seem to be less labor-intensive when aided by contemporary computer technology, but they were time-consuming and effortful in antiquity and required a lot of knowledge, wisdom even, to do so.

---

26 See the summary in Blair 2010, 14–24; Dorandi 2007 (2017).
27 E.g., https://www.ontotext.com/knowledgehub/fundamentals/dikw-pyramid/, accessed 18 August 2021.

Although we need not agree with this visual translation of data processing, it helps raise questions about how people in late antiquity hierarchized stages of knowledge construction. As has already been mentioned, drafts were not much appreciated in late antiquity and thus were reused, washed off, or simply left to disintegrate. It appears that an aesthetic and material hierarchy regarding the process of text production was in play. Certain texts were associated with a particular format, like the Torah with a scroll, for instance.[28] If so, what was the status of tablets, ostraca, even rotuli that contained only an excerpt of a text or a text in its preliminary stages? Were these artifacts and texts considered to be proper writings or of a different quality, maybe even "oral"? Thinking along ways of knowledge hierarchization may further point to imbalances where the historian sees knowledge or wisdom in places where the ancients saw data or information, and vice versa.

Current definitions and demarcations of data, information, and knowledge vary. Wisdom is defined as a form of knowledge that is unteachable, or at least unmanageable by information systems, since it consists of personal experience and skill rather than just data and information. Therefore, wisdom is often omitted from the discussions of knowledge hierarchies, and I similarly will exclude it here. Indeed, the more recent the definitions of the components of the pyramid are, the more they are marked by electronic computations, which focus predominantly and, in light of the hierarchy, somewhat paradoxically on the complex potential of data.[29] Simpler and somewhat older definitions may therefore be more useful for historical purposes. In these discussions, data can be anything between signs and "elementary descriptions of things, events, activities, and transactions."[30] Information is defined as organized data that is supposed to convey some overriding meaning. Knowledge, in turn, is said to consist of data *and* information, that is, accumulated learning, which, together with experience, can be applied to make decisions, identify and solve problems.[31] In terms of knowledge construction, these demarcations can be used fruitfully in thinking about a text's formation and purpose. Was the text meant to provide information, or was it a collection of data? How do the choices made in turning data into information reflect prior knowledge and strategies of data processing qua education?

---

28 See Picus, this volume.
29 See Braf 2002, 75.
30 Braf 2002, 74.
31 See Braf 2002, 74. I picked what seemed to be the most useful definitions for the present purpose from her summary of (often overlapping) definitions by prior scholars.

I would like to illustrate how these demarcations could be used with a brief example from the Babylonian Talmud's tractate Shabbat. The work, which dates to the fifth or sixth century CE, is a compilation of earlier traditions, like most, if not all, late-antique works of this size.[32] The scholarly consensus tends to attribute the formation of this work to oral transmission, although the use of tablets and other writing material as occasional tools for knowledge preservation has been acknowledged.[33] The section I would like to discuss in terms of data, information, and knowledge falls, at least to some extent, outside of this discussion because it is one of the rare instances in which the use of a written document is explicitly mentioned.

According to the text itself, then, what is discussed is an astrological hemerology "found in Joshua b. Levi's notebook" (Aramaic *pinkas* from Greek *pinax*). It is a homogenous list that first discusses the influence of the stellar constellation on a person born on a certain day of the week before turning to the hours of the day. As it appears now in the Talmud, however, it seems that the list has been tampered with for the sake of turning its data into information: the hemerology is periodically interrupted by quotations. These interferences in the list show that someone considered the information provided by the list as mere data that needed reconfiguration. The list, which in itself is already data turned into information, is brought into conversation with information derived from personal experience, weaving both together into knowledge that would serve future decision-making on an even more complex basis than the list itself attempted to do. In the following annotated extract from this passage, the original list is rendered in *italics*, insertions are in Roman, and the compilers' comments are underlined.

> *Behold, one who [is born] on the first [day] of the week, will be a man without one [thing] in him.* What is "without one thing in him"? [What] if one would say "without one virtue"?
> But Rav Ashi said: "I was [born] on [the] first day of the week! Rather, [the text should read] 'but without one evil [thing in him]!'"
> But Rav Ashi said: "I and Dimi bar Kakuzta were [both born] on the first [day] of the week. I am a king, [yet] he is the head of thieves! Rather [it means that the person will be] entirely good or entirely evil."

---

32 The date is debated, some scholars placing the closing date of the work into the first half of the eighth century CE. Notwithstanding minor changes, which are unavoidable in a manual copying and transmission process, I believe that the work was finished during the period indicated above and in a much more concise process than assumed up until now (see my forthcoming monograph).
33 See Jaffee 2001, 128–140.

> One who is born on the second day of the week will be a quarrelsome man. What is the reason? Because the waters were divided on it [the second day].
> One who is born on the third day of the week will be a rich man; he will [also] be a fornicating [man]. What is the reason? Because the plants were created on the [third] day ... (b. Shabb. 156a)[34]

If the hemerology and the quotations are both considered data, then the information they each transmit on their own is that who one will become depends on which day of the week one was born. Together, however, they teach that how the lot has to be interpreted depends on additional data such as personal experience and observation. By turning data into information that appeals to the learners' better judgement, knowledge is generated. Additionally, both sets of data, hemerology and quotations, are now arranged in a way that teaches the skill of arguing. This can also be seen from the critical remark by the compilers (underlined in the above passage). Thereby, knowledge is not only produced but is simultaneously shown by way of *mimesis*, how it should be applied by someone who *knows*.

This passage in tractate Shabbat continues for a bit in the same way with the stereotyped content of the notebook interrupted by associative quotations before adding short hermeneutical expositions and stories. They are each concerned with astrology and whether stellar constellations apply to the people of Israel. Such thematic agglutinations of formally disparate material stimulates questions about how the text came into being in the first place. Are the quotes that interrupt the stereotyped content of the notebook transcripts of an actual discussion styled after *apo phones* transcripts of lessons as they were produced by students of the medical school in Alexandria (550–650 CE), for example, or the student questions inserted in the lectures of Didymus the Blind?[35] Or are they excerpts from other written sources (maybe *apo phones* themselves) that were used associatively along the content of the notebook? Apart from the rough common subject, the latter procedure seems more likely, due to the stylistically disparate nature of the inserted material.

Fragmenting texts by content, or simply sorting tablets, scraps, or ostraca, which due to their constrained format can only contain excerpts, would have served two purposes: the literary storage of data pertaining to the same topic in one place (tablets joined with string, or a scroll) and the creation of new knowledge by way of arrangement. Indeed, the discursive style adopted by the

---

[34] Translation follows Gardner 2008, 317, slightly adapted. For another discussion of this passage, see Rubenstein 2007.
[35] See Szabat 2015, 261, and Stefaniw 2019, 62–64, respectively.

Talmud teaches the art of conversation and argument building on top of the literal content. The work mimics how this information could be turned into knowledge. Since we find stories with similar or even identical structures and vocabulary distributed associatively all over the Talmud, it is more likely that we face a composition of multiple written sources rather than the product of an actual conversation.[36] The form of the late-antique notebook, especially consisting of multiple tablets that were tied together, is suitable for rearrangement. Once untied, the tablets could easily be stored together with others according to content. At the moment of compilation, attached keywords would be consulted and thematic threads created by way of arranging and rearranging tablets.

The loose nature of tablets, ostraca, or papyrus scraps, the most ordinary writing materials, indeed enabled compilers to compose by moving them around, thereby using the information on the tablets as data to generate a different cluster of information. That way, compilers could easily experiment with different arrangements before settling for one, saving valuable time and more costly material such as papyrus sheets or parchment needed for drafting.[37] Ultimately, this enabled complex and sometimes hidden structures, such as underlying numerical patterns, as they have long fascinated scholars.[38] Templates for such data management are found in the bookkeeping of large estates, for example, where receipts constantly had to be classified and then drafted into weekly, monthly, and yearly overviews of expenses and income.[39]

The process of collecting notes and excerpts on small slips, tablets, or ostraca and storing them according to keywords, numbers, letters, or even dates must have been rather obvious to the ancients. This would explain the overall silence about the exact process. It was likely a form of collective tacit knowledge indispensable if one wanted to smoothly navigate everyday life: a form of knowledge

---

36 Thus, two stories relating how Chaldeans made a prediction according to the stars that once came true and once did not are found in b. Shabb 156b, and a third one is in b. Shabb. 119a. Another example consists of recipes of a certain style that are found, for example, in b. Git. 68b–69b; b. Avod. Zar. 28a–29a; b. Shabb. 109b–110b.
37 See Locher/Rottländer 1985. Dershowitz 2021 shows how many apparent "jumblings" in the biblical text point to the use of many loose text carriers in the composition and transmission of the text.
38 Jacobs 1983; Pasternak/Yona 2016; Valler 1995.
39 See Rathbone 1991, 335–341. There are several ways to think about how thematic excerpts were kept together: in the same place but managed by an index list; loosely tied together according to subject; sewed or folded together (e.g., papyrus). See Blair 2010, 99, for similar strategies in the seventeenth century. The literary and visual documentation of such archiving strategies is a modern phenomenon.

embodied in society that informs new inventions and transfers of knowledge but can never be fully made explicit.[40] Based on the available sources, it seems that the Swiss polymath and "father of modern bibliography" Conrad Gessner was the first to describe the method he applied to craft his impressive work of indexing all books and authors ever known. In an entry titled "de indicibus librorum" in the second part of his magnum opus, in the *Pandecta*, he writes that (1) everything important that one reads should be copied on a piece of paper; (2) every idea should occupy a separate line; (3) the ideas should be cut apart so they can be arranged and rearranged at will and into clusters and subdivisions; and (4) the final order should then be copied and fixed directly.[41]

History, we have learned in the past decades, is not a linear development, and much less does it follow a teleological aim. Rather, technologies come and go, are reinvented, renovated, and forgotten again. Gessner was maybe the first to describe this method using the material of his time, (thin!) paper and scissors — but he was certainly not the first to use it. Based on the mistakes in the text of Pliny the Elder's *Natural History*, Alfred Locher and Rolf Rottländer have suggested that this first-century author applied a very similar method. Although Pliny did not use scissors but dictation and slim wooden tablets rather than paper, they describe the process as practically identical.[42] Indeed, while people after Gessner discovered the handy and standard size of playing cards imprinted only on one side to write down their notes, which allowed them to skip the step of cutting their notes apart, Pliny may have found some of his excerpts already tailored to the size of a tablet, papyrus scrap, or ostracon.[43] This might have been the case with the hemerology found in Joshua b. Levi's notebook, which stretched over several pages qua tablets and was thereby already portioned to be interrupted by other quotes and excerpts.

Why was this method not documented earlier, if it was already known and practiced in the time of the Roman Empire? As mentioned above, it may have been because it was part of the collective tacit knowledge. Alternatively, it may have been documented, but we have no access to this documentation. Then

---

40 On forms of tacit knowledge, see Collins 2010, 119–138. On innovations for data management, see Coogan this volume.
41 See Krajewski 2011, 13.
42 See Locher/Rottländer 1985. Others have criticized their model as too neat; see Dorandi 2007 (2017).
43 On the use of playing cards, see Krajewski 2011, 33; and Blair 2010, 94. Locher/Rottländer 1985 suggest that Pliny might have used the thin wooden slats that have been found in contemporary military camps (e.g., Vindolanda and Vindonissa) and which Martial refers to as Vitellian tablets in his *Epigr.*, 14.8–9.

again, classifying is not everybody's cup of tea. Gottfried Wilhelm Leibniz, for example, used Gessner's system when working as a librarian, and he purchased a closet to sort paper slips as designed by Thomas Harrison in the 1640s for his own projects.[44] Leibniz's successor as the librarian in Wolfenbüttel, however, none less than Gotthold Ephraim Lessing, preferred to stroll through the library instead of updating registers and to discover neglected books and topics by accident.[45] Undoubtedly, cataloguing data facilitates and accelerates knowledge production, while accidental finds and spontaneous associations and combinations may produce more innovative and creative results. Both ways of processing data have their advantages and disadvantages and the ability to attend to different tastes in a society or to a prevailing aesthetics of knowledge production. After all, it was not just Lessing's individual mood to stroll through the library and bring long-forgotten books to light: he was also acclaimed for it.[46]

2 Texts as Artifacts and Tools that Shape Knowledge

To illustrate processes of knowledge construction, Yoshiteru Nakamori chose the example of a particular Japanese chess player's method for creating new tactics.[47] The chessboard and playing pieces, however, did not seem to play a significant role in Nakamori's assessment of how ideas are transformed into deployable and communicable knowledge. And yet they are the center scaffolding, to piggyback on Larsen's terminology, around which new tactics are constructed. After all, the board and the pieces are the prime reason for the development of new tactics; their material qualities and limits stimulate and constrain at the same time in addition to the firm rules of the game. Moreover, visualization of ideas is frequently the first step in the process of transforming tacit knowledge into explicit knowledge.[48] A chessboard, with its clear pattern and consistent pieces, clearly helps the process of developing new tactics, either through experimentation with the physical game or by drafting a mental image.

---

44 See Krajewski 2011, 16–23 (with picture).
45 See Krajewski 2011, 32–33.
46 See Krajewski 2011, 33.
47 Nakamori 2019. See discussion below.
48 See Battistutti/Bork 2017.

Similarly, ancient thinkers often resorted to diagrams and tables to visualize their knowledge and to identify paths for the solution of a problem. It was obviously easier to calculate fractions and unit conversions with a visual aid — numbers arranged in a table or list, for example — than without.[49] Indeed, we might suspect that diagrams and tables also preceded the arrangement of excerpts in the preparation of composite works, such as, for example, the *Ecclesiastical History* discussed by Rebecca Stephens Falcasantos in this volume. Diagrams and tables serve as "external representations" of new and innovative knowledge and allow for manipulation and experimentation with what are otherwise bound to remain shadowy ideas.[50] Since pictures and signs are capable of conveying ideas much faster than texts, it is not surprising that the intellectual turmoil of late antiquity was negotiated graphically.[51]

Tables and diagrams organize the space of knowledge, whether on a tangible surface or imagined. Ancient thinkers used this capacity to create associative loci in their minds that helped them remember things; the places created an *ordo rerum* in the mind to which new items could be associated.[52] This idea of assembled and assorted knowledge loci is mirrored by the material involved in knowledge construction. Indeed, Cicero himself was aware of this connection when he wrote, "We shall employ the localities and images respectively as a wax writing tablet and the letters written on it."[53] The most basic material locus in (on) which to preserve knowledge for the ancients is obviously the tablet, ostracon, or papyrus scrap. Like the chessboard, they impose structuring boundaries. Tablets and other material places of knowledge can easily be grouped according to a certain order: an encyclopedic compilation, such as Socrates's *Ecclesiastical History* or the Babylonian Talmud. The final arrangement of these material bits and cognitive places of knowledge is ultimately the product of carefully planned text architecture. Without such planning, the meaningful structures obtained by way of recycled excerpts could not have been achieved.

Although they do not talk about this process — again we may suspect collective tacit knowledge in play — ancient authors obviously planned and drafted their work ahead of time, some with stunning success. The order of Pliny the Elder's *Natural History*, for example, is well known and may be too familiar by now

---

49 See Roby, this volume.
50 See Guerra/Ostergaard 2016, 237.
51 See Garipzanov 2015.
52 On the ancient theory of memorizing by loci, see Small 1997, 83. On actual and conveyed places of knowledge, see Jacob 2018.
53 Cicero, *De or.* 2.354, trans. Sutton/Rackham.

to evoke astonishment. Still, it must have taken a lot of advance planning, sorting, and defining of "places" to achieve a macrostructure that starts with the planets and ends with minerals, while moving associatively through every known natural substance in between. Another example are the two books that constitute Lucian of Samosata's *True Story*, which have puzzled scholars ever since because the sequence of motifs in each book mirrors the one in the other exactly.[54] For *The Learned Banqueters*, Athenaeus crafted dialogues between dinner guests out of excerpts and arranged them thematically. Christian Jacob has suggested that Athenaeus "started to organize his reading notes and collection of excerpts in categories such as 'wine,' 'cups,' 'fishes,' 'courtesans,' 'water,' 'parasites,' etc."[55] In her close reading of the Talmudic tractate Avodah Zarah, Mira Beth Wasserman discovered a macrostructure that organizes the material "as a journey down a cosmic ladder, moving from the heights of humans' spiritual aspiration down through descending rungs of creaturely existence. As the tractate begins, narratives about individuals who find redemption in the next world predominate. Later, the talmudic discussion shifts its orientation downward, from the supernal realm of souls and spirit to the material world of embodied, animal existence. Finally, the deliberations drill down into the inanimate domain of objects, investigating the physical properties of idols and other things."[56] The creative work of compilers, or authors working with excerpts, obviously began long before they started composing, such as the selection of topics and the drafting of a macrostructure (sequence of topics) or maybe even a microstructure (an associative pattern, a dialogue structure, or the arrangement of material according to the four rhetorical elements).[57] The easiest solution, at least on the macrolevel, was to follow an already existing text. It may not be surprising, therefore, that commentary literature abounds in late antiquity.

How did the designs for such text architectures come about? Michael Roberts once observed that "poets looked to the visual arts for inspiration; they understood composition in visual terms."[58] Roberts refers here to aesthetic models rather than the mimesis by poets of the technique and mechanical procedures applied by artists. Yet, it might be safe to assume that methods for the composition of aesthetically appealing and intellectually challenging texts (i.e., text

---

54 See Anderson 1976, 8–11.
55 Jacob 2000, 551 n. 182.
56 Wasserman 2017, 32–33.
57 The rhetorical elements in a composition are as follows: the introduction (*prooimion/exordium*), the narration of the case (*diēgēsis/narratio*), the proofs (*probatio/pistis*), and the peroration (*epilogos/peroratio*).
58 Roberts 1989, 118.

architecture) were similarly adapted from the visual arts such as painting, weaving, tessellating, or actual architecture.

Indeed, already the etymology of the Latin word for text (*textus*), as well as the one used to denote Talmudic tractates (*massekhet*) point to some conceptual connections, since in both cases the terms denote fabric.[59] Ellen Harlizius-Klück has long pointed out that the art of weaving served in many, and especially also distinctly mathematical, ways as a framework (pun intended!) to build knowledge or *episteme*.[60] Most interesting for the present purpose is her emphasis on the importance of the regulatory beginning in weaving, the *starting border*, which organizes the warp threads. These threads determine the success of the structure and envisioned pattern of the whole fabric — a mistake in the starting border will affect the whole weave. Tellingly, an emphasis on beginnings is notable throughout ancient discourses, whether they initiate a speech; a new year, month, or week; or a ceremony. The word *hymnos*, for example, is linguistically closely related to the *hymên*, the starting border.[61] The starting border, in turn, is the result of careful planning, drafting, and small-scale experimenting by the weaver (usually female).[62]

Similar activities of warping, *ordior* in Latin, appear to have preceded the composition of texts.[63] In his work on "revision" in ancient texts, Sean Gurd found that authors treated the need for revision as the result of imperfect planning.[64] Accordingly, late-antique scholia on Homer and Euripides show a deep "concern to evaluate an author's reasons for expanding on a theme or a topic ... why certain subjects are treated at length while others are not."[65] Thus, while careful planning is obviously expected, the actual process remains concealed. The general nonchalance with which the topic is addressed seems rather pretentious, since the ideal was spontaneous creation rather than minute and laborious preparation.[66] Rare hints allude to the (probably many) tablets that were consulted before their data was used to craft new knowledge.[67] A similar situation regarding drafts and descriptions of processes preceding the actual work can be found in the context

---

59 See Stemberger 2011, 126.
60 See Harlizius-Klück 2004.
61 See Harlizius-Klück 2016, 103–110.
62 See Harlizius-Klück 2004, 101–102.
63 See Scheidegger Lämmle 2015, 172.
64 Gurd 2012, 17–18.
65 Gurd 2012, 82.
66 See Gurd 2012, 9–11.
67 See the analysis of Pseudolus's reference to *sed quasi poeta, tabulas cum cepit sibi* (like a poet who consults his tablets) in Scheidegger Lämmle 2015, 175.

of art, be it weaving, painting, or producing mosaics.⁶⁸ Drafts, unlike the final piece, are not meant to last. They are often customized, unique, and subject to changing trends.⁶⁹ Against this lack of evidence of how it was done, the construction of texts became even more laborious during late antiquity. And the ties to weaving become apparent in the times' liking of centos: texts that treat words from ancient writers like the threads with which they create a completely new text. Optatian's artful grid poems even treat individual letters as weft and yarn with which he weaves a text with an intext.⁷⁰

In ancient weaving, weft and yarn are to the fore: they constitute the fabric and hold together the loom, which is otherwise just a bundle of sticks and beams.⁷¹ Like the yarn is tied to these beams in the weaving process, letters are tied to their writing surface. The latter were mostly loose, as the most common writing surfaces in late antiquity were wooden tablets, ostraca, or papyrus scraps. As such, these primary writing surfaces were as temporary as the loom. The loose and disparate nature of the so-distributed knowledge can be both a disadvantage, since they risk getting lost in the archive or on the street, and an advantage because of their flexibility and portability. Similar to tesserae, they were mobile and could be moved around, thereby facilitating experimenting with different structures and patterns before being fixed in mortar, that is, a scroll or quires. And the three-dimensionality of tablets and ostraca must have led to a physical interaction with these texts like tools.⁷²

Experimentation with tablets and ostraca is again a working step that follows upon original planning. Such planning not only has advantages that speak to the soundness and creativity of an author. Rather, once the pattern of the plan is in a stage where it can be communicated or, speaking in terms of weaving again, once the pattern begins to appear on the starting band, others can take up the thread and continue. Indeed, in the historiography of late antiquity, we are confronted with a significant number of people who are never mentioned as taking an active role in knowledge construction but who seem to have been the driving forces behind its material realization, maybe even its conceptualization. Those who first come to mind are, of course, slaves, women, and men of lower social status. Considering

---

68 See Burdajewicz 2020, 66–68.
69 Tellingly, the only papyrus that may have served as a model book, the "Artemidorus Papyrus," was found in a lump with other papyri, "possibly used to stuff an animal mummy." Burdajewicz 2020, 67. On the ephemeral nature of sketches in the textile industry, see Bogensperger 2016, 259.
70 On centos, see Mulligan 2018, 242–243; Schottenius Cullhed 2016.
71 See Harlizius-Klück 2004, 101.
72 See Pinker 1984, 1–2.

the material givens of the time and the fact that some authors had surprisingly long publication lists, it seems impossible that mega works such as the *Ecclesiastical History* were carried out by a single person. Yet, coauthors and co-conceptualizers are hardly mentioned.[73] The same is true for women, who often acted as patrons and sponsors but were generally not mentioned, at least not in terms that made their role as providers obvious.[74] Ultimately, it was the anonymous mass of literate people, as well as semi- or maybe unliterate craftsmen, providers of writing supplies, that were responsible for the manufacture of knowledge, its wider circulation and preservation.

3 Chapter Overview

Asked to engage with knowledge construction, the contributors to this volume have confirmed the stimulating potential of thinking about and along various aspects of knowledge construction. Daniel Picus, for example, looks at how rabbinic texts derive content based on the "vessel" that contains it, its form and shape. At the heart of his investigation are rabbinic interpretations of two prophetic visions of scrolls mentioned in the Bible, one flying (Zech. 5:1) and one that was eaten, "written front and back, and written upon it were lamentations, dirges, and woe" (Ezek. 2:8–3:3). Centuries later, these visions were "read" quite differently from the (probable) original intention of the biblical text, thereby "illustrating both changing conceptions of how knowledge is constructed and transmitted, and shifting networks for power and knowledge."[75] The physical aspects of the scroll with which the rabbinic readers are left, and who seem to read the texts in a decontextualized and fragmented manner (maybe not from a scroll?), bring their associations with scroll, front and back writing, lamentations, and dirges to the fore. Picus finds the rabbinic language infused with physicality that connects knowledge to "a thing written and read."[76] The scroll, for example, appears to

---

[73] This is true for slave work more generally; see Charles 2020. On invisible servile labor with a focus on interpreters, see Moss 2021. The late-antique educational system, however, witnessed a dramatic shift away from the slave teachers of the early imperial period to the professional teacher. That shift climaxed in the fourth century before taking another turn, this time to a "home-schooling" system, especially among Christian families that were skeptical about the content on which traditional pedagogy was based; see Lenski 2019, 134–149.
[74] See Layton 2002, 491–500.
[75] Picus, this volume, 32.
[76] Picus, this volume, 32.

represent "a certain type of authorized, divine knowledge" similar to "the rabbinic idea of the Torah as a 'text' that contains everything."[77] The physical form and shape associated with particular knowledge is a crucial part of its reception. It is this container that determines the usefulness and the actual usage of the contained knowledge. Moreover, it is in and of itself a semiotic device that signals content and enables people to know unread books.

Jeremiah Coogan examines an easily overlooked visual tool for knowledge construction: the column-and-row table. Ubiquitous and indispensable today, the use of columns and rows to organize texts seems to be an innovation of the third century CE. Adapted from prior usage in astronomy and other more technical fields, the table was deployed by Origen to correlate the Hebrew text of the Bible with several Greek translations. Eusebius of Caesarea used tables to organize the data of world history for his synchronizing work, the *Chronological Tables*. He further used tables to coordinate parallel passages in the four New Testament Gospels. A set of ten tables allowed for an unprecedented cross-referencing. In all three cases, the table provided an information architecture that could be used by multiple invisible coworkers. The table proves to be a real "textual machine"! Coogan also finds the concept of the column or row (*shitah*) also present in the discourse of Palestinian rabbinic sages, where it is used to refer to rightly situated and coordinated or, conversely, displaced and disorganized knowledge. The *shitah* appears to be such a strong visual aid in the construction of knowledge that it helps organizing and structuring knowledge, even if the table, which the row helps create, is only imagined.

In her paper on the scientific content of the letters by the "sophist turned monk" Isidore of Pelusium (375–435/40 CE), Elizabeth M. Conner addresses a still often underestimated tool for collaborative knowledge construction: the letter. Challenged by *scholastici* outside the monastery, Isidore was forced to navigate between his prior sophistic knowledge and his new Christianized paradigm. This resulted in new interpretations of Hellenistic scientific knowledge from an emerging and still ambiguous Christian-monastic perspective. Thus, Isidore himself is so deeply immersed in the classical categories of knowledge production that he uses Platonic arguments to oppose ideas that conflict Christian doctrine. It appears that the "classical" is an inescapable vocabulary of articulating knowledge in the service of polemic. The continuity of classical arguments appears to have been ensured by summarizing doxographies and catalogues of arguments, as can be judged from the repeated use of the same arguments, often in unsophisticated and compressed form. The likely core of Isidore's epistolary corpus, approximately

---

77 Picus, this volume, 47.

2,000 letters compiled perhaps a century after the monk's death and conserved by the "sleepless monks of Constantinople," suggests again the letters' ongoing contribution to monastic pedagogy.[78]

The constant reconfiguration of earlier knowledge by authors and readers, and readers turned authors, is also an issue in Rebecca Stephens Falcasantos' paper on one of Isidore's contemporaries: Socrates of Constantinople. His *Ecclesiastical History* is a miscellany composed of textual material as disparate as imperial letters, conciliar documents, and polemical orations. What is original about Socrates's text is, therefore, the arrangement of this prior material, his highlights, and emphases rather than Socrates's own writing. This text is in itself an interesting case of knowledge construction. Yet, Falcasantos moves beyond Socrates's applied compositional techniques and intentions to the reception of the edgy information about the monstrous, bloody actions committed by Bishop Macedonius of Constantinople and Arianizers more generally among Socrates's copyists. It appears that Socrates copied much of the respective material from Athanasius and added to the latter's polemic, thereby pulling his readers "into the orbit of Arian degeneracy."[79] Socrates's text is not only full of monstrosities in terms of content but also in terms of the text's form, which left the seams visible between quotation, summary, and Socrates's own commentary. The copyist of Plut. 70.7 used paratextual tools to tame Socrates's "textual monster" and to turn it (again) into a navigable archive for the reader. By atomizing the text by means of *kephalaia* (headings) and annotations in the margins, the copyist seemingly prepared the text for the next "reader turned author" who would want to excerpt information from the text. It looks like the future deconstruction of the assembled piecemeal knowledge is already anticipated.

Nicola Reggiani investigates linguistic, paralinguistic, and nonlinguistic strategies used to structure and enhance medical knowledge as found in papyri. This is a prolific field for looking at knowledge construction, since, to remain effective, medical knowledge must be in a constant discourse with the past, the present, and the possible, anticipated future. Information regarding a certain condition needs to be clearly bundled and allocatable. For this purpose, recipe collections use horizontal lines or line displacements to differentiate optically between two recipes. Monograms were developed to replace words that typically introduced the condition and the therapy, thereby highlighting and separating

---

[78] On the habit of retaining and collecting one's own letters, see van Hoof 2017, esp. 114–116; Schwitter 2017; on Isidore's letters and the "Sleepless monks of Constantinople," see Larsen 2017, 296 and 296 n. 98.
[79] Stephens Falcasantos, this volume, 107.

these two distinct parts of the recipe. Medical papyri, whether recipe books (*receptaria*) or more theoretical discussions, further included devices that enabled readers to engage actively with the content of the papyri. Reggiani identifies marginal notes referencing textual variants. This implies that these papyri were critically compared with other manuscripts which contained alternative views about how to cure a particular disease. Corrections of the language used in the papyri similarly testify to an intense interaction with the texts. Several strategies were applied for such interferences, such as interlinear and supralinear interventions and overdots and strokes. Some papyri provide section titles, short summaries in the margins, notes about the usefulness of the passage, or personal notes. Reggiani's analysis shows that, by way of paratextual devices, any text could be turned into a site where knowledge could be constructed by physicians from different places and times. Conversely, knowledge could be deconstructed by way of interference from the margins. It appears that it was not only the human body, or certain *materia medica*, that could be "epistemic objects," that is, objects used to produce knowledge.[80] Rather, the medical treatise itself served as an epistemic object.

Obviously, knowledge does not evolve consistently but is a constant back-and-forth between success and failure, accident, and taste. The never-ending trial of knowledge is perhaps best illustrated in the realm of applied mathematics, which often comes down to a binary between right and wrong. Courtney Ann Roby makes the case for the utility not of signs of successfully applied knowledge but of failure, that is, mistakes. She uses the latter to dive deep into the reasoning behind some of the miscalculations in the newly published papyrus P. Math.[81] These mistakes indicate that the author of this papyrus was a person with solid mathematical everyday skills such as the conversion of measurements or basic arithmetic, who challenged himself (?) with more difficult tasks. For example, he tried to calculate the amount of grain a vaulted granary could contain with the volume of a complicated, uncategorizable shape and with the number of bricks in a tower. An inner monologue becomes visible when the "solver," as Roby calls the author, breaks down numbers after an excessive and obviously wrong result. This breakdown of numbers, which results now in the calculation of an unrealistically tiny granary, was clearly supposed to help the solver verify his strategy. Yet, like contemporary math students, the solver remains tied to the super procedure he chose for solving the problem in the first place, which leads again to the same mistake. Unlike current students, however, our ancient solver seems to

---

80 For the term "epistemic object," see Tybjerg 2017.
81 P. Math was published by Bagnall/Jones 2020.

have faced these problems alone and without a teacher: the mistakes remain uncorrected. We are left to wonder what the solver's incentives were to push his mathematical competences further. Actual plans to build a granary? Peer pressure or social factors that are nowadays no longer associated with mathematical skills?

Indeed, mathematics, despite having taken a distinctly applied turn in late antiquity, also found their way into the period's rhetorical agon, as Monika Amsler's paper argues. Her contribution is a rather programmatic investigation into diverse factors that may have served as incentives for the composition of numerical maxims as they are found in the Babylonian Talmud. Classified by earlier scholarship as mnemonic devices of arbitrary content, these maxims have not received much attention. Indeed, the maxims, which often appear in thematically associative bundles, are not very gripping. Once made the center of scholarly attention, however, they raise interesting questions about their original purpose, about authorial merits, leisurely activities, continued education, and the significance of numbers in late antiquity. It appears that the maxims may, for example, be the result of creative collaboration when they are placed in the context of games played at dinner parties or public graffiti. It is quite feasible that someone would have taken the initiative and challenged colleagues or passers-by to enumerate, for example, "five things said about garlic," "eight things [that] reduce the semen," or "ten things that cause hemorrhoids."[82]

Lillian I. Larsen's paper looks at how modern scholarship has shaped accounts of monastic knowledge construction through emphasis or, in this case, neglect in totalizing narratives, particularly that of Henri-Irénée Marrou (1956). A positivistic reading of the sources taught Marrou that monks were more concerned with forgetting their prior, pagan education than with learning, thereby bringing "back into Christian tradition the virtues of the simple and unlettered" (Marrou 1956, 330). Larsen traces Marrou's interpretation of even the most explicit references to school monks and sketches of programs as singular and negligible back to an orientalist view of the unliterate, peasant, and yet mystical Egyptian desert. By contrast, Marrou reads the Western monastic literary remains as evidence of a highly literate community. "Ironically," writes Larsen, "by virtue of climate the richest range of extant school evidence is ... 'eastern' ... in provenance."[83] Larsen goes on to depict the educational program as it can be conjectured from the writings of Eastern monastic leaders and shows how it is corroborated by archaeological finds of school exercises in the monasteries. The program

---

[82] b. B. Qam. 82a; b. Git. 70a; and b. Ber. 55a, respectively.
[83] Larsen, this volume, 230.

is, in fact, not unlike the one put forward by Western grammarians and orators such as Quintilian, for example. According to this program, education started with the letters of the alphabet, their shape and sound, and proceeded from there to the syllables needed for reading. Students were then taught how to read names, words — not the simple ones, though — and ultimately sentences and sayings. In writing exercises, students were challenged to turn sentences into sayings, and sayings into short stories. Even complex inquiries into a topic retained this structure and would start with a sentence or saying. Those early "building blocks" obviously remained fundamental in the way individuals constructed their knowledge and negotiated their opinions.

In "Grammar in the School of Diodore of Tarsus," Robert Edwards approaches the remaining commentaries by Diodore of Tarsus not as exegetical texts that provide scholars with a glimpse of his particular method, but as artefacts that were produced to fulfill a role important enough that people invested time, labor, and money. By way of analyzing the content of the commentaries, by tracking down what other people wrote about Diodore's working methods and habits, and by comparing the nature of the extant commentaries with similar ones (e.g., Didymus the Blind), Edwards settles for a school context. Indeed, Diodore's biblical commentaries, often classified as employing a literal exegetical method against the allegorical one used by the Alexandrinians, frequently explain the grammar of a certain passage. Looking more closely at Diodore's commentary on the Psalms, Edwards points out that the commentary is not merely influenced by grammar, as prior scholarship would have it, but that it *is* grammar. The social and discursive nature of Diodore's commentaries and teaching, then, can be gleaned in that the grammatical examples are sometimes repeated, as if to rehearse with the students or to raise the issue again for those who missed a previous class. But then it also appears from various sources that Diodore taught a "polemical theology," a necessary skill for his students in order to successfully defend their beliefs against "heretics." Ultimately, the content of Diodore's curriculum conforms to the Roman area rhetorical exercises, as is to be expected based on the educational biography of the teachers, but the textual basis and the purposes have changed. Like Lillian Larsen's contribution to this volume, Edwards' assessment of Diodore's teaching shows that educational aims have not just been adapted to Christian ideas and customs. Rather, education and the emerging Christianized society with all the challenges it fostered mutually enforced and shaped each other. Ultimately, education does not happen in a vacuum.

The papers engage with the different forms of knowledge as they were identified in theories of knowledge construction, such as tacit, intuitive, explicit, personal, and social knowledge. Picus's project of describing knowledge associated with a form goes somewhat ahead of the rabbinic sages themselves, who are not aware of their use of collective *tacit knowledge*: knowledge that is undisputed but cannot (or at least not fully) be articulated.[84] Tacit knowledge, like exegetical knowledge, is mostly situational. That is why it is often so difficult to connect an author's sound argument in one place to the one made in another and to discern underlying principles. Tacit knowledge is related to *intuitive knowledge*, that is, ideas and imagination that are difficult to express since they are still new. Coogan shows how established and articulated *explicit knowledge* may pass through stages of intuitive knowledge again when confronted with a new technology: the effect that Eusebius's tables will have on the readers of the Gospels could only have been surmised. Conner places the eloquent Isidore of Pelusium on a continuum between the explicit knowledge stored in the ancient archive and his still intuitive knowledge of what Christian education should look like. Falcasantos shows how Socrates of Constantinople struggles to make other people's explicit knowledge seem like his own, deploying it tactically to make it confirm to his own rationale about the succession and importance of events. Roby's P. Math solver works to enrich his *personal knowledge*, which, according to Nakamori, builds on established, available knowledge, intuitive knowledge, and social knowledge. The aim of personal knowledge is to acquire new, valid knowledge for himself.[85]

As mentioned above, Nakamori observed the process of knowledge construction based on how a chess player develops new tactics. For this purpose (and simply to play chess), the player interacts with the chessboard and figurines but also with the game partner. The development of new tactics is thereby strongly marked by social knowledge. Without the dialectics between game partners, the experience of success and pushback, ideas and impulses cannnot be turned into tactics. This multidimensionality of knowledge construction is illustrated in Larsen's and Edward's papers: while the former engages ancient material to show how Egyptian monks acquired personal knowledge to build and consolidate the social status of their community, the latter maintains that an exegetical method does not exist for its own sake, but is socially constructed. Similarly, Amsler places rabbinic sages in a context of *social knowledge*, in which ideas are validated and put into words by a group through public acclamation and rejection.[86]

---

[84] See Nakamori 2019, 97; Braf 2002, 78. On "collective tacit knowledge," see Collins 2010, 119–138.
[85] See Nakamori 2019, 95.
[86] On *social knowledge* see further Nakamori 2019, 94–96.

4 Epilogue

We cannot, of course, always make knowledge construction and its components the primary focus of our research. But keeping in mind questions of knowledge construction may help reduce the tendency to identify a single cause as responsible for one or even several effects. The awareness of the constructedness of knowledge, not only our own but also the one we investigate, encourages contextual analysis, especially regarding resources. What does the author (or painter, sculpturer, or producer of a mosaic, for that matter) know, and what are they anticipating? What can they know or imagine, and what do they think they know? How does the available technology shape this knowledge?

The latter question has recently been addressed in theories of distributed cognition, which posit that the mind is shaped by things by way of analogy and metaphor drawing. Without physical objects, humans would be stuck, uninspired and unable to invent.[87] What appears to be a somewhat basic acknowledgement meanwhile remains a hypothesis, contested by the very strong implementation of the Cartesian divide between the human mind and material things, between subject and object, in Western reason.

Rarely, ancient sources themselves give us a glimpse into such analogy-drawing, the entanglement of the human mind with physical objects and with their visual and perceptive affordances. Thus, Andrew Riggsby observed that Varro, before giving the sole instruction recorded in Latin texts to produce a table, "had offered the reader a concrete physical analogy — the checkerboard-like playing surface for the game of latrunculin (LL 10.22). As far as we can tell, the rules of the game assign no significance to the rows and columns as such, so the board is not a table in itself. At the same time, though, it provides the reader with a "scaffolding" and in particular it frames the fully two-dimensional extension of the eventual table."[88] Others, like Aelian, realized the importance of visual representation — in his case of tactical theory — for students that learned without instructor (*hyphēgētēs*) and supplied his discussion with sketches.[89]

The advantages of thinking along the lines of factors of knowledge construction more broadly and, especially, more physically may not necessarily result in a reversal of the initial thesis or of a scholarly consensus arrived at by more monocausal approaches. But it can help to ground these results more firmly and,

---

[87] E.g., Malafouris 2013.
[88] Riggsby 2019, 78.
[89] Roby (forthcoming). Roby notes the same argument in Ptolemy, *Harmonica* III.3.64–71.

especially, more directly within "the culture we are studying."[90] Thinking about knowledge construction could do for historians what the kind reminder on the train does for passengers: both can remind those leaving (either the analysis or the train) to look back and check whether something has been forgotten.

Without corroborating detail, Barbara Tuchman once wrote, "Historical narrative and interpretation, both, may slip easily into the invalid. It is a disciplinarian."[91] This "corroborative detail" can be found in the realm of texts, geographical or material givens, artifacts, or social structures. Indeed, unlike texts, which can more easily be forced to agree with the historian's interpretations, material artifacts seem more reluctant in that they simply cannot always do what we want them to.[92] Thinking with knowledge construction allows, this volume suggests, a more comprehensive look for such details by the scholar crafting models of broad explication.

What we offer here is ultimately a chessboard and some tokens. May they serve the reader in developing new strategies and in turning tacit knowledge into explicit knowledge in areas and fields that were, out of ignorance or space restrictions, left out of this volume.

Bibliography

Althoff, J./Berrens, D./Pommerening, T. (eds.) (2019), *Finding, Inheriting, or Borrowing? The Construction and Transfer of Knowledge in Antiquity and the Middle Ages*, Bielefeld.

Anderson, G. (1976), *Studies in Lucian's Comic Fiction*, Leiden.

Bagnall, R.S./Jones, A. (eds.) (2020), *Mathematics, Metrology, and Model Contracts: A Codex from Late Antique Business Education (P.Math.)*, New York.

Battistutti, O.C./Bork, D. (2017), "Tacit to explicit knowledge conversion", *Cognitive Processing* 18, 461–477.

Berkovitz, A.J./Letteney, M. (eds.) (2018), *Rethinking 'Authority' in Late Antiquity Authorship, Law, and Transmission in Jewish and Christian Tradition*, Abingdon.

Blair, A.M. (2010), *Too Much to Know: Managing Scholarly Information before the Modern Age*, New Haven.

Bogensperger, I. (2016), "How to Order a Textile in Ancient Times: The Step before Distribution and Trade", in: K. Droß-Krüpe/M.-L. Nosch (eds.), *Textiles, Trade and Theories: From the Ancient Near East to the Mediterranean*, Münster, 259–270.

---

90 Elsner 2014, 3, writing about the merits of thinking along the lines of ancient rhetorical principles when analyzing the period's art.
91 Tuchman 1981, 34.
92 Kotrosits 2020, 4.

Braf, E. (2002), "Knowledge or Information: What Makes the Difference?", in: K. Liu/R.J. Clarke/ P.B. Andersen/R.K. Stamper/E.-S. Abou-Zeid (eds.), *Organizational Semiotics: Evolving a Science of Information Systems*, Boston, 71–90.

Burdajewicz, J. (2020), "Travelling Painters' Workshops in the Late Antique Levant: Preliminary Observations", in: M. Ivanova/J. Hugh (eds.), *Transmitting and Circulating the Late Antique and Byzantine Worlds*, Leiden, 44–77.

Burnett, C./Mantas-Espana, P. (eds.) (2014), *Mapping Knowledge: Cross-Pollination in Late Antiquity and the Middle Ages*, Cordoba.

Charles, R. (2020), *The Silencing of Slaves in Early Jewish and Christian Texts*, London.

Chin, C.M. (2008), *Grammar and Christianity in the Late Roman World*, Philadelphia.

Chin, C.M. (2015), "Cosmos", in: C.M. Chin/M. Vidas (eds.), *Late Ancient Knowing. Explorations in Intellectual History*, Oakland, 99–116.

Chin, C.M./Vidas, M. (eds.) (2015), *Late Ancient Knowing*, Oakland.

Cicero (1942), *On the Orator: Books 1–2*, trans. W.E. Sutton/H. Rackham, Cambridge, MA.

Collins, H. (2010), *Tacit and Explicit Knowledge*, Chicago.

Coogan, J. (2021a), "Gospel as Recipe Book Nonlinear Reading and Practical Texts in Late Antiquity", *Early Christianity* 12, 40–60.

Coogan, J. (2021b), "Transforming Textuality: Porphyry, Eusebius, and Late Ancient Tables", *Studies in Late Antiquity* 5, 6–27.

Crawford, M.R. (2019), *The Eusebian Canon Tables: Ordering Textual Knowledge in Late Antiquity*, Oxford.

Dershowitz, I. (2021), *The Dismembered Bible: Cutting and Pasting Scripture in Antiquity*, Tübingen.

Doody, A./Föllinger, S./Taub, L. (2012), "Structures and Strategies in Ancient Greek and Roman Technical Writing: An Introduction", *Studies in History and Philosophy of Science* 43, 233–236.

Dorandi, T. (2007; 2nd reprint 2017), *Nell'officina dei classici. Come lavoravano gli autori antichi*, Rome.

Elsner, J. (2014), "Introduction", in: J. Elsner/M. Meyer (eds.), *Art and Rhetoric in Roman Culture*, Cambridge, 1–34.

Formisano, M. (2013), "Late Latin Encyclopaedism. Towards a New Paradigm of Practical Knowledge", in: J. König/G. Woolf (eds.), *Encyclopaedism from Antiquity to Renaissance*, Cambridge, 197–215.

Formisano, M./P. van der Eijk (eds.) (2017), *Knowledge, Text and Practice in Ancient Technical Writing*, Cambridge.

Gardner, G. (2008), "Astrology in the Talmud: An Analysis of Bavli Shabbat 156", in: E. Iricinschi/ H.M. Zellentin (eds.), *Heresy and Identity in Late Antiquity*, Tübingen, 314–338.

Garipzanov, I. (2015), "The Rise of Graphicacy in Late Antiquity and the Early Middle Ages", *Viator* 46, 1–22.

Guerra, J./Ostergaard, S. (2016), "Technopoiesis as Complex Dynamic Knowledge Construction. A Biopoetic Explanation of the Creative Convolution of Human, Natural, and Technological Sciences", *Icono* 15, 235–255.

Gurd, S.A. (2012), *Work in Progress: Literary Revision as Social Performance in Ancient Rome*, Oxford.

Harlizius-Klück, E. (2004), *Weberei als episteme und die Genese der deduktiven Mathematik in vier Umschweifen entwickelt aus Platons Dialog Politikos*, Berlin.

Harlizius-Klück, E. (2016), "Denkmuster in der antiken Weberei. Eine Spurensuche", in: H. Harich-Schwarzbauer (ed.), *Weben und Gewebe in der Antike: Materialität - Repräsentation - Episteme - Metapoetik*, Oxford, 87–108.

Hicks, D. (2010), "The Material-Cultural Turn: Event and Effect", in: D. Hicks/M.C. Beaudry (eds.), *The Oxford Handbook of Material Culture Studies*, Oxford, 25–98.

Jacob, C. (2000), "Athenaeus the Librarian", in: D. Braud/J. Wilkins (eds.), *Athenaeus and his World: Reading Greek Culture in the Roman Empire*, Exeter, 85–110.

Jacob, C. (2018), *Des mondes lettrés aux lieux de savoir*, Paris.

Jacobs, L. (1983), "The Numbered Sequence as a Literary Device in the Babylonian Talmud", *Hebrew Annual Review* 7, 137–149.

Jaffee, M.S. (2001), *Torah in the Mouth: Writing and Oral Tradition in Palestinian Judaism 200 BCE – 400 CE*, Oxford.

Kehnel, A./Panagiotopoulos, D. (eds.) (2015), *Schriftträger - Textträger: Zur materialen Präsenz des Geschriebenen in frühen Gesellschaften*, Berlin.

Knorr Cetina, K. (1981), *The Manufacture of Knowledge: An Essay on the Constructivist and Contextual Nature of Science*, Oxford.

Knorr Cetina, K.D./Mulkay, M. (eds.) (1983), *Science Observed: Perspectives on the Social Study of Science*, Beverly Hills.

Knorr Cetina, K./Schatzki, T.R./von Savigny, E. (eds.) (2001), *The Practice Turn in Contemporary Theory*, London.

Knust, J. (2017), "Miscellany Manuscripts and the Christian Canonical Imaginary", *Memoirs of the American Academy in Rome. Supplementary Volume: Ritual Matters: Material Remains and Ancient Religion* 13, 99–118.

König, J./Whitmarsh, T. (eds.) (2007), *Ordering Knowledge in the Roman Empire*, Cambridge.

König, J./Woolf, G. (eds.) (2017), *Authority and Expertise in Ancient Scientific Culture*, Cambridge.

Kotrosits, M. (2020), *Lifes of Objects. Material Culture, Experience, and the Real in the History of Early Christianity*, Chicago.

Krajewski, M. (2011), *Paper Machines: About Cards & Catalogs, 1548-1929* (trans. P. Krapp), Cambridge, MA.

Larsen, L. (2017), "The Letter Collection of Isidore of Pelusium", in: C. Sogno/B. Storin/E. Watts (eds.), Berkeley, 286–308.

Latour, B. (1991), "The Brlin Key or How to do words with things", in: P.M. Graves-Brown (ed.), *Matter, Materiality and Modern Culture*, London, 10–21.

Latour, B. (1999), *Pandora's Hope: On the Reality of Science Studies*, Cambridge.

Latour, B. (2007), "Can We Get Our Materialism Back, Please?", *Isis* 98, 138–142.

Latour, B./Woolgar, S. (1979), *Laboratory Life. The Construction of Scientific Facts*, Beverly Hills.

Layton, R.A. (2002), "Plagiarism and Lay Patronage of Ascetic Scholarship: Jerome, Ambrose and Rufinus", *Journal of Early Christian Studies* 10, 489–522.

Lehmhaus, L. (2015), "Listenwissenschaft and the Encyclopedic Hermeneutics of Knowledge in Talmud and Midrash", in: J.C. Johnson (ed.), *In the Wake of the Compendia: Infrastructural Contexts and the Licensing of Empiricism in Ancient and Medieval Mesopotamia*, Berlin, 59–100.

Lehoux, D. (2012), *What Did the Romans Know? An Inquiry into Science and Worldmaking*, Chicago.

Lenski, N. (2019), "Searching for Slave Teachers in Late Antiquity", *Révue Des Études Tardo-Antiques* 12, 127–191.

Locher, A./Rottländer, R.C.A. (1985), "Überlegungen zur Entstehungsgeschichte der Naturalis Historia des älteren Plinius und die Schrifttäfelchen von Vindolanda", in: M. Kandler (ed.), *Lebendige Altertumswissenschaft: Festschrift für Hermann Vetters*, Vienna, 140–147.

Lundhaug, H./Lied, L.I. (2017), "Studying Snapshots: On Manuscript Culture, Textual Fluidity, and New Philology", in: H. Lundhaug/L.I. Lied (eds.), *Snapshots of Evolving Traditions: Jewish and Christian Manuscript Culture, Textual Fluidity, and New Philology*, Berlin, 1–19.

Malafouris, L. (2013), *How Things Shape the Mind: A Theory of Material Engagement*, Cambridge.

Martin, D.B. (2005), "Introduction", in: D.B. Martin/P.C. Miller, *The Cultural Turn in Late Ancient Studies: Gender, Asceticism, and Historiography*, Durham, 1–20.

Miller, P.C. (2009), *The Corporeal Imagination: Signifying the Holy in Late Antiquity*, Philadelphia.

Moss, C. (2021), "Fashioning Mark: Early Christian Discussions about the Scribe and Status of the Second Gospel", *New Testament Studies* 67, 181–204.

Mulligan, B. (2018), "Epigrams, Occasional Poetry, and Poetic Games", in: S. McGill/E.J. Watts (eds.), *A Companion to Late Antique Literature*, Hoboken, 241–258.

Nakamori, Y. (2019), "Knowledge Construction Methodology", in: Y. Nakamori (ed.), *Knowledge Construction Methodology: Fusing Systems Thinking and Knowledge Management*, Singapore, 93–126.

Onotext (n.d.), "What is the Data, Information, Knowledge, Wisdom (DIKW) Pyramid?", accessed online under https://www.ontotext.com/knowledgehub/fundamentals/dikw-pyramid/ [last access date February, 6 2023].

Pasternak, A.-R./Yona, S. (2016), "Numerical Sayings in the Literature of the Ancient Near East, in the Bible, in the Book of Ben-Sira and in Rabbinic Literature", *Review of Rabbinic Judaism* 19, 202–244.

Pinker, S. (1984), "Visual cognition: An introduction", *Cognition* 18, 1–63.

Rathbone, D. (1991), *Economic Rationalism and Rural Society in Third-Century A.D. Egypt: The Heroninus Archive and the Appianus Estate*, New York.

Riggsby, A.M. (2019), *Mosaics of Knowledge. Representing Information in the Roman World*, New York.

Roberts, M. (1989), *The Jeweled Style: Poetry and Poetics in Late Antiquity*, Ithaca.

Roby, C.A. (forthcoming), "Model Wars: Theorizing War in Greek and Roman Manuals", in: A. König and N. Wiater (eds.), *Visualising War*, Cambridge.

Rubenstein, J.L. (2007), "Talmudic Astrology: Bavli Šabbat 156a-b", *Hebrew Union College Annual* 78, 109–148.

Scheidegger Lämmle, C. (2015), "Einige Pendenzen. Weben und Text in der antiken Literatur", in: H. Harich-Schwarzbauer (ed.), *Weben und Gewebe in der Antike: Materialität – Repräsentation – Episteme – Metapoetik*, Oxford, 165–208.

Schottenius Cullhed, S. (2016), "Reading textual patchwork", in: H. Harich-Schwarzbauer (ed.), *Weben und Gewebe in der Antike: Materialität - Repräsentation - Episteme – Metapoetik*, Oxford, 235–243.

Schwitter, R. (2017), "Letters, Writing Conventions, and Reading Practices in the Late Roman World", *Analysing Literary Reception in Late Antiquity and Beyond. Linguarum Varietas: An International Journal* 6, 61–77.

Small, J.P. (1997), *Wax Tablets of the Mind. Cognitive Studies of Memory and Literacy in Classical Antiquity*, London.
Stefaniw, B. (2018), "Knowledge in Late Antiquity: What is it Made of and What Does it Make?", *Journal for the Study of Late Antiquity* 2, 266–293.
Stefaniw, B. (2019), *Christian Reading: Language, Ethics, and the Order of Things*, Oakland.
Stemberger, G. (2011), *Einleitung in Talmud und Midrasch* (9th ed.), Munich.
Szabat, E. (2015), "Late Antiquity and the Transmission of Educational Ideals and Methods: The Greek World", in: W.M. Bloomer (ed.), *A Companion to Ancient Education*, Chichester, 252–266.
Taub, L. (2017), *Science Writing in Greco-Roman Antiquity*, Cambridge.
Taub, L./Doody, A. (eds.) (2009), *Authorial Voices in Greco-Roman Technical Writing*, Trier.
Tuchman, B.W. (1981), *Practicing History*, New York.
Tybjerg, K. (2017), "Exhibiting Epistemic Objects", *Museum & Society* 15, 269–286.
Valler, S. (1995), "The Number Fourteen as a Literary Device in the Babylonian Talmud", *Journal for the Study of Judaism in the Persian, Hellenistic, and Roman Period* 26, 169–184.
Van Hoof, L. (2017), "The Letter Collection of Libanius of Antioch", in: C. Sogno/B.K. Storin/E.J. Watts (eds.), *Late Antique Letter Collections. A Critical Introduction and Reference Guide*, Oakland, 113–130.
Wasserman, M.B. (2017), *Jews, Gentiles, and other Animals: The Talmud After the Humanities*, Philadelphia.
Wissa, M. (ed.) (2017), *Scribal Practices and the Social Construction of Knowledge: In Antiquity, Late Antiquity and Medieval Islam*, Leuven.

Daniel Picus
Better Left Unread: Rabbinic Interpretations of Prophetic Scrolls

Abstract: This paper analyzes classical rabbinic interpretation of two visions from the prophetic corpus of the Hebrew Bible. Both of these visions — one from Ezekiel, and one from Isaiah — involve the unexpected presence and examination of a mysterious scroll whose contents, while known, are never explicitly read. Rabbinic interpretations of these scrolls further this lack of focus on the written contents of the scrolls by emphasizing their material, physical dimensions: their relationship to other scrolls, their size and shape, and their putative relationship to the body of God. I argue that this focus on the scrolls as material objects in later interpretation suggests that the rabbis conceive of the knowledge contained therein as a material component of the world. This hints at a larger set of assumptions at play in rabbinic literature, in which divine wisdom acts as a blueprint for the world.

1 Introduction

Twice in the prophetic corpus of the Hebrew Bible — the collection of oracles, narratives, prophecies, and poems collectively known to the ancient rabbis as the "*Nevi'im*" — a prophet has a vision of a scroll he does not read.[1] These visions are not statements about the literacy of the prophets in question, but rather testaments to the multivalent layers of meaning present in the image of a scroll.[2] Neither of the scrolls are said to be blank: both visions provide a general statement about the scroll's contents, but the vision makes it quite clear that it

---

1 Ezekiel 2:8–3:3; Zechariah 5:1–4.
2 There is a substantial amount of scholarly discourse on the question of early Israelite literacy, but such questions are not of great concern to us here. More important is the widespread understanding of the materials and implements of reading and writing. For an account of the intertwined relationship between literacy and biblical composition, see Schniedewind 2004, 84–90. Schniedewind carefully discusses the lack of images of writing and reading in the earlier prophets, like first Isaiah and Hosea, and the later association of writing with prophetic activity, which is what we see in Ezekiel and Zechariah. Importantly, he also points out that even these earlier prophets made oracles that were recorded, collected, and edited by a scribal class.

∂ Open Access. © 2023 Daniel Picus, published by De Gruyter. This work is licensed under the Creative Commons Attribution 4.0 International License.
https://doi.org/10.1515/9783111010311-002

is not the writing that lends import to the scroll. It is the scroll itself, as an object, an artifact, and a vision, that carries meaning. These two visions of scrolls and their subsequent reception in rabbinic literature provide us with an opportunity to investigate ideas about the role of texts and written materials as conveyers of knowledge that goes beyond the written word.

The prophet gives meaning to these unread scrolls. He makes them part of a broader message: for Zechariah, the flying giant scroll is a curse, whose effects are all-encompassing and broad, affecting all those in the land who steal and swear;[3] for Ezekiel, who consumes his scroll, the scroll is at first "dirges, lamentations, and woe," but it becomes nourishment, comfort, and sweetness.[4] The scrolls are not mere symbols, although their symbolic functions surely encompass potential allegorical interpretations. They are the message, material emblems of the transmission of knowledge from the deity to the prophet — and then, put into words and written on text, transmitted from the prophet to the people. They are images that "work" because of the particularities of how knowledge was transmitted in Ancient Israel.[5] As the norms for the transmission and production of knowledge change, so too do the images that bolster and underscore the legitimacy of that production and transmission. The images at play in the biblical text itself, rooted in a particular time and place, take on a different meaning in the later rabbinic context, in which the transmission of knowledge occurs in rubrics largely organized by a Roman culture in the wake of the Hellenistic age.[6] Such changes remind us that though the significance of a literary image is culturally contingent on a particular reading, the significance is not *limited* to a single reading. The different ways that later rabbis envision the significance of the images at play here are an instructive reminder of this fact.

I use these scrolls and their later materializations in late ancient rabbinic literature as an entry point into thinking about the intertwined nature of materiality and knowledge in late antique Judaism, as overlaid onto similar discourses in the Hebrew Bible and rabbinic literature. A scroll is a concrete, material object, and in the ancient world, a reasonably common one (at least, among the

---

[3] Zechariah 5:3.
[4] Ezekiel 3:3.
[5] Sanders 2017 has argued cogently for a model of Near Eastern knowledge transmission rooted in the structures of the Aramaic scribal class.
[6] Annette Yoshiko Reed has documented much of this transition and its ramifications: see Reed 2020. While her analysis is focused heavily on the 3rd century CE, the complicated lineages she traces are part of the substrate of rabbinic literature.

literate, cultured elite).⁷ Knowledge, on the other hand, is abstract — or so we often treat it. What can a scroll in a vision, a scroll written about by a prophet, and then interpreted, reinterpreted, and retold by later rabbis, tell us about the way knowledge, writing and prophecy interact? What can this intersection tell us about the rabbis who formulated it? In this essay, I argue that moments in rabbinic literature such as these — the later interpretations of prophetic scrolls — offer glimpses into the rabbis' expansive conception of knowledge as an underlying principle of the material world, contained not only in writing, texts, Torah, the ossification of processes of knowledge transmission, and the ever-controversial books, but also in the forms, contexts, vessels, and shapes of the material world itself. The flying and consumed scrolls of Zechariah and Ezekiel are not symbols or floating signifiers: they are knowledge itself, and knowledge in both the particular and the expansive sense. After briefly contextualizing the rabbinic movement within broader trends of knowledge, expertise, and education in the later Roman empire and introducing the biblical texts in question, I move on to examine classical Palestinian and Babylonian rabbinic texts that take up these prophetic visions in detail. From there, I move to a more expansive discussion of rabbinic texts that conceive of knowledge as embedded in the material foundations, and even origins, of the world, before concluding by articulating how discourses of knowledge transmission are intertwined with, and inseparable from, discourses of materiality.

2 Rabbis, Books, and Knowledge

The rabbis of the late-antique eastern Mediterranean strategically used discourses surrounding the practice of reading to craft an image of their own authority that transcended, and even claimed to reject, other forms of book-oriented knowledge in the Eastern Mediterranean. This strategy does not mean that the rabbis were unfamiliar with the practice of reading, or even broader, text-based strategies of pedagogy and knowledge production. On the contrary, they were implicated in, and familiar with, the materials, technologies, and practices of reading that were current in the broader Roman Empire and Mediterranean basin of late antiquity.⁸ The selective use of language involving texts,

---

7 For older, but fuller accounts of the scroll form, see Cavallo/Chartier 1999, especially 83–89. See also the foundational work in Roberts/Skeat 1983, 5–10.
8 For the most important discussion of early rabbis as Roman provincial elites, see Lapin 2012.

composition, and reading can be understood as a strategy of self-formation and authorization that sets them up as privileged outsiders to an educated world circumscribed, in the early centuries of the Common Era, by the Greek tradition of *paideia*.[9] This particular relationship *to* paideia was tempered by earlier discourses of Aramaic pedagogy that are visible in texts of the Hebrew Bible, as well as other ancient Near Eastern literature. What makes the rabbinic discourse of knowledge transmission distinctive is a particular understanding of transmitted wisdom and knowledge as a material substance, an understanding that is visible at particular moments in rabbinic literature, especially in biblical interpretation.

One aspect of the rabbis' strategic use of reading is in their construction of knowledge in concrete, material terms. The rabbis of the early *midrashim* and *Talmudim* understood knowledge as something physical, rather than abstract. That physicality was present in language that understood knowledge as a thing written and read, present in the accoutrements of the scribe and scholar — but certainly not limited to them.[10]

In some ways, the prophetic visions under discussion here can be read as standard images of "books" and literary production, but the rabbis derive their message in ways far beyond the writing they contain. Crucially, the rabbis "read" these scrolls *differently* than the ways in which the biblical prophets seem to read them, illustrating both changing conceptions of how knowledge is constructed and transmitted, and shifting networks for power and knowledge. These are both moments, for the rabbis, where the prophet is focused on the object of a scroll as a medium of transmission, and the scroll's location and material qualities as signifiers, as opposed to the textual content therein. The content is ultimately significant as well, of course: but the significance of what is written, according to rabbinic interpretation, does not overshadow the material medium of transmission itself. The scroll itself becomes the message. By considering these texts as texts that construct knowledge in a particular, material way, we have an opportunity to think about the stakes of knowledge as material for late ancient rabbis.

---

9 Brown 1992, 35–70.
10 This understanding was not limited to the rabbis, of course: the issue is simply that the materiality of rabbinic knowledge has yet to be fully described and analyzed. See Carr 2008 for more on this. My thinking on the materialization of the transmission of knowledge as critical for understanding the materiality of knowledge has been heavily influenced by Annette Reed. See, in particular, the discussion surrounding Reed 2020, 74–75.

The scrolls I discuss here are not, I think, scrolls that the rabbis understood as "actually existing," or as having direct analogues in the extratextual world. This allows us (and the rabbis) to consider them a bit more conceptually in relation to their own construction of knowledge. What can a scroll in a vision tell us about the way knowledge, writing, and prophecy interact? What can this interaction tell us about the rabbis who formulated it? Perhaps most importantly, it tells us that despite a baseline level of suspicion with which "new" written material was typically treated,[11] writing provided a useful vocabulary for the rabbis to frame their own understanding of knowledge as a material, concrete element: a literal blueprint and building block for the world in which they lived. Learning involves new knowledge by definition, but the rabbis were careful to frame that new knowledge within particular, specific discourses and settings. When confronted with an image in which the new information conveyed is tied inextricably to written material, the rabbis creatively ensure that the message the scroll conveys is present not in the written text to be read, but the material elements, presence, and movement of the scroll itself.

3 The Scrolls of the Prophets

Writing and the written word were laden signifiers in the ancient Near East. They were associated with priests and scribes, and a class of religious practitioners whose skills made them uniquely capable of communicating with deities, as well as interpreting their will made manifest in the world.[12] Even across the span of the "biblical period" (which is, of course, many periods, and several centuries), writing and reading remain both important markers of a certain educated class status, and links to divine and extra-human knowledge, both within biblical texts and in related literature.[13] Scrolls appear as prophetic signs twice in the Hebrew Bible: in Ezekiel 2–3, and Zechariah 5. Scrolls in general, of

---

11 Wollenberg 2017. Wollenberg argues that texts as sources of *new* information were regarded as highly suspicious. On the other hand, texts as receptacles of known information — well-known, studied, partially memorized and constantly recited stories, poems, and laws (such as the *Tanakh*) — were read in highly ritualized fashions, and understood as sacred, both conceptually and materially. While a Torah *could* be read for new information, as Wollenberg shows in her discussion, the idealized, positively-coded reading practice was either part of a highly formalized study, or a ritual lectionary.
12 See, for example, Satlow 2014, 31–51, Schniedewind 2004, 34–34.
13 Reed 2020, 11–21; 87–131.

course, appear much more regularly: Jeremiah's scribe Baruch writes one in Jeremiah 36, Deuteronomy 17 instructs a king to write a scroll of the law to keep with him at all times, and Numbers 5, the ritual of the suspected adulteress (or *sotah*), involves the writing, and then consumption, of a scroll for the performance of the ritual.[14] In this section, I will focus on the first two examples, from Ezekiel and Zechariah.

Before doing so, however, it is worthwhile to note that as remarkable as these textual moments seem to us, they are not as out of the ordinary as they seem. While they use images and materials (namely, writing surfaces and implements) unique to themselves, the performance of, and interpretation of, prophetic actions as "signs" was commonplace in prophetic literature of the Hebrew Bible.[15] In the context of their composition, these textual excerpts should be read as part of the broader realm of textual discourse that uses performed, viewed, and interpreted signs in order to convey divine messages.[16]

The book of Ezekiel begins with the prophet's vision of the divine chariot leaving Jerusalem, carrying the presence of God with it, bearing it towards the Exile in Babylon. In chapter 2, the Presence of God speaks directly to the prophet, giving him a charge to speak to the Children of Israel.[17] His message is contained in a scroll, written front and back, and rather than simply showing it to Ezekiel, the Divine Presence demands that he consume it. The relevant text reads thus:

> "Open your mouth, and eat what I am giving to you." And I looked, and behold, there was a hand extended out towards me, and behold, in it was a scroll. And he spread it out before me, and it was written front and back, and written upon it were lamentations, dirges, and woe. And he said to me, "Mortal, what you find, eat; eat this scroll, and go, speak to the House of Israel." And I opened my mouth, and he fed me this scroll. And he said to

---

14 The biblical text refers to this writing surface as a *sefer*, but given its size and use, it is entirely possible that it was merely a scrap. While this is a likely incomplete discussion of scrolls in particular, there are, of course, other written materials present in the biblical text: the tablets of the Ten Commandments, written amulets, and others. See Picus (forthcoming).
15 See, for example, Nissinen 2019, 57–64 and Lundbom 2010, 144–145.
16 Friebel 1999, 14 refers to all non-verbal forms of communication in a prophetic book as a "sign-act;" these actions must be *intended* to relay information. I am grateful to Kerry Sonia for this reference.
17 Previous interpretations of the book of Ezekiel's beginning have seen the vision of the chariot, or *merkavah*, followed by the scroll, and then by Ezekiel's call narrative at the end of chapter 3, and the language of speechlessness that pervades it, as metaphoric of his ministry as a whole: the move from oral to textual prophecy, and the prophet's own inability to speak prophecies other than those of destruction and woe. Freibel discounts these interpretations, reading the prophet's speechlessness as a sign-act (Freibel 1999, 169–188).

me, "Mortal, feed your stomach, and fill your belly with this scroll, which I am giving to you." I ate it, and it was as sweet honey in my mouth. (Ezek. 2:8–3:3)[18]

Two elements of this vision immediately leap out as worthy of note. The Divine Presence hands Ezekiel a scroll inscribed on the front and the back. This scroll was presumably made of papyrus: parchment did not become a common or widespread writing surface in ancient West Asia until the Hellenistic period, and Ezekiel's vision pre-dates that by several centuries. Even so, writing appearing on both sides of the scroll would have been significant regardless of its material.[19] In addition to making the scroll much more difficult to manipulate and read, most writing surfaces were only prepared for writing on one side.[20] Beyond this, a rolled document being written on both sides would run the risk of ink smearing and becoming illegible. This is a text written without regard for the rules of the scribal trade, either written outside of their remit, or using imagined materials that neither smudge nor bleed. The double-sided nature of the scroll as a prophetic sign, of course, is meant to highlight the magnitude of woe and lamentation that Ezekiel will prophesy for the Judahite community in exile — but the mechanics of this double-siding are indicative of far more. If we ask ourselves how the image would have resonated with an audience that knew writing, it seems clear that any numinous qualities would have resided in both the writing *on* the scroll, and the double-sided scroll itself. Even if the biblical author is unconcerned with the unreal dimensions and qualities of the scroll, these are elements that matter deeply to the rabbis.

After being presented with this double-sided scroll, Ezekiel is instructed not to read it, but to eat it. This is a powerful metaphor of consumption, but it is also more than that: Rather than reading the dirges and lamentations that are on the scroll, Ezekiel internalizes (and ultimately transforms) them completely. Their

---

18 Translation is author's own, based on the NJPS and NRSV. Hebrew text taken from the *Biblia Hebraica Stuttgartensia*.

פצה פיך ואכל את אשר אני נתן אליך ואראה והנה יד שלוחה אלי והנה בו מגלת ספר ויפרש אותה לפני והיא כתובה פנים ואחור וכתוב אליה קנים והגה והי ויאמר אלי בן אדם את אשר תמצא אכול אכול את המגלה הזאת ולך דבר אל בית ישראל ואפתח את פי ויאכלני את המגלה הזאת ויאמר אלי בן אדם בטנך תאכל ומעיך תמלא את המגלה הזאת אשר אני נתן אליך ואכלה ותהי בפי כדבש למתוק

19 Roberts and Skeat are quite clear that scrolls in antiquity could be either papyrus or parchment, and that neither papyrus codices nor parchment scrolls would have gone against ancient expectations (Roberts/Skeat 1983, 5). Even so, papyrus was the more common writing surface in the Levant prior to the Hellenistic era.

20 See Lewis 1974, 39–69. While papyrus written on both sides certainly exists (see n. 41), Lewis suggests, according to ancient sources, that papyrus was *generally* understood to be inscribed on one side.

nature becomes a part of his prophetic charge in the same way that Isaiah's lips are purified with a burning coal in his call narrative.[21] A text is also consumed in Numbers 5, as part of the *Sotah* ritual. Sarit Kattan Gribetz traces this particular image in later rabbinic interpretation, showing how consumption is a particularly gendered way for the rabbis to discuss learning without bringing reading into the equation.[22] Ezekiel's consumption of the scroll, if it *is* intended to suggest a gendered mode of knowledge transmission, does so subtly — at least in comparison to the later rabbinic understanding of the *Sotah*, and other late ancient texts that understand eating as a particularly feminized mode of acquiring knowledge.[23]

The second prophetic image involving an unread scroll comes from Zechariah. Zechariah is a prophet of the Exile proper — his prophecies seem to have been written down later than Ezekiel's. In chapter 5, Zechariah relates a vision of a flying scroll.

> And again, I raised my eyes, and I saw, behold, a scroll was flying. And he said to me, "What do you see?" And I said, "I see a flying scroll, twenty cubits long, and its width is ten cubits." And he said to me, "This is the curse which goes out over all the land. For everyone who steals, as is on one side, has gone unpunished, and everyone who swears, as is written on the other side, has gone unpunished. I have sent it out, (oracle of Yahweh of Hosts) and it shall come to the house of the thief, and to the house of the one swearing in my name in vain, and it shall lodge within his house, and utterly end their timber and their stones. (Zech. 5:1–4)[24]

The image of consumption is gone from Zechariah's vision of the flying scroll, but its double-sidedness remains. Zechariah adds an almost absurd size to the scroll — its width is only half its length, which is rare enough, but that width is already ten cubits: fifteen feet![25] If the miraculous nature of the scroll as high-

---

21 Isaiah 6:5–7. This call narrative, importantly, also takes place during a vision of the heavenly host.

22 Gribetz 2018. Rabbinic literature is, at times, concerned with keeping women separate from certain elements of Torah study and reading; *consuming* the text skirts this issue completely. Gribetz also notes that similar metaphors arise in early Christian discussions of ascetic women.

23 See also Boyarin 1994, 126–130.

24 ואשוב ואשא עיני ואראה והנה מגלה עפה ויאמר אלי מה אתה ראה ואמר אני ראה מגלה עפה ארכה עשרים באמה ורחבה עשר באמה ויאמר אלי זאת האלה היוצאת על פני כל הארץ כי כל הגנב מזה כמוה נקה וכל הנשבע מזה כמוה נקה הוצאתיה נאם יהוה צבאות ובאה אל בית הגנב ואל בית הנשבע בשמי לשקר ולנה בתוך ביתו וכלתו ואת עציו ואת אבניו

25 It need hardly be stated that this is far beyond the norm for the size of a scroll. Pliny states that there are never more than twenty sheets in a papyrus scroll, with the width varying con-

lighted by being written on both sides is downplayed, its miraculous nature, derived from its sheer size, is front and center. The fact that it is flying, of course, is similarly miraculous, and is an anomalous image. While its double-sided nature, as well as images of consuming scrolls, appear elsewhere in the Hebrew Bible, flight is unique.

This was an image that troubled early interpreters even prior to the rabbis. The Septuagint, for example, translates "scroll" (מגילה/*megillah*) as "δρέπανον," meaning "sickle," or "scythe."[26] Myers and Myers state this is due to confusion with Joel 4:13, in which the word מַגָּל/*maggal*, which contains the same consonants as *megillah*, or scroll, means "sickle."[27] The word *megillah* was unlikely to be problematic to the translators in and of itself: other occurrences are translated as "κεφαλὶς βιβλίου." This is a reasonably common term for a scroll in ancient Greek, and certainly a preferred term for various LXX translators.[28]

The author or compiler of the text of Zechariah itself, of course, knows that this is an image that requires explanation: that is why the angelic interpreter of verses 3 and 4 explains the image's meaning, both to Zechariah and to the reader. The scroll itself is a curse — again, an image and association that we see in Numbers 5. Its size suggests the curse's magnitude, while its flight enables one to imagine just how far-reaching the curse inscribed on it might be. Myers and Myers point out that the length — twenty cubits — is not outside the realm of possibility, but a width of ten cubits is surely symbolic.[29] The dimensions of ten by twenty cubits, they argue, carry direct resonances to the dimensions of Solomon's Temple as described in 1 Kings; specifically, we should read it as a reference to the size of the *ulam*, or porch, or perhaps the dimensions of the golden *cherubim* that sheltered the Ark of the Covenant with their wings.[30] This is an association that the rabbis will also make.

The actual content of the scroll, beyond extremely vague language, is left undescribed. We know that it is against thieves and those who swear false oaths in the name of God — but very little else, including the actual wording. The

---

siderably (but never going over something close to a foot). See Pliny, *Naural History* xiii. 77–78; *apud* Lewis 1974, 37–39.
26 Rahlfs/Hanhard 2006.
27 Myers/Myers 1987, 277–278.
28 The word κεφαλὶς on its own properly refers to the beginning of a column, but combined with βιβλίου seems to indicate an entire scroll. It does seem that the LXX translators use the word metonymically. Cf. Lewis 1974, 78.
29 Myers/Myers 1987, 279.
30 Myers/Myers 1987, 280. The porch was symbolic of the meeting between priest and populace, as the only (or perhaps most notable) location where such meetings occurred.

wording of the curse, it seems clear, is not the important aspect: rather, the fact that it was written down, on a scroll, and that the scroll plays a part in Zechariah's vision are the aspects that the text's compiler, and later the rabbis, found most important.

As seen in the resonances between this text and Numbers 5, the *Sotah* ritual, connections between writing and cursing were common in the ancient Near East. Isabel Cranz explores this relationship, arguing that Zechariah 5, in conjunction with Ezekiel 2–3, relies on this widespread logic of cursing.[31] She connects these prophetic visions of scrolls to other narrative moments relating written documents and curses; Jeremiah 36:2–4, for example, relates Baruch the son of Neriah's recording of Jeremiah's curses, and the covenant ceremony of Deuteronomy 27–28 involves the establishment of stone slabs inscribed with the stipulations of an extensive curse.[32] This close association derives, Cranz argues, from ancient Near Eastern oath-swearing ceremonies.[33] Even beyond rituals of covenant and cursing, though, we can see that writing in the Hebrew Bible is never far from the numinous.

Even in the Biblical text itself, these two visions were tied to networks of knowledge that relied both on the establishment of a professional class of scribes and religious professionals, as well as a more casual and widespread understanding of their practices. The association of writing with religious, administrative, and even divine power means that prophetic images of writing were particularly potent, and ripe for interpretive creativity.[34] Inheriting a text that was largely constructed under the rubrics of an Ancient Near Eastern scribal pedagogy, but themselves inhabiting a world where knowledge production was largely shifting to a Hellenistic pedagogic model, the rabbis received these images through their reception of the Biblical text. They reinterpret, and indeed, re-understand the function of the scrolls therein in order to make them fit into their own conception of knowledge as hanging precariously between the bookish and the non-bookish, all the while remaining a strikingly material substance.

---

31 Cranz 2016.
32 Cranz 2016, 411; see also Quick 2017.
33 Cranz 20016, 415–416.
34 Satlow discusses the varieties of authority texts and writings could contain: oracular, normative, and literary. See Satlow 2014, 4–5.

4 Rabbinic Interpretations

Sifre to Numbers

The earliest rabbinic interpretation of one of these visions appears in *Sifre Bamidbar*, or the *Sifre to Numbers*, a tannaitic rabbinic commentary on the book of Numbers, likely formed in the latter 3rd century.³⁵ This interpretation relates a completely disparate text to the vision of Ezekiel 2–3, and it does so through investigating themes of knowledge and its transmission through material objects. The text being interpreted, or the text of the lemma, is Numbers 12:6, which comes after Aaron and Miriam complain about Moses's prophetic authority: God summons the three of them to the Tent of Meeting and declares, "Listen to my words: If there will be prophets of Yahweh among you, I will make myself known to them in a vision, I will speak to him in a dream."³⁶ The interpretation is long — as rabbinic interpretations often tend to be — but it circles around the themes of prophecy, speech, and writing, by interpreting the scroll written front and back with reference to Moses being denied a vision of God's face (Exodus 33:17–23), while still being referred to as a prophet who spoke to him face-to-face (Numbers 12:6). God's body is even brought into the equation. Rather than relaying the entire interpretation at length, I will briefly summarize Sifre Numbers 103:1, and then focus on elements that are particularly important for our purposes.

Sifre Numbers 103:1 is a lengthy discourse interpreting Numbers 12:6–8, both continuously, and piecemeal. It begins by parsing the words the deity himself uses to speak to Moses, Aaron and Miriam, identifying a textual curiosity: when God speaks to rebuke Aaron and Miriam, he does so *politely*.³⁷ The word נא/*na* in biblical Hebrew, which God uses in Numbers 12:6, is a marker of a polite request — surely Yahweh is not in the habit of making requests!³⁸ As with so many of Yahweh's actions, however, the rabbis interpret it normatively, rather than descriptively. God speaks politely to Miriam and Aaron because humanity should speak politely to each other. In what seems like a jump, the passage next turns to prophecy and vision. This isn't a jump at all, however: it is simply a continuation into the next verse, where God is explaining to Moses, Aaron, and Miriam why Moses has a different sort of access to divine knowledge

---

35 Strack/Stemberger 1996, 297.
36 ויאמר שמעו נא דברי אם יהיה נביאכם יהוה במראה אליו אתודע בחלום אדבר בו
37 Specifically, he uses the term נא/*na*.
38 Brown/Driver/Briggs 1906, 609.

than they do — and indeed, how that access works. God speaks to Moses clearly, rather than through visions or dreams. The *Sifre* then claims that he is trusted even more than God's ministering angels, although Rabbi Yose then objects: Moses is trusted the most, with only the ministering angels being trusted more.

Moses's access to divine wisdom is so unique, that Rabbi Yose places his trustworthiness above the trustworthiness of the angels that minister to God himself. The rabbis then argue about the actual mechanics of Moses's unique access to God. God states that he speaks to Moses "mouth to mouth." This phrase suggests a direct conversation between Moses and the deity, but this is tempered with another suggestion on the part of the rabbis: perhaps, instead of a revelation of direct speech from God, Moses spoke with the divine presence. After all, Exodus makes it quite clear that a direct conversation with God can be deadly. This is a significant moment: the rabbis of the *Sifre* (the *tannaim*) are positing the divine presence as a mediator between Moses and the word of God. The actual mechanics of this are difficult, however: the divine presence as a mediator makes some sense, provided it is understood as distinct from God's body itself. Therefore, discussion then turns to what it means for a human being to look at God and not be able to live, a reference to Exodus 33. Unsurprisingly, the rabbis look for puns here: "And live" is understood as being not a verb, but rather a plural noun ("and the living things"): *va-ḥai* becoming *v-ḥayot*. The rabbis move from discussing the mechanics of prophecy to a discussion of death at the hands of a divine revelation, or perhaps a face-to-face epiphany — but they do so entirely within the remit of a prophetic call narrative, Ezekiel 3, while also referencing the *ḥayot*, or beasts, of Ezekiel 1. A verse from the Psalms is brought in to close out this particular portion of the discussion, while still keeping it connected to the broader prophetic theme: The divine presence, the psalm makes clear, makes itself visible to humanity at the hour of death.

The interpretation continues on with the next words from Numbers 12:8. God is still explaining Moses's uniqueness in Numbers, and the rabbinic text moves from riddles, which God does not use for Moses, to the fact that Moses sees God's likeness: his image, or תמונה/*temunah*. It is this "image," or likeness, that finally links our text to the double-sided scroll of Ezekiel 2–3. In Exodus 33, God shows Moses his back instead of his face, and the rabbis, in a remarkable exegetical leap, connect that to the scroll written both front and back. At this point, I quote the *Sifre* itself.

> The Torah teaches, "and he beholds the likeness of Yahweh" (Numbers 12:8). This is a vision of his back. You might ask, "What is this, a vision of his back? Perhaps it is a vision of

his face?" The Torah teaches, "And I will remove my palm, and you shall see my back" (Ex. 33:23).[39]

The likeness of Yahweh is not his face, but his back, since Scripture cannot contradict itself,[40] and Exodus makes it clear that Moses *never* sees God's face. The rabbis of the *Sifre* make another radical jump, then, into Ezekiel — this time focused on the idea of the "back," a term in Hebrew that can also mean "behind," or "after."

> "And he spread it out before me, and it was written front and back" (Ezek. 2:10). And don't even those who are light of intellect, and commoners, act thus, when they are writing [write on the front and back]? Why does the Torah say "front and back?" "Front" is in this world, and "back" is in the world to come." "Front" is the security of the righteous, and their afflictions in this world, and "back" is the gift of the reward of the righteous, and the punishment of the wicked, in the world to come.[41]

The image of the scroll written on two sides from Ezekiel 2 is transformed in the *Sifre* — if not in content, then certainly in reception. A scroll written on both sides, as noted earlier, is a rarity in the Biblical world, and an indication of something miraculous and fine: an ink that doesn't transfer, a papyrus or parchment that allows for writing on more than one face. Here, however, the rabbis understand it very differently. A scroll with writing on both sides is not a piece of writing to take note of: it is a piece of scrap paper, the province of the simple, or the commoner.[42] Even still, the rabbis understand the presence of writing on both sides as symbolic: it represents this world and the world to come, and can likely also be understood as the duality between the righteous and the wicked in both timelines. It is the association with scrap paper, however — and perhaps even of unknown written texts with negative outcomes in general, especially in religious contexts — that adds this vision's next dimension in the rabbinic imagination.

---

39 Sifre Numbers 103:1

ת"ל ותמונת ה יביט זה מראה אחוריים אתה אומר זה מראה אחוריים או אינו אלא זה מראה פנים ת"ל והסירותי את כפי וראית את אחורי

40 This is, of course, one of the foundational claims of the early biblical interpreters, including the rabbis: see Kugel 2007, 14–17.

41 Sifre Num. 103:1   ויפרוש אותה לפני והיא כתובה פנים ואחור והלא אף קלי הדעת וההדיוטות עושים כן כותבים ומה ת"ל פנים ואחור פנים בעולם הזה ואחור לעולם הבא. פנים בשלוותם ויסורים של צדיקים בעולם הזה ואחור מתן שכרן של צדיקים ופורענותם של רשעים לעולם הבא

42 A few examples of papyrus scrolls like this exist, called *opisthographs*. See, for example, Perrot 2020.

"And written upon it were lamentations, dirges, and woe" (Ezek. 2:10). The lamentations of the wicked, as it is written, "This is a lamentation, and it shall be intoned" (Ezek. 32:16). "Dirges," of the righteous, as it is written, "To the music of the ten-stringed harp, to the music of the lute, with melody and lyre together" (Ps. 92:4). "And woe," of the wicked, as it is written, "Calamity upon calamity is coming" (Ezek. 7:26).[43]

The text is particularly terse and difficult to understand here. The implication, however, is that the writing on the double-sided scroll — the dirges, lamentations, and woe — are directly connected to the fates of the righteous and the wicked, which in turn are connected thematically to the rabbinic understanding of God's face, and God's back. The double-sidedness of Ezekiel's scroll is the message: it is the present and the future, the benefit of living in God's presence, and the calamity of living in a world on which God has turned His back. The vision itself is a merism, in which the opposition of front and back with the present world and the world to come, and the extremes of divine favor, serve to contain the extensive possibilities of divine knowledge in a single vision of a single scroll. This is highlighted by the verses the *tannaim* cite: in the midst of a message of woe, the rabbis also cite Psalm 92, a joyous praise-psalm of the Sabbath day, to describe the "dirges" of Ezekiel's prophecy.

It is almost as if the rabbis are trying to impart two messages. The first is that whether a prophet is like Moses, and speaks directly to the deity, or like later prophets who only encounter him in a dream, is unimportant. The content of the message comes from God one way or another; whether it is from direct speech, or a divine image of a floating scroll, the origin of either is the same. As the text says: "The Torah does not say 'Against my servant Moses,' but rather that 'You have spoken against Me,' speaking against my servant Moses."[44] The scroll is never *read*, however, despite its presence in this interpretation: the fact of it conveys the prophet's message, and even the biblical verses cited do not appear on it, but rather describe its contents in general terms.

The second message is one of woe and devastation, even in the midst of God's glory. It is a remarkable thematic movement for a passage that begins with a statement about polite speech, but this wide, sweeping movement is also tightly connected: prophetic discourse, polite speech, and the divine presence are all linked through the materiality of knowledge, brought together intelligibly by the image and presence of a scroll written on both sides. The section of *Sifre Bamidbar* just quoted above appears in later sources: we will see it again in

---

43 Sifre Num. 103:1   וכתוב אליה קינים והגה והי קינים של רשעים שנאמר קינה היא וקננוה והגה של
צדיקים שנא' עלי עשור ועלי נבל עלי הגיון בכנור והי של רשעים שנאמר הוה על הוה באה
44 *Sifre Bamidbar* 103:1.

the Babylonian Talmud, in a tradition that combines interpretation of Ezekiel 2 with Zechariah 5, and it is perhaps one of our clearest indicators of the rabbis' understanding knowledge as material. We move next, though, to a midrash from the subsequent period of rabbinic activity, the amoraic period, which cites Zechariah's giant scroll.

Leviticus Rabbah

Zechariah's flying scroll appears in a slightly later collection of midrash: Leviticus Rabbah, which is Palestinian, and was likely compiled in the fifth century CE.[45] Leviticus Rabbah is typically known as a "homiletic" midrash, as opposed to an "exegetical" midrash, although these distinctions are becoming less and less common.[46] The text is composed of two interpretive formats. The first format is what is classically known as the "proem," or *petiḥa/petiḥta* in Hebrew and Aramaic. In this highly intricate form, one verse from scripture — often, but not always, from Psalms or Proverbs — is linked through a process of homiletic "chaining" to another verse, with numerous intermediary verses expounded on the way.[47] The other format is significantly less crafted: this is a lemmatic commentary, identified by snippets of a verse from the text being commented upon (in this case, Leviticus), and interpretations identified by the word *gufa* (which is also the Aramaic word for "body"), which mark a word or phrase's "meaning."

Leviticus Rabbah 6:3 is an exegesis of Leviticus 5:1, which relates a law about the responsibilities of one with information when someone is publicly accused. The text reads: ונפש כי תחטא ושמעה קול אלה והוא עד או ראה או ידע אם לוא יגיד ונשא עונו, which translates to, "And when a person sins — and one hears a public imprecation, and he is a witness, or has seen or learned of the matter — if he does not testify, he bears the guilt." We can, I think, already see the themes that will connect the flying scroll to this verse from the Pentateuch: the flying scroll is a manifestation of the public imprecation, making it incumbent on all with knowledge to witness and to act. The text in question begins:

> Gufa: Do not let a false vow be a light thing in your eyes, for behold Zechariah saw it, "And I raised my eyes and I saw, behold, a scroll was flying," (Zech. 5:1). What does flying

---

45 Strack/Stemberger 1996, 291.
46 Visotzky 2003.
47 The classic treatment of the *petihta* is Heinemann 1971. See also Cohen 1981 and Vitotzky 2003, 23–30, where he argues for the essential incoherence of this category.

> mean? Floating. As it says, "And it flew to me, one of the Seraphim [and in its hand was a live coal, which he took from the altar with a pair of tongs]," (Isaiah 6:6). "And he said to me, 'What do you see?' And I said I see a flying scroll, [twenty cubits long, and ten cubits wide]." (Zech. 5:2). Rabbi Abbahu said, "Even the skin of an elephant and the skin of a camel are not this size," and you say here "This is the curse which goes out over all the land," (Zech. 5:3), from here it went out from the entrance to the sanctuary, which we learned [a technical term which means this is a reference to the Mishnah] has an entrance that is forty cubits high and twenty wide.[48]

The flying scroll of Zechariah is initially linked directly to Isaiah's call narrative: while Isaiah was purified, and given a message, by a burning coal touched to his lips, the rabbis are trying to make Zechariah's vision of the scroll into a similarly momentous event. The size of the scroll is, according to them, a direct reference to the fact that it flew out of the entrance of the Temple in Jerusalem — which is even larger than this seemingly gargantuan scroll. The explanation continues, explaining why this vision — these two visions, really — are related to a section of the Pentateuch that discusses testimony and false vows.

> Rabbi Aibo said, "How come when man swears on a Torah scroll, we bring before him empty skin bottles? To show that yesterday, this bottle was full of sinews and bones, and now it is entirely empty. Thus will one who causes his companion to wear a false oath in the end go out entirely empty of his possessions." Rabi Assa said this is about a false oath, and Rabbi Yonah said this is even in regards to the truth.[49]

The connection between Zechariah's scroll and Leviticus 5:1 is made clearer here: the practices in question, at least in the rabbis' day, involve swearing on a Torah scroll. Rabbi Aibo references an interesting practice that we don't see elsewhere: whenever an oath is taken on a Torah scroll, empty wineskins are present as well. Functionally, these might be there after a libation, which was common enough as part of oath-taking practices in the ancient eastern Mediterranean — but Rabbi Aibo certainly does not understand them that way.[50] The passage continues, but enough of our themes have been revealed to end here. The flying scroll's size is an important element of its physicality, because the

---

[48] LevR 6:3: גופא אל תהי שבועת שוא קלה בעיניך שהרי זכריה חמי ליה ואשא עיני והנה מגילה עפה מה עפה שייטא כמה דתימא ויעף אלי אחד מן השרפים ויאמר אלי מה אתה ראה ואמר אני ראה מגלה עפה אמר רבי אבהו אפילו עורו של פיל ועורו של גמל אינן במדה כאן זאת האלה היוצאת על פני כל הארץ מהיכן יצאת מפתחו של אולם דתנן פתחו של אולם גבהו ארבעים אמה ורחבו עשרים אמה

[49] LevR 6:3: אמר רבי איבו מפני מה משביעין האדם בספר תורה ומביאין לפניו נודות נפוחים לומר אתמול היה הנוד הזה מלא גידים ועצמות ועכשיו הוא רק מכלן כך המשביע לחברו לשקר סוף שיצא ריקם מכל ממונו רבי אסא אמר על שקר רבי יונה אמר אפילו על אמת

50 See Sommerstein/Torrance 2014.

size associates it with the doorway of Solomon's temple's sanctuary. Its existence as a material scroll written on front and back also places it in direct contradistinction to the empty skin bottles and the Torah scroll used for oaths. Bereft of both their wine and the flesh that once animated them as living creatures, the skin bottles are nevertheless not valueless and empty. Like the giant scroll, they provide meaning in their very presence and materiality.

The wineskins' double emptiness connects to the double significance of the scroll of Zechariah's vision: its flight in Zechariah is the vastness of the curse, although the rabbis connect it to the prophetic call, while the size and the area the scroll demarcates are nothing less than a reference to the Temple itself. It is a powerful hermeneutic. The wineskins are important because of what they lack, and the scroll is important (and perhaps even comprehensible) despite whatever may be written upon it. Again, these might not be unique signs in prophetic discourse or rabbinic interpretation, but they center around a written object while studiously ignoring the fact of writing. This makes them significant elements in an attempt to think about the ideology of writing among the classical rabbis.

Babylonian Talmud

The final two rabbinic interpretations I will discuss here both come from the Bablyonian Talmud, or Bavli. Bavli Gittin 60a deals with the image from Zechariah, while bEruvin 21a interprets both visions — a fitting conclusion to this section. The Babylonian Talmud is a notoriously difficult text to study. Nominally a commentary on the Mishnah (albeit one that goes far beyond our standard ideas of commentary), the period of its composition, editing, and redaction extends from the 3rd century all the way to the cusp of the seventh or eighth. Each passage is composed of layers that come from different periods of rabbinic activity, and sometimes even different locations: here we attempt to read them holistically, and in the context of the later layers of redaction and editing that would have taken place in Babylonia.

Our passage in Bavli Gittin comes in the middle of a lengthier discussion that involves a variety of material texts and the restrictions and stipulations surrounding them. There is a debate over whether lectionary readings from the prophets, for example, must be read from the scrolls of the prophets, and not lectionary scrolls (the latest layer of the Bavli, the *stam*, mandates that lectionary scrolls are appropriate), as well as whether or not it is appropriate to write out individual portions of the Torah for children to study. Such practices, of course, are familiar to us from the world of monastic education, but the Talmud gives us a glimpse into the debate over them in rabbinic communities.⁵¹

This particular discussion stems from an assertion made anonymously, in a *baraita* (a non-Mishnaic tannaitic tradition): that the Torah was given scroll by scroll, which presumably means book by book, rather than all at once, as a single document. The ramifications of this discussion are significant for the rabbis: the mode in which the Torah was transmitted can determine whether or not it is acceptable to copy it down in individual parts, or whether it must always be copied as a whole. This passage, though short, is particularly complex, because it relies on a midrashic association between individual instantiations of words in distinct verses. In this case, the linked words are "scroll" (*megillah*) and "take" (*laqo'aḥ*).

> Rabbi Yochanan said in the name of Rabbi Bena'ah, "The Torah was given scroll by scroll, as it is said, 'Then I said, 'Behold I have come with the scroll of the book that is written for me.''" (Ps. 40:8). Resh Lakish says that the Torah was given as a complete/sealed book, as it is said, "Take this Torah scroll," (Deut. 31:26). And on the other hand, isn't it written, "Take?" as well? [The implication here is that Resh Lakish's argument is irrefutable because of this word, so how does Rabbi Yochanan counter it?] That is about after it was joined. And on the other hand, isn't it written, "With a scroll of the book written for me?" This shows that the entire Torah is called a scroll, as it is written, "And he said to me, 'What do you see? And I said, I see a scroll flying.'" (Zech. 5:2).⁵²

This is a remarkable assertion on the part of the rabbis: not only are they claiming to have knowledge about what the content of Zechariah's scroll is, beyond the general indication that it contains a "curse": they are identifying it as the scroll of the Torah itself. This fact is assumed to be so self-evident that it is used as evidence for another claim: that the Torah is only called a "scroll" when the entire manuscript is meant. This could be a reference to Deuteronomy 28 and the broader tradition of covenant curses that are contained in the Hebrew Bible.⁵³ This interpretation, indeed, seems most likely, even if it is not the only one available to us. I think that there is *also* a conflation here between scrolls as

---

51 For an insightful introduction to this monastic material, see Lillian Larsen's contribution in this volume, and cited literature.

52 b. Git. 60a: א"ר יוחנן משום רבי בנאה ניתנה תורה מגילה מגילה שנא' אז אמרתי הנה באתי במגילת ספר כתוב עלי ר"ש בן לקיש אומר תורה חתומה ניתנה שנאמר לקוח את ספר התורה הזאת ואידך נמי הכתיב לקוח ההוא לבתר דאידבק ואידך נמי הכתיב במגילת ספר כתוב עלי ההוא דכל התורה כולה איקרי מגילה דכתיב ויאמר אלי מה אתה רואה ואומר אני רואה מגילה עפה

53 Quick 2017.

representative of a certain type of authorized, divine knowledge and the rabbinic idea of the Torah as a "text" that contains everything.

The last text, which brings together both biblical passages under examination, comes from the Babylonian Talmud, tractate Eruvin. It is worth noting that despite the obvious similarities between these two passages, this is the first place where we see both interpreted together, or juxtaposed, in classical rabbinic literature.

Bavli Eruvin deals, in an overarching sense, with the concept of borders and limitations: an 'eruv is the Sabbath boundary, a rabbinic invention which creates an area of habitation in which an observant rabbinic Jew can, according to *halakhah*, unproblematically carry items during the Sabbath. This does not mean, of course, that every word of Talmud on Eruvin's hundred and five double-sided folios deals with boundaries and limitations of this sort — but there is a striking prevalence of themes focused on measurements, the human body, and other boundaries. We see this concern manifested in several ways here. The overarching concern is the expanse of God's intellect, and the ability of humans to comprehend it: the spaces where the borders of divine knowledge rub up against the boundaries of human perception.

This selection comes five pages into a *sugya* that, in classic Talmudic fashion, spins off from a short Mishnaic passage about how to build a boundary around a well in such a way that drawing water from it is an acceptable activity on the Sabbath.[54] Even within the context of the *sugya*, as long and complex as it is, this particular section feels like something of a surprise: amidst lengthy discussion of the exact length of various perimeters and travel distances between locations, Rav Hisda presents a *drash*, or interpretive commentary, on a verse from the Psalms. The link is verbal: the "width" of the commandment is at stake here, and in the context of an almost mundane discussion of spatial sizes and distance, the physical size of Zechariah's scroll takes on a cosmic significance, along with the fences and roads discussed earlier in the *sugya*.

> Rav Hisda said, "Mari bar Mar would expound: What does this mean, "I have seen an end for everything, but your commandment is very wide" (Psalm 119:96). David said this thing, but he did not interpret it; Job said it, but he did not explain it; Ezekiel said it, but he did not explain it, until Zechariah son of Iddo came, and explained it. David [as the traditional author of the Psalms] said it, but did not explain it, as it is written: "I have seen an end for everything, but your commandment is very wide." Job said it, but he did not

---

54 m. Eruv. 2:1.

explain it, as it is written: "Its [the end of the Almighty's] measure is longer than the earth, and wider than the sea" (Job 11:9).[55]

This is a particularly self-conscious bit of midrashic play. In asking for an interpretation of Psalm 119:96, the classic move would be to interpret it with reference to another biblical verse that makes use of some of the same vocabulary, or perhaps the same theme. Various verses from other biblical books are presented here, but the *drash* rejects them all as having no explanatory power, until the verse from Zechariah is brought forth: only with Zechariah is the notion of "width" both quantified and defined. Before Zechariah is invoked, though, verses from Job and Ezekiel are presented as being synonymous with Psalm 119:96. This synonymity is interesting, as it creates parallels where the reader might not have seen them before, providing insight into just how the rabbis of the Talmud chose to represent their own understanding (or one of their many playful understandings) of the text.

The verse from Job provides two axes of measurement for the extent of the divine measurement. Two large, seemingly endless, bodies are invoked: the earth, and the sea. This is a classic literary merism, as the two are opposed in such a way that suggests the totality of the world. Also important is the fact that we are still not entirely sure what is being measured. The text from the Psalms identifies the "commandment," or *mitzvah* of God, but the verse from Job, especially in a decontextualized context, is much vaguer, and has no referent. We can assume that the referent is the commandment from Psalms, but as the passage continues, it seems likely that the rabbis had something else in mind.

> Ezekiel said it, but did not explain it, as it is written: "And he spread it out before me, and it was written front and back, and written upon it were lamentations, dirges, and woe" (Ezek. 2:10). Lamentations [*qinnim*]: This is the warning of the righteous in this world, and thus he said, "It is a lamentation, and they lament with it" (Ezek. 32:16). Dirges [*hegeh*]: This is the reward of the gift of the righteous in the future, and thus he said, "With the melody [*higgayon*] of the lyre" (Ps. 92:4). Woe: This is the warning of the wicked in the future, and thus he said, "Calamity [*hoveh*] upon calamity is coming" (Ezek. 7:26).[56]

---

55 b. Eruv. 21a: אמר רב חסדא דריש מרי בר מר מאי דכתיב לכל תכלה ראיתי קץ רחבה מצותך מאד דבר זה אמרו דוד ולא פירשו אמרו איוב ולא פירשו אמרו יחזקאל ולא פירשו עד שבא זכריה בן עדו ופירשו אמרו דוד ולא פירשו דכתיב לכל תכלה ראיתי קץ רחבה מצותך מאד אמרו איוב ולא פירשו דכתיב ארוכה מארץ מדה ורחבה מני ים

56 b. Eruv. 21a: אמרו יחזקאל ולא פירשו דכתיב ויפרוש אותה לפני והיא כתובה פנים ואחור וכתוב אליה קינים והגה והי קינים זו פורענותן של צדיקים בעולם הזה וכן הוא אומר קינה היה וקוננוה והגה זו מתן שכרן של צדיקים לעתיד לבא וכן הוא אומר עלי הגיון בכנור והי זו היא פורענתן של רשעים לעתיד לבא וכן הוא אומר הוה על הוה תבא

The addition of the scroll from Ezekiel is confusing. It differs in style from the previous two prooftexts: individual words are re-interpreted with still more prooftexts from different biblical books, and the verse in question does not contain the root רחב/*r-h-v*, which signifies "width," and is present in the initial verse and the verse from Job. The Ezekiel interpretation, in fact, is almost identical to that found in the Sifre to Numbers, and indicates that this tradition circulated between texts and tradents in late antiquity. It is possible, however, and even likely, that it was inserted here not because of the texts that came before it, but as an antecedent to the interpretation that came after. It is tied to the passage's theme not through measurement, but through the materiality of a giant scroll, and concern over its physical properties.

> Until Zechariah son of Iddo came and interpreted it, as it is written: "And he said to me, 'What do you see?' And I said, 'I see a flying scroll, twenty cubits long, and its width is ten cubits,'" (Zechariah 5:2). And if you unfurl it, is it not twenty cubits by twenty cubits? And it is written: "It was written front and back" (Ezekiel 2:10). And if you split it, how much would it be — forty by forty cubits. And it is written: "Who measured the waters with his palm, and the heavens with a span…?" (Isaiah 40:12). We find that the entire world is but one three thousand two hundredth of the Torah.[57]

The notion of "width" is finally concretized with Zechariah's verse, and its interpretation is linked to the cosmic valence of the Torah itself. The scroll is conflated with Ezekiel's scroll, written front and back, and gone is any imagery of consumption: rather, the scroll is either unrolled to its full length, or "peeled," the front split from the back so that both writing surfaces are visible at once, and the size of the scroll doubled.[58]

There seems to be a tradition lying behind this one, suggesting that the scrolls of Zechariah and Ezekiel are the same scroll, and that they are God's Torah — or perhaps the original Torah. This idea, I think, helps us make sense of the rest of the passage: the measurement of the world is given in God's measurements, the divine palm and span — and the divine Torah is significantly larger than both of these. The entire world is but a small portion of the original

---

57 b. Eruv. 21a, cont.: עד שבא זכריה בן עדו ופירשו דכתיב ויאמר אלי מה אתה רואהר אני רואה מגילה עפה ארכה עשרים באמה ורחבה עשר באמה וכי פשטת לה הויה לה עשרין בעשרין וכתיב היא כתובה פנים ואחור וכי קלפת לה כמה הויה לה ארבעין בעשרין וכתיב מי מדד בשעלו מים ושמים בזרת תכן וגו" נמצא כל העולם כולו אחד משלשת אלפים ומאתים בתורה

58 Instead of adding the length and width of two new parchment sheets together, it seems that the length and width have been doubled individually. For more on mathematical mistakes and what they teach us in this context, see Courtney Roby's article in this volume.

Torah scroll in size, and it is also, suggestively, but a small portion of the divine Torah scroll itself.

These rabbinic interpretations, spanning a time range from the first to the fifth or sixth century, and a span of land from Palestine to Babylonia, show us a range of understandings that are remarkably similar to each other. Even with one early Palestinian tradition (*Sifre Bamidbar* 103:1) being reused wholesale in the Babylonian Talmud, these teachings reveal a growing conception of knowledge as material, and perhaps even artifactual. The scrolls, for us, stand in as an index of how certain types of knowledge were received, transmitted, and conceptualized. The absence of a tradition regarding the exact wording on the scrolls is indicative of the way a conception of knowledge as material is working in rabbinic interpretations of this motif.

Only in the *Sifre* tradition, repeated in the Bavli, is the content of the scroll even mentioned. Rather than being specifically delineated, a verse from Ezekiel is presented as a general summary of its contents: "dirges, lamentations, and woe." General as they are, however, two of these categories are textual types that come with highly formal, stylized, and ritualized practices and actions: dirges and lamentations. Both of these have their roots in traditions of communal mourning and lamentation,[59] and while such traditions might have changed dramatically from the time of Ezekiel's composition to the Tannaitic period, it is clear that the rabbis participated in traditions of lamentation and mourning as well.

The prophetic scrolls with writing are "artifactual," and suggest a *type* of knowledge, rather than something specific. Rabbinic interpretation focuses on their material qualities, with size and location being the most prominent. The knowledge they contain and transmit comes from the embodied reactions that these scrolls are meant to engender: the lamentation of a particular city's destruction, the dirge for a particular death or period of mourning. The *Sotah* scroll presents a parallel example to this: in the Mishnah, the rabbis disagree vehemently over the actual words that the scroll is meant to contain,[60] while the ritual itself, at least in its broad strokes, is relatively stable.

Another common theme in the rabbinic reinterpretation and reuse of the scrolls of Ezekiel and Zechariah is the focus on their size. The Bavli, as just shown, uses the stated size of the scroll, and then expands it in order to connect the size of the scroll to the size of the Torah itself — although in this case, the Torah in question is a primordial Torah, and not a synagogue scroll. Leviticus

---

[59] Olyan 2004, 29–39; 49–51.
[60] m. *Sotah* 2:3–4.

Rabbah connects the size of the scroll to the entrance to the Sanctuary, yet again underscoring a connection between the image of the scroll and the particularity of knowledge relating to size and distance. This focus on numbers and particularity appears in the later generations of rabbinic interpretation, rather than in our earliest tradition; whether it represents a largescale development, however, remains to be seen. What we *can* say, however, is that Leviticus Rabbah and the Babylonian Talmud both connect these prophetic scrolls to objects with loaded ideological valences, and cosmic significance: the Temple and the Torah. Those connections are made materially — through size, through shape, and through proximity. Both of these referents, I think, are understood as microcosms — although in the Torah's case, it might be more correct to say that it is a macrocosm. Either way, the scroll in the prophetic vision is a model of something larger that leads the reader towards it: the Temple, or the Torah, which encompasses the world in turn. It is to this implicit connection between the Torah and the world, and the Torah *as* the world, that I turn next, before concluding.

5 A Blueprint of Wisdom

A well-known late ancient rabbinic midrash on the first verse of Genesis begins not with sweeping claims of God's majesty and power as the creator of the world, but with a lexicographical query into a word that appears in Proverbs 8:30: אָמוֹן/*amon*.[61] Proverbs 8 is a lengthy discourse spoken by "Wisdom," sometimes referred to as "Lady Wisdom;" in verse 30, she is charting her own pre-existence of the universe, and her role in the divine creation. The verse in question reads, "And I was at his side, an *amon*, and I was his delight every day, playing before him at all times." A few verses earlier, the speaker's pre-existence is made clear: she states, "I was there when he established the heavens, when he set the horizon upon the ocean" (Proverbs 8:27). This context is necessary for understanding the rabbinic readings for *amon*. Even alone, the necessity of context combined with the formalized atomization present in the rabbinic reading reveals a remarkable tension between orderly, narrative read-

---

[61] Gen. Rabb. 1:1. The early rabbis were not the only interpreters to have difficulty with this word, or even this entire passage: commentators disagree about its meaning. Michael V. Fox presents possibilities that generally fall into three camps: "artisan," as indicated by the rabbis, "constant," and "nursling" or "child" (which is the preference of the KJV and the NRSV). Fox 2000, 285–289.

ing, and the broader rabbinic conception of scripture as an endless ocean of verses in constant ebb and flow against each other. By attempting to define *amon* in the context of the world's creation, Genesis Rabbah is emphasizing one aspect of Proverbs 8, even as it transports it to another biblical book entirely.

Rabbi Oshaya, in whose name the rabbinic tradition is given, provides three possible translations for the rare word in question.[62] The first possibility is "tutor," translated with a Hebrew transliteration of the Greek *paidagogos*, פדגוג. The tradition goes on to list "hidden" and "great" as the other possibilities before offering an entirely different exegesis. This tradition, marked by the rabbinic phrase "*d'var aḥer*," or "another thing,"[63] relates the word *oman* to *uman*, composed of the same consonants. It reads thus:

> Another interpretation: *oman* is an *uman*. The Torah says, "I was the tool of the workmanship/faith of the Holy One, Blessed Be He." In the custom of the world, when a human king builds a palace, he does not build it from his own knowledge, but from the knowledge of an *uman*, and the *uman* does not build it from his own knowledge, but he has parchments and notebooks to know how to make rooms, how to make gates. Thus the Holy One, Blessed Be He, looked at the Torah and created the world, and the Torah said "In the beginning, God created" (Gen 1:1). And "beginning" means nothing other than "Torah," and how you might say, "God acquired me at the beginning of his way" (Prov 8:22).[64]

According to Rabbi Oshaya, we should read the first verse of Genesis as "With the Beginning, God created," and understand "Beginning" as the Torah: an identification that the text makes explicitly, along with the connection of "Torah" with "wisdom." It is a particularly material sort of wisdom, however: the wisdom of a craftsman, who lays out plans and blueprints, creating conceptual and physical models of what is to come. The Torah, according to the very beginning of Genesis Rabbah, is nothing other than the physical blueprint of the world. It is also synonymous with wisdom, and it is the beginning of all. The world, then, is built on wisdom — but more than that, it is built *with* wisdom, and from wisdom.

---

62 See above, n. 139.
63 A phrase which signifies a different interpretation of the same passage.
64 Gen. Rabb. 1:1: דבר אחר אמון אמן התורה אומרת אני הייתי כלי אמנתו של הקדוש ברוך הוא בנהג שבעולם מלך בשר ודם בונה בירה אינו בונה אותה מדעת עצמו אלא מדעת אמן והאמן אינו בונה מדעת עצמו אלא דפתראות ופנקסאות יש לו לדעת היאך הוא עושה חדרים היאך הוא עושה פשפשין כך הוה הקדוש ברוך הוא מביט בתורה ובורא את העולם והתורה אמרה בראשית ברא אלהים ואין ראשית אלא תורה היאך מה דאת אמר ה" קנני ראשית דרכו

The biblical book of Proverbs is marked at various points by a concern for pedagogy and transmission: when read, the text itself speaks to the listener, formulating itself as a collection of wisdom being transmitted from a father to his children.[65] The text from Genesis Rabbah, likely dating from the fourth century, expands and modifies Proverbs' pedagogical bent. The text itself is the transmitted teaching of one generation to the next; but Rabbi Oshaya adds to that here, making the entire Torah, of which Proverbs is clearly part, into a teacher, a covering, a sense of magnitude, and ultimately, a blueprint. The transmission of knowledge from father to son becomes a part of the scaffolding upon which the world is built, incorporating, in the process, the ideas of shelter and enormity. The interplay between text-as-context and text-as-material is dizzying; the reader is ultimately left with a sense of the rabbis' understanding of wisdom as a divine artifact and tool of creation, while at the same time being the result of a process grounded in the basic realities of human existence.

This text highlights an important and under-examined feature of rabbinic discourse: the fluidity with which intellectual qualities we consider abstract, such as knowledge and wisdom, are portrayed as both physical, material substances and immaterial ideas. This fluidity can be ascribed, in part, to a slippage that at times seems to occur between the method of transmission, and the material being transmitted; Annette Reed has discussed this in earlier Jewish literature, particularly as a function of scribal discourse in the development of forms of knowledge that constitute angels and demons.[66] Aramaic literature in the Second Temple period, she argues, was characterized by a close attention to dynamics of how wisdom and knowledge was transmitted. Oral transmission from teacher to student was prioritized, and written texts came to be understood as material forms of this dynamic of transmission. Scrolls and texts were not knowledge itself, but rather a material manifestation of the process by which knowledge moved from one subject to the next.

Rabbinic discourses of pedagogy, transmission, and the construction of knowledge make use of this discourse, which in turn makes use of older biblical language and ideas about the inculcation of knowledge and wisdom between subjects.[67] It adds additional layers, however, dependent on the context and setting of a particular rabbinic text's composition: amoraic texts from Palestine

---

[65] There is much work on this subject, but see the overview in Fox 2000, 80–82 for a helpful start.
[66] Reed 2020, 113–115. Reed is here talking about the coalescence of ideologies of pedagogy and transmission into attitudes about writing and material books.
[67] Carr 2005, 126–134.

participate in the discourse of *paideia*, for example, while later Babylonian texts situate knowledge as a product of formal academies — an intervention clearly dependent on the establishment of the early Medieval Islamic academies.[68] My goal here has not been to disentangle and separate these discourses in a particular set of rabbinic texts: indeed, they are so closely intertwined that such an enterprise would be ultimately meaningless. Rather, I present them as plausible background for the shifting and elusive ways that late ancient rabbis spoke about knowledge and wisdom as sometimes material, sometimes ephemeral, sometimes concrete, and always precious.

Learning was described in a variety of manners in classical rabbinic literature, but a common way to describe it, consistent with some of the interpretations seen here, was with sheer physical size: a famous example describes the intellect of an early generation as being as wide as the Temple gateway, the next generation as wide as the sanctuary door, and the current generation as wide as the eye of a needle.[69] This highly material construction of knowledge was made possible by an understanding of the *realia* of learning and reading — scrolls, parchment, papyrus, pens, the human voice, memory — not just as texts to be read or words to be heard, but rather as material objects that could signify in a variety of ways. It is for this reason that the writing on the scrolls of Ezekiel and Zechariah do not matter as much for what words are present: the fact of them, and the fact of the scroll itself, signifies as much as a text might have, just in a different fashion. This paper has served as a test case for this broad assertion: it should be reasonably uncontroversial to point out that knowledge was material for the rabbis, but analyzing the rabbinic interpretation of a few biblical passages focused on prophetic visions of scrolls as bearers of knowledge helps to tease out the specifics of that construction.

My contention here is both very large, and very small. My large claim is that the rabbis understood knowledge as material: as something contained in material, physical subjects and objects, that could be divided, subdivided, moved, and removed. Its presence in those objects could be understood and drawn out. In this way, the world is built on knowledge. My smaller claim, which hopefully helps to bolster and serve as a foundation for the larger, is that rabbinic interpretations of symbolic scrolls in prophetic texts are an aspect of this material understanding of knowledge. These scrolls are more than symbolic: they are urgent messages, containers of divine knowledge, and flying objects that are

---

[68] For an overview of Palestinian rabbinic educational practices, see Hirshman 2012. On the Babylonian context, the classic work is Goodblatt 1975. See also, however, Brody 1998.
[69] b. Eruv. 53a.

anything but floating signifiers. They are understood as concrete and real, and every aspect of their materiality conveys information: while they are not necessarily "better" left unread, understood properly, there is simply no need to read them.

Bibliography

Alt, A. et al. (eds.) (1997), *Biblia Hebraica Stuttgartensia*, Stuttgart.
Boyarin, D. (1994), *A Radical Jew: Paul and the Politics of Identity*, Berkeley.
Brody, R. (1998), *The Geonim of Babylonia and the Shaping of Medieval Jewish Culture*, New Haven.
Brown, F./Driver, S./Briggs, C. (1906), *The Brown-Driver-Briggs Hebrew and English Lexicon*, Boston.
Brown, P. (1992), *Power and Persuasion in Late Antiquity: Towards a Christian Empire*, Madison.
Carr, D. (2005), *Writing on the Tablet of the Heart: Origins of Scripture and Literature*, New York.
Cavallo, G./Chartier, R. (eds.) (1999), *A History of Reading in the West*, Amherst.
Cohen, N. (1981), "Structure and Editing in the Homiletic Midrashim", *AJS Review* 6, 1–20.
Cranz, I. (2016), "Magic and Maledictions: Zechariah 5, 1–4 in its Ancient Near Eastern Context", *Zeitschrift für die alttestamentliche Wissenschaft* 128:3, 404–418.
Fox, M. (2000), *Proverbs 1–9: A New Translation with Introduction and Commentary*, New York.
Friebel, K.G. (1999), *Jeremiah's and Ezekiel's Sign-Acts: Rhetorical Non-Verbal Communication*, Sheffield.
Goodblatt, D. (1975), *Rabbinic Instruction in Sasanian Babylonia*, Boston.
Gribetz, S.K. (2018), "Consuming Texts: Women as Recipients and Transmitters of Ancient Texts", in: A.J. Berkovitz/M. Letteney (eds.), *Rethinking 'Authority' in Late Antiquity: Authorship, Law, and Transmission in Jewish and Christian Tradition*, London, 178–206.
Heinemann, J. (1971), "The Proem in the Aggadic Midrashim", *Scripta Hierosolymitana* 22, 100–120.
Hirshman, M. (2012), *The Stabilization of Rabbinic Culture, 100 C.E.–350 C.E.: Texts on Education and Their Late Antique Context*, New York.
Kugel, J. (2007), *How to Read the Bible: A Guide to Scripture, Then and Now*, New York.
Lapin, H. (2012), *Rabbis as Romans: The Rabbinic Movement in Palestine, 100–400 CE*, New York.
Lewis, N. (1974), *Papyrus in Classical Antiquity*, Oxford.
Lundbom, J.R. (2010), *The Hebrew Prophets: An Introduction*, Minneapolis.
Myers, C.L./Myers, E.M. (1987), *Haggai, Zechariah 1–8 (The Anchor Bible Commentaries)*, Garden City.
Nissinen, M. (2019), *Prophetic Divination: Essays in Ancient Near Eastern Prophecy*, Berlin.
Olyan, S. (2004), *Biblical Mourning: Ritual and Social Dimensions*, New York.
Perrot, A. (2020), "Reading an Opisthograph at Qumran", in: A. Krauß et al. (eds.), *Material Aspects of Reading in Ancient and Medieval Cultures: Materiality, Presence, and Performance*, Berlin/Boston, 101–114.

Picus, D. (forthcoming), "Reading Material: Textual Objects as Ritual Artifacts in Tannaitic Literature", *AJS Review*.
Quick, L. (2017), *Deuteronomy 28 and the Aramaic Curse Tradition*, New York.
Rahlfs, A./Hanhard, R. (2006), *Septuaginta* editio altera, Stuttgart.
Reed, A.Y. (2020), *Demons, Angels, and Writing in Ancient Judaism*, New York.
Roberts, C.H./Skeat, T.C. (1983), *The Birth of the Codex*, New York.
Sanders, S.L. (2017), *From Adapa to Enoch: Scribal Culture and Religious Vision in Judea and Babylon*, Tübingen.
Satlow, M. (2014), *How the Bible Became Holy*, New Haven.
Schniedewind, W. (2004), *How the Bible Became a Book: The Textualization of Ancient Israel*, New York.
Sommerstein, A./Torrance, I. (eds.) (2014), *Oaths and Swearing in Ancient Greece*, Boston.
Strack, H.L./Stemberger, G. (1996), *Introduction to the Talmud and Midrash*, Minneapolis.
Visotzky, B. (2003), *Golden Bells and Pomegranates: Studies in Midrash Leviticus Rabbah*, Tübingen.
Wollenberg, R.S. (2017), "The Dangers of Reading As We Know It: Sight Reading As a Source of Heresy in Early Rabbinic Traditions", *Journal of the American Academy of Religion* 85:3, 709–745.

Jeremiah Coogan
Tabular Thinking in Late Ancient Palestine: Instrumentality, Work, and the Construction of Knowledge

Abstract: In late antiquity, a revolution in information technology transformed the practices and possibilities of knowledge. At the cutting edge of this development, several third- and fourth-century figures in Roman Palestine deployed the emerging technology of the column-and-row table as a novel tool of historical and literary scholarship. The Christian scholars Origen and Eusebius and the rabbinic sages of the Palestinian Talmud adapted this specialist technology from grammar and astronomy, and put it to work to structure complex textual corpora. As a "textual machine," the table generated new possibilities of knowledge. Bringing together literary and material evidence, this study analyses the "how" (working methods) and the "who" (human actors) involved in these innovative late ancient projects. I interrogate the pragmatics and the ethics of late ancient tabular thinking in order to locate these projects within broader histories of knowledge construction, in late antiquity and beyond.

1 Introduction

In his 2011 monograph, *Paper Machines: About Cards & Catalogs, 1548–1929*, Markus Krajewski narrates the development of card catalogues and similar in-

---

This project has received funding from the European Commission's Horizon 2020 research and innovation programme under Marie Skłodowska-Curie grant agreement no. 891569, "Expanding the Gospel according to Matthew: Continuity and Change in Early Gospel Literature." It also received the support of the Oxford Centre for Hebrew and Jewish Studies, where some of these ideas were presented in March 2021. An earlier version was presented as "Tabular Thinking and the Practice of Commentary in Late Ancient Palestine" at the Schlindwein Family Tel Aviv University–Notre Dame Research Workshop: "Interpretive Cultures in Late Antiquity: Hellenistic, Roman, Jewish & Christian Perspectives," University of Notre Dame (13–14 May 2019). The author is grateful to Monika Amsler, Hallel Baitner, Markus Bockmuehl, Martin Goodman, Joseph Howley, Benjamin Kantor, Blake Leyerle, David Lincicum, Candida Moss, Hindy Najman, Vered Noam, Andrew Riggsby, Ishay Rosen-Zvi, James VanderKam, and Moulie Vidas for generous engagement with these ideas in various forms. Parts of this chapter adapt discussion in Coogan 2022, ch. 2.

∂ Open Access. © 2023 Jeremiah Coogan, published by De Gruyter. This work is licensed under the Creative Commons Attribution 4.0 International License.
https://doi.org/10.1515/9783111010311-003

dex systems, tracing a history of use and innovation that extends from the early modern period to the twentieth century.[1] The invention of the card catalogue enabled new practices of knowledge. Cataloguing systems facilitated the large-scale categorization of information about people and things, with ramifications far beyond the scholar's study or the university library. One might think of widespread systems for managing census and population data that emerged in the later nineteenth century, of the emergence of income tax schemes (first organized with card catalogues), or of the millions of individual cards used to collect words and definitions for the *Oxford English Dictionary* or the *Thesaurus Linguae Latinae*. Card catalogues provided an architecture to assemble information from many sources and to coordinate the efforts of many people. These "paper machines" offered new possibilities of organizing information and, thereby, new ways of knowing the world.

The modern card catalogue was not the first such innovation in information technology. The systematizing impulse of Krajewski's "paper machines" has a rich variety of ancient and medieval antecedents. Over the past decade, scholars have analyzed diverse strategies for organizing a world that is "too much to know"[2] and have mapped complex patterns of distributed cognition in Mediterranean antiquity.[3] Building on these developments, I examine the late ancient emergence of the column-and-row table as a technology for constructing historical and literary knowledge. As part of a larger transformation of knowing in late antiquity, the innovative deployment of the table afforded new spatial approaches to organizing information and producing knowledge.[4]

---

1 Krajewski 2011. For other recent histories of textual technologies, see Robertson 2019; Lynch/Robertson 2021; Robertson 2021.

2 "Too much to know": Blair 2010. Blair focuses on early modern reference books and the navigational devices that helped people use them. (Eusebius of Caesarea's fourth-century Gospel apparatus, discussed below, is an earlier example of such a navigational device.) As Blair demonstrates, these tools facilitated new projects of knowledge. In recent years, scholarly interest in the history of organizing information has exploded. See Franklin-Brown 2012; Kennedy 2016; Riggsby 2019; Dershowitz 2021; Reader 2021; Wellmon 2021.

3 The foundational work on distributed cognition is Hutchins 1995; Hutchins focuses on two case studies of nautical navigation. On distributed cognition in the ancient Mediterranean, see Anderson *et al.* 2019, as well as the ongoing work of Serafina Cuomo. Applying such cognitive models to writing in the ancient Mediterranean (thinking about the "extended mind" of a single human actor), see Yuen-Collingridge 2018.

4 On a "late ancient revolution" in information technology, see Riggsby 2019, 216–222. Significant studies of late ancient transformations in textuality and knowledge include Grafton/Williams 2006; Chin 2008; Chin/Vidas 2015b; Vidas 2017; Stefaniw 2019. On "affordances," see

Across fields from informatics to the history of science to literary studies, scholars often distinguish between "information" and "knowledge."[5] On these terms, *information* consists of (more or less) raw material, data that can be collected, organized, analyzed, and so forth.[6] *Knowledge* is what people make out of this information through a variety of practices, institutions, and technologies. The distinction is not between "unmediated" or "objective" data and "constructed" or "subjective" knowledge. Both information and knowledge are contingent. Collections of data are often flawed and inevitably partial. Knowledge is inescapably situated, deploying concepts or models to make sense out of limited information for particular ends.[7] Given the contingency involved in every aspect of cognition, a rigid division between information and knowledge will not hold up to scrutiny. Instead, we might imagine a continuum, by which the experienced data of the world are organized into increasingly complex and embedded forms of knowledge. What is vital for the present project are the technologies and the human knowers involved in structuring information into new configurations and, thereby, in constructing knowledge. Knowledge takes the shape that it does, in part, because of how people put it together.

Levine 2015, 6–7. This language derives from environmental psychologist James Gibson (Gibson 1966, developed in Gibson 1979, 127–137).

5 See, e.g., The Postclassicisms Collective 2020, 113–127 ("Knowing"); Wellmon 2021. The most influential account is Kuhn 2012 [1962], building on Polanyi 1958. On knowing in late antiquity, see Chin/Vidas 2015b. As Chin and Vidas write, recent scholarship has often understood "the activity of knowing as thoroughly conditioned, indeed created, by larger patterns of discourse and embedded in systems of social and cultural power" (2015a, 2). Leading the way in a major development in the history of late antiquity, the essays in Chin and Vidas 2015b combine this wider perspective with attention to specific, local, and embodied practices of knowing.

6 Debates continue about how to define and distinguish data, information, and knowledge. Blair articulates a contrast between "discrete and small-sized items that have been removed from their original contexts" — that is, information — and knowledge, which requires "an independent knower" to make sense of that information (Blair 2010, 2). As discussed by Amsler in the introduction to this volume, some draw a sharper distinction between (unsorted) "data" and (minimally organized) "information."

7 As Wellmon writes, knowledge deploys "concepts, methods, or theories" (often submerged or unrecognized) in making sense of available information (2021, 134). For the language of "situated knowledges," see the foundational essay of Haraway 1988. As Haraway writes, "[h]istories of science may be powerfully told as histories of the technologies. These technologies are ways of life, social orders, practices of visualization" (Haraway 1988, 587). Thinking with Haraway, we might describe late ancient tabular thinking as a "situated knowledge" emerging out of particular conditions and enabling particular possibilities because of its reliance on particular configurations of human labor. "Practices of visualization" are particularly relevant to the modes of knowing afforded by the table.

In this study, I examine the role of tables in late ancient scholarship, investigating both the "how" (the technologies and working methods) and the "who" (the human actors) involved in several innovative late ancient projects of knowledge construction.[8] Attending to both the technologies and the human actors involved in the construction of knowledge is crucial for understanding the late ancient social and intellectual contexts in which people developed and deployed this tabular mode of knowing.

The pragmatics and the ethics of knowledge cannot be separated. Technologies and practices for constructing knowledge are often collaborative, involving the labor, expertise, and agency of numerous individuals. This work is distributed across time, space, agents, and artifacts. As Chad Wellmon writes, knowledge is "bound up not just in minds but also in media, technologies, practices, and institutions."[9] Yet ancient and modern projects of knowledge often obscure the people, technologies, and processes involved in complex cognitive work. The present study examines two different kinds of instrumentality: the table as a late ancient tool of knowledge and the human knowers who made this textual machine work. Scholars often overlook both as "merely" instrumental. Both occlusions, moreover, reflect an aversion (ancient and modern) to the embodiment of knowledge. Yet their ethical significance is not the same. To obscure a technology (like the abacus, the drawing compass, or the column-and-row table) differs dramatically from exploiting and erasing human agency and labor. We must actively resist the dehumanizing fiction that Brendon Reay calls "masterly extensibility," which treats subordinated (often enslaved) individuals simply as tools, as extensions of the bodies and wills of others.[10] The

---

[8] Despite their enormous impact, late ancient tables have received scant attention and their technological features remain under-analyzed; see, however, Grafton/Williams 2006, 86–232 (Origen and Eusebius); Crawford 2019, esp. 56–95 (Origen and Eusebius); Riggsby 2023 (Origen); Mansfeld/Runia 1997–2010, 1:111–116 (Ptolemy, Origen, and Eusebius); Coogan 2022 (grammar, Ptolemy, Origen, and Eusebius).

[9] Wellmon 2021, 135. For an account of the interlocking structures of philology in nineteenth-century Europe, involving "practices, instruments, and cooperation," see Kurtz 2021, 751. Kurtz's account of varied *instrumenta* in the cooperative enterprise of philology offers a comparandum for late ancient knowing. Modern studies of distributed cognition illuminate how teams of people collaborate with each other and with varied technologies to form complex units for processing information and making decisions; these systems are not reducible to the contributions of any single individual (Hutchins 1995).

[10] While enslavement in the ancient Mediterranean differed in various ways from enslavement in other contexts, we cannot overlook its exploitative nature. On "masterly extensibility," see Reay 2005. As described by Joseph Howley, the "despotic discourse" of the Roman Mediterranean regarded human workers as cogs in a machine (Howley forthcoming). See, for example,

erasure of technologies and bodies in favor of an idealized solitary thinker is older than the Cartesian ideal of the European Enlightenment. It is grounded not only in the buffered self of modernity, but in what Joseph Howley has described as the "epistemic firewall" of ancient "despotic discourse," which separates the elite knower from the embodied labor of others.[11] By attending to the often-overlooked technologies involved in late ancient projects of knowledge construction, I intend also to redirect attention to people whom we might otherwise overlook.

In what follows, I define the table and describe its limited uses in Mediterranean antiquity before the third century CE. Then I turn to a revolution in knowledge that centers on figures working in third- and fourth-century Palestine: Origen (ca. 185–ca. 255 CE) in the third century, Eusebius (ca. 260–339/40 CE) in the early fourth century, and the rabbinic sages associated with the Palestinian Talmud (redacted late fourth century). These are among the first known figures to organize texts using tables, but the tabularity of their projects has often been neglected. After analyzing how these projects organize textual knowledge, I conclude by discussing the social and intellectual implications of late ancient tabular thinking.

2 Tables in the Roman Mediterranean

Modern readers encounter tables in manifold mundane contexts. We use them as bus timetables and budgets, gradebooks and coffee shop menus. We might find many everyday tasks inconvenient without this ubiquitous technology. But familiarity may lead us to overlook how tables organize information. What is it that makes the table such a powerful technology? Building on the work of An-

---

Aristotle, *Nicomachean Ethics* 1161a30–b6, which equates humans and physical tools. See further Candida Moss on the textual interchangeability of enslaved catapult operators and the catapults themselves in P. Berol. 11632 (Moss 2021b) and Sarah Blake on "prosthesis" as a model for the exploitation of enslaved bodies in antiquity (Blake 2012). On ancient tendencies to obscure and modern tendencies to ignore enslaved individuals in the Roman Mediterranean, see Fitzgerald 2021. On how present-day scholars might acknowledge those whom sources actively efface, see Dan-el Padilla Peralta's description of "epistemicide" (Padilla Peralta 2020) and the work of Moss (2021b), drawing on Saidiya Hartman's "critical fabulation" (Hartman 2008).

11 Howley forthcoming. This is not only an ancient prejudice; compare Geoghegan 2020 on the erasure of human cognitive work in modern information technologies. As Geoghegan argues, this erasure is often racialized, gendered, and connected to other bodily difference.

drew Riggsby, I define a table as a regular arrangement of columns and rows that structures information in two directions.[12] The crucial feature is the table's bidirectional significance: one can read both vertically and horizontally to obtain meaningful information. In these terms, the table differs from the list, which structures material in only one direction.[13] Because the table generates new meaningful juxtapositions, one can think with a table.

Although tables are familiar today, they were rare in the Roman Mediterranean.[14] People used tables in a handful of specialized contexts; in each case, tables were part of practical modes of knowing, embedded in particular communities of practice. Tables are first attested in the Mediterranean world around the turn of the era as a specialist technology for organizing scientific information. Astronomical tables on papyrus are extant from the first century BCE.[15] As Courtney Roby observes, the table was a mechanism for the collaborative production and maintenance of knowledge. Because the requisite observational time spans, especially without the precision of modern instruments, transcend the lifetime of any human astronomer, astronomical tables require astronomers to collaborate in collecting data and demand an information structure robust enough to enable different contributors over time to integrate observational

---

12 Riggsby 2019, 44–45; cf. Coogan 2022, 40.

13 Note the subversive possibilities of the nonlinear reading afforded by the index or the table of contents, e.g., Roy Gibson's discussion of subversive reading engendered by the index in manuscripts of Pliny (Gibson 2014). On nonlinear reading and late ancient tables of contents, see Coogan 2021a; 2021b.

14 Riggsby argues that tables were "vanishingly rare" until the third century CE (Riggsby 2019, 43). He focuses on Latin sources (2019, 42–82). Greek evidence in the first and second centuries CE is more widespread, but Greek tables were still confined to handful of technical contexts.

15 The *Handy Tables* of the second-century CE astronomer Ptolemy are a well-attested and successful example; see, *inter alia*, the papyrus fragments published in Jones 1999. Although I focus on tables that organize literary and historical information, late ancient Christian figures also used column-and-row tables for astronomical purposes. Paschal calculations offer some of the earliest evidence for Christians using tables. Through Eusebius' *Ecclesiastical History*, we discover third-century figures who employed mathematical astronomy to produce paschal canons. Hippolytus of Rome prepared "a canon (κανόνα) for a sixteen-year cycle" (Eusebius, *Hist. eccl.* 6.22.1) and Anatolius of Laodicea devised a nineteen-year cycle, published in a work known as Κανόνες περὶ τοῦ πάσχα (partially preserved in Eusebius, *Hist. eccl.* 7.32.14–19; cf. Jerome, *Vir. ill.* 73), created ca. 264 CE. In addition to a Greek excerpt preserved by Eusebius, a version of Anatolius' work is preserved in the Hiberno-Latin treatise *De ratione paschali* (PG 10, 209–222). As reflected by this Latin version, Anatolius' work contained a short treatise and two tables: the first provided a lunar calendar; the second provided the dates of Easter for the repeating cycle.

data.¹⁶ While astronomical tables are attested first, we also find numerical tables in geography, arithmetic, and other disciplines (τέχναι).¹⁷

As part of the τέχνη of grammar, tables also appeared in the schoolroom. The table was part of the toolbox of the grammarian, used for declension tables and glossaries.¹⁸ As Eleanor Dickey has demonstrated, arranging parallel texts in adjacent columns was an innovation that emerged out of ancient language learning, especially as a way of organizing bilingual information.¹⁹ Prior to the third century CE, however, we do not find the table as a technology for coordinating multiple texts.

As we consider late ancient tables, there are two things to observe. First, there are actual tables — composed of columns and rows, populated with information. Second, numerous late ancient texts reflect tabular dynamics of vertical sequence and horizontal comparison even when no formal column-and-row tables are preserved. Both kinds of evidence impel us to attend to the technological practices and the social structures involved in the construction of knowledge.

3 Origen's *Hexapla*

In the third and fourth centuries CE, multiple scholars based in Caesarea Maritima in Roman Palestine experimented with tables. Origen of Alexandria and — as I argue — a number of collaborators aligned multiple versions of Hebrew and Greek scriptures in a massive tabular project known as the *Hexapla* ("sixfold").²⁰ The *Hexapla* correlated divergent but roughly parallel texts: Hebrew scriptures and several Greek translations. Following initial Greek translations of Hebrew

---

16 Roby 2019, 43–44. Ptolemy similarly describes tabular arrangement as a way of inviting subsequent correction (διόρθωσις) and refinement of geographical data. In *Geogr.* 2.1.3, he invites subsequent users of his tables to correct the positional data and describes how his table can facilitate this revision.
17 See, e.g., Cribiore 1993; Roby 2018; Azzarello 2019. We find a handful of related uses: military duty rosters, surveying grids, and so forth; see Riggsby 2019, 50, 52.
18 Dickey *et al.* 2013; Dickey 2015; 2019. Classroom tables are not discussed in Morgan 1998 or Cribiore 2001.
19 Dickey 2015; cf. Brock 1970.
20 On Origen and the table, see Riggsby 2023; Mansfeld/Runia 1997–2010, 1:111–116; Grafton/Williams 2006; Crawford 2015, revised and expanded in Crawford 2019, 57–74; Coogan 2022, 42–47. Other important discussions of Origen's textual scholarship (e.g., Neuschäfer 1987; Martens 2012) do not engage the table as a technology.

scriptures beginning in the third century BCE, subsequent revisions had been made using various Hebrew texts. Different translation techniques and several distinct projects of revision led to a situation of textual diversity in Greek. While multiple texts were conceptually parallel, they often differed in detail and sequence. Origen responded to this complex situation with a table, using parallel columns to juxtapose multiple Greek versions with a Hebrew text.

The format of the *Hexapla* is unfortunately attested only by muddled literary descriptions and by two partial and palimpsested manuscripts,[21] one from the Cairo Genizah and the other in the Ambrosian Library in Milan.[22] They date from the seventh and ninth centuries CE, respectively. Both contain parts of the Psalms. Although the manuscripts are fragmentary, they enable us to reconstruct how Origen's project appeared on the manuscript page. Across every two-page opening, the *Hexapla* included six columns: a Hebrew text, a transliteration of the vocalized text into Greek characters, and four Greek translations.[23]

Although the *Hexapla* was an ambitious project of textual scholarship, it is unlikely that it was ever intended for distribution. Neither a handy *vade mecum* like ancient astronomical tables nor an ephemeral classroom genre like the grammatical table, the *Hexapla* was enormous. Anthony Grafton and Megan Williams estimate that a *Hexapla* containing the whole Hebrew Bible would

---

21 Ancient references to the *Hexapla* and *Tetrapla* are assembled in Field 1964 [1875], 1.xii. They include Origen, *Comm. Matt.* 15.14; *Ep. Afr.* 1–5; Eusebius, *Hist. eccl.* 6.16.1–4; Epiphanius, *Mens.* 7 [Greek ed. Moutsoulas 1973, 164–165; Syriac ed. Dean 1935, 21–22 (50c–d)]; *Pan.* 64.3.5–7; Jerome, *Comm. Tit.* 3.9; *Ep.* 102; *Vir. ill.* 54. On these sources and the history of scholarship, see Grafton/Williams 2006, 86–133.
22 The first manuscript (Rahlfs 2005) is Cambridge University Library Taylor-Schechter 12.182 (LDAB 3490; *editio princeps*: Taylor 1900, 1–50). The second manuscript (Rahlfs 1098) is Milan, MS Ambrosianus O. 39 sup. (*editio princeps*: Mercati 1958). Three other manuscripts preserve very limited evidence for the *Hexapla*'s columnar format: Rome, Vat. Barb. gr. 549 (Rahlfs 86), esp. fol. 94v; Milan, MS Ambrosianus B. 106. sup. (Rahlfs 113), fol. 7v; and Rome, Vat. gr. 1747 (Rahlfs 271), p. III. (I am grateful to Benjamin Kantor for discussing these three manuscripts with me.) Other manuscripts attest the *Hexapla* indirectly or include readings from multiple Greek versions, but do not reflect the tabular format of Origen's project. An important example is the fourth-century P. Amh. Gr. I.3c (Rahlfs 912; LDAB 3475), which preserves Gen 1:1–5 in Old Greek and Aquila.
23 For some biblical books (especially the Psalms and Minor Prophets), further Greek translations were included as additional columns. See Eusebius, *Hist. eccl.* 6.16.2–3; Epiphanius, *Mens.* 7 [Greek ed. Moutsoulas 1973, 164–165; Syriac ed. Dean 1935, 21–22 (50c–d)]; *Pan.* 64.3.6; Jerome, *Comm. Tit.* 3.9. These additional columns are not preserved in the extant *Hexapla* manuscripts.

require forty codex volumes of 400 pages each.[24] Although the *Hexapla* might have been copied, late ancient authors describe consulting it in Caesarea rather than using manuscripts elsewhere.[25]

As a table for organizing multi-lingual information, the *Hexapla* resembled earlier tabular glossaries and bilingual texts.[26] Origen might have known such tabular layouts from language pedagogy during his own education or during his career as a teacher.[27] Some scholars have proposed that Origen devised his *Hexapla* as a tool for learning to read the Hebrew scriptures.[28] This is unlikely. Including four or more Greek columns would have been superfluous if the *Hexapla* was primarily a crib; a single translation would suffice. Origen's decision to employ a framework primarily used for language learning does not require that the *Hexapla* was a tool for learning Hebrew. Others have more plausibly proposed that – regardless of Origen's own purposes for his project – his *Hexapla* was inspired by, or even built upon, existing bilingual tables designed to help readers access the Hebrew text. Nonetheless, the expansive project cannot be reduced to a tool for language pedagogy.

The *Hexapla* was an innovative matrix that coordinated textual data in two dimensions. A user could read horizontally across any row to compare the wording of a unit and could also consult each text vertically in its own column. This novel tabular arrangement afforded systematic comparison while preserving the possibility of linear reading.[29] The massive table made existing information

---

24 This estimate is based on the forty-line, complete-opening format of the Cairo palimpsest, in comparison with similar features in the Milan palimpsest; see Grafton/Williams 2006, 88. This extensive project would have been beyond the financial means of most. Questions of what exactly constituted the "Hebrew Bible" at this stage (and for whom) do not substantially change the massive size of the project.

25 The ambitious project may never have been completed. Pamphilus and Eusebius were working on it more than fifty years after Origen's death. See the colophons discussed in Grafton/Williams 2006, 324 n. 42 and, more extensively, in Marsh 2023.

26 Sebastian Brock perceptively suggested more than fifty years ago that the *Hexapla* was analogous to Latin-Greek parallel texts of Vergil (Brock 1970).

27 According to a farewell panegyric offered by one of his students, Origen's teaching included astronomy and geometry ([Pseudo-]Gregory, *Orat. paneg.* 8); both disciplines employed tables. Note Origen's emphasis on the value of astronomy and geometry in *Ep. Greg.* 1. Compare later reports of Origen's pedagogical breadth in Eusebius, *Hist. eccl.* 6.18.2–4 and Jerome, *Vir. ill.* 54. On the scope of Origen's own education, see Epiphanius, *Pan.* 64.1.1–2.

28 See the summary of positions in Martin 2004; Grafton/Williams 2006.

29 As James VanderKam observes, reading linearly down the page at forty words per opening would be inconvenient when done for any length of time. While the possibility of vertical reading puts each horizontal row in meaningful context and enables the painstaking labor of producing an edition, the *Hexapla* is not designed to be read *in extenso*. Cf. Martens 2012, 46.

available for new uses. The *Hexapla* was a purpose-built textual machine for a specific project, designed to facilitate comparison of parallel texts. As Francesca Schironi and Peter Gentry have both argued, the *Hexapla* juxtaposed Greek and Hebrew versions as a massive preparatory stage for the production of the *Tetrapla*, a non-columnar edited text (ἔκδοσις) of the Greek Bible supplied with critical signs and marginal annotations of variant readings.[30] This instrumental role may explain why ancient descriptions of Origen's project devote so little attention to its tabular features. The *Hexapla* was not the finished product. Instead, it was a ground-breaking textual machine that deployed the technology of the table to afford the efficient, systematic comparison of parallel texts.

The technology of the table was crucial in another way, as well. The *Hexapla*'s tabular format enabled collaboration. As a grid for textual data, it allowed multiple individuals to fill in the matrix.[31] As Andrew Riggsby observes, "[I]t is possible to come up with a table by introspection, but it is easier with a pen and pencil, and easier still in an environment in which different people are adding information to a given document at different times."[32] The simultaneous involvement of multiple individuals facilitated Origen's ambitious project.[33] Debates about the purpose and production of the *Hexapla* often center on Origen's own knowledge of Hebrew. But in light of tabular collaboration, this is unnecessary. Origen's linguistic competence is less important than the availability of one or more unacknowledged collaborators who *did* have the requisite skills.

---

30 Schironi 2012; 2015; Gentry 2016. The clearest evidence for the text-critical purpose of Origen's project and for the intermediate function of the *Hexapla* derives from the presence (and absence) of critical signs. So-called Aristarchean signs appear in Origen's discussion of his project, in other late ancient literary evidence referring to the *Hexapla*, and in a number of manuscripts of the Greek scriptures. They do not appear in the manuscript evidence for a columnar *Hexapla*. Nor should we expect them to. Aristarchean signs marked additions, omissions, or transpositions, but indicating these phenomena with critical signs was redundant in a table where the reader could visually compare the running texts. The table enables users to visualize textual similarity, difference, and correspondence. The signs belong instead in Origen's critical edition, where a single text is annotated with alternate readings, additions, and omissions – all marked with sigla. Such an arrangement is visible in P. Grenf. 1.5, which dates from the later third or early fourth century CE (Schironi 2015). The critical signs are the result of using the *Hexapla* to create a new text.
31 In his model of distributed cognition, Hutchins identifies the cognitive process as occurring both in the mind and outside the body of the participants, mediated through varied external devices or representations (Hutchins 1995, 292). That is precisely what we see here.
32 Riggsby 2023.
33 Compare the exploitation of enslaved workers which enabled the prodigious intellectual output of Pliny the Elder. Pliny "did all this work – reading, searching, comparing, excerpting, compiling – with the assistance of an enslaved staff" (Howley 2020, 23).

Origen's technological approach relates directly to the collaborative context of textual production. In terms of distributed cognition, the table's unifying information structure coordinates multiple forms of expertise. Table technology enables the *Hexapla* to be what Hutchins describes as an "open tool," subject to use and verification by more than one individual.[34] The *Hexapla* reflects a mode of textual scholarship, a practice of constructing knowledge, that involves the labor of multiple individuals.

Modern scholars tend to imagine collaborative projects in antiquity as the results of school circles, and this may sometimes be the case.[35] But a collaborative process need not imply willing students. Might we imagine other configurations of labor and agency? According to Eusebius, Epiphanius, and Jerome, Origen exploited the work of at least fourteen enslaved individuals as scribes and copyists.[36] We should not ignore this fact in scholarship on the massive editorial project that produced the *Hexapla* and *Tetrapla*. The table provided a way to coordinate a complex working process involving many hands and eyes.[37] It organized the skill and labor of these unacknowledged workers to offer new architectures of knowledge.

---

34 Hutchins 1995, 170.
35 I diverge from Riggsby (Riggsby 2023), who hypothesizes that the *Hexapla* evokes a classroom environment with the reader in a student position *vis-à-vis* Origen. While this may be the result for the rare individuals to encounter the *Hexapla* later — including figures like Eusebius who imagined themselves as the students of Origen — it does not offer the best model for the initial production of the *Hexapla*. On the idea of a Caesarean "school" under Origen: *Hist. eccl.* 6.32 and 6.36 with Knauber 1968; Crouzel 1970; Neuschäfer 1987; Jacobsen 2012; Martens 2012; Penland 2013; Schott 2013a; 2013b; Rogers 2017; Bäbler 2018; Satran 2018. On Jewish and Christian scholarly circles in Caesarea more broadly: Lapin 2005. Lapin cautions against attributing undue institutional status to the circles around Origen and Pamphilus. As Rogers and Penland both emphasize, much of what we know about Origen's circle reflects Eusebius' retrojection and requires caution.
36 Eusebius, *Hist. eccl.* 6.18.1–2; 6.23.1–2; cf. 6.36.1; Epiphanius, *Pan.* 64.3.4 [Holl 1915–2006, 2.405–406]; Jerome, *Ep.* 43.1; *Vir. ill.* 56; 61.3. Origen often receives exclusive recognition for the work of these specialists, funded by his patron Ambrose. On enslavement and early Christian literary production, see Haines-Eitzen 1998; Moss 2021a.
37 Given Origen's exploitation of enslaved literary workers and the prevalence of elite dictation (on which see, e.g., Arns 1953, 37–62; Herescu 1956; Schlumberger 1976; Horsfall 1995; McDonnell 1996; Cavallo 2000; Dorandi 2000), we might expect that Origen relied on enslaved workers in the production of the *Tetrapla* also.

4 Eusebius' Tables

Another scholar from late ancient Palestine, Eusebius of Caesarea, deployed the table for innovative projects of knowledge construction. Working in the first half of the fourth century, Eusebius devised a number of tabular projects, including his *Chronological Tables*, which synchronized events from world history, and his Gospel canons, a set of cross-reference tables that coordinated the four New Testament Gospels.[38] Both of these projects deployed the emergent technology of the table to configure existing material in innovative ways and to invite new possibilities of historical and textual knowledge.

Eusebius' *Chronological Tables* (Χρονικοὶ κανόνες) organized world history, synchronizing events, eras, and empires in parallel columns. Synthesizing numerous sources, they structured historical data into a framework that coordinates both time and space: the linear movement of time proceeds vertically, while geographical distinctions are represented horizontally.[39] Like Origen's *Hexapla* and earlier linguistic tables, the *Chronological Tables* deployed the technology of the table to organize cross-cultural and cross-linguistic information. Parallel columns often reflect distinct sources. (As we saw with the *Hexapla*, here also the table may coordinate not only varied sources but also the labor of multiple collaborators.) The *Chronological Tables* were distributed as the second half of Eusebius' two-part *Chronography*; the massive table in the second volume structures the various regnal lists and other chronological data that are excerpted, summarized, and annotated in the first volume.[40] The *Chronological Tables*, like the *Hexapla*, are a textual machine. But while the *Hexapla* was preparatory to a conventional edition, Eusebius innovates by publishing his tabular project as the product. This is a form of open data: Eusebius constructed a database to organize his research and made this available to subsequent readers, facilitating ongoing use and adaptation of the *Chronological*

---

[38] In the preface to his *Onomasticon*, Eusebius describes another potentially tabular project, a glossary of Hebrew and Greek place names. Another work attributed to Eusebius, his *Psalms Pinax*, categorizes individual psalms by attributed authorship; this work is a list rather than a table. The text is published in Wallraff 2013. The sole extant copy (titled Πίναξ ἐκτεθεὶς ὑπὸ Εὐσεβείου τοῦ Παμφίλου) is a prefatory paratext to the Psalter in the tenth-century manuscript Oxford, Bodleian Library, Auct. D. 4. 1, fols 24v–25r.

[39] On the *Chronological Tables* (sometimes known as the *Chronicon*) and information technology, see Grafton/Williams 2006; Grafton/Rosenberg 2010; Riggsby 2019, 218–222; Coogan 2022, 54–56.

[40] On the exploitation of enslaved workers for excerpting and note-taking, see Howley 2020, 23.

Tables and also subsequent production of historiographic texts by others.[41] The *Chronological Tables* organize their disparate sources to offer a particular vision of divinely ordered history, culminating in a single column for a unified *imperium*. The instrumental, tabular medium of the project, inviting ongoing appropriation and reconfiguration, amplified the influence of the Eusebian teleology expressed in the information architecture of the *Chronological Tables*.[42]

Another of Eusebius' projects, his Gospel canons, was massively successful from late antiquity until the modern period.[43] This set of ten tables ("canons") offers a system of cross-references for reading the Gospels according to Matthew, Mark, Luke, and John as a single fourfold whole. Eusebius' Gospel canons are the first system of cross-references ever devised. Eusebius' canons resemble Origen's *Hexapla* in their aim of organizing parallel texts. Yet Eusebius' project differs in crucial ways. Rather than rearranging the Gospels into a single massive table, Eusebius provided a system of marginal numbers that segment the four New Testament Gospels into sections.[44] The ten tables correlate these numbered sections.[45] Each number metonymically represents a section of Gospel text. The tables thus encapsulate the relationships between the four Gospels on just a few pages. In this, Eusebius' succinct system resembles a handy glossary or a set of astronomical tables more than it resembles the expansive datasets of the *Hexapla* or the *Chronological Tables*. The result is an elegant tool for tabular reading. Each linear ("vertical") Gospel text remains intact, expanded by a par-

---

41 Eusebius provided an information architecture that would be updated and expanded by others, including Jerome of Stridon's translation into Latin, an early translation into Armenian, and various later Greek, Latin, and Syriac chronographies; see Adler 1989; Grafton/Williams 2006.
42 On the theological and political implications of Eusebius' project, see Crawford 2020 (with cited sources).
43 On Eusebius' Gospel canons, see especially Grafton/Williams 2006; Coogan 2017; Crawford 2019; Coogan 2022.
44 The marginal annotations consist of two numbers for each section. The first number enumerates sections in each Gospel sequentially from the beginning of that Gospel. The second number identifies which of the ten reference tables coordinates a section with parallel sections from other Gospels.
45 Each of Eusebius' ten canons organizes a different pattern of relationships. Canon I tabulates material found in all four Gospels. Canons II–IV identify material found in various combinations of three Gospels. Canons V–IX identify material found in various combinations of two Gospels. Canon X consists of four sections, each identifying material found in one Gospel only.

atextual reference system that invites the reader to compare parallels horizontally.[46]

Eusebius' innovative tabular *instrumentum studiorum* enables the reader to identify parallel material and to read in new sequences. Moreover, because the ten canons each map different configurations of parallels, Eusebius' apparatus prompted varied projects of pattern-oriented "distant reading" in late ancient and medieval scholarship on both the Gospels and other texts.[47] Through the widespread transmission of the Eusebian system, tabular reading became part of the Gospel book itself, inviting ongoing engagement by readers in late antiquity and beyond.[48]

Both of these Eusebian projects are complex tabular systems for managing interrelated bodies of information, and perhaps for coordinating the labor of multiple human bodies. We know less about the human and economic conditions of Eusebius' *oeuvre* than we do for Origen's.[49] Yet, in light of the widespread exploitation of enslaved literary workers in the Roman Mediterranean and the use of the table as a tool of collaboration, Eusebius' tabular projects may have similarly depended on the unacknowledged work and expertise of others.[50] The table emerges again as a textual machine that both coordinates

---

[46] As traced in Crawford 2019 and Coogan 2022, numerous readers through late antiquity and the Middle Ages, encountering the Gospels in over a dozen languages, used Eusebius' Gospel canons for tabular reading.

[47] By "distant reading" I mean pattern-oriented analysis of large corpora (often in visual or quantitative ways), as opposed to the "close reading" that often characterizes textual scholarship. With the advent of digital humanities, distant reading sometimes studies corpora too large to analyze efficiently without computers, but it need not involve computers *per se* (see Piper 2020). For examples of late ancient and medieval distant reading using the Eusebian apparatus, see Coogan 2022, 33–36.

[48] Eusebius' Gospel tables are developed in part from an earlier project devised by Ammonius of Alexandria, who had rearranged the Gospels into parallel layout. See Crawford 2019, 56–95; Coogan 2022, 59–93.

[49] A *Life of Eusebius* reportedly penned by his successor Acacius is lost; the work is mentioned by the fifth-century historian Socrates of Constantinople, *Hist. eccl.* 2.4.

[50] This is especially true for the *Chronological Tables*, where the tabular structure might have provided a framework to organize the labor of multiple collaborators and multiple written sources. Elsewhere in Eusebius' corpus, we also discern the traces of uncredited workers. See Schott 2013b, 358–359, arguing that Eusebius' *Praep. ev.* reflects the work of multiple individuals. One might propose that these uncredited assistants were students or fellow clergy rather than enslaved or servile literary workers. Yet, given what we know about the role of enslavement in ancient reading and writing, we must resist the tendency to privilege the more palatable alternative in historical reconstructions.

existing information and facilitates new projects of constructing knowledge by a range of different users.

5 Tabular Thinking in the Palestinian Talmud

Origen, Eusebius, and their uncredited collaborators deployed the technology of the table for innovative modes of textual scholarship. But late ancient Palestine offers further examples that reflect tabular thinking, even though physically inscribed tables are not preserved in the extant sources. When we read closely, we find that the rabbinic sages who figure in the Palestinian Talmud were engaged in constructing knowledge with columns and rows.[51] The technology of the table again invites us to examine both modes of knowledge and human knowers.

The Amoraic sages addressed several of the same conceptual and textual problems that Origen and Eusebius did.[52] They were, as Moulie Vidas argues, engaged in "the development of a set of scholarly tools and formulations which address access to or textual problems with rabbinic traditions, a development which resembles in some sense what we find in 'book cultures' of other scholarly traditions."[53] This innovation was interwoven with another one, "the development of a discourse that centered on the way rabbinic knowledge was produced or generated by specific individuals or groups rather than by undifferentiated processes of transmission and production."[54] The scholarly

---

[51] The text dates in something like its current form to the late fourth century. On the date of the Palestinian Talmud and the material that it contains, see Strack *et al.* 1996, 171–176. The traditional periodization of figures and texts locates the Palestinian Talmud in the Amoraic period (ca. 200–500 CE). The material that reflects tabular thinking is overwhelmingly attributed to Amoraic sages rather than to those of the earlier Tannaitic period.

[52] Given the importance of tabularity for ancient astronomy, it is striking that we lack evidence for late ancient rabbinic use of astronomical tables. This might reflect both the instrumentality of such tables (such that, once consulted, the tables did not need to be mentioned in rabbinic discussions of astronomical and calendrical questions) and the limited range of genres that characterize the extant early rabbinic corpus. While a lunar phase diagram is mentioned in m. Roš Haš. 2:8 (see Leicht 2014), reference tables do not appear in Tannaitic or Amoraic texts. Medieval rabbinic texts employ tables (Stern and Burnett 2014).

[53] Vidas 2017, 28. The analogy is strengthened if we understand the figure of the rabbi to replace the physical book as a locus of textual knowledge (Dohrmann 2020, §§ 32–34). Organizing rabbinic dicta thus becomes equivalent to organizing parallel texts.

[54] Vidas 2017, 28.

projects of Origen, Eusebius, and their collaborators — which organized parallel literary texts and historical sources — correspond to both of these transitions that Vidas identifies.

The rabbinic sages of 3rd- and 4th-century Palestine reflect an analogous mode of tabular thinking. This parallel pattern of rabbinic thought does not require direct interaction between early Christian figures like Origen or Eusebius and their respective rabbinic contemporaries.[55] Nor do I argue that the tabular thinking of these third- and fourth-century Palestinian sages depends on the better-attested tabular projects of their Christian contemporaries. It suffices that these figures all participated in the rapid transformations in textuality and knowledge that were taking place in the late ancient Mediterranean world. The *Hexapla*, the *Chronological Tables*, the Eusebian canons, and the Palestinian Talmud each reflect this late ancient shift in knowing.

In light of these broader developments, I develop the implications of an example first identified by Moulie Vidas: the language of שיטה (*shitah*; שיטא in Aramaic).[56] The term has its basic meaning as something like "line." In Jewish Palestinian Aramaic it appears as an inscriptional term, almost always in the plural. It refers to "lines" (שיטין) of writing in bills of divorce or other legal documents (e.g., y. B. Bat. 10:1, 17c; y. Git. 3:2, 44d; y. Git. 9:6, 50c). Instructions for writing a Torah scroll stipulate that four (horizontal) "lines" or "rows" (שיטין) must be left between books of the Pentateuch (e.g., y. Meg. 1:8, 71d). The term שיטה can also refer to a vertical column of text. The most common example is in discussions of bilingual bills of divorce, in which Greek and Hebrew columns are placed side by side (e.g., y. B. Bat. 10:1, 17c). This, we note, approximates the format of the multi-column translations discussed above: tabularity is, again, about organizing linguistically divergent information in a shared space. In short, the שיטה appears both as the horizontal inscriptional line (that is, the row) and as the vertical column of text.

---

55 Scholarship over the past half-century (e.g., Baer 1961; de Lange 1976; Kimelman 1980; Horbury 2014) has frequently proposed direct exchange, especially between Origen and his contemporaries. On Origen's exchanges with "sages" (σοφοί), see *Ep. Afr.* 6–7. Note also Niehoff 2019 on R. Abbahu ("most likely active under Diocletian," 297), who is depicted in Amoraic literature as knowing Greek and engaging in the Roman legal-administrative culture of third-century Caesarea; R. Abbahu was Eusebius' contemporary. Some rabbinic circles operated in similar ways to the rhetorical circles of the Second Sophistic or to the philosophical circles around figures like Plotinus, Origen, and Eusebius; see Tropper 2004; Lapin 2005; Hidary 2017.

56 Vidas 2017. I am grateful to Moulie Vidas for discussing his work on שיטה with me in June 2018.

But שיטה also appears in conceptual contexts that do not describe physical writing. Frequently it refers to a "line" of thought. For example, "they answered him by his שיטה: 'by your שיטה [...]'" (y. Shevu. 9:9, 39a). Such usages lead to the gloss "usage, system" that appears in modern lexica of late ancient Hebrew and Aramaic.[57] We see a reflection of this systematizing impulse at various points in the Palestinian Talmud. A school or line of thought can be described as a שיטה (e.g., y. Demai 3:4, 23c; y. Pe'ah 7:6, 20b).[58] In some cases, the term describes the logical extension of a "line" of thinking (e.g., y. Or. 1:1, 60d). Often, it is used when a sage steps out of line or breaks his system. We read repeatedly "there he says" (תמן הוא או׳) but "here he says" (וכא הוא או׳ הכן); to describe such inconsistencies, the Palestinian Talmud tells us that the sage's שיטה has been "changed" or "exchanged" (using מוחלפת or another passive form of the verb הל"ף).[59] This usage does not appear in the Mishnah or in other Tannaitic literature, suggesting that it emerges in Amoraic (that is, late ancient) thought. In reaching two apparently inconsistent halakhic conclusions, a sage is imagined to switch one "line" (שיטה) of thinking for another. A sage who ordinarily rules in one way (corresponding to one column) might diverge from the norm for a given question (a particular row on the table) and offer an opinion that corresponds to the other imagined column. (We might imagine a "strict" column and a "lenient" column for a given halakhic question, although stringency and leniency are not the only possible categories.) This idiom — and its relevance for tabular thinking — becomes clearer in the occasional cases when two sages are imagined exchanging שיטין with one another (e.g., y. Shabb. 12:5, 13d). The mode of thinking reflects not simply a notional column (שיטה), but multiple columns in parallel, a meaningful table that works both down and across. Pattern-oriented halakhic analysis is systematized into a tabular structure of rows and columns.

This rabbinic idiom corresponds with the developments in late ancient tabular thinking that I have traced in the work of Origen, Eusebius, and their collaborators. Yet we lack direct evidence that the sages or their disciples were

---

[57] This is the first entry in Sokoloff's *Dictionary of Jewish Palestinian Aramaic* (Sokoloff 2002, 547a) and the second in the *Comprehensive Aramaic Lexicon* (http:cal.huc.edu; accessed 11 October 2018). This usage appears frequently in Palestinian and Babylonian texts. "System" or "method" also happens to be the normal meaning in modern Hebrew.

[58] For discussion of this terminology, but without engaging its tabularity, see Moscovitz 2009, 422–425.

[59] For example, in y. Pe'ah 7:5, 20b, the redactional voice informs the reader that the שיטה of R. Judah has changed. The passage goes on to attempt to resolve the contradiction; the table is used first to map a perceived inconsistency in the system and then to restore consistency to it.

drawing tables — on wax tablets, parchment notebooks, or any other medium.⁶⁰ The spatial mode of constructing knowledge reflected in the language of שיטה may instead have been an ephemeral schoolroom exercise, similar to drawing a grammatical paradigm or a multiplication table. Even so, it is far easier to draw out such ideas — on a chalkboard for us, on a wax tablet or a dusty floor for our ancient predecessors — than to imagine or discuss them in the "pure abstract."⁶¹ This mode of tabular thinking requires visualization to work.

These tables are not, insofar as we can discern, part of the literary output of rabbinic thought.⁶² We do not see the rabbinic table deployed as a published *instrumentum*, nor do we discern its systematic use in large-scale ("industrial," as it were) projects of knowledge production. In its non-publication, the table of halakhic opinions is distinct from astronomical tables or the Eusebian Gospel canons. It differs even from the *Hexapla*, which was an intermediate product

---

60 Several scholars have proposed that sages and their students employed such media in the process of teaching and learning. Taking notes and reviewing lectures using tablets or notebooks were widespread practices around the Roman Mediterranean (e.g., Arrian's *Discourses of Epictetus*; cf. Wollenberg 2017 on rabbinic use of written texts as *aides-mémoires*). These technologies were available to the rabbinic sages. The writing tablet (טבלא) appears frequently in rabbinic texts. The parchment notebook (דפתרא) also appears (e.g., m. Soṭah 2:3). On a couple of occasions, the Palestinian Talmud records halakhic appeal to material recorded in a notebook (פנקס = πίναξ) (y. Ma'as. 2:4, 49d; y. Kil. 1:1, 27a). As Natalie Dohrmann summarizes, "It is clear from the literary remains that [the sages'] teachings reached colleagues and acolytes, were collected, copied into notebooks, memoires, and curricula, excerpted, combined, and reissued in a range of new contexts" (Dohrmann 2020, § 34). We might imagine that such notes included sketched out tables or other diagrams as well. More speculative have been proposals about the relationship between such ephemeral notes and the eventual transmitted rabbinic corpora (e.g., Jaffee 2001, 140–147). As Dohrmann argues, although early rabbinic corpora elide many textual practices to present a dramatically narrowed bibliographic universe, the rabbinic "sense of foreboding in the face of the proliferation of knowledge" and the corresponding "attempt to manage" this complexity reflect the broader landscape of Roman imperial textuality (Dohrmann 2020, § 37). If rabbinic book-phobia participates in the pervasive anxieties of imperial Roman textuality (rather than indicating a complete retreat from textuality itself), then this should not mislead us into imagining that the sages lacked access to varied technologies for taking notes, reviewing material, or analyzing data.

61 Compare Netz 2002 on the physical manipulation of ideas. (Serafina Cuomo's ongoing work also involves discussion of the abacus as a tool of distributed cognition.) As Netz observes, the "abacus" as a technology does not require a specific physical artefact. An imagined division of space or a few lines in the dirt will do. Expert abacus practitioners can perform advanced calculations simply by visualizing an abacus (Netz 2002, 326). The tabular thinking that I propose for the Amoraic sages is similarly flexible regarding physical media.

62 This may reflect both the sages' frequent skepticism about transmitting Oral Torah in writing and the instrumental role of the late ancient table.

neither intended for nor suited to extensive distribution, since Origen's project was durable. Rather than a textual machine for assimilating large amounts of data, the language of שיטה reflects the table as a technology for more localized systematization. It indicates a different social situation, less the textual workshop of Origen or Eusebius, more the classroom of the grammar table, the glossary, and the table of squares. Even so, these rabbinic texts preserve the metaphorical traces of tabular thinking as a late ancient technology for systematizing information and constructing knowledge.[63]

6 Conclusions: Tabularity, Instrumentality, and Agency

The use of the table for textual scholarship was a late ancient innovation. Yet modern scholars have often overlooked how the table transformed textual knowledge. In this essay, I show how late ancient thinkers put the technology of the table to work for creative ends. Origen, Eusebius, and the Amoraic sages each reconfigured existing material to afford new possibilities of knowledge. Their projects of constructing knowledge involved different kinds of information and operated within divergent social contexts, but in each case the table organized sources of information and coordinated human work in projects of constructing knowledge.

The table invites distinctive modes of comparison and visualization. Each of these novel late ancient projects employed the technology of the table in order to afford their users with new — or newly efficient and accessible — patterns, juxtapositions, and comparisons, bringing disparate information into new structuring wholes. Origen's *Hexapla*, Eusebius' *Chronological Tables*, Eusebius' Gospel canons, and the ephemeral tables of the Palestinian Talmud were each instrumental to the production of knowledge. Origen's *Hexapla* provided a tabular grid to organize knowledge in preparation for a consolidated edition of the Greek Bible. Eusebius' tables afforded new practices of comparative reading and reference. Rabbinic tables mapped patterns and anomalies in received dicta. The late ancient table was a technology for configuring and reconfiguring

---

63 On literary texts preserving instrumental technologies and cognitive processes, see Netz's discussion of the abacus (Netz 2002, 325).

knowledge, making anomalies, patterns, and structures visible. To borrow Krajewski's terminology, these tables were papyrus or parchment "machines."[64]

Attending to the table as a textual machine should compel us to attend to the human agents who made that machine work. The pragmatics and the ethics of late ancient tabular thinking intersect. This essay is thus an exercise in "looking *directly at*" what we usually look "*through*."[65] In drawing attention to a technology that is often overlooked precisely because of its instrumentality, I have also tried to draw our attention to how human workers — often uncredited — interacted with these tables. Our evidence here is limited. We know more about Origen's exploitation of enslaved literary workers than we do about the people involved in Eusebius' literary endeavors. The role of enslaved or subaltern workers in rabbinic knowing is even less clear. Yet, as a machine for constructing knowledge, the table afforded a way of coordinating the efforts and expertise of multiple workers — and modern reconstructions must attend to these histories of work and agency.

Each of the late ancient tabular projects that I survey in this study reconfigured existing material for new ends. Origen organized divergent textual forms of the Jewish scriptures. Eusebius organized historical information about different ἔθνη and narratives about Jesus attributed to particular evangelists. The rabbis of the Palestinian Talmud organized halakhic knowledge attributed to particular sages. These tabular projects constructed knowledge by coordinating material attributed to varied texts and individuals. They reflect not merely a desire to put into order, but a documentary or bibliographic way of thinking that seeks to structure inherited knowledge — and this mode of constructing knowledge works because of the possibilities for visualization that the column-and-row table affords. These modes of knowing are facilitated by the technology of the table, not just as a metaphor, but as a way for people — often multiple people working together — to arrange information in spatial ways that afford reading and knowing in newly shared, systematic, and productive ways. Like Krajewski's "paper machines," the late ancient table is a mechanism that creates knowledge. Attending to comparative dimensions of tabularity reveals parallels between scholarly practices and textual communities in late ancient Palestine and invites attention to how technologies participated in a late ancient transformation in knowledge.

---

64 Krajewski 2011, 8–9.
65 Here I adapt the words (with emphasis) of Howley 2018, 175.

Bibliography

Adler, W. (1989), *Time Immemorial: Archaic History and its Sources in Christian Chronography from Julius Africanus to George Syncellus*, Washington.
Anderson, M./Cairns, D./Sprevak, M. (2019), "Distributed Cognition and the Humanities", in: M. Anderson/D. Cairns/M. Sprevak (eds.), *Distributed Cognition in Classical Antiquity*, Edinburgh, 1–17.
Arns, P.E. (1953), *La technique du livre d'après saint Jérôme*, Paris.
Azzarello, G. (2019), "Μισούμενα on the *Misoumenos*: Neglected Tables of Fractions in P.Oxy. XXXIII 2656", *Trends in Classics* 11, 241–255.
Bäbler, B. (2018), "Für Christen und Heiden, Männer und Frauen: Origenes' Bibliotheks- und Lehrinstitut in Caesarea", in: P. Gemeinhardt/I. Tanaseanu-Döbler (eds.), *"Das Paradies ist ein Hörsaal für die Seelen": Institutionen religiöser Bildung in historischer Perspektive*, Tübingen, 129–152.
Baer, Y.A. (1961), "Israel, the Christian Church, and the Roman Empire: From the Time of Septimius Severus to the Edict of Toleration of A.D. 313", in: A. Fuks/I. Halpern (eds.), *Studies in History*, Jerusalem, 79–149.
Blair, A. (2010), *Too Much to Know: Managing Scholarly Information Before the Modern Age*, New Haven.
Blake, S. (2012), "Now You See Them: Slaves and Other Objects as Elements of the Roman Master", *Helios* 39, 193–211.
Brock, S.P. (1970), "Origen's Aims as a Textual Critic of the Old Testament", *Studia Patristica* 10, 215–218.
Cavallo, G. (2000), "Écriture et pratiques intellectuelles dans le monde antique", *Genesis* 15, 97–108.
Chin, C.M. (2008), *Grammar and Christianity in the Late Roman World*, Philadelphia.
Chin, C.M./Vidas, M. (2015a), "Introduction", in: C.M. Chin/M. Vidas (eds.), *Late Ancient Knowing: Explorations in Intellectual History*, Berkeley, 1–13.
Chin, C.M./Vidas, M. (eds.) (2015b), *Late Ancient Knowing: Explorations in Intellectual History*, Berkeley.
Coogan, J. (2017), "Mapping the Fourfold Gospel: Textual Geography in the Eusebian Apparatus", *Journal of Early Christian Studies* 25, 337–357.
Coogan, J. (2021a), "Gospel as Recipe Book: Nonlinear Reading and Practical Texts in Late Antiquity", *Early Christianity* 12, 40–60.
Coogan, J. (2021b), "Transforming Textuality: Porphyry, Eusebius, and Late Ancient Tables", *Studies in Late Antiquity* 5, 6–27.
Coogan, J. (2022), *Eusebius the Evangelist: Rewriting the Fourfold Gospel in Late Antiquity*, Oxford.
Crawford, M.R. (2015), "Ammonius of Alexandria, Eusebius of Caesarea and the Origins of Gospels Scholarship", *New Testament Studies* 61, 1–29.
Crawford, M.R. (2019), *The Eusebian Canon Tables: Ordering Textual Knowledge in Late Antiquity*, Oxford.
Crawford, M.R. (2020), "The Influence of Eusebius' *Chronicle* on the Apologetic Treatises of Cyril of Alexandria and Augustine of Hippo", *Journal of Ecclesiastical History* 71, 693–711.
Cribiore, R. (1993), "A Table of Squares", *Bulletin of the American Society of Papyrologists* 39, 23–25.

Cribiore, R. (2001), *Gymnastics of the Mind: Greek Education in Hellenistic and Roman Egypt*, Princeton.
Crouzel, H. (1970), "L'école d'Origène à Césarée: Postscriptum à une édition de Grégoire le Thaumaturge", *Bulletin de littérature ecclésiastique* 71, 15–27.
de Lange, N.R. (1976), *Origen and the Jews: Studies in Jewish-Christian Relations in Third-Century Palestine*, Cambridge.
Dean, J.E. (ed.) (1935), *Epiphanius'* Treatise on Weights and Measures: *The Syriac Version*, Chicago.
Dershowitz, I. (2021), *The Dismembered Bible: Cutting and Pasting Scripture in Antiquity*, Tübingen.
Dickey, E. (2015), "Columnar Translations: An Ancient Interpretive Tool that the Romans Gave the Greeks", *Classical Quarterly* 65, 807–821.
Dickey, E. (2019), "A Re-Examination of New Testament Papyrus P99 (Vetus Latina AN glo Paul)", *New Testament Studies* 65, 103–121.
Dickey, E./Ferri, R./Scappaticcio, M.C. (eds.) (2013), "The Origins of Grammatical Tables: A Reconsideration of P.Louvre Inv. E 7332", *Zeitschrift für Papyrologie und Epigraphik* 187, 173–189.
Dohrmann, N.B. (2020), "Jewish Books and Roman Readers: Censorship, Authorship, and the Rabbinic Library", in: K. Berthelot (ed.), *Regarding Roman Power: Imperial Rule in the Eyes of Greeks and Romans, Jews and Christians, and Others*, Rome, 417–442.
Dorandi, T. (2000), *Le stylet et la tablette: Dans le secret des auteurs antiques*, Paris.
Field, F. (1964) [1875], *Origenis Hexaplorum*, Hildesheim.
Fitzgerald, W. (2021), "The Slave, between Absence and Presence", in: T. Geue/E. Giusti (eds.), *Unspoken Rome: Absence in Latin Literature and its Reception*, Cambridge, 239–249.
Franklin-Brown, M. (2012), *Reading the World: Encyclopedic Writing in the Scholastic Age*, Chicago.
Gentry, P.J. (2016), "Did Origen Use the Aristarchean Signs in the *Hexapla*?", in: W. Kraus/M.N. van der Meer/M. Meiser (eds.), *XV Congress of the International Organization for Septuagint and Cognate Studies, Munich, 2013*, Atlanta, 133–148.
Geoghegan, B.D. (2020), "Orientalism and Informatics: Alterity from the Chess-Playing Turk to Amazon's Mechanical Turk", *Ex-position* 43, 45–90.
Gibson, J.J. (1966), *The Senses Considered as Perceptual Systems*, Boston.
Gibson, J.J. (1979), *The Ecological Approach to Perception*, Hillsdale.
Gibson, R. (2014), "Starting with the Index in Pliny", in: L. Jansen (ed.), *The Roman Paratext: Frame, Texts, Readers*, Cambridge, 33–55.
Grafton, A./Rosenberg, D. (2010), *Cartographies of Time*, New York.
Grafton, A./Williams, M.H. (eds.) (2006), *Christianity and the Transformation of the Book: Origen, Eusebius, and the Library of Caesarea*, Cambridge.
Haines-Eitzen, K. (1998), "'Girls Trained in Beautiful Writing': Female Scribes in Roman Antiquity and Early Christianity", *Journal of Early Christian Studies* 6, 629–646.
Haraway, D. (1988), "Situated Knowledges: The Science Question in Feminism and the Privilege of Partial Perspective", *Feminist Studies* 14, 575–599.
Hartmann, S. (2008), "Venus in Two Acts", *Small Axe* 12 (2), 1–14.
Herescu, N.I. (1956), "Le mode de composition des écrivains («dictare»)", *Revue d'études latines*, 132–146.
Hidary, R. (2017), *Rabbis and Classical Rhetoric: Sophistic Education and Oratory in the Talmud and Midrash*, Cambridge.

Horbury, W. (2014), "Origen and the Jews: Jewish-Christian and Jewish-Greek Relations", in: J.K. Aitken/J.N. Carleton Paget (eds.), *The Jewish-Greek Tradition in Antiquity and the Byzantine Empire*, New York, 79–90.
Horsfall, N. (1995), "Rome Without Spectacles", *Greece and Rome* 42, 49–56.
Howley, J.A. (2018), *Aulus Gellius and Roman Reading Culture: Text, Presence, and Imperial Knowledge in the* Noctes Atticae, Cambridge.
Howley, J.A. (2020), "In Rome", in: L. Price/M. Rubery (eds.), *Further Reading*, Oxford, 15–27.
Howley, J.A. (forthcoming), "Despotics: Theory and Practice of Domination in the Ancient Agronomists".
Hutchins, E. (1995), *Cognition in the Wild*, Cambridge.
Jacobsen, A.-C. (2012), "Conversion to Christian Philosophy: The Case of Origen's School in Caesarea", *Zeitschrift für antikes Christentum* 16, 145–157.
Jaffee, M. (2001), *Torah in the Mouth: Writing and Orality in Palestinian Judaism 200 BCE to 400 CE*, Oxford.
Jones, A. (1999), *Astronomical Papyri from Oxyrhynchus (P. Oxy. 4133–4300a): Edited with Translations and Commentaries*, Philadelphia.
Kennedy, K. (2016), *Textual Curation: Authorship, Agency, and Technology in Wikipedia and Chambers's* Cyclopaedia, Columbia.
Kimelman, R. (1980), "Rabbi Yoḥanan and Origen on the Song of Songs: A Third-Century Jewish-Christian Disputation", *Harvard Theological Review* 73, 567–595.
Knauber, A. (1968), "Das Anliegen der Schule des Origenes zu Cäsarea", *Münchener theologische Zeitschrift* 19, 182–203.
Krajewski, M. (2011), *Paper Machines: About Cards & Catalogs, 1548–1929*, Cambridge.
Kuhn, T. (2012) [1962], *The Structure of Scientific Revolutions*, Chicago.
Kurtz, P.M. (2021), "The Philological Apparatus: Science, Text, and Nation in the Nineteenth Century", *Critical Inquiry* 47, 747–776.
Lapin, H. (2005), "Jewish and Christian Academies in Roman Palestine", in: K.G. Holum/A. Raban (eds.), *Caesarea Maritima: A Retrospective After Two Millennia*, Leuven, 496–512.
Leicht, R. (2014), "Observing the Moon: Astronomical and Cosmological Aspects in the Rabbinic New Moon Procedure", in: S. Stern/C. Burnett (eds.), *Time, Astronomy, and Calendars in the Jewish Tradition*, Leiden, 27–39.
Levine, C. (2015), *Forms: Whole, Rhythm, Hierarchy, Network*, Princeton.
Lynch, D./Robertson, C. (2021), "Pinning and Punching: A Provisional History of Holes, Paper, and Books", *INSCRIPTION* 2, 15–25.
Mansfeld, J./Runia, D.T. (eds.) (1997–2010), *Aëtiana: The Method and Intellectual Context of a Doxographer*, 4 vols., Leiden.
Marsh, B.J., Jr. (2023), *Early Christian Scripture and the Samaritan Pentateuch*, Berlin.
Martens, P.W. (2012), *Origen and Scripture: The Contours of the Exegetical Life*, Oxford.
Martin, M.J. (2004), "Origen's Theory of Language and the First Two Columns of the *Hexapla*", *Harvard Theological Review* 97, 99–106.
McDonnell, M. (1996), "Writing, Copying, and Autograph Manuscripts in Ancient Rome", *Classical Quarterly* 46, 469–491.
Mercati, G. (ed.) (1958), *Psalterii Hexapli reliquiae. Pars prima. Codex Rescriptus Bybliothecae Ambrosianae O 39 Sup. phototypice expressus et transcriptus*, Rome.
Morgan, T. (1998), *Literate Education in the Hellenistic and Roman Worlds*, Cambridge.

Moscovitz, L. (2009), *The Terminology of the Yerushalmi: The Principal Terms* [Hebrew], Jerusalem.

Moss, C.R. (2021a), "Fashioning Mark: Early Christian Discussions about the Scribe and Status of the Second Gospel", *New Testament Studies* 67, 181–204.

Moss, C.R. (2021b), "Between the Lines: Looking for the Contributions of Enslaved Literate Laborers in a Second-Century Text (P. Berol. 11632)", *Studies in Late Antiquity* 5, 432–452.

Moutsoulas, E.D. (1973), "Τὸ 'Περὶ μέτρων καὶ σταθμῶν' ἔργον Ἐπιφανίου τοῦ Σαλαμῖνος", *Θεολογία* 44, 157–198.

Netz, R. (2002), "Counter Culture: Towards a History of Greek Numeracy", *History of Science* 40, 321–352.

Neuschäfer, B. (1987), *Origenes als Philologe*, 2 vols., Basel.

Niehoff, M.R. (2019), "A Hybrid Self: Rabbi Abbahu in Legal Debates in Caesarea", in: M.R. Niehoff/J. Levinson (eds.), *Self, Self-Fashioning, and Individuality in Late Antiquity: New Perspectives*, Tübingen, 293–330.

Padilla Peralta, D. (2020), "Epistemicide: The Roman Case", *Classica* 33, 151–186.

Penland, E.C. (2013), "The History of the Caesarean Present: Eusebius and Narratives of Origen", in: J.M. Schott/A.P. Johnson (eds.), *Eusebius of Caesarea: Tradition and Innovations*, Cambridge, 83–95.

Piper, A. (2020), "Enumerative", in: L. Price/M. Rubery (eds.), *Further Reading*, Oxford, 145–151.

Polanyi, M. (1958), *Personal Knowledge: Towards a Post-Critical Philosophy*, Chicago.

Reader, S. (2021), *Notework: Victorian Literature and Nonlinear Style*, Stanford.

Reay, B. (2005), "Agriculture, Writing, and Cato's Aristocratic Self-Fashioning", *Classical Antiquity* 24, 331–361.

Riggsby, A.M. (2019), *Mosaics of Knowledge: Representing Information in the Roman World*, Oxford.

Riggsby, A.M. (2023), "Learning the Language of God: Tables in Early Christian Texts", in: L. Ayres/M.W. Champion/M.R. Crawford (eds.), *The Intellectual World of Christian Late Antiquity: Reshaping Classical Traditions*, Cambridge.

Robertson, C. (2019), "Granular Certainty, the Vertical Filing Cabinet, and the Transformation of Files", *Administory* 4, 71–86.

Robertson, C. (2021), *The Filing Cabinet: A Vertical History*, Minneapolis.

Roby, C. (2018), "Geometer, in a Landscape: Embodied Mathematics in Hero's *Dioptra*", in: M. Siliaros (ed.), *Revolutions and Continuities in Greek Mathematics*, Berlin, 67–88.

Roby, C. (2019), "Physical Sciences: Ptolemy's Extended Mind", in: M. Anderson/D. Cairns/M. Sprevak (eds.), *Distributed Cognition in Classical Antiquity*, Edinburgh, 37–56.

Rogers, J.M. (2017), "Origen in the Likeness of Philo: Eusebius of Caesarea's Portrait of the Model Scholar", *Studies in Christian-Jewish Relations* 12, 1–13.

Satran, D. (2018), *In the Image of Origen: Eros, Virtue, and Constraint in the Early Christian Academy*, Berkeley.

Schironi, F. (2012), "The Ambiguity of Signs: Critical σημεῖα from Zenodotus to Origen", in: M.R. Niehoff (ed.), *Homer and the Bible in the Eyes of Ancient Interpreters*, Leiden, 87–112.

Schironi, F. (2015), "P. Grenf. 1.5, Origen, and the Scriptorium of Caesarea", *Bulletin of the American Society of Papyrologists* 52, 181–223.

Schlumberger, J. (1976), "'Non scribe sed dicto" (HA T 33,8): Hat der Autor der Historia Augusta mit Stenographen gearbeitet?" in: G. Alfoldy/E. Badian/R. Syme (eds.), *Bonner Historia Augusta Colloquium 1972–1976*, Bonn, 221–238.

Schott, J.M. (2013a), "Introduction: Origenist Textualities", *Journal of Early Christian Studies* 21, 323–327.
Schott, J.M. (2013b), "Plotinus's Portrait and Pamphilus's Prison Notebook: Neoplatonic and Early Christian Textualities at the Turn of the Fourth Century C.E.", *Journal of Early Christian Studies* 21, 329–362.
Sokoloff, M. (2002), *A Dictionary of Jewish Palestinian Aramaic of the Byzantine Period*, Ramat Gan.
Stefaniw, B. (2019), *Christian Reading: Language, Ethics, and the Order of Things*, Berkeley.
Stern, S./Burnett, C. (eds.) (2014), *Time, Astronomy, and Calendars in the Jewish Tradition*, Leiden.
Strack, H.L./Stemberger, G./Bockmuehl, M.N. (1996), *Introduction to the Talmud and Midrash*, Minneapolis.
Taylor, C. (1900), *Hebrew-Greek Cairo Genizah Palimpsests from the Taylor-Schechter Collection, Including a Fragment of the Twenty-Second Psalm According to Origen's Hexapla*, Cambridge.
The Postclassicisms Collective (2020), *Postclassicisms*, Chicago.
Tropper, A.D. (2004), *Wisdom, Politics, and Historiography: Tractate Avot in the Context of the Graeco-Roman Near East*, Oxford.
Vidas, M. (2017), "A Place of Torah", in: C.E. Fonrobert/I. Rosen-Zvi/A. Shemesh/M. Vidas/J.A. Redfield (eds.), *Talmudic Transgressions: Engaging the Work of Daniel Boyarin*, Leiden, 23–73.
Wallraff, M. (2013), "The Canon Tables of the Psalms: An Unknown Work of Eusebius of Caesarea", *Dumbarton Oaks Papers* 67, 1–14.
Wellmon, C. (2021), "Knowledge", in: M. Kennerly/S. Frederick/J.E. Abel (eds.), *Information: Keywords*, New York, 133–147.
Wollenberg, R.S. (2017), "The Dangers of Reading as We Know It: Sight Reading as a Source of Heresy in Early Rabbinic Traditions", *Journal of the American Academy of Religion* 85, 709–745.
Yuen-Collingridge, R. (2018), "Between Autograph and Copy: Writing as Thinking on Papyrus", *Book History* 21, 1–28.

Elizabeth Mattingly Conner
Leading Sources of Knowledge at the Monastery: Isidore of Pelusium

Abstract: This paper will examine debates about the leading sources of knowledge and scientific inquiry among lettered ancient provincials, Christian and pagan, through the lens of a subset of the letters of an understudied yet voluminous epistolographer, an ex-sophist turned monk, Isidore of Pelusium (375–435/40 CE). In missives to literati associates, Isidore continued to play the role of "sophist-philosopher" by dramatizing his technical knowledge of scientific and medical authors and flaunting his possession of this competence which still constituted a verifiable form of the cultural capital of *paideia* among Christian and non-Christian literati.[1] Placing these missives in the broader context of contemporary monastic polemical outreach methods and the use of doxographies and anthologies at the monastery in the environs of Alexandria and Gaza, Isidore's apparent opposition to empiricism on closer examination suggests pervasive ambivalence about the true sources of learned authority and persistent immersion in Classical models of authorizing knowledge.

1 Introduction

Competence in medical and scientific discourse constitutes a dimension of late antique epistolography rather neglected in modern scholarly discussion. Epistolary commerce enabled vibrant discussions among various types of literati (ranging from sophists to philosophers to architects, doctors, and iatrosophists) about mechanical devices as well as scientific and medical ideas, stretching from the nature of the universe to discussion of the relationships between various types of matter, to the Galenic definition of the soul.[2]

We can observe in a smattering of late antique sources keen interest in scientific speculation and mechanical gadgets. In fifth and early sixth century CE

---

[1] Van Hoof 2013, 387.
[2] The conventions of learned Greek and Latin epistolography may have engendered technical or scientific discussion. As Morello and Morrison observe "the differences in power, competence, or technical expertise which can be dramatized in such role-playing make the letter form especially suited for the transmission of knowledge or of advice... one of the strongest affinities of the epistle is with a variety of didactic traditions." Morello *et al.* 2007, viii.

∂ Open Access. © 2023 Elizabeth Mattingly Conner, published by De Gruyter. This work is licensed under the Creative Commons Attribution 4.0 International License.
https://doi.org/10.1515/9783111010311-004

Gaza, Christian sophists Aeneas (b. 430) and Procopius (ca. 465–528, not to be confused with the historian Procopius of Caesarea) captured their admiration for mechanical devices, specifically a water-lifting device and water-clock, (presumably both at Gaza in Palaestina Prima) by means of ekphrastic description. Not surprisingly for these custodians of Greek rhetoric, *ekphrasis* provided a means for these literati to authorize their fascination with mechanical devices, although the use of *ekphrasis* in scientific writing deserves further attention.[3] Aeneas' epistolary *ekphrasis* in *Letter* 25 of a waterwheel on his property clearly registers his fascination and admiration for both the machine itself and for its inventor.[4] Similarly, in his *ekphrasis* on the animated water clock dedicated to Heracles in the city center of Gaza, Procopius of Gaza applies various strategies recommended in rhetorical instruction books or *progymnasmata* to engage his audience's imagination and emotional engagement, including hyperbolic statements and discussion of clock movement.[5] Neither sophist is particularly interested in understanding the technical operation of these devices presumably because of their professional concerns and the assumption of the superiority of rhetorical discourse.

Sources from the Latin West contemporary to the sophists from Gaza express that technical and scientific knowledge could inspire fascination and fear. Epistolary testimony addressed by the statesman and intellectual Cassiodorus (487–585) to Boethius (477–524) conveys the fear and awe of late ancient provincials in the face of scientific and technical knowledge. *Letter* 1.14 drafted by Cassiodorus to petition the help of Boethius in constructing a clock for Gundobad of Burgundy contains remarks that suggest how a man vested with mathematical and mechanical competence was perceived by lettered peers without such training.[6] At 8.59–60 Cassiodorus quips, "it is wonder enough that a man might understand these things; what shall we say of him who can perform

---

[3] In discussion of *ekphrasis* in the context of the Second Sophistic, Roby 2013, 109–125, has recently pointed out Ptolemy's use of *ekphrasis* in mathematical and astronomical texts to persuade readers of the veracity of his theories and to help them to visualize hypothetical experiments; and Bäbler's review: *BMCR* 2014.11.44.
[4] On this letter, see Watts 2017, 388.
[5] For the most recent publication of the Greek text of Procopius' *ekphrasis* on the water clock including an introduction, annotation, and a translation in French, see Amato 2014, 119–156. See also the Greek text, Italian translation, commentary, and notes in Amato 2010a, 204–213; 276–80nn76–113. For scholarship concerning this text, see Diehls 1917, Amato 2010b, 21–30 and Bäbler/Schomberg 2010, 528–559. On the use of hyperbole and movement in late antique and Byzantine *ekphrasis*, see Webb 1999, 64, 69–71.
[6] See Rousseau 1996, 877.

them?" At lines 7 and 10, Boethius is said to have the power to imitate the heavens and at 10 "what a strange power is that of his art, while it claims to play it has the supreme power to disclose the secrets of nature."[7] Hence Cassiodorus attaches a sort of almost religious wonder and fear to the craft and knowledge of a mathematician and mechanician.

Probably in the early fifth century, in a letter sent with the gift of an astrolabe to Paeonius, a military magistrate at Constantinople, the philosopher and bishop Synesius of Cyrene (373–414?) offered a Neoplatonic defense of the natural sciences because they serve philosophy. For Synesius, the study of astronomy is a lofty science that propels one toward the even loftier field of knowledge of the ineffable things about God (*tēs aporrhētou theologiā*). Astronomy "makes available the blessed body of the heavens, for the happy body of heaven has matter underneath it, of which the movement (of the heavens) appeared to the leaders in philosophy to be an imitation of the Mind."[8] By "Mind" (*Nous*), Synesius means here the idea of the Demiurge, the first efflux descending from the One in the Neoplatonic hierarchical hypostasis. This intelligible realm is the "self-specification and articulation" of the One.[9] Implying a mystical experience as the *telos* of scientific study of the heavens, Synesius affirms that the spiritual sparks native to the human soul long to seek out their divine source.[10] Astronomy itself discloses the secrets etched in the cosmos which reproduce the noetic realm.

This paper will engage with debates about epistemology and attitudes toward the appropriate role of scientific knowledge among late ancient literati through the lens of the letters of Synesius' contemporary, an understudied yet voluminous epistolographer, a former sophist turned monk, Isidore of Pelusium (375–435/40 CE).[11] The over 2,000 surviving letters of Isidore,[12] many of which

---

[7] "O artis inaestimabilis virtus, quae dum se dicit ludere, naturae praevalet secreta vulgare!" Fridh *et al.* 1973, 53.
[8] ὕλην τε γὰρ ὑποβέβληται τὸ μακάριον οὐρανοῦ σῶμα, οὗ καὶ τὴν κίνησιν νοῦ μίμησιν εἶναι τοῖς κορυφαιοτάτοις ἐν φιλοσοφίᾳ δοκεῖ. *Ad Paeonium de dono astrolabii* 4.1, in Stramondo, 1964.
[9] Bregman 1982, 36. On Synesius' various uses of the Nous, including his assimilation of the Neoplatonic Trinity (One, *Nous*, Soul) to the Christian Trinity, see Bregman, 33, 36, 63, 79–83, 91, 103, 112, 165–166, 179, 180, 183.
[10] Bregman. This is a paraphrase of Bregman's discussion of the *epistrophē* in Synesius' Hymn 1.
[11] For discussion of Isidore's biography, see Larsen 2017, Évieux 2000, and Évieux 1995.
[12] Isidore's letters number over 2000. The recent Source Chrétiennes (SC) editions include Évieux 1997: Letters 1214–1413; Évieux 2000: Letters 1414–1700; Évieux/Vinel 2017: Letters 1701–2000.

highlight the continuing intellectual involvement of the monk in provincial aristocratic intellectual and cultural life, confound hagiographically driven depictions of the monastery "as locus where individuals sought to forget poetry and secular knowledge."[13] At issue in this essay will be a dossier of Isidore's letters pertaining to astronomical and medical knowledge addressed to Christian literati which testify to monastic engagement with knowledge and debate about the leading forms of knowledge in late antiquity.

In numerous letters, Isidore cultivates a depiction of his monastic retreat in the environs of Pelusium in the eastern Nile Delta as a complete and utter rupture with the city (*pheugein*), placing high rhetorical boundaries between the city and the monastery.[14] Ultimately, however, such epistolary rhetoric contradicts Isidore's deployment of letters to exercise social influence in ecclesial, monastic, and civic affairs.[15] Isidore's missives addressed to other monks and clergy as well as urban intellectuals — *scholastikoi* and sophists — and high-ranking councilmen and civil authorities preserve his own *apophthegmata*, advice, and various social and political interventions. Like the corpora of John and Barsanuphius from the environs of Gaza at Tawatha and Nilus of Ancyra, Isidore's letters written from ascetic retreat illuminate the role of letters as vehicles of continued involvement in polis affairs and the impossibility of a complete social separation from the city for the former urban leader.[16] As a former urban leader in the form of Pelusium's professor of rhetoric, and as a Christian leader, Isidore exploited epistolography to pursue leadership and thereby remained a power broker serving the citizens of Pelusium, its greater administrative province of Augustamnica I, and its adjacent monastic communities.

While projecting an epistolary posture of communal disengagement emphasizing his flight (*pheugeĩn*) from the polis of Pelusium, the desert monk pursued letters with learned provincials as pedagogical and polemical claims to regulate valid forms of knowledge. In this subset of letters, it will be demonstrated that, not unlike other literati who displayed in letters various forms of technical knowledge, specific ethical and communal goals shaped Isidore's framing of knowledge and his depiction of what fields of learning ought to define the leading forms of knowledge. In these letters, Isidore's relationship to

---

13 Larsen 2017, 293 n. 67 quoting Marrou 1982, 330.
14 Isidore refers to the monastery as an alternative political order: for examples flight to the monastery is conceptualized as flight to the heavenly *politeia* of Eden (e.g., *Letters* 282 and 266).
15 For detailed discussion of Isidore's network, see especially Évieux 1995 and Larsen 2017, 289–294.
16 Concerning the epistolography of Barsanuphius and John, see Hevelone-Harper 2005.

science and medicine as a dimension of learned aristocratic culture is deeply ambivalent: his attachment to Platonic induction results in hostility to empiricism while at the same time he applies technical traditions to solve intellectual problems and mold biblical exegesis. Lastly, placing these thematic alignments in a broader educational and discursive context, this essay surveys the monastic use of scientific and philosophical anthologies and doxographies as well as the polemical outreach methods staged by monks in conversations with Christian literati in the environs of Alexandria and Gaza during the fifth-sixth centuries CE. From this vantage point, the apparent "anti-intellectualism" of monks and Christian leaders indicates ongoing ambivalence about the superior sources of knowledge and abiding attachment to the cultural capital of Hellenic *paideia*.

2 Cosmological Speculation and the *Aristē Politeia*

Isidore advertises his knowledge of certain astronomical traditions yet is careful to respond to these traditions with his own moral analysis. Isidore's *Letter* 1435 superscribed to Johannes the deacon, offers us an opportunity to view a hybrid epistolary sociolect drawn from classical tragedy, Scripture, and ancient astronomical traditions. Responding to his friend's request for help explicating Jude 13, quoted in the letter as "errant stars for which the obscurity of darkness keeps watch for eternity,"[17] Isidore suggests an allegorical interpretation of the passage by explaining that "stars" metaphorically represent human beings who have sinned by choice and reap eternal punishment.[18] In his exegesis of the issue of errant stars or planets, Isidore threads together scientific traditions concerning wandering stars and fixed stars developed by thinkers such as the doxographer Aetius, and demonstrations transmitted, for example, by Posidonius of Apamea, by the astronomer Cleomedes, and by Vitruvius.[19] Offering a moral valence to celestial bodies, Isidore asserts that these entities perform their revolutions in agreement and perfect harmony, and, contrary to pagan belief,

---

17 ἀστέρες πλανῆται οἷς ὁ ζόφος τοῦ σκότους εἰς αἰῶνα τετήρηται.
18 φημὶ τοίνυν ὅτι περὶ ἀνθρώπων συγγνώμης πταιόντων ὑψηλότερα ἦν τῷ ἐπιστείλαντι ὁ λόγος, οὐ περὶ ἄστρων καὶ νεφελῶν, κυμάτων τε καὶ δένδρων, οἷς δὴ παραδείγμασι κέχρηται· "I believe the author of the letter spoke of men committing mistakes exceeding forgiveness, not the stars and clouds, waves and trees, which he uses as examples." In addition to errant stars, Isidore refers here to the other natural objects appearing in Jude 1:12–13.
19 References in Evieux 1997, 2.46n1, 47 n. 2, 51 n. 1.

they are not themselves deities but instead are arranged in an ordered whole by a creator. Those who are not persuaded, Isidore advises, should listen to Plato who averred "Good is the demiurge of this universe" (*Timaeus* 28c) and Euripides' who has Jocasta say that "the sun and night are servants to mortals" (*Phoenician Women* 546).[20] According to Isidore, such Greek thinkers articulated a cosmological vision shared by Jews and Christians wherein heavenly bodies have a cause and a creator who rules their movement and order. Stitching together the strands of classical texts and Greek scientific tradition, Isidore underscores his erudition and authorizes his scriptural exegesis by harmonizing Christian cosmology with revered Greek scientific and philosophical lineages as well as the poetry of the tragic stage.

By projecting a moral valence onto the physical universe, Isidore constructs an exegetical response for his friend that asserts a cosmology created and structured by God, thereby desacralizing the cosmos and refuting the pagan theology of astral bodies as divine beings. Along the way, Isidore pursues a discussion of astronomical theory that plays upon a moral meaning in the wandering stars — the planets — as erring. Referring to pagan astronomers (*hoi deinoi*), Isidore states that regarding astronomical bodies experts in the field "offer to the many explanations neither likely nor persuasive; for they [their explanations] fight with the visible testimony of the eyes."[21] He proceeds to explain how these experts say that these planets hasten to complete their own circuits from west to east yet defeated by the opposing motion of the faster fixed stars, they are carried westward again. These experts, Isidore says, use the following example: "just like when a wheel is moving swiftly, an ant advancing in motion opposite to the wheel will accomplish nothing — for it is carried by the swiftest motion of the wheel — thus also the planets are affected by the motion of the fixed stars."[22]

---

20 εἰ δ' οὐ πείθονται, ἀκουέτωσαν Πλάτωνος μὲν λέγοντος· «Ἀγαθός ἐστιν ὁ τοῦδε τοῦ παντὸς δημιουργός», Εὐριπίδους δέ· Εἶθ' ἥλιος μὲν νὺξ τε δουλεύει βροτοῖς, καὶ παυέσθωσαν τῆς τοσαύτης ἀσεβείας. And those who are not persuaded should listen to Plato who said, "Good is the demiurge of this world, and Euripides who said, "the sun and night are servants to mortals," and thus put an end to such impiety. For citations of Plato and Euripides, see Evieux 1995, 2: 52.

21 οὔτε εἰκότα οὔτε πιθανὰ τοῖς πολλοῖς λέγουσι· τῇ γὰρ ἐναργείᾳ καὶ τῇ διὰ τῶν ὄψεων μαρτυρίᾳ μάχονται.

22 ὥσπερ τροχοῦ ὀξέως κινουμένου, μύρμηξ τὴν ἐναντίαν αὐτῷ κίνησιν πορευόμενος οὐδὲν τοσοῦτον ἀνύει–ἐκνικᾶται γὰρ ὑπὸ τῆς τοῦ τροχοῦ ὠκυτάτης κινήσεως–οὕτω καὶ οἱ πλανῆται πρὸς τὴν τῶν ἀπλανῶν διάκεινται κίνησιν.

In adducing the analogy of the ant on a cartwheel, Isidore appears to flaunt his knowledge of this example drawn from an astronomical compendium.[23]

In a brief digression, Isidore seizes this teaching analogy to ridicule pagan practice of associating gods with various animals and hints that the use of this analogy among pagan astronomers embeds a repudiation of their own habits. Mockingly, Isidore comments "that they (i.e., the pagans) are refuted because now they make them into gods, now they compare them to the ants, I am only going to suggest."[24] Switching gears, Isidore indicates that he will leave that issue unresolved for now, though he continues to pursue astronomical discussion in tandem with aggressive criticism of pagan theology. Confronting the pagan theological imprint of his own cosmological vocabulary, Isidore discusses why Scripture uses the same words for the sun, moon, and planets as the pagans use for their deities. He states because Scripture uses this name, either properly or improperly, or by following the general habit, I think, maybe when they rank among the planets the sun and the moon, and five other stars, which many do not know, Saturn, Jupiter, Mercury, and Mars, and of course Lucifer (Venus), people more foolish than you have assigned them the names of characters who were powerful on earth, who led a life of shame and died without glory.[25]

Isidore indicates the convention of denoting heavenly bodies with the same words that indicate names of the gods and inserts his own moral assessment of the degeneracy of the pagan deities. He continues to set out astronomical argu-

---

23 See, e.g., Posidonius of Apamea, the astronomer Cleomedes, Vitruvius. See also Mansfeld *et al.* 1997, 311 and 311 n. 59; Évieux 1997, 2:47 n. 2; Kertsch 1997, 164. Isidore may, however, draw this example from an intervening Christian source rather than a compendium; more below, and see Kertsch 1997, 160–163, on the parallels between Isidore *Letter* 1435 and Origen's *Philocalia*. Bayer originally argued that Isidore made direct use of the manuals of Arius Didymus and Aëtius, but this cannot be demonstrated definitively; see Mansfeld *et al.* 1997, 309; Bayer 1915, 66–72.
24 Ep. 1435. τὸ μὲν οὖν ἐλέγχειν αὐτοὺς ὅτι ποτὲ μὲν αὐτοὺς ὡς θεοὺς ἐκθειάζουσι, ποτὲ δὲ μύρμηξι παραβάλλουσι, μόνον ἐπισημηνάμενος.
25 ἐγὼ δ' οἶμαι, διὰ τὸ χρήσασθαι καὶ τὴν Γραφὴν τούτῳ τῷ ὀνόματι, ἢ κυριολεκτοῦσαν, ἢ καταχρωμένην, ἢ τῇ τῶν πολλῶν συνηθείᾳ ἑπομένην, ὅτι, ἴσως ἐπειδὴ τὸν ἥλιον καὶ τὴν σελήνην, καὶ ἄλλους πέντε ἀστέρας, οὐ πολλοῖς γνωρίμους, Φαίνοντά τε καὶ Φαέθοντα, Στίλβοντα τε καὶ Πυρρόεντα, ναὶ μὴν καὶ Φωσφόρον εἰς τοὺς πλανήτας τάττουσιν οἱ σοῦ ἀνοητότεροι, τινῶν ἐπὶ γῆς δυναστευσάντων, καὶ αἰσχρῶς βεβιωκότων, καὶ ἀκλεῶς τὸν βίον καταστρεψάντων τὰς προσηγορίας ἐπέθεσαν. Kertsch 1997, 163, has pointed out that Isidore's use of the terms κυριολεκτεῖν and καταχρᾶσθαι we see also in Origen *Philocalia* 26.8.9. I would also add that *Philocalia* 26.8, akin to this passage in Isidore *Letter* 1435, is concerned with the topic of understanding names and whether or not to take them literally.

ments regarding the movements of the fixed bodies and offers explanations for the meanings of their names, but ultimately asserts that the cosmos is the product of the devising of God the Creator. Referring back to the thoughts of *hoi deinoi*, Isidore adduces the evidence of Isaiah 45:12 concerning God's cosmic hegemony framed in the Platonic language of the Demiurge: "Whether this or that is true, it [i.e., the movements of stars and planets] is the proclamation of the Demiurge who thus ordered and made the laws, as He himself declares 'I command the stars.'"[26] Compounding this demonstration, Isidore offers with a Platonic overlay the evidence of the Psalmist who, "pointing out how the divine prescription on earth has been infringed when men go off on their own accord into transgression, while in the heavens it is preserved, says 'for eternity, O Lord, your Word will remain in the heavens.'"[27] God orders not just beings that some claim possess reason and will but all elements of the material universe, as Scripture at Psalms 77:23 states "The Lord command the heat," "he command the clouds," "he commands the worm."[28] Isidore proceeds to aver that astronomical theories contribute nothing to showing us how to live:

> That they (the stars and planets) are therefore beings gifted with reason, as some claim, or spheres of fire, or disc-shaped bodes lit by the ethereal fire, or condensations of a fire-shaped sphere, or incandescent masses — this is indeed the opinion of some philosophers — or chariots receiving immaterial and hyper-cosmic light coming from beyond the world, I do not argue forcefully — in fact I think it does nothing to accomplish the good way of life.[29]

The issue of the moral *politeia*, which Isidore uses elsewhere to denote the monastic lifestyle, comprises for him a key frustration with astronomical inquiry.

---

26 πλὴν εἴτε τοῦτο, εἴτε ἐκεῖνο ἀληθὲς εἴη, τοῦ Δημιουργοῦ ἀνακηρύττει τὴν ἐπιστήμην τοῦ οὕτω τάξαντος καὶ νομοθετήσαντος ὡς καὶ αὐτὸς μέν φησιν· «Ἐγὼ τοῖς ἄστροις ἐνετειλάμην».
27 δεικνύων ὡς ἐν γῇ μὲν παρέβαθη τὸ θεῖον πρόσταγμα, τῶν ἀνθρώπων εἰς παρανομίας αὐτομολησάντων, ἐν οὐρανῷ δὲ ἐφυλάχθη, ἔφη· «εἰς τὸν αἰῶνα, Κύριε, ὁ λόγος σου διαμένει ἐν τῷ οὐρανῷ.» Cf. Psalms 118.89; see Évieux, 2:49. The issue of will also corresponds to Origen *Philocalia* 19–20; see also Kertsch 1997, 161–162.
28 «Ἐνετείλατο Κύριος καύσωνι», καὶ «Ἐνετείλατο νεφέλαις», καὶ «Ἐνετείλατο σκώληκι», cf. John 4:8, Psalms 77:23, and John 4.7; see Évieux 1997, 2:51.
29 εἴτε οὖν λογικά ἐστι ζῷα, ὥς φασί τινες, εἴτε πύρινοι σφαῖραι, εἴτε δισκοειδῆ σώματα, ἐκ τοῦ αἰθερίου πυρὸς ἐξαφθέντα, εἴτε σφαιροειδεῖς πυρὸς πιλήσεις, εἴτε μυδροί – τινὲς γὰρ τῶν φιλοσόφων τοῦτ' ἐδογμάτισαν – εἴτε ὀχήματα δεκτικὰ τοῦ ἀΰλου καὶ ὑπερκοσμίου φωτός, οὐ σφόδρα ἰσχυρισαίμην – οὐδὲν γὰρ τοῦτο πρὸς ἀρίστην πολιτείαν συντελεῖν ἡγοῦμαι. These six examples bear resemblance to the views of Aëtius in pseudo-Plutarch's *Placita philosophorum* and Stobaeus *Eclogae physicae*, but certainly were not derived from these sources. They are closer to the examples Philo provides in *On Dreams* 1.21. See Mansfeld/Runia, 311 and 311 n. 62.

The overriding concern for the moral lifestyle resounds also in *Letter* 2.273, where Isidore faults astronomical speculation for offering nothing for the *aristē politeia*. This *topos* of natural science as useless because it does not contribute to a moral life was a broader discursive trend in patristic authors such as Eusebius and Theodoret.[30] Engaging with scientific texts, Isidore's treatment of heavenly bodies in this letter may be drawn from primers such as those of Cleomedes, Theon, Smyrnaeus, and Geminus.[31] Additionally, this letter includes language resembling astronomical language on the shape of the earth in pseudo-Plutarch's *Placita*.[32] For example, Isidore's use of κύλινδρος is reminiscent of Anaximander's language of the earth's column-like shape, and Isidore's use of the comparison "like a winnowing fan" (λικνοειδής) is similar to Democritus' "disc-like in surface but hollow in the middle."[33] These examples, however, Isidore takes from Basil's last *Homily on the Hexaemeron* (9.1.480.10–16).[34] Thus Isidore signals that he is conversant in astronomical traditions and offers a moral parallel to such scientific traditions.

Isidore, like other Church Fathers, broadcasts a veneer of astronomical language by including teaching analogies and other *doxai* originally appearing in astronomical texts. He feels compelled to demonstrate some competence in the astronomical lore that he ultimately debunks because of both its serious pagan resonances and his view that it offers nothing for the correct moral lifestyle. On the other hand, however, Isidore's ridicule of the polytheistic language of these scientific authors is also softened with appeals to the wisdom of specific Hellenic authors whose thought may be harmonized with Christian attitudes.

---

30 See Eusebius *Praeparatio Evangelica* 15, and Theodoret *Curatio affectionum Graecarum* 4.24; cf. Mansfeld *et al.* 1997, 139, 276, 310, and 310 n. 53.
31 Mansfeld, 310.
32 Mansfeld, 310 and 310 n. 55.
33 Mansfeld, 310 and 310 n. 56. Apart from a lexical entry in the *Suda*, the term λικνοειδής is also found in Basil, *In hexaemeron hom.* 9.1 (ed. Giet SC26bis, p. 480) and some later lexicons (Ps-Zonaras, Gennadius Scholarius).
34 Basil's examples are close to the opinions of Aëtius in the *Placita*; see Mansfeld *et al.* 1997, 310–311. Évieux postulates that Isidore likely encountered the writings of the Cappadocians in the course of the Pelusian's early retreat to Nitria during which time Isidore also took up concentrated study of scripture; see Évieux 1995, 279–281 and Larsen 2017, 288, 301 n. 19–20.

3 Matter and the Soul

Letters among educated provincials were forums for philosophical and scientific speculation about the relationship between matter and soul and the concomitant issue of the relationship between matters of various forms such as liquids and solids. In *Letter* 1475 to Dorotheus, a doctor and deacon, Isidore responds to a friend who apparently "wished to learn something clear and agreed upon both in the Holy Scriptures and in the 'wiser' writers of those outside (pagans)."[35] The net is cast fairly wide in terms of permitted sources. Isidore pledges that he will endeavor, so far as he is able, to say much in few words. Dorotheus has asked Isidore to explain "wherefore is it clear that the incorporeal things are less likely to undergo change and are stronger than corporeal beings?"[36] Isidore responds that "to the extent that those bodies that are nearer to incorporeality are stronger and less subject to change than those that are denser, the incorporeal things are less likely to undergo change than not only the denser things but also the lighter things."[37] To support this assertion Isidore cites the example of how a stone, which is denser than water, can no longer be united if it is broken, but water when divided is brought together again, for it is less dense and to this extent it does not undergo change.[38] Density correlates positively with mutability. The lighter example (*paradeigma*) of air, Isidore continues, cannot be separated: "if air is enclosed in a container or a wine skin and is thrown into the depths of water, it does not put up with it, but comes to the surface and swims up and wishes to manifest itself and hunts after that which is like it."[39] Isidore expresses wonderment that Dorotheus marvels how bodiless things are stronger given Isidore's proofs that air is less dense than water and water is less dense than stone and therefore is less subject to change.

This discussion of the relationship of bodiless and corporeal entities and their relative densities and vulnerability to change next leads into evidence of

---

35 Ep. 1475. ἐπειδὴ χρῆμα σαφὲς καὶ ὁμολογούμενον καὶ ταῖς ἱεραῖς Γραφαῖς καὶ τοῖς σοφωτέροις τῶν ἔξωθεν διὰ παραδειγμάτων ἠθέλησας μαθεῖν ...
36 Ep. 1475. ἐπεὶ τοίνυν ἔφης· πόθεν δῆλον ὅτι τὰ ἀσώματα τῶν σωμάτων ἐστὶν ἀπαθέστερα καὶ ἰσχυρότερα.
37 Ep. 1475. φημί, ὅσῳ τὰ ἐγγὺς τῆς ἀσωματότητος σώματα ἰσχυρότερα καὶ ἀπαθέστερά ἐστι τῶν παχυτέρων σωμάτων, τοσούτῳ καὶ τὰ ἀσώματα οὐ μόνον τῶν παχυτάτων, ἀλλὰ καὶ τῶν λεπτοτάτων ἐστὶν ἀπαθέστερα.
38 Ep. 1475. οἷον ἡ πέτρα τοῦ ὕδατός ἐστι παχυτέρα, διὸ ῥηγνυμένη οὐκέτι συνάπτεται, τὸ δὲ ὕδωρ διαιρεθέν, πάλιν συναφθὲν ἑνοῦται· ὅσῳ γὰρ λεπτότερον, τοσούτῳ ἀπαθέστερον.
39 Ep. 1475. ἐὰν γοῦν ᾖ εἰς κέραμον ἢ εἰς ἀσκὸν ἀποκλεισθείη, καὶ εἰς βυθὸν ῥιφείη, οὐκ ἀνέχεται, ἀλλ' ἐπιπολάζει καὶ ἐπινήχεται, καὶ τὴν ἐπιφάνειαν ζητεῖ, καὶ τὸ συγγενὲς θηρᾶται.

the immutability of the soul – an inherently bodiless entity. Isidore contends then that the soul, also bodiless and invisible like air, provides the body with inner strength and physical strength. When the soul departs from the body, however, the body not only remains motionless, dead, but it decomposes. Affirming the power of his friend's profession and linking its practice to the soul, Isidore next links the art (*technē*) of the physician to the soul's immutability: the bodiless power (*dunamis*) of Dorotheus' *technē* itself is stronger than the body. As soul has the power to fortify the body, whenever the medical art departs from the body the treatment remains most ineffective (*achrēstotatē*); like the body, a remedy can only live when enlivened by the *dunamis* of the physician's *technē*, and the remedy effectively dies when this *dunamis* departs. In this way, the medical art and the soul itself share the capacity to animate matter itself. By the letter's end, Isidore's conversation interweaving philosophical and scientific ideas about soul and matter engages with his friend's profession as a physician and praises its power to manipulate and arrange human bodies.

4 Platonic Repudiation of Galen's Mortal Soul

Isidore was also rankled by specific definitions of the soul offered by Galen. *Letter* 1791 (*PG* 4.125), published so far only in Migne, also preserves Isidore's side of an epistolary discussion with a doctor and *scholasticus* named Prosechius focused on rebuffing a Galenic conception of the soul as mortal, testifying that knowledge of Galen, perhaps even first-hand knowledge, belonged in the repertoire of late antique sophists of the Greek East.[40] Alternatively, it is inviting to suggest that Isidore accessed Galenic passages by means of a doxographical or collected work. Isidore opens by adducing the authoritative testimony of "Pythagoras and Plato and those other wise men who were held in high repute following the necessary art of the techniques of demonstration."[41] These men, Isidore avers, "rightly give the opinion that the soul is more of a guide than the

---

40 *Pace* Évieux 1995, 148 n. 61, who, following *PG* 78:1197–98n99, reproduced the misidentification of the relevant text of Galen as *De placitis Platonis et Hippocratis*, 1.II. As I indicate below, Isidore is mainly concerned in this letter with Galen's treatise *The Faculties of the Soul Follow the Mixtures of the Body*.
41 Ep. 1791. Πυθαγόρας μὲν, καὶ Πλάτων, καὶ οἱ ἄλλοι ἔνδοξοι παρ' Ἕλλησι σοφοί, ἀποδεικτικαῖς ἀνάγκαις ἑπόμενοι.

body, calling soul the artificer, the body the instrument."[42] Referring collectively to these Greek philosophers as *hoi sophoi*, Isidore remarks that even if these men missed the truth concerning some things — probably the error of their paganism — on the issue of the relationship between body and soul, however, they hit the mark (lit. "were led to the target").[43] Isidore then identifies the scientific interlocutor who irritates him: Galen, who did not escape the notice of those who were reading intelligently (that is, Isidore himself). Deploying the analogues of lyre and lyre-player, Isidore contends that Galen "considering the lyre itself to be harmonious, not the lyre-player, declared the soul to be mortal."[44] Galen, according to Isidore, asserted that "because the powers of the soul follow the mixture (compounding) of the body, he ended by saying that the soul was not bodiless and immortal but, I do not know how, that the mixture was the soul."[45]

Isidore refers directly here to Galen's definition of the soul as a mixture which he articulated in his treatise *The Faculties of the Soul Follow the Mixtures of the Body* (*Quod animi mores sequuntur temperamenta corporis*).[46] In this late pamphlet, one of the two extant Galenic texts which focused on the nature of the soul (the other is *De placitis Hippocratis et Platonis*), Galen asserted that the soul and its capabilities are dependent on the temperaments or mixtures (*kraseis*) of the body.[47] Following the Aristotelian conception of the soul as the form (*eidos*) of the body, Galen asserts that as the body is comprised of matter (*hylē*) and form (*eidos*), and, as Aristotle also thought, "the physical body comes to be from the inborn four qualities in matter, and it is necessary to regard the form as the mixture of these qualities, so also I suppose the soul to be a mixture of the four elements," or hot, cold, wet, and dry (*QAM* 774).[48] From this, Galen posits "if the reasoning faculty is a form of the soul, it is mortal; for it is itself a

---

42 Ep. 1791. ἡγεμονικωτέραν τὴν ψυχὴν τοῦ σώματος εἰκότως ἀπεφήναντο· καὶ ἐκάλεσαν τὴν μὲν τεχνίτην, τὸ δὲ ὄργανον.
43 Ep. 1791. ἐν τούτῳ κατὰ σκοποῦ ἠνέχθησαν.
44 Ep. 1791. ἁρμονίαν αὐτὴν λύραν οὐ λυρῳδὸν ἡγησάμενος θνητὴν ἀπεφήνατο.
45 Ep. 1791. ὅτι τῇ κράσει τοῦ σώματος ἕπονται αἱ τῆς ψυχῆς δυνάμεις, εἰς τὸ φάναι τὸ μηδὲ εἶναι ψυχὴν ἀσώματον καὶ ἀθάνατον ἐτελεύτησεν, τὴν κρᾶσιν τὴν ψυχὴν οὐκ οἶδ' ὅπως ὁρισάμενος.
46 This text will be henceforth abbreviated *QAM*.
47 For a useful overview of Galen's views of the soul, see Donni 2008, 184–209.
48 Ep. 1791. τῶν τεττάρων ποιοτήτων ἐγγιγνομένων τῇ ὕλῃ τὸ φυσικὸν γίγνεσθαι σῶμα, τὴν ἐκ τούτων κρᾶσιν ἀναγκαῖον αὐτοῦ τίθεσθαι τὸ εἶδος, ὥστε πως καὶ ἡ τῆς ψυχῆς οὐσία κρᾶσίς τις ἔσται τῶν τεττάρων εἴτε ποιοτήτων.

certain mixture of the brain" (*QAM* 774–775).⁴⁹ On the other hand, "if the soul is immortal, as Plato wished, why is it separated from the body when the brain becomes excessively cold or hot or dry or wet."⁵⁰ That is, why does the soul leave the body when the body undergoes certain physical changes? As will be demonstrated below, Isidore quotes this argument virtually verbatim in *Letter* 1791. Isidore's epistolary diatribe aims to steer his learned friend clear from the Galenic nets. Drawing a distinction between Galen's philosophical and medical contributions, Isidore warns Prosechius "we must not pay attention to him in this!"⁵¹ Concerning Galen's medical work Isidore recognizes his renown and merit, but regarding the soul, Isidore rails:

> Let him not contend with the wiser men, let him not go into the *agon*, where he does not have the physical training or the skill; nor let someone who is an athlete judge music. Having emptied the whole of his intellect concerning bodies, let him not teach concerning the soul, and let him not believe that the bringing about the harmony of the elements is the soul.⁵²

Isidore registers his offense at Galen's philosophical forays into *agones* for which he has no experience or capability with curt minatory imperative phrases framed by Classical analogies of competition.

If Galen's hypothesis were in fact true, reasons Isidore, then with the body the soul would be extinguished. Perhaps imitating Plato's Socrates, Isidore addresses Galen with ironic superlative address,⁵³ wondering "what would this good man (*beltistos*) say to the poets and philosophers and speechwriters how in every way and by every means there will be punishments in the (last) judgment; for what kind of reward does he rightly contrive for those living in this world?"⁵⁴ If the soul is mortal, Galen obviates the possibility of rewards or punishments in the afterlife. Similar to his concerns in *Letter* 1435 and 2.273 dis-

---

49 *QAM* 774–775. εἰ μὲν οὖν τὸ λογιζόμενον εἶδος τῆς ψυχῆς ἐστι, θνητὸν ἔσται· καὶ γὰρ καὶ αὐτὸ κρᾶσίς τις ἐγκεφάλου ...
50 *QAM* 775. εἰ δ' ἀθάνατον ἔσται, ὡς ὁ Πλάτων βούλεται, διὰ τί χωρίζεται ψυχθέντος σφοδρῶς ἢ ὑπερθερμανθέντος ἢ ὑπερξηρανθέντος ἢ ὑπερυγρανθέντος τοῦ ἐγκεφάλου.
51 ἀλλ' οὐ προσεκτέον αὐτῷ ἐν τούτῳ.
52 Ep. 1791. μὴ ἁμιλλάσθω τοῖς σοφωτέροις, μηδὲ καταβαινέτω εἰς ἀγῶνα, οὗ καὶ ἀνάσκητός ἐστι καὶ ἀμελέτητος, μηδὲ ἀθλητὴς ὢν τὴν μουσικὴν κρινέτω, μηδὲ περὶ τὰ σώματα ὅλην ἑαυτοῦ κενώσας τὴν σύνεσιν περὶ ψυχῆς δογματιζέτω, μηδὲ πιστευέσθω ἐν τῷ κατασκευάζειν τὴν ἁρμονίαν τῶν στοιχείων εἶναι ψυχήν.
53 On Plato's use of superlative titles in Socratic conversations see Dickey 1996.
54 Ep. 1791. τί οὖν φαίη ὁ βέλτιστος περὶ τῶν παρὰ ποιηταῖς καὶ φιλοσόφοις καὶ λογογράφοις φιλοσοφηθέντων, ὡς πάντῃ τε καὶ πάντως ἐσομένων ἐν τῇ κρίσει κολαστηρίων; Ποῖον δὲ γέρας τοῖς τῇδε βιοῦσιν ὀρθῶς ἐπινοήσει.

cussed above regarding the uselessness of astronomical theory for living the good life, Isidore here perceives Galen's "mortal soul" as an assault on his entire lifestyle. Employing the terms *ponoi* and *politeuein*, the verbal form of *politeia*, which we have seen above as denoting the monastic lifestyle, Isidore quips "thus for those who live in this manner, for the most part, contests are provided filled with the greatest of labors and sweats, until the end."[55] What is the meaning of these trials for the virtuous if the soul is mortal? And what about those who live without virtue: "how is the punishment determined for those who pursue every evil until death and enjoy wealth and fame?"[56] Isidore wonders how Galen would interpret the Homeric poet's assertion that "the spirit remains, and it has gone to the House of Hades"; how would he translate "there thus also is a dwelling place in Hades."[57] Invoking also Euripides' *Alcestis*, Isidore asks how Galen would interpret Euripides whom Prosechius determines to be wise, who said "May it be good for you in the House of Hades also."[58]

Isidore asks how, if the soul is an order (*harmonia*), "how does it change to discord, and accomplish an inelegant and discordant song?"[59] The soul presides over various types of conduct which Isidore classes as either harmonious or discordant. Moral behavior — virtue (*aretē*) — generates harmonious song and moral baseness a discordant song. Why, wonders Isidore, would Galen himself consider it necessary to praise or censure those pursuing wisdom and frivolous arts respectively if indeed the soul were simply a mixture?

Isidore suggests that the soul has an agency over the body for which Galen does not account and is puzzled that Galen cites in his own defense the changes that happen every day between soul and body. Isidore observes how individuals often reverse former habits, since "many licentious men take wing and fly up to moderation. And many men fly down to lasciviousness. For the mixture would not change."[60] Why, contends Isidore, if the soul were a mixture or order would it change as in the examples of many men who were licentious in their youth

---

55 Ep. 1791. τοῖς γὰρ οὕτω πολιτευομένοις, ὡς τὰ πολλά, ἆθλα μέγιστα πόνων καὶ ἱδρώτων μεστά, ἕως τῆς ἐνθάδε τελευτῆς προετέθη.
56 Ep. 1791. ποῖ δὲ τὴν τιμωρίαν ὁριεῖ τοῖς κακίαν μὲν πᾶσαν μεταδιώκουσιν, ἕως δὲ θανάτου καὶ πλούτου καὶ τιμῆς ἀπολαύουσι.
57 Ep. 1791. «Ψυχή τε πταμένη Ἀϊδόσδε βεβήκει»; Πῶς δὲ «Ἦ ῥά τί ἐστι καὶ εἰν Ἀΐδαο δόμοισιν». In a manner not unlike Galen's invocation of brief testimony from Homer and Theognis in the *QAM* at 778, Isidore selects in this passage quotations from Homer and Euripides.
58 Ep. 1791. εὖ σοι γένοιτο καὶ ἐν Ἅιδου δόμοις.
59 Ep. 1791. εἰς ἀναρμοστίαν μεταπίπτει, καὶ ἄμουσον καὶ ἀπηχὲς ἀποτελεῖ μέλος.
60 Ep. 1791. πολλοὶ μὲν γὰρ ἀσελγεῖς εἰς σωφροσύνην ἀνέπτησαν· πολλοὶ δὲ σώφρονες εἰς λαγνείαν καταπεπτώκασιν· οὐ γὰρ δὴ ἡ κρᾶσις μετέπεσε.

but return to decorum at the prime of life? Isidore reasons "the mixture would not alter itself thus but would bring to successful issue its resolve."[61]

With concern for the length of his letter, Isidore transitions to what he considers to be his strongest refutation of Galen. At this point Isidore provides a quotation of Galen almost identical to the passage quoted above at *QAM* 775: "If the soul is immortal as Plato wished, why is it separated from the body when the brain grows excessively hot or cold or dry or wet?"[62] Isidore then leaves this statement and proceeds to attack the deductive methods of Galen's inquiry, citing how on the basis of the pulse Galen proclaims to some people that they will die and to others that they will live, but he makes a mistake because some of these individuals come back to life and some die. Declaring his hostility to empirical experimentation and endorsing the inductive method of Plato, Isidore asserts that by Galen's approach "the truth escapes the art which proceeds by guesswork."[63]

Harm to the body does not necessarily result in the destruction of the soul. Formidable pharmacological assaults, such as "noxious drugs administered by a sorcerer, do not make the soul go away."[64] Deploying this argument in response to Galen's assertion at *QAM* 776 that the drinking of hemlock cools the body, Isidore retorts "in this way, the soul does not always depart from the body having grown cold."[65] Defending his philosophical ally, Isidore speculates that there exists "a divine bond that binds together things that are much different from each other and an unsaid partnership of soul toward the body, and ineffable fellow-feeling (*sympatheia*) of the divine being toward the mortal instrument, as it seemed to Plato himself."[66] Such a partnership operates "so that the soul will seriously take care of the body, not so that the soul will be puffed up with fleshiness, but so that it will be healthy."[67] If the soul does not care for the

---

61 Ep. 1791. οὐ τῆς κράσεως ἐν τούτῳ μεταβληθείσης, ἀλλὰ τῆς προαιρέσεως κατορθωσάσης.
62 Ep. 1791. Εἰ ἀθάνατός ἐστι, φησίν, ἡ ψυχή, ὡς ὁ Πλάτων βούλεται, διὰ τί χωρίζεται ψυχρωθέντως σφοδρῶς ἢ ὑπερζεσθέντος ἢ ὑπερξηρανθέντος ἢ ὑπερυγρανθέντος τοῦ ἐγκεφάλου. The omega in ψυχθέντω is most likely the result of a scribal error; the cod. Vat. contains ψυχθέντος, see *PG* 78:1202 n. 9.
63 Ep. 1791. οὕτως τὴν τέχνην στοχαστικὴν οὖσαν τἀληθὲς διαφεύγει.
64 ὅτι πολλῶν δηλητηρίοις φαρμάκοις καταηγοητευθέντων αἱ ψυχαὶ οὐκ ἀπέπτησαν.
65 Ep. 1791. οὕτως οὐ πάντως ψυχθέντος τοῦ ἐγκεφάλου χωρίζεται ἡ ψυχή.
66 Ep. 1791. ὅτι θεῖός ἐστι δεσμὸς συνδέων τὰ πολὺ ἀλλήλων διαφέροντα, καὶ κοινωνία ἄρρητος ἀσωμάτου ψυχῆς πρὸς σῶμα, καὶ συμπάθεια ἄλεκτος ἀθανάτου οὐσίας πρὸς θνητὸν ὄργανον, ὡς καὶ αὐτῷ τῷ Πλάτωνι δοκεῖ.
67 Ep. 1791. ἵν' ἡ ψυχὴ περὶ πολλοῦ ποιῆται τὸ ἐπιμελεῖσθαι τοῦ σώματος, οὐχ ὥστε πολυσαρκίᾳ ἐξογκοῦσθαι, ἀλλ' ὥστε ὑγιαίνειν.

body it shares in the bad temperament (*dyskrasia*, "ill-mixing") of the body due to its fellow-feeling (*sympatheia*). In this way, the soul exercises its agency over the body and suffers if it shows poor regard for it. Likely alluding to Platonic examples drawn from Galen's quotation at *QAM* 811–12 of Plato's *Laws* 674a–b, Isidore alleges that "the bad temperament of the body (*dyskrasia*) and drunkenness transmit the misfortune to the soul, just like a helmsman in heavy sea does not show off his own knowledge and is inundated."[68] In this way, Isidore argues that the soul is not inextricably bound to matter. If the soul is the proper mixture of the body, one cannot account for the failures that occur between the body and the psyche. Isidore is careful to acknowledge, however, that these demonstrations do indicate that the soul's capacities are hindered by the body, "since neither the best musician having a muse-less lyre, or when he has fallen into the sea, will perform a harmonious song."[69]

In conclusion, Isidore authorizes his arguments via the vote of the Creator (*Demiourgos*), whose words in Matthew 10:28 and Luke 12:4 place their seal on the soul's immortality: "don't have fear before those who are killing the body but do not have the power to kill the soul."[70] Underscoring again a concern about the interconnection between the soul's immortality and one's lifestyle, Isidore exhorts his friend, "as the soul is immortal, let us live and act accordingly."[71]

This epistolary harangue offers an instructive register of the fierce grip of the Platonic worldview on Isidore and like-minded Early Christian contemporaries. Isidore was not only offended by the idea that Galen's definition of the soul as mortal undermined his *politeia*, specifically his monastic lifestyle, but also in part because he preferred the idealism of the Platonic model. In his criticism of Galen's empirical method, Isidore reveals a discomfort and perceived threat — likely shared by many of his contemporaries — with observation and experimentation as paths to knowledge. For Isidore, one of the problems with empiricism was that it appeared like guesswork; observable data offered a bewildering complexity of results that seemed inconsistent and thus untrustworthy. This letter also registers the emotional quality of Isidore's response to Galen. Mark-

---

[68] Ep. 1791. ἡ δὲ, καθάπερ κυβερνήτης ἐν πολλῷ κλύδωνι, ταράττεται, καὶ τὴν οἰκείαν ἐπιστήμην οὐκ ἐπιδείκνυται συμβυθισθεῖσα. In particular, the discussion of drunkenness and the image of the helmsman (κυβερνήτης) steering a ship likely corresponds to Galen's use at *QAM* 811–812 of these Platonic examples from *Laws* 674a–b.

[69] Ep. 1791. ἐπειδὴ μηδὲ μουσικὸς ἄριστος, ἄμουσον λύρον ἔχων, ἢ εἰς πέλαγος ἐμπεσὼν ἐναρμόνιον ἀποτελέσει μέλος.

[70] Ep. 1791. μὴ φοβηθῆτε ἀπὸ τῶν ἀποκτεινόντων τὸ σῶμα, τὴν δὲ ψυχὴν μὴ δυναμένων ἀποκτεῖναι.

[71] Ep. 1791. ὡς ἀθανάτου τοιγαροῦν οὔσης τῆς ψυχῆς, οὕτω καὶ διακεώμεθα καὶ διαπραττώμεθα.

ers, such as the flow of his epistolary speech punctuated by curt imperatives and the patronizing use of the superlative *beltistos* (my good sir), articulate Isidore's cognitive dissonance in rejecting the definitions offered by the premier ancient medical expert in late antiquity and beyond.[72]

5 Polemical Outreach and Intellectual Engagement at the Monastery

The "snapshots" of intellectual interaction captured in these selected letters complicate hagiographic idealizations of monastic anti-intellectualism which still appear forcefully in contemporary scholarly discussion.[73] In his repudiation of Galen – a powerful, if not the most powerful medical commentator in late antiquity – on theological grounds, Isidore turns to a thoroughly classical mode of attack: Platonic induction. Thus, Isidore's assault on Galen embraces Hellenic intellectual tradition to support Christian ideas of the immortality of the soul.

At this point it is useful to place Isidore's correspondence within a wider discursive context of educational engagement in eastern monastic circles in late antiquity. In the late fifth and early sixth century Aeneas of Gaza and Zacharias Scholasticus (465–536) of Maiouma (the port city of Gaza) appear to have been part of two generations of Gazan literati who frequented the cells of the anti-Chalcedonian ascetics Isaiah and Peter the Iberian in the environs of Gaza. Zacharias was especially close to Peter and Isaiah, composing biographies of each of these monks after their deaths and Zacharias also claims that Isaiah taught Aeneas how to interpret Plato, Aristotle, and Plotinus.[74] These literati likely accessed at monasteries in the Gazan hinterlands ready-made Christian arguments against Platonism, perhaps drawn from anthologies, with which to engage philosophically trained literati and teachers. We do not know specifically the intellectual training of these monks, but they might have learned such invective from collections summarizing Christian arguments against Platonism.

The monasteries around Gaza and Alexandria seem to have attracted audiences with visiting literati more generally. John Rufus refers to various intellec-

---

72 On Galenism and its dominating role in medical theory in late antiquity, see Nutton 2004, 292–309.
73 See, e.g., Larsen 2017, 286–287.
74 *Life of Isaiah* 8; see Watts 2006–2007, 161.

tuals (sophists, *scholastikoi*, and students) who visited Palestinian and Egyptian anti-Chalcedonian monasteries during the 450s–470s.[75] Peter the Iberian also journeyed to Phoenicia to visit Christian students who probably included Zacharias when they were at Berytus studying law.[76]

Edward Watts theorizes that Zacharias, deriving much of his *Ammonius* from Aeneas' *Theophrastus*, shaped his dialogue to appeal to the concerns of a broader student audience associated with Peter the Iberian. The eschatological concerns evinced in Zacharias' *Ammonius* may well reflect the immersion of these literati — as well as other Palestinian and Egyptian students — in the distinctive anti-Chalcedonian culture which John in his *Plerophories* attributes to Peter the Iberian.[77]

In addition to the details concerning Christian students provided by Zacharias' hagiography of Severus, we have Aeneas' *Theophrastus* and Zacharias' *Ammonius*.[78] While clearly immersed in Platonism, Aeneas and Zacharias both struck to undermine specific Platonist doctrines which contradicted Christian teaching. For both, the vehicle of this polemic was the archaizing form of the Platonic dialogue. The basic goals for the Gazan literati in these texts were to demonstrate that the world was not co-eternal with God and that God would not be diminished by the destruction of the universe.

It is difficult to assess the philosophical training of Aeneas and Zacharias based upon these dialogues. Dubbing the *Ammonius* more of a "cabaret act" engineered to entertain and impress fellow Christian students at Alexandria rather than a systematic Platonist rejection of elements of Neoplatonic thinking, Richard Sorabji speculates that Zacharias might not have had a very extensive philosophical training during his studies with the pagan philosopher Ammonius in Alexandria. Zacharias and even Aeneas earlier might also have gathered some of their philosophical arguments from discussions with rhetorically and philosophically trained monks in the environs of Alexandria and perhaps Gaza. Zacharias claims at *Life of Isaiah* 8 that Aeneas learned how to interpret Plato, Aristotle, and Plotinus from Isaiah. As was discussed above, the monasteries around Alexandria and Gaza drew various literati visitors and student visitors whom monks probably catechized and instructed, offering them ready-made arguments with which to engage philosophically trained literati and teachers.

---

[75] *Plerophories* 13, 14, 57, 38, 77, 78; see Watts 2006–2007, 158 and 158 n. 27.
[76] *Life of Peter the Iberian* 114, cited in Watts 2006–2007, 158.
[77] Watts 2006–2007, 161–164.
[78] For a recent translation into English and commentary on these texts, see Geertz *et al.* 2012; Champion 2014.

Certain monks at Enaton in Egypt appear interested to weaken Ammonius in particular. Zacharias' fellow pupil at Alexandria, Paralius, a student of grammar, learned at Enaton specific arguments to wield against philosophy teachers at Alexandria, among them Ammonius.[79] We do not know specifically the intellectual training of these monks, but they or Zacharias might have learned such invective from collections summarizing Christian arguments against Platonism. Sorabji suggests that the uneven quality of Zacharias' arguments — a few that were well-developed but many unsophisticated and sometimes in a highly compressed form — might well indicate his use of a catalogue of summarized arguments and/or his learning from a "crash course" in philosophy. Procopius of Gaza may also have drawn his arguments against the eternity of the world in his commentary on Genesis from such a catalogue of arguments.[80] These sorts of catalogues could take the form of *florilegia* (collections of excerpts from various texts) of the teachings of the Church Fathers, summaries of pagan teaching, and summaries of Christian responses to pagan teaching. Christian scholars often depended for their knowledge of pagan philosophy and scientific traditions upon catalogues of summaries of these traditions in doxographies.[81]

In sum, it is quite suggestive to place Isidore's monastic conversations about scientific and philosophical issues within this broader context of monastic intellectual discourse in the Greek East. In this view, Isidore's conversations about astronomical and medical issues appears as one iteration of a rich regional discursive pattern of monastic engagement with students and literati professionals concerned with elements of Hellenism perceived as contradicting Christian teaching. This apparent "anti-intellectualism" of learned monks and Christian leaders, however, betrays ambivalent immersion in Classical sources and ideas in part because of their enduring cultural authority.

Bibliography

Amato, E. (ed.) (2010a), *Rose di Gaza: gli scritti rhetorico-sofistici e le epistole di Procopio di Gaza*, Alessandria.
Amato, E. (ed.) (2010b), "La produzione letteraria di Procopio", in: E. Amato (ed.), *Rose di Gaza gli scritti rhetorico-sofistici e le epistole di Procopio di Gaza*, Alessandria, 10–45.
Amato, E. (ed.) (2014), Procope de Gaza. *Discours et fragments*, Paris.

---

79 Geertz *et al.* 2012, xxiii.
80 Geertz *et al.* 2012, xxiii–xxiv.
81 Geertz *et al.* 2012, xxiv.

Bäbler, B./Schomberg, A. (2010), "Prokop: Die Kunstuhr in Gaza", in: E. Amato (ed.), *Rose di Gaza: gli scritti rhetorico-sofistici e le epistole di Procopio di Gaza*, Alessandria, 528–559.
Bayer, L. (1915), "Isidors von Pelusium klassische Bildung", PhD diss. Paderborn.
Bregman, J. (1982), *Synesius of Cyrene: Philosopher Bishop*, Berkeley.
Brown, P. (1992), *Power and Persuasion in Late Antiquity: Towards a Christian Empire*, Madison, WI.
Champion, M. (2014), *Explaining the Cosmos: Creation and Cultural Interaction in Late Antique Gaza*, Oxford.
Dickey, E. (1996), *Greek Forms of Address: From Herodotus to Lucian*, Oxford.
Diehls, H. (1917), *Über die von Prokop beschriebene Kunstuhr von Gaza mit einem Anhang enthaltend Text und Übersetzung der Ἔκφρασις ὡρολογίου des Prokopion von Gaza*, Berlin.
Donni, P. (2008), "Psychology", in: R.J. Hankinson (ed.), *The Cambridge Companion to Galen*, Cambridge, 184–209.
Évieux, P./Vinel, N. (2017), *Lettres: Isidore de Peluse*, Paris.
Évieux, P. (2000), "From Rhetoric to Monasticism: The Personal Itinerary of Isidore of Pelusium", in: W. Meyer/P. Allen/L. Cross (eds.), *Prayer and Spirituality in the Early Church*, Brisbane, 143–57.
Évieux, P. (1997), Lettres: *Isidore de Péluse*, Paris.
Évieux, P. (1995), *Isidore de Peluse*, Paris.
Fridh, Å.J./Halporn, J.W. (eds.) (1973), *Magni Aurelii Cassiodori Senatoris Opera Variarum Libri XII*, Turnhout.
Gertz, S./Dillon, J./Russell, D. (eds.) (2012), *Aeneas of Gaza, Theophrastus with Zacharias of Mytilene Ammonius*, Bristol.
Hevelone-Harper, J. (2005), *Disciples of the Desert: Monks, Laity, and Spiritual Authority in Sixth-Century Gaza*, Baltimore.
Kertsch, M. (1997), "Isidor von Pelusion in der sog. Catena Andrea (Clavis PG C 176) zu Jud. 12/13", *Jahrbuch für Antike und Christentum* 40, 158–167.
Larsen, L. (2017), "The Letter Collection of Isidore of Pelusium", in: C. Sogno/B. Storin/E. Watts (eds.), *Late Antique Letter Collections*, Berkeley, 286–308.
Mansfeld, J./Runia, D. (1997), *Aëtiana: the Method and Intellectual Context of a Doxographer*, Leiden.
Marquardt, J. (ed.) (1967), *Claudii Galeni Pergameni Scripta minora*. Bibliotheca scriptorium graecorum et romanorum teubneriana. Amsterdam.
Migne, J.P. (ed.) (1844–1866), *Isidore of Pelusium: Epistulae. Patrologiae graecae cursus completes*, vol. 78, Paris.
Morello, R./Morrison, A. (2007), *Ancient Letters: Classical and Late Antique Epistolography*, Oxford.
Nutton, V. (2004), *Ancient Medicine*, London/New York.
Roby, C. (2013), "L'*ekphrasis* e l'immaginazione scientifica in Tolomeo", in: S. Marino/A. Stavru (eds.), *Ekphrasis Estetica: Studi e ricerche 1*, Rome, 109–125.
Rousseau, P. (1996), "The Death of Boethius and the Charge of Maleficium", *Studi Medievali* 20, 871–889.
Sogno, C./Storin, B./Watts, E. (eds.) (2017), *Late Antique Letter Collections: A Critical Introduction and Reference Guide*, Berkeley.
Stramondo, G. (ed.) (trans.) (1964), *Synesio: A Paeonio sul dono*, Catania.

Van Hoof, L. (2013), "Performing paideia: Greek Culture as an Instrument for Social Promotion in the Fourth Century A.D.", *The Classical Quarterly* 63, 387–406.
Watts, E. (2017), "The Letter Collection of Aeneas of Gaza", in: C. Sogno/B. Storin/E. Watts (eds.), *Late Antique Letter Collections*, Berkeley, 384–393.
Watts, E. (2006–2007), "Creating the Ascetic and Sophistic Mélange: Zacharias Scholasticus and the Intellectual Influence of Aeneas of Gaza and John Rufus", *ARAM* 18–19, 153–164.
Webb, R. (1999), "The Aesthetics of Sacred Space: Narrative, Metaphor, and the 'Ekphraseis' of Church Buildings", *Dumbarton Oaks Papers* 53, 59–74.

Rebecca Stephens Falcasantos
Fabricating Monstrosity: Archival Manipulation and the Production of Orthodoxy in Socrates of Constantinople's *Ecclesiastical History*

Abstract: This chapter considers how the late antique historian's praxis influences a reader's knowledge of orthodoxy and heterodoxy. In the first half, I examine how Socrates of Constantinople's arguments make prominent Arianizers into monstrous figures in Book 2 of his *Ecclesiastical History*, as synthesized from his textual archive. The second half of the article considers how Socrates's early readers may have engaged the *History* as an archival text through a close examination of the earliest surviving manuscript of Socrates, the late 9th- or early 10th-century Biblioteca Medicea Laurenziana Plutei 70.7. I specifically attend to when and how episodes about the villains of Book 2 are noted in the manuscript. This evidence of scribal intervention, I propose, illuminates the process by which earlier polemical accusation became archived fact, which informed the reader's knowledge about the limits of orthodoxy and the dangers of heresy.

1 Introduction

As more of the intellectual and governing class embraced Christianity during the fourth and fifth centuries CE, Roman cultural institutions experienced profound shifts. Among the consequences of these shifts was the reorganization of knowledge around assertions of Christian theology, including the categorization of social networks in terms of orthodoxy and heterodoxy. Such reorganizations are particularly evident in heresiological literature, with its frequently elaborate ethnographic mapping of heretical groups and their reported "perverted" theology and habits.[1] But such mapping also occurs in Christian historiography, wherein perceived heretics are not simply presented as villains but as monstrous agents who have inflicted lasting wounds on orthodox populations. Among these productions is the *Ecclesiastical History* of Socrates of Constanti-

---
1 For the ethnographic impulse in heresiology, see Berzon 2016, esp. 42–54.

ə Open Access. © 2023 Rebecca Stephens Falcasantos, published by De Gruyter. This work is licensed under the Creative Commons Attribution 4.0 International License.
https://doi.org/10.1515/9783111010311-005

nople, composed in Greek during the mid-fifth century.[2] Like the texts of the heresiological tradition, the *History* is an act of world-building, by which the author populates his city and empire with dangerous others who both tempt the faithful away from Christ and commit extreme violence: they cause fatal street riots, force-feed their Eucharist to the orthodox, and mutilate holy bodies. These figures are effectively monsters, in that they serve as warnings of boundaries not to be crossed, their grotesqueness found not in their physical features, but in their moral depravity and the atrocities they cannot help but commit.[3] In effect, Socrates uses these characters as sites of negotiation in constructing knowledge of orthodoxy and heterodoxy.

But such characters are not the only disruptive feature of the *History*. The text itself is a somewhat unwieldy, composite artifact that preserves a pastiche of source material: imperial letters, conciliar documents, polemical orations, reportedly eyewitness accounts, and what may be information from local archives, all held together within Socrates's own loose framing remarks. Approaching this material is consequently complicated and at times frustrating. Because of the contrast between the rhetorical complexity of his sources and his own comparatively simple Greek, his work has frequently been treated primarily as an archive for reconstructing ecclesiastical affairs from the reign of Constantine through the first decades of the fifth century. Indeed, a source-critical analysis of Socrates's *History* is itself an important subject of inquiry in that it helps us understand late antique literary culture and provides access to texts that do not otherwise survive. However, we also need to examine *how* Socrates utilizes his sources to construct a particular view of the past and the consequences it has for interpreting his present. Of note is Socrates's intentional curation of extracts from earlier sources into bounded episodes. His editorial decisions reproduce earlier, highly stylized (and perhaps false) accusations about the violent tendencies of his sources' perceived opponents, casting them as certain fact.

This article examines these aspects of Socrates's work, namely, his active arrangement of earlier material to amplify the dangers presented by the heterodox and its influence on a reader's knowledge of orthodoxy and heterodoxy. To

---

[2] As far as we can determine, the *History* was completed sometime between 439 and 446. See Leppin 1996, 273–281, and Leppin 2003, 223; 224–225; Urbainczyk 1997, 20; Van Nuffelen 2004, 10, 61; Wallraff 1997, 209–221. All translations are the author's unless otherwise noted.

[3] While Socrates rarely mentions the physical features of any of his characters, the moral depictions of his "villains" can be read in terms of hybridity, ideological deviance, and the moral grotesqueness of "monsters" as explored in Cohen 1996, 3–25.

do this, I consider, first, Socrates's compositional strategies, and second, evidence of subsequent reader engagement with the *History*. Regarding the former, I focus on Book 2, where Socrates presents the central villains of his history, those he identifies as Arianizers.[4] A noticeable core of the material in this book comes directly from the writings of Athanasius, much quoted verbatim, with additional, unsourced material that mirrors the episodes found in Athanasius's polemic. Those added episodes reiterate established narratives of violence, implicating other individuals — particularly the bishop Macedonius of Constantinople — through similar actions and thus pulling them into the orbit of Arian degeneracy. It should be noted upfront that for the present purposes, I am not concerned with the veracity of any of the incidents of violence Socrates relates. Rather, my interest is the narrative effects produced from building a text not simply by consulting earlier sources, but by stitching together extensive quotation, summary, and original commentary, while leaving the seams visible. I argue that this work amplifies earlier polemic to a degree that fashions the *History*'s heterodox characters into monstrous entities that provide reminders of where the limits of orthodoxy lie.

Following this examination, I consider how Socrates's early readers may have engaged this material by examining the paratextual information conveyed in our earliest surviving manuscript of Socrates, Biblioteca Medicea Laurenziana's Plutei 70.7, a late ninth-century manuscript originating from Constantinople or its immediate environs.[5] I specifically attend to where and how the episodes of Book 2 are noted in the manuscript, including in its *kephalaia* (titles) and marginal notations provided by the manuscript's scribe. Such markers suggest that at least in this manuscript particular topics, individuals, and episodes were deemed significant enough to draw the reader's attention. This evidence of active engagement, I propose, illuminates how the copyist participated in the ongoing production of knowledge about orthodoxy in the way his paratextual apparatus did more than simply provide a technology for navigating a complicated text, but reshaped a textual representation of the past.

---

4 These individuals should be, strictly speaking, those who supported the Alexandrian presbyter Arius and spread his teaching that the Son was a creature and thus not *homoousios* with the Father. In Socrates's narrated social landscape, however, this category is significantly broader than it was for those involved in the conciliar politics of the fourth century, for Socrates blithely dumps any Christian who challenges the *homoousios* or its proponents into this category.
5 For a summary of the manuscript as it attests to Socrates, see Hansen 1995, xii–xviii (but note Hansen dates it to the tenth century). Subsequent examination has identified the manuscript's hand with that of scribe active in the late ninth or early tenth century. See Agati 2001, 47–48; Porciani 2011, 87–88; Speranzi 2016, 132.

2 Monsters in the Margins

One of the features of Socrates's *History* is the stacking of short episodes of violence into extended narrations of conflict between religious groups, marked with a variety of framing devices, as well as pronounced shifts in location, tone, focalization, and even verb tense. This episodic rhythm is due in part to Socrates's praxis as a historian: he actively extracts, redacts, summarizes, and compiles a narrative of the past from source material from a variety of genres, including polemical treatises, letters, credal pronouncements, and reportedly eye witness accounts and local traditions. He discusses his methodology several times. At the opening of Book 2, for example, Socrates informs his readers that he had originally proposed to provide the "naked facts" of the disputes following the Council of Nicaea, but that this approach could not do justice to the harms suffered by the proponents of Nicaea, arguing that those who have suffered these harms (in particular, Athanasius) should be trusted and their words given weight. Similar comments appear in the preface to Book 5, where Socrates explains his rationale for presenting the history as he does, interweaving ecclesiastical and governmental affairs: first, he writes to make his audience aware of past events; second, to prevent his readers from becoming bored of conflicts between bishops; and third, to demonstrate how the affairs of the churches and the public affect each other.[6]

The narrative structures and pacing resulting from Socrates's praxis is apparent in each book of the *History*, even if the execution is at times somewhat awkward. In this regard, Book 2 is not particularly exemplary, aside from the fact that it, along with Book 1, contains more documentary sources (namely, imperial letters and creeds) than the later books. Narrative sequences are interwoven with chapters devoted to the extensive quotation of documentary evidence, consisting primarily of synodal pronouncements and imperial letters.[7] As I note above, however, I focus on Book 2 because it is arguably the book that establishes (from Socrates's position) the monstrous nature of Arianizers, fulfilling the preliminary arguments set out in Book 1 and doing the pronounced work of pushing these characters to the margins of human society.

---

6 Socrates, *HE* 5. *pref*. 2–3.
7 In referring to chapters, I am, of course, following modern editorial hands here. Socrates himself did not divide the *History* into clearly demarcated chapters, although he frequently supplies narrative devices to mark transitions from one event or topic to the next, many of which become chapter breaks during transmission.

The pacing of Book 2's narrative is pronounced, with individual episodes strung together into a clear plot that frequently suggests causal relationships between events and a dynamic frame that pushes the reader through synodal proclamations. Amidst the chaotic landscape of Arian usurpations, exiled bishops, and burning churches, we can identify five primary excursuses on credal formulations or doctrinal discussions:
1) Chapter 8 and 10, on the Synod of Antioch (with an interlude on Eusebius of Emesa),
2) Chapter 18–20, on a series of creeds published by various bishops and the synod of Sardica,
3) Chapter 29–30, on the Synod of Sirmium,
4) Chapters 36–37, on the Synods of Milan, Ariminum, and Nicomedia (with a preface on Aëtius and the Eunomians in Chapter 35), and
5) Chapters 39–41, on the Synod of Seleucia.

This list of synods and their documents is somewhat deceptive because of the conventions of chapter division in modern editions. While more chapters in the second half of the book are devoted to directly addressing synods, obscured is the fact that the latter chapters (especially chapters 30 and 37) are by far the longest in Book 2 and provide extensive reproductions of synodal documents. Narratives of violence frequently serve as framing devices between these excursuses. For example, Socrates frames the third and fourth excursus with two lengthy accounts of excessive violence involving Macedonius and George (2.27–28 and 2.38), and an interlude of several chapters concerning the torture of Hosius (2.31), the Jewish revolt in Diocaesarea (2.32), and political instability (2.33–34).

Despite this extensive attention to synodal activity, the narrative framing provides several coherent plots for someone reading the text for an unfolding account of events and Socrates's historical arguments. One of the most significant in Book 2 is a dual plotline concerning the episcopacies of Alexandria and Constantinople, the core of which is found in chapters 2.10 through 2.21, with a coda appearing in 2.27–28 and 2.38. As I will return to this narrative cycle to consider the processes shaping our text into an archive in the second half of the chapter, a brief summary is necessary here. The account begins with the followers of Arius appointing Gregory of Cappadocia to the episcopal throne of Alexandria following Eusebius of Emesa's refusal of that position (2.10). Gregory's installation (2.11), however, is not an easy affair. The local general Syrianus and his army of five thousand surround the church of Dionysius, where Athanasius and his congregation are observing a vigil. Athanasius contrives his escape, providing Gregory the opportunity to enter the church. The people respond by setting the church ablaze. The following chapters (2.12–2.13) shift attention to Constantinople, which remains embroiled in disputes over the successor of its bishop Alexander. In a sequence of events paralleling what has occurred in Alexandria, the general Hermogenes expels the Nicene Paul, with the people of Constantinople responding by burning the general's house and dragging him to death through the streets. The emperor Constantius expels Paul, cuts the city's grain dole, and accepts Macedonius's seizure of the episcopal throne (2.13). The narrative then returns to Alexandria, where the Arianizers, dissatisfied with Gregory's efforts and disturbed by his role in the fire at the church of Dionysius, replace him with George of Cappadocia (2.14). (Socrates provides no hint here, but in 2.38 George will far surpass Gregory's violence). Paul and Athanasius travel to Rome to appeal to the bishop Julius, who proclaims that the two bishops should be restored to their respective sees (2.15). Socrates then provides a brief notice on the riots and deaths that occur at the instigation of George's supporters when Athanasius returns to Alexandria, before digressing into a discussion of the lies and omissions of Arianizers and Macedonius's supporter Sabinus. With 2.16, we are again in Constantinople, this time to witness the praetorian prefect's expulsion of Paul and the deaths of 3,150 of Paul's supporters during a riot at Hagia Eirene. Athanasius and Paul again make their way to Rome to appeal to Julius (2.17). At this point, Socrates inserts his second synodal excurses (2.18–20, 2.23), interrupted by a lengthy defense of Eusebius of Caesarea, including extensive excerpts from Eusebius's work (2.21).

Socrates eventually returns to the George-Macedonius cycle in the second half of Book 2, where the full villainy of the two bishops is exposed. Upon regaining control of Constantinople's churches (2.27), Macedonius "incites a Christian war" parallel to the war being waged by those attempting to usurp the imperial throne, expelling the supporters of the *homoousios* and then launching a persecution on par with "those who previously had compelled veneration of cult statues" (2.27.1, 4). Socrates then turns to reports of George's actions by way of an extended passage cited from Athanasius (2.28). This effectively decenters Socrates as narrator and focalizes instead the voice of Athanasius (as he had promised in the introductory comments to Book 2). Having arrived in Alexandria during Lent, George begins attacking Athanasius's followers as soon as Easter Week had passed:

> Virgins were thrown into prison, bishops were put in chains and led off by the soldiers, houses and food were seized from orphans and widows, and attacks were made against the houses. The Christians were struck at night, their houses were seized, and clerics' brothers were endangered on their account. Even these things were terrible, but after-

wards, more terrible things were dared. In the week following holy Pentecost, the people, who had fasted, went out to pray in the cemetery because they all refused communion with George. But this same villain, hearing of this, provoked the general Sebastianus, a Manichaean. Then, with a crowd of soldiers carrying shields, naked swords, bows, and arrows, he set out against the people on the Lord's Day... Setting up a large fire and stationing the virgins nearby, he demanded that they proclaim that they were of the creed of Arius. When he saw that they were prevailing and thought nothing of the fire, he stripped them naked and mutilated their faces until they were barely recognizable. Then he seized forty men and tortured them in an even more unusual way: he cut branches from palmtrees, but kept their thorns, and flogged their backs so aggressively that some of them had to undergo surgery multiple times because the thorns had lodged in their wounds; other men could not withstand it and perished. Now they exiled all the survivors and the virgins to the Great Oasis, but did not allow the bodies of those who died to be returned to their households according to the rule of proper conduct, but hid them as they wished, throwing them without burial in order to make it seem that they forgot such a great cruelty (2.28.4–11).

Socrates follows the recitation of George's evils with a series of (sometimes lengthy) chapters documenting synods occurring in both halves of the empire, interrupted by relatively brief discussions of military affairs. Then, in 2.38, he provides the culmination of his arguments in a lengthy account of Macedonius's activities in Constantinople. Having effectively stolen the city's episcopacy earlier, he has become even more emboldened by the synodal decrees and begun appointing his allies as bishops in neighboring cities. Socrates provides a graphic account of how Macedonius "turned the provinces and cities upside down":

He was performing countless evils to those who did not choose to heed his teachings, and he was persecuting not only those of the church who were distinguished, but also the Novatians, knowing that they, too, accepted the *homoousios*... Many of the men notable for their reverence were being arrested and tortured, since they refused to share communion with him. After the tortures, they compelled men by violent means to partake of the mysteries, for prying open the men's mouths with wood, they shoved the mysteries down their throats; and those who suffered this considered it a torture greater than other punishments. Also seizing women and children, they forced them to be baptized. If any refused or otherwise resisted, flogging immediately followed, and after the flogging, [there were] chains and the rack and other terrible things... They placed the women who refused to partake of the mysteries in a box and cut off their breasts. They branded the breasts of other women, sometimes with iron and other times with eggs heated intensely in fire. This [punishment] from those who claimed to Christianize was unknown among the punishments of the Hellenes (2.38.5–9).

Included in the list of Macedonius's other atrocities here are the destruction of Novatian churches in Constantinople, the deployment of soldiers to harass Novatians in the Paphlagonian town of Mantinium, and even an attempt to move the sarcophagus of Constantine to the church of Hagios Akakios. These last two events lead to open fighting and bloodshed, with the Mantineans successfully defending themselves with only hatchets and scythes (2.38.29–32) and street fights turning deadly in Hagios Akakios's courtyard (2.38.40–42). Even as lengthy as they are, these episodes do not occupy nearly as much space as their neighboring expositions on synods and creeds. However, compared to many of the previous notices of violence, which are short, punctuated, and relatively vague, these episodes are quite extensive and detailed. If Socrates's readers had any doubts as to either George's or Macedonius's tyranny, these events should resolve them.[8]

Beyond the mere argument against those Socrates casts as Arianizers, this plotline allows us to consider how the historian is re-shaping knowledge of the past as he collates earlier sources. While some of his material for this narrative cycle appears in the earlier history written by Rufinus, his dependence on Rufinus is surprisingly limited, considering his comments in 2.1 and how reliant he is on Rufinus for his chronology in other portions of the *History*. Instead, the bulk of the narrative and its details are consolidated into a coherent narrative from various works by Athanasius. The events surrounding Gregory's election and installation (2.10–11) are pieced together from Athanasius's *De synodes Arimini in Italia et Seleuciae in Isauria* 22–23, *Apologia de fuga sua* 20, 24, and 33, *Historia Arianorum* 11.1, and *Epistula encyclica* 3.3. Athanasius's travels to Rome (2.15 and 2.17) appear in *Apologia de fuga sua* 25 and 33 and *Apologia contra Arianos* 3–20. It is not entirely clear whether Socrates was working directly with those sources, as he indicates only once, in 2.28 while recounting George's brutality in Alexandria, that he is quoting his source. Timothy D. Barnes has argued that Athanasius had compiled a dossier of his works, conciliar documents, and letters, and other fifth-century historians clearly worked from similar collections, if not that very dossier.[9] Given Socrates's comments in 2.1, it seems plausible that he was working with just such a collection, even if he also had access to other copies of Athanasius's work.

---

8 George's character receives further confirmation in 3.2, when he suffers a proportionate death at the hands of an angry mob: following the desecration of the *adyton* of Alexandria's Mithreum, which incidentally exposed evidence of human sacrifices by the cult's participants, the city's Hellenizers attacked Christians, culminating in forcibly removing George from his church, tying him to a camel, and then burning him with the camel. See further discussion in Drake 2010, 173–193. Macedonius is eventually deposed for his crimes in *HE* 2.42; Socrates does not provide an account of his death.
9 Barnes 1993, 37; 110–112; Burrus 2000, 64–68.

Details about the Constantinopolitan episcopacy, on the other hand, are largely unsourced. Athanasius, and after him Jerome, offers only brief mentions of Paul, primarily regarding his accompanying the Alexandrian bishop to Rome.[10] Sources for Macedonius are even more difficult to track. While short notices of some events can be found in Rufinus and Jerome, Socrates's *History* is the first surviving source for these details.[11] The most charitable reconstruction is that Socrates expanded on the brief mentions of his named sources by incorporating details from unnamed sources: imperial or ecclesiastical archives, eyewitnesses, and local traditions, or perhaps the writing of Sabinus, whose compilation of synodal documents does not survive and whom Socrates castigates for misrepresenting events.[12] The account of Macedonius's actions against the Novatians in 2.38 Socrates attributes to personal conversations with Auxanon, an aged contemporary whom he claims witnessed the events (2.38.11). Whatever his sources for the Constantinopolitan material were, however, the effect of his editorial hand is striking. Macedonius's character is substantiated by his connections with George, connections that may be primarily narrative, but implied to be personal because of the close narratological interweaving. In his own work, Athanasius clearly marks George of Cappadocia as a tyrant who has no qualms about overexercising his authority. Socrates's accounts of Macedonius's actions present the Constantinopolitan bishop as having similar tendencies.

It is overly simplistic to observe that Socrates is simply presenting material from the sources he had collected. Along with knowledge of a documentary nature (whether imperial documents or direct, attributed quotation of literary works), Socrates participates in and reproduces a history of polemic. This is particularly evident in his reproduction — and amplification — of earlier Christian tropes linking persecution to insanity, contentiousness, and conflagration. In the roughly two generations prior to Socrates these associations had been transferred from "pagan" authorities to Arius's sympathizers, and Socrates developed this association further. Book 1 of the *History* abounds with evidence of the duplicity of Arius and his supporters, from Socrates's earliest warnings about the coming "civil war between Christians" in *HE* 1.4.6 to Arius's pretended acceptance of the *homoousios* (for which God punishes him with a shitty

---

10 Athanasius, *Apologia de fuga sua* 3, *Historia Arianorum* 7; Jerome, *Chronicon* 324 (317f–i).
11 See Rufinus *HE* 10.28; Jerome, *Chronicon* 342, 359 (317h–i, 323h).
12 Whether Sabinus is Socrates's source here is unclear. References to Sabinus and his collection appear in Socrates, *HE* 1.8.28, 1.9.28; 2.15.8, 2.17.9–10, 2.20.5, 2.39.8; 3.10.11, 3.25.19; 4.12.41, and 4.22.1.

death in the book's final pages) (1.38.8–9). Throughout Book 2 it becomes increasingly clear that the Arianizers are not simply devious fraudsters, but the new persecutors of true Christians. In the first report of Arianizing intrigue after Constantine's death (2.2), Eusebius of Nicomedia and Theognis of Nicaea employ an unnamed presbyter, previously exiled for supporting Arius, to insinuate himself into the palace and become intimate with the empress and her eunuchs.[13] Echoing the progress of Arius's teachings in the previous book, this single presbyter is the spark (σπινθήρ) through which Arius's teachings ignites contentiousness (φιλονεικία) at court, which quickly becomes strife (ἔρις) that engulfs not only the city, but the entirety of the eastern provinces (2.2.4).[14] The double refrain of fire and conflict reverberates throughout book 2, as strife over Arius's teachings is "kindled" (ἐξαφθὲν) and individual Arianizers are described as having "fiery" (διαπύρως) dispositions.[15]

But Arianizers are not simply hot-heated in Socrates's history, nor are their teachings merely incendiary. Their leaders are also pyromaniacs who have no hesitations about setting people or property aflame, sometimes in ways that unsettle their supporters. Consider, for example, the brief episcopacy of Gregory in Alexandria. Initially supported by Arianizers in the city (and installed by the threat of military force) (2.11), Socrates reports that Gregory is rejected by the Arianizers three chapters later for burning a church (2.14).[16] Again, this report aligns with persecution tropes, for, as Jennifer Barry has recently noted, the burning of a sacred space signals the initiation of imperial persecution in fourth-century Christian literature, including Socrates's source for this incident (Athanasius, *Epistula encyclica* 7).[17] As the narrative of Book 2 proceeds, property destruction becomes violence against bodies. People are slaughtered in riots in Antioch (2.8.5), Alexandria (2.15), and Constantinople (2.16, 2.38.40–43). The Alexandrian bishop George of Cappadocia and the Constantinopolitan bishop

---

13 Compare this episode to the earlier insinuation of Arian teaching in the household of Constantine's sister Constantia in Socrates, *HE* 1.25 (following Rufinus, *HE* 10.12).
14 Cp. Socrates, *HE* 1.6.
15 Socrates, *HE* 2.2.5, 2.12.5, 2.25.4, 2.35.4. See similar language about the opponents of Alexander of Alexandria earlier at 1.6.31.
16 Presumably, this structure is the church of Dionysius, which was burned not by Gregory but by "the people of Alexandria" because they were angered by the attempted arrest of Athanasius (at least as Socrates narrates the incident in the earlier chapter). It should be noted, however, that Gregory was not expelled from Alexandria, but rather died in 345. See note in Hansen 1995, 105.
17 See Barry 2020, 14.

Macedonius mutilate the bodies of those loyal to the *homoousios*, sometimes by fire.[18]

Much of this imagery comes directly from Athanasius, whom Socrates privileges for the "record" of events, as he admits at the beginning of Book 2 and we have already seen. But as Virginia Burrus has noted, Athanasius himself had manipulated his own involvement in the controversy — perhaps even reshaping what was a local controversy into a more decisively transregional one — in order to lend credibility to his own contested episcopacy.[19] "Only after the crisis of Gregory's entry into Alexandria in late 338," Burrus observes, "did Athanasius rediscover 'Arius' (who had been dead since 335 or 336) and the usefulness of the label 'Arianism... The *Encyclical Letter to All Bishops*, which he seems to have written in 339 ... following the appointment of Gregory as bishop of Alexandria, frames Gregory as an 'Arian' but still does not explicitly mention Nicaea."[20] But it was not until around 350, she argues, that Athanasius began to fully develop and deploy a memory of Nicaea against another rival bishop that he characterized as Arian.[21] As Barry demonstrates, a significant part of Athanasius's strategy was to deploy precisely those earlier associations of imperial persecutors with insanity and fire against his Christian opponents discussed above.[22] Athanasius's success in controlling the narrative is suggested by the fact that later authors invoked the memory of Athanasius's "persecution" to assert their own legitimacy and shaped their own struggles according to Athanasius's example — as, for example, Pseudo-Martyrius and Palladius do in their eulogaic apologies for John Chrysostom.[23] In the process, the distinctions between heroes and villains are crystalized, the latter frozen into monstrous (mis)representations.

Saying that Socrates is convinced by Athanasius's account of the past may risk overstating evidence for authorial intentionality. The ecclesial and intellectual environment of fifth-century Constantinople had already been shaped through generations of homoousian discourse that reinforced Athanasian claims. As an inhabitant of that world Socrates was subject to its discursive processes. In other words, Socrates did not simply compose a history, but was himself shaped by the polemic of previous generations — narratives that he

---

18 See Socrates, *HE* 2.27.4–7, 2.31.3, 3.38.5–43.
19 Burrus 2000, 60.
20 Burrus 2000, 60.
21 Burrus 2000, 61–62.
22 Barry 2020, 27–29.
23 Pseudo-Martyrius, *Oratio funebris in laudem Joannis Chrysostomi*, 93; Palladius, *Dialogus de vita Joannis Chrysostomi*, 9.196–205. See discussion in Barry 2019, 126–130.

presents (perhaps even trusts) as factual accounts of events following Nicaea. Socrates not only accepted Athanasius's account as historical fact, but he has also appropriated it as an archetype for arranging his own presentation of the past. Even if Socrates derives his material on Macedonius from another source, his dual plot involving the two bishops amplifies these tropes further. In arranging his narrative as he does, Socrates replicates and reinforces Athanasius's assertion that those associated with Arius were never truly Christian, but rather the devious agents of Satan, and inherently effeminate and "out of their minds" (παράφρονες).[24] The parallel narratives about George and Macedonius mutually reinforce the violent characters of both "heretics," until they become acute in the second half of Book 2. Torture builds upon torture, blood mingles with blood, and the intwined accounts solidify into one that solidifies the monstrosity of these two "heretics."

The resulting argument appeals to his audience's sense of violation and outrage in order to place these characters outside the normal boundaries of human society. Consequently, the Arianizers come to function as monsters, in the sense that they occupy a category of actors whose deviance marks social boundaries and warns against the transgression of those boundaries. Socrates himself never refers to these characters as monsters, but like many monsters, these figures occupy the margins of human society and perform a type of hybridity — not in their physical appearance (for Socrates never mentions their appearance), but rather in their tendency to act as beasts or demons. This is true even when they have somehow broken into the center of human society and gain control over the mechanisms of governance and cult, for in their irrationality and depravity they overturn proper order and bring chaos, war, and death. Their deviance lies not in their own bodily deformity but in their moral deformity, and they not only disfigure the bodies of their victims, but they also threaten to mutilate "orthodoxy" and the empire as a whole. This narrative strategy also had the potential to similarly demonize their "heirs," that is, individuals in Socrates's own day who identified with — or whom others might identify with — the Macedonians or other "Arianizing" clergy. Particularly important here is his presentation of harm and trauma at the hand of vicious actors to construct definitive knowledge of the past and, through that, knowledge of the present.[25] The Arianizers, especially George and Macedonius, become agents interested *only* in applying pressure to those around them, to force heresy and apostacy or

---

24 Athanasius, *Apologia de fuga sua* 7; Socrates, *HE* 2.28.12. For a summary of Athanasius's construction of Arians, see Burrus 2000, 51–52.
25 For the reduction of moral agents in narratives of harm, see Presser 2013, 22.

to exercise their own power. In other words, Socrates maps orthodoxy by casting these individuals as monsters and stationing them at its margins, relying on their disfiguring actions to serve as a warning to those who encounter them.

While Socrates's *History* is populated with a large cast of deviant characters, including Hellenizers, Jews, Manichaeans, and even a few tyrannical Nicene bishops, the most pervasively insidious and destructive are those whom Socrates identifies as Arianizers. The Arianizers's subversiveness and violence continue to appear in subsequent books, albeit increasingly displaced, until focus on the Arianizers's plots gives way to the machinations of Alexandrian bishops, Nestorius, and others in Book 7. This coincides, not accidentally, with the near disappearance of the Arianizers themselves from Socrates's landscape, whether by their acceptance of the homoousios or the dilution of Arius's teachings.[26] But their torch is passed along to the villains of later books, to their imagined heirs, including individuals contemporaneous to Socrates.

3 Monsters in the Archive

From this examination of Book 2, it is evident that Socrates manipulated the sources that constituted his archive to craft sustained arguments about the monstrous nature of those he regarded to be arch-heretics. But how did Socrates's readers interact with that narrative? Did they read Socrates's *History* for its arguments, as I have offered above? Or did they approach it primarily in highly atomized way, interacting with it as a bounded archival record of the past (and as many scholars today still tend to do)?[27] My goal in this second half of the chapter is to think about how readers may have received, organized, and packaged the knowledge provided by Socrates through a close examination of our earliest surviving Greek manuscript of Socrates, Biblioteca Medicea Laurenziana Plut. 70.7.[28] To that end, I focus on the manuscript's presentation of *Ecclesiasti-*

---

26 See, for example, the acceptance of the *homoousios* by the Macedonian community in Synnada to avoid persecution (7.3) and the theological shifts in Constantinople's Arian community brought the presbyters Timothy and George (7.6).
27 This is not to say that modern scholars *only* treat the text in an atomized way. Significant counter examples include Gardiner 2013, 244–269; Irshai 2013, 149–153; Van Nuffelen 2004, 342–346; and others who engage details supplied by Socrates with a healthy attention to his agenda.
28 A high-resolution digital facsimile of this manuscript is available through the Biblioteca Medicea Laurenizana's website at http://mss.bmlonline.it/Catalogo.aspx?Shelfmark=Plut.70.7.

cal History 2.10–21, 2.27–28, and 2.38, that is, the "George-Macedonius cycle" discussed above, including its credal documents and the defense of Eusebius of Caesarea at 2.21. A survey of the paratextual apparatus for these selections from Book 2 reveals interesting details about how Plut. 70.7's copyist imposed a superstructure onto Socrates's text that could shape how it was read. While I recognize the scribe may have replicated and added to structuring elements already present in his exemplar(s), for the sake of my argument I will approach the scribe's production of the manuscript as a historical moment and the decision to retain any features of the exemplar (including the text itself) as an act of shaping engagement — including, as will become apparent below, the impulse to atomize the text, to offer summaries and notations that fashioned it into a more easily navigable record of historical events and documents.[29] This activity, I argue, helped tame a cumbersome and at times unruly "textual monster," while encouraging readers to approach the text as an archive to be skimmed and referenced.

Dating to the late ninth century, Plut. 70.7 was likely copied in a scriptorium in Constantinople or its immediate environs. Maria Luisa Agati has identified the copyist as the same scribe who produced volumes for Arethas and an otherwise unknown Dionysius.[30] Folios 1 through 187 contain Eusebius of Caesarea's *Ecclesiastical History* (ff. 1–173r) and the *Martyrs of Palestine* (ff. 173r–187v), the latter being a text frequently appended to the former.[31] Like Eusebius's work in the first half of the volume, Socrates's text (ff. 188r–391v) is written in two columns, in a semi-angular minuscule. Provided at the beginning of each book is a table of its *kephalaia* (chapter titles). Book 2 occupies folios 227v through 277r; the selections I am surveying here appear on folios 232v through 243v, 249v–251v, and 263r–265v. Throughout the volume abbreviated kephalaia appear in the top (or occasionally the bottom) margin of the column in which that chapter begins and is anchored to the text by chapter numeration. The scribe also provides rubrics, annotations, scholia, and other sigla to guide subsequent readers. At least three later hands added to these notations, providing their own glosses, repairs, and corrections. The reader should also note that the modern chapter divisions as established in the *editio princeps* and currently

---

Last accessed 28 October 2022. I extend my gratitude to my student intern, Emma Candland, for helping transcribe and catalog the manuscript's marginalia and paratextual features during Summer 2021 and to Amherst College for providing funds for this work.

29 See comments in Nichols 1997, 10–11, 14.
30 Agati, 2001, 47–48; Speranzi 2016, 132.
31 Schwartz 1999, cxlvii–cliii; Schott 2019, 27.

followed in Hansen's critical edition do not fully align with our manuscript's numeration.[32] In the following discussion I will therefore provide three notations: (1) the folio number, (2) the chapter as assigned in Plut. 70.7 (labeled as κ), and (3) the modern numeration (labeled as *HE*).

As my interest is the earliest discernable moves to transform the text into an archive, I will focus on the first stratum of reader engagement, that is, the copyist's structuring and visual ordering of the text through kephalaia and marginal notations. Distinguishing between the decisions of the scribe and the precedent of his exemplar is difficult, particularly because we do not have earlier manuscripts for comparison. Even so, we can make some tentative speculations about how the scribe engaged the text. For example, the inclusion of both Eusebius and Socrates in the same volume suggests the scribe accepted Socrates's assertion that his history should be read as a continuation of Eusebius's.[33] It also seems to me that at least two copies of Socrates lie behind the text and paratextual apparatus of Plut. 70.7. The kephalaia in the tables for the first three books of Socrates tend to be succinct, running only two or three lines. This is a marked contrast with the kephalaia in the tables for the four later books, which are quite lengthy. This difference is also reflected in the division of chapters. The earlier books follow roughly the same chapter division as modern editions of the text, whereas the later books are divided into far fewer chapters. This suggests that the *kephalaia* originated from two sources, one for Books 1 through 3 and another for Books 4 through 7. It is impossible to determine whether this means that our scribe himself had two copies of the *History* at his disposal or that those two sources were already combined in his exemplar. At the very least, however, it strongly suggests that neither the titles nor chapter divisions originated with Socrates, but were subsequent additions.[34]

As mentioned, the scribe employs a number of ways to divide and annotate his text. The broadest imposition of order in the book is made by dividing the text into discrete units through its *kephalaia*. As is the case in the rest of the manuscript, the *kephalaia* of Book 2 are visually set apart from the text, nearly always in rubric (red uncials) in the upper margin. In most cases the heading supplied in the margins is verbatim, or nearly so, to that provided in the table at

---

[32] As discussed below, Book 2's chapter numerations between Plut. 70.7 and modern editions coincide until *HE* 2.10.
[33] Porciani 2011, 88.
[34] A cursory comparison of *kephalaia* for Book 2 in the eleventh-century BML Plut. 69.5 reveals at least some titles shared with Plut. 70.7. Further comparison of *kephalaia* across the available manuscripts is warranted.

the beginning of the book (ff. 227v–228v). Divergence in Book 2's titles largely appear in the abridgment of the in-text title, most likely, I imagine, due to the demands of space. These abridgments do not result in the loss of information, with a few exceptions.[35] Beyond *kephalaia* and headings, the scribe offers subtitles, which appear in the margins in a black, uncial script. These generally mirror the *kephalaia* in form and length, including their tendency to begin with ὅτι, περί, or ὡς. Related are frequent marginal lemmata, similarly written in a black uncial.[36] These notations appear to serve as indexing notations aimed at orienting the reader within the progression of the narrative and helping them quickly locate events or topics of interest. For example, several notations alert the reader to episcopal succession or to characters within the text.[37] The distinction between subtitle and indexing lemma is often blurred, and both registers seem to assume the functions Gérard Genette assigns to intertitles.[38] A further important paratextual register consists of scholia and glosses that direct the readers to particular textual loci. Occasionally these notations provide the reader with outside information, but more often, they summarize the immediate contents of the text. In a few instances, a scholion offers a brief exclamatory response, often disparaging in tone, that provides a glimpse of the scribe's reactions to Socrates's material or to the author himself. Finally, the abbreviation ΣH (written as a lunate sigma enclosing an eta, for σημείωσαι, "take notice"), in the scribe's hand as well as in later hands, appear throughout the text, occasionally in conjunction with the marginal commentary outlined above. The scribe's ΣH are generally distinguishable from those of later hands by the presence of one or more rippled dashes.[39] While I will include relevant instances of a ΣH in the following discussion, more study is warranted to understand the types of information that interested the scribe for such notice.

As will be observed below, the scribe's treatment of quoted documents is inconsistent. Sometimes documents are marked conspicuously with rubricated

---

35 Compare, for example, the titles for κ.8, in which the abbreviated title drops the long title's emphasis on Eusebius of Nicomedia's responsibility for the Synod of Antioch.
36 There are three instances of indexing annotation written in minuscule on ff. 234v and 234r. As they provide the same type of information as other indexing annotations, it is not immediately clear why the scribe did not write these in uncial.
37 See for example, ff. 231r, 248r, and 272r.
38 Genette 1997, 294–318.
39 An observation made by D. Speranzi in an unpublished catalog entry for the online *Codices Graeci Antiquiores. A Palaeographical Guide to Greek Manuscripts to the Year 900*. As of September 2021, information for the project was located at the now defunct https://sites.google.com/site/codicesgraeciantiquiores/. My thanks to Jeremy Schott for sharing this detail with me.

intertitles situated in the columns or the presence of diple (>) at the left edge of each line.⁴⁰ In other cases, the scribe does not provide such pronounced forms of visual identification. For example, while some of the letters in the series in *HE* 2.23 (ff. 243v–248r) receive rubrication, others in this same series are noted by short glosses or are even simply numbered in the margins. Still other documents are marked only with a new paragraph, signaled by *ekthesis*, or the extension — and occasionally the enlargement — of the first letter of the line into the left margin.⁴¹

Let us turn, then, to our selection, with an eye to the map drawn by the scribe. *HE* 2.10 begins on f. 232v, roughly a third of the way down the left-hand column (see fig. 1). While the passage is marked with a faint chapter number (10) and the associated rubric "ἔκθεσις τῆς ἐν Ἀντιοχείᾳ συνόδου (the proclamation of the Synod at Antioch)" appears in the upper margin, the chapter is not set off with a new paragraph, which is unusual for chapter divisions in Book 2. (The reader should like to know that this is where Plut. 70.7's chapter divisions begin to disagree with modern chapter divisions.) Interestingly, the title of f. 232v does not agree with the title in the kephalaia table, which refers instead to the appointment of Gregory as Alexandria's bishop. But on f. 233v we find another kephalaia rubric, also marked as κ.10, signaling just that episode (this location coincides with the beginning of *HE* 2.11 in modern editions). The reason for the duplicated κ.10 is unclear. Perhaps the scribe erroneously misread an indexing lemma as a chapter title, resulting its placement as a chapter rubric.⁴² This hypothesis is supported by other indications for credal statements in the same chapter. Further down f. 232v, the scribe has placed a ΣH next to Socrates's comments about the alteration of the creed at Antioch (*HE* 2.10.2), accompanied by a summarizing gloss in miniscule noting that the synod made no

---

40 Examples of inter-text rubrication appears on ff. 232v, 237v, 247r, and 247v. Similar rubrication appears in Book 1, on ff204r, 205v, and 206v. Diple appear only three times in Book 2: f. 241v (κ.20; *HE* 2.21.3, quoting Eusebius's *Vita Constantini* 3.13); ff. 242r–243r (κ.20; *HE* 2.21.7–12 and 14–21; quoting Eusebius's *De ecclesiastica theologia* 1.8 and 9 [attributed by Socrates to *Contra Marcellum*]); and ff. 250r-251r (κ.26; *HE* 2.28.3–14, quoting Athanasius's *Apologia de fuga sua* 6–7). We see diple more frequently in Book 1.
41 I note here that our manuscript does not include Constans's letter to Constantius that some later manuscripts place at the end of *HE* 2.22. At some point, however, a later reader (not the copyist himself, I think) has marked the location with an obolus, suggesting recognition of the omission. Interestingly, the reader did not add the text of the letter in the margins.
42 Another possible error appears on f. 266v, where the in-text title for κ.38 (*HE* 2.40) is missing entirely. The beginning of that chapter, however, is indicated by the scribe. As the chapter concerns Acacius's machinations at the council of Seleucia, I wonder if the omission was intentional.

innovation to the creed, but produced two credal statements. Here the creed is set off simply by *ekthesis*, that is, it is written as a single, contained paragraph that continues onto f. 233r. The second creed from Antioch receives a rubric inserted in the left column (ἄλλη ἔκθεσις, "another creed"). In short, we should expect both κ.10' on f. 232v and the rubric on f233r to both be inter-text signals intended to aid the reader in finding the synodal documents.[43] Remarkably, neither creed receives comment, but is rather simply indexed to aid the reader in location. The scribe seems to focus instead on connecting the Frankish movement into Gaul with the general disorder of the synod (*HE* 2.10.21–22), inserting on f. 233v both a ΣΗ and a marginal anchor directing the reader to a miniscule gloss in the left margin: "ὅτι ἐν τη ταραχῆ των εκκλησιῶν ὡς ἐπίπαν ἐν ζάλη τοῦ κοινοῦ (at the disorder of the churches almost everywhere was in general distress)."

K.10" (*HE* 2.11 in the modern numeration) receives little scribal attention aside from a top-margin chapter rubric indicating that it concerns Gregory's use of imperial troops to attack Athanasius, and a ΣΗ marking the locus of his attack on Athanasius's vigil (*HE* 2.11.3). The following chapters, in contrast, receive more attention. K.11 begins on the right column of f. 234r and is given the title "ὅτι Ἐυσεβίου τελευτήσαντος, ὁ ἐν Κωνσταντιουπολει λαὸς Παῦλον ἐνεθρόνισεν αὖθις, οἱ δε Ἀρειανοὶ Μακεδόνιον (when Eusebius died, in Constantinople the people again enthroned Paul, and the Arians Macedonius)." Alongside the passage relating Eusebius of Nicomedia's death, the reader is directed to a scholion reiterating this information, as well as the additional comment that "στάσις ἐκ τούτου ἐμφύλιος (there was civil war from this)." The chapter continues to the folio's verso, where the scribe has offered a brief indexing notation at the top of the left margin next to Ursacius's and Valens's recantation of Arian teachings (*HE* 2.12.4). In the next chapter, κ.12, "περὶ τῆς Ἑρμογένους τοῦ στρατηλάτου ἀναιρέσεως (concerning the death of the general Hermogenes)," the scribe notes several details: the treaty between the Romans and the Franks (marked by a ΣΗ), Paul's second expulsion from the city, and the 80,000 units of grain Constantinople normally received prior to Constantius's sanctions. When we return to Alexandria in the next, short chapter for George's replacement of Gregory, the scribe again takes little note aside from a ΣΗ drawing attention to the church fire (*HE* 2.13). He has no interest in George's Cappadocian origin or in recording episcopal succession as we occasionally find elsewhere.[44]

---

43 Compare the rubrication of imperial letters in *HE* 2.23.49–58 (f. 247r–247v).
44 See, for example, ff. 231v and 248v.

With κ.14, the reader returns to Athanasius and Paul, who, as the chapter rubric in the lower margin of f. 235r announces, have received letters from Julian of Rome and returned to their respected cities. In the margins, another indexing notation draws attention to Athanasius's and Paul's second restoration and the seventh synod held in Antioch. At the top of f. 235v's left margin is a lengthy scholion that appears to have received some repair by a later hand:

> Σκόπει ὅτι καὶ ὑπὲρ δικαίων λέγοντες οἱ 'Ρωμαῖοι, οὐδὲ ὑπὲρ τούτων οὐδ' ὑπὸ τῶν τυχόντων παρεδέχοντο. Σκόπει δὲ καὶ τὸ ἀδιάκριτον [αὐτῶν], ὅτι ὥσπερ τους ἀνευθύνους Παῦλον καὶ Ἀθανάσοιον, οὕτως καὶ τοὺς ὑπευθύνους ὡς ἁυτον Μαρκελλον ἐδικαίουν. Ἀλλ' εἰ καὶ παρὰ τῶν τυχόντων επισκπῶν, ὅμως σφοδρὰν ἐπιτίμησιν δέχονται. ὡς εἴ γε παρὰ ἀξιολογω τούτων, καὶ ὑπὲρ δικαίων ἐδέχοντο τὴν ἐπιτίμησιν, πάλαι ἂν τῆς φιλοπρωτείας ἐπαυσαντο.

> See that even the Romans who speak about the verdicts do not recognize anything concerning these men or from what happened. And see, too, their indecisiveness, that just as Paul and Athanasius were innocent, so too were they responsible because they vindicated Marcellus himself. But although among those who were bishops, nevertheless they received excessive criticism. Because if they were among people of importance and received criticism about the verdicts, they would have ended their former ambitions.[45]

The scribe's source here is not certain, but behind it is perhaps a lost letter from the Synod of Sirmium outlining the judgments against Athanasius, Paul, and Marcellus and subsequent vindications.[46] The abbreviated title for κ.15 focuses on Constantius's expulsion of Paul from Constantinople, omitting the longer summary's mentions of both Philip's involvement in the affair and Macedonius's installation as bishop. But the scribe flags Paul's third expulsion, this time at the hands of the prefect Philip (HE 2.16.3), as well as Socrates's comments about Paul's Macedonian ancestry (HE 2.16.6) and the massacre in Hagia Eirene (HE 2.16.13). Athanasius's third exile is noted in both the rubric for κ.16 and in an indexing notation at HE 2.17.3.

While not as directly involved in the George-Macedonius cycle, the synodal excursus in HE 2.18–20 and the defense of Eusebius in HE 2.21 provide an interesting comparison to preceding chapters. First, the synodal excursus of 2.18–20 (κ.17–19) is remarkable in the scribe's near lack of interest in the credal material. Instead, annotations focus on information about Athanasius and Paul. Not

---

[45] A ΣΗ that appears to be from a later hand anchors the scholion to a passage concerning how Macedonius's supporters blame Athanasius for the conflict (2.15.8). Further to the left, a third hand has added another, much larger ΣΗ.
[46] See discussion of the letter in Amidon 1997, 52–53.

only are the two men centered in the title of κ.17 (*HE* 2.18), but the scribe also provides a short explanatory scholion on f. 237v clarifying that after they had received no aid from the Roman throne (presumably the scribe refers to the bishop of Rome here), they sought help from the emperor. At the end of the same chapter, the scribe provides a short biographic notation for Photinus (f. 238r). The next annotations the reader of the first strata of marginalia encounters are several folios later. But of the creeds contained in this section, the scribe offers only an in-column rubric (ἄλλη ἔκθεσις) for the creed composed by a small number of bishops at Constans's request (*HE* 2.18.3), dedicated chapter titles for κ.18 and 19, and a very few ΣΗ on f. 240r marking discussion about Patripassionists in the "μακρόστιχος ἔκθεσις (long-lined creed)" (*HE* 2.19.20– 22).[47] Otherwise, the scribe provides no notations, leaving the reader a remarkably barren textual landscape between ff. 237v and 240v.[48] More robust marginalia appear again on f. 241r, with notices on a divergent reading attributed to Sozomen (*HE* 20.5)[49] and summary indexing for the Synod of Philippopolis (*HE* 2.20.8–9) and the deception of Marcellus at Sardica (*HE* 2.20.13). The scribal intervention with Socrates's apology for Eusebius of Caesarea (*HE* 2.21) is more pronounced. On the one hand, this is one of only three chapters in Book 2 where the scribe marks quoted material (here quotations from Eusebius) with diple. On the other hand, our scribe breaks from his penchant for indexing with derision, first calling the defenses of Eusebius "ψυχραὶ καὶ ἀσθενεῖς (silly and weak)" on f. 241v, and later, on f. 243v, exclaiming "οια φλυαρα (what nonsense)!"[50]

The codas to the George-Macedonius cycle (*HE* 2.27–28 and 38) appear on ff. 249v–251v and 263r–265v. *HE* 2.27 and 28 both belong to the same chapter, κ.26, summarized with the rubric "ὅτι Παύλου ἐξορισθέντος Μακεδόνιος αὖθις κατασχὼν πολλὰ κακὰ τοῖς τὸ ὁμοούσιον φρονοῦσιν πεποίηκεν (when Paul was banished, Macedonius, holding power, again brought about many evils upon those supporting the homoousios)." Almost immediately the reader encounters a gloss noting "πανταχοῦ ὁ Μακεδονίου μιαιφόνος τρόπος (the entirely blood-

---

[47] While Socrates does not identify the location of the synod that produced this creed, his source, Athanasius's *De synodis* 26, implies that the bishops had again met in Antioch.
[48] This section did elicit the attention of later readers, evident in brief notations and discussions in later hands and other "signs of active reading" (to borrow a phrase from Liv Ingeborg Lied via personal correspondence), including vertical lines marking passages of interest.
[49] The parallel is Sozomen *HE* 3.11. Note, however, that the critical edition of Sozomen agrees with Socrates and does not record a variant reading for the passage. Perhaps the scribe had a copy of Sozomen with the variant reading; another possibility is that the scribe (or the source scholion) has confused the accounts of Sardica and Ariminum (Sozomen, *HE* 4.17).
[50] The comment is written in uncial, with no accents or breathing marks.

thirsty character of Macedonius)" (f. 249v; see fig. 2). There is a remarkable lack of interest in Athanasius's accusations about George's violence, quoted at length by Socrates in 2.28, aside from diple marking material quoted from Athanasius (this is the second chapter in Book 2 with this feature). Interestingly, however, the passage does not even warrant its own chapter, but is rather presented as part of a chapter about Macedonius. The details that draw the scribe's pen instead are Vetranio's failed elevation to the purple (*HE* 2.28.10) and Gallus's elevation as Caesar, with its accompanying celestial portent (*HE* 2.28.21–22).

The lengthy chapter on Macedonius (κ.36; *HE* 38), in contrast, receives multiple notations, beginning with its kephalaia alerting the reader to Macedonius's "cruelty" (περὶ τῆς Μακεδονίου ὠμότητος, f. 263r). On f. 263v, alongside the account of Macedonius's mutilation of women (*HE* 2.38.9), the scribe exclaims "ἄθεον καὶ ὠμόν (ungodly and savage)!" (see fig. 3). As the reader proceeds through the chapter, the scribe's annotations draw attention not to the forced communions or mutilations, but to other bishops installed by Macedonius and the Arianizers — Cyril of Jerusalem, Eleusis of Cyzicus, and Marathonius of Nicomedia — and those who suffered Macedonius's attacks — the Novatian bishop Agelius, Auxanon (another Novatian), and the Novatian community in Mantinium. The scribe also notes the relocation of the Novatian Anastasia church from Constantinople's Pelargos neighborhood to its suburb Sicai and comments on f. 264v that Socrates "λέγει μικροῦ Ναυατιανους καὶ τοὺς ἀπὸ τῆς καθολικης ὁμονοῆσαι ("says the Novatians and those from the Catholic [church] are nearly united"). This commentary is perhaps surprising, given how pronounced the violence in this section of the chapter is, but the scarcity of annotations here only makes the existing notations more noticeable. Importantly, these notations draw attention to incidents that, amid so many other more gruesome events, might be otherwise overlooked, particularly the relocation of the Novatian Anastasia and the Mantinian affair.

From this survey, we see the copyist make numerous textual interventions that are simultaneously visual and textual cues that direct the reader, atomizing the text into digestible, scannable segments and making it a navigable archive.[51] I cannot address every detail here, but we can see some key themes emerge. First, it is no surprise that synods and credal proclamations should elicit some level of interest. We see this not only in the rubrication of synodal documents here, but also elsewhere in Book 2. For example, the scribe keeps a running

---

51 See Nichols 1990, 8.

count of the synods, as well as summary comments.⁵² And yet, it is curious that these documents do not receive more textured mapping than we find in the episodes that serve as Socrates's framing narrative. It is also interesting to note the contrast in the scribe's treatment of Socrates's source material, whereby quotations from Eusebius and Athanasius are given significant weight and clearly marked as quoted material, but the documentary evidence (credal statements and epistle), which Socrates also (supposedly) reproduced from other sources, are more firmly presented as part of the textual background. While excerpts from Eusebius and Athanasius receive clear attention, Socrates's quotations of other texts (including biblical texts) are not marked by diple. In such cases, the documents and source materials almost — if not entirely — fade into the background noise of the text. If these creeds signal the limits of orthodoxy, if they are the products of defeated monsters, then the scribe's relative silence further signals their defeat. These documents effectively become documentary evidence, available to interested readers, but ultimately artifacts of ancient disputes relegated further to the past.

And what of Socrates's monsters, of Gregory, George, and Macedonius? While Socrates had a pronounced interest in Macedonius, the actions of George and Gregory were central to his arguments about the monstrosity of Macedonius and the Arianizers more generally. The scribal apparatus, however, imposes a marked shift in the text's emphasis. Rather surprisingly, George and Gregory receive very little notice from our scribe. At most, they receive mention in a few kephalaia and cursory σημείωσαι. Instead, the scribe's focus is on events related to Macedonius: Constantius's reduction of grain rations, the massacre at Hagia Eirene, the attacks on Novatians, and, in a passage not examined here, the assassination of Paul of Constantinople (*HE* 2.26.5; f. 249r). The scribe pulls a few other opponents to the foreground — for example, Ursacius and Valens, Photinus, and Marcellus — but sustained focus remains on Macedonius. Perhaps this attention is simply because of the manuscript's proximity to Constantinople (which, of course, intersects with Socrates's own interest in the city). Even so, the attention is surely not without consequence.

In a programmatic essay on material philology, Stephen Nichols observes, "One can alter some words in a song that one sings without changing it in an

---

52 For example, his assignation of blame for the "most ungodly (δυσσεβέστατον)" synod at Antioch to "the turncoat (ὁ κόθορνος) Acacius" (f. 272v; κ.43; *HE* 2.45.9). Numeration of synods appear on ff. 235r, 241r, and 265v. Also noted are the six condemnations and nine excommunications issued at Seleucia (*HE* 2.40.44–45) and the nine credal statements listed by Socrates in *HE* 2.41.18–23.

altered context. By writing it down amidst other songs with which it will be immediately compared, one may radically change many aspects of how we understand the song, even without changing its lyrics."[53] So, too, with a text — including our text. Through the paratextual apparatus, our scribe brings some elements forward from the clutter of the narrative, while pushing others backward — or even effectively erasing them altogether. In this way, the scribe redraws the map of the archive, encouraging his reader to visit new sites and forget old ones, as though old Nebraskan rail towns pushed to the negative space of the map when bypassed by the interstate. Similarly, as a result of scribal intervention, some of Socrates's monsters — Gregory, George, even heretical creeds — are subdued and tamed, pushed from the spotlight, yet lurking in the text for any who step past the margins. Others hold their station on the margins, offering warnings to those who consult the archive. While I have not analyzed here the evidence of later reader engagement with this scribal map, we do find traces of readers who set their own guideposts that further reshaped the text.[54]

4 Conclusion

What we have examined here is a sequence of transformations in the textual record, in which source documents are compiled into a narrativized text and subsequently atomized and indexed into an easily navigable format. In the simplest terms, this is a move from textual archive (Socrates's sources) to text (Socrates's *History*) to archival text (Plut. 70.7). But the layers and agendas involved make these moves far from simple.

In the first half of this article, we observed how Socrates transformed lingering accusations from Athanasius against his adversaries into facts, contributing to the ongoing solidification of orthodoxy and heterodoxy as meaningful social categories. His activity in this regard — not quite composition, but also not merely compilation — depends on his already having been persuaded by Athanasius's claims, as well as the orthodoxy of Nicene Christianity.[55] Of course, Socrates is not an aberration in either his commitments to Nicene Christianity

---

53 Nichols 1997, 19.
54 See for example, a series of longer discussions left on ff. 239r–240v by the thirteenth-century hand, identified by Hansen as hand 2; see Hansen 1995, xv.
55 It should be noted that for Socrates, imperial authority is as important as (and often more important than) whether a Christian leader is orthodox. Consider, for example, his negative evaluations of John Chrysostom (6.21) and Cyril of Alexandria (7.7.4).

and assumptions about its place in mid-fifth-century Roman society or in his strategies to reinforce those commitments for himself and his readers. This observation is true even if we consider outstanding questions regarding his observed sympathies and possible affiliation with individuals in Constantinople's Novatian community. Nevertheless, it is important to acknowledge the ways that Socrates is a *product* of over a century of Christian discourses and epistemology and how much he is actively constructing knowledge. We have ample evidence of "orthodox" orderings of the world from the fourth and fifth centuries, in a plurality of modes (doctrinal treatises, invective and apologia, historiography, collections of synodical canons and imperial legislation). Their representations produced the illusion of relatively coherent collectives or networks of Nicene ("orthodox") and heretical voices. It is a world excavated, cleaned, and reconfigured from a complicated, layered, contentious cesspool. It is also an understanding of the world of which Socrates is both a product and an active producer.

Socrates's *History* readily shows its composite nature, stacking narrative episodes next to documents. Sometimes its chronological progression and causal links are thick, but at other times they are incredibly thin. This unevenness in construction has encouraged negative literary judgments about Socrates's literary skill, as well as a certain willingness to trust him as a reporter, even if his chronology or testimony is at times found wanting or erroneous and despite acknowledgment of his sympathy for Novatians. What has received less discussion is that it facilitates not only the same atomization and indexing that we find occurring to other texts, but a strong archival sense — or rather, the weaker narrative structures provide the illusion that the text can be approached as archive first and a unified narrative second. We see these tendencies emerge in the paratextual apparatus of Plut. 70.7, where the scribe has provided (or passed along) a map for those who wish to consult the text. At the same time, the technologies of reading culture add new layers and agendas, changing the text's fabric as emphasis shifts. A reader's engagement with the text would depend on several factors: the reader's motivations, interests, time, and ability. Plut. 70.7's paratexts — kephalaia, subtitles, scholia — provide information that helps readers navigate the chaos and clutter of Socrates's *History*, but also shapes their interpretations of the text and the knowledge it offers.

Bibliography

Agati, M.L. (2001), "'Digrafismo' a Bisanzio. Note e riflessioni sul X seculo", *Scriptorium* 55, 34–56.
Amidon, P. (1997), *The Church History of Rufinus of Aquileia, Books 10 and 11*, New York.
Barnes, T.D. (1993), *Athanasius and Constantius: Theology and Politics in the Constantinian Empire*, Cambridge.
Berzon, T.S. (2016), *Classifying Christians: Ethnography, Heresiology, and the Limits of Knowledge in Late Antiquity*, Oakland.
Burrus, V. (2000), *Begotten Not Made: Conceiving Manhood in Late Antiquity*, Stanford.
Barry, J. (2019), *Bishops in Flight: Exile and Displacement in Late Antiquity*, Oakland.
Barry, J. (2020), "We Didn't Start the Fire: The Alexandrian Legacy Within Orthodox Memory", *Journal of Orthodox Christian Studies* 3, 13–30.
Cohen, J.J. (1996), "Monster Culture (Seven Theses)", in: J. Cohen (ed.), *Monster Theory: Reading Culture*, Minneapolis, 3–25.
Drake, H.A. (2010), "The Curious Case of George and the Camel", in: D. Luckensmeyer/P. Allen (eds.), *Studies of Religion and Politics in the Early Christian Centuries*, Strathfield, New South Wales, 173–193.
Gardiner, L. (2013), "The Imperial Subject: Theodosius II and Panegyric in Socrates' *Church History*", in: C. Kelly (ed.), *Theodosius II: Rethinking the Roman Empire in Late Antiquity*, Cambridge, 244–269.
Genette, G. (1997), *Paratexts: Thresholds of Interpretation*, J. Lewin (trans.), Cambridge.
Hansen, G.C. (1995), *Sokrates Kirchengeschichte*, GCS n.f. 1, Berlin.
Irshai, O. (2013), "Christian Historiographers' Reflections on Jewish-Christian Violence in Fifth-Century Alexandria", in: N. Dohrmann/A. Reed (eds.), *Jews, Christians, and the Roman Empire: The Poetics of Power in Late Antiquity*, Philadelphia, 137–153.
Leppin, H. (1996), *Von Constantin dem Großen zu Theodosius II. Das christliche Kaisertum bei den Kirchenhistorikern Sokrates, Sozomenus, und Theodoret*, Göttingen.
Leppin, H. (2003), "The Church Historians (I): Socrates, Sozomenus, and Theodoret", in: G. Marasco (ed.), *Greek and Roman Historiography*, Leiden, 219–254.
Nichols, S.G. (1990), "Introduction: Philology in a Manuscript Culture", *Speculum* 65, 1–10.
Nichols, S.G. (1997), "Why Material Philology?", *Zeitschrift für Deutsche Philologie* 116, 10–30.
Porciani, L. (2011), "Storici greci a Bisanzio: alcuni problemi di ricenzione del classico", in: M. Bernabò (ed.), *Voci dell'Oriente. Miniature e testi classici da Bisanzio alla Biblioteca Medicea Laurenziana (Firenze, Biblioteca Medicea Laurenziana, 4 marzo-30 giugno 2011)*, Florence, 55–88.
Presser, L. (2013), *Why We Harm*, New Brunswick.
Speranzi, D. (2016), "Il Laurenziano Pluteo 4.9 e il copista di Dionisio", *Scripta* 9, 127–146.
Schott, J. (2019), *Eusebius, The History of the Church: A New Translation*, Oakland.
Schwartz, E. (1999), "Überschriften und Kephalaia", in: Schwartz (ed.), *Eusebius Werke* II.3, Berlin, cxlvii–cliii.
Urbainczyk, T. (1997), *Socrates of Constantinople: Historian of Church and State*, Ann Arbor.
Van Nuffelen, P. (2004), *Un héritage de paix et de piété: étude sur les histoires ecclésiastiques de Socrate et de Sozomène*, Leuven.
Wallraff, M. (1997), *Der Kirchenhistoriker Sokrates. Untersuchungen zu Geschichtsdarstellung, Methode und Person*, Forschungen zur Kirchen- und Dogmengeschichte 68, Göttingen.

Figures

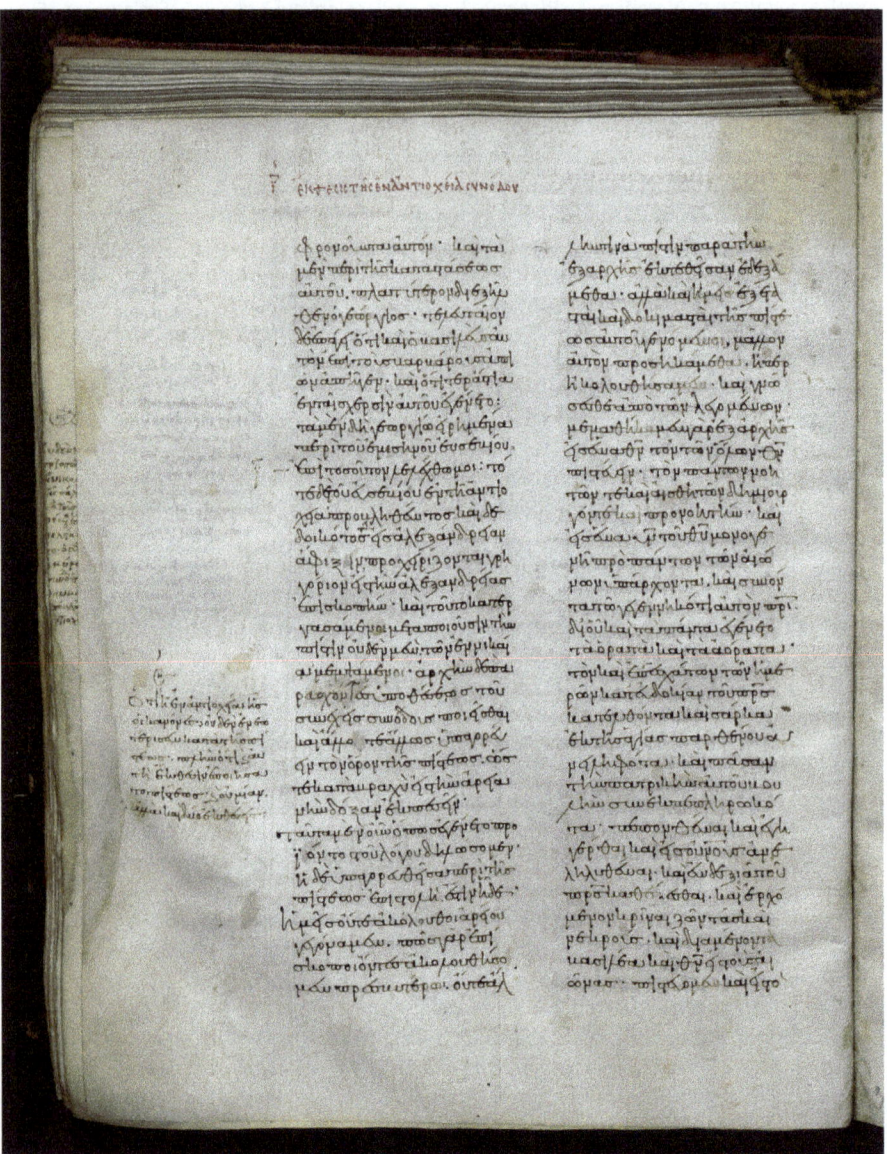

Fig. 1: BML Plut. 70.7, f. 232v. Chapter title in left column is rubricated.

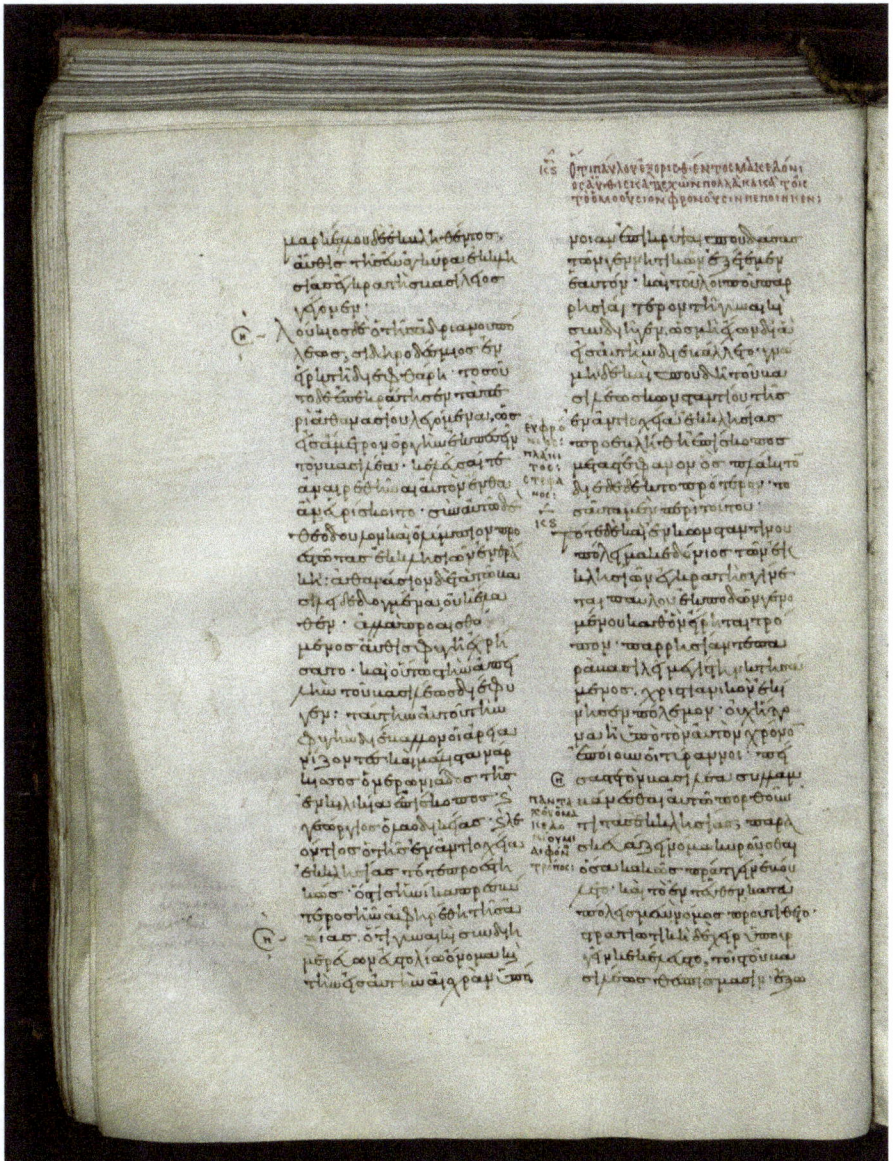

Fig. 2: BML Plut. 70.7, f. 249v. Chapter title in right column is rubricated.

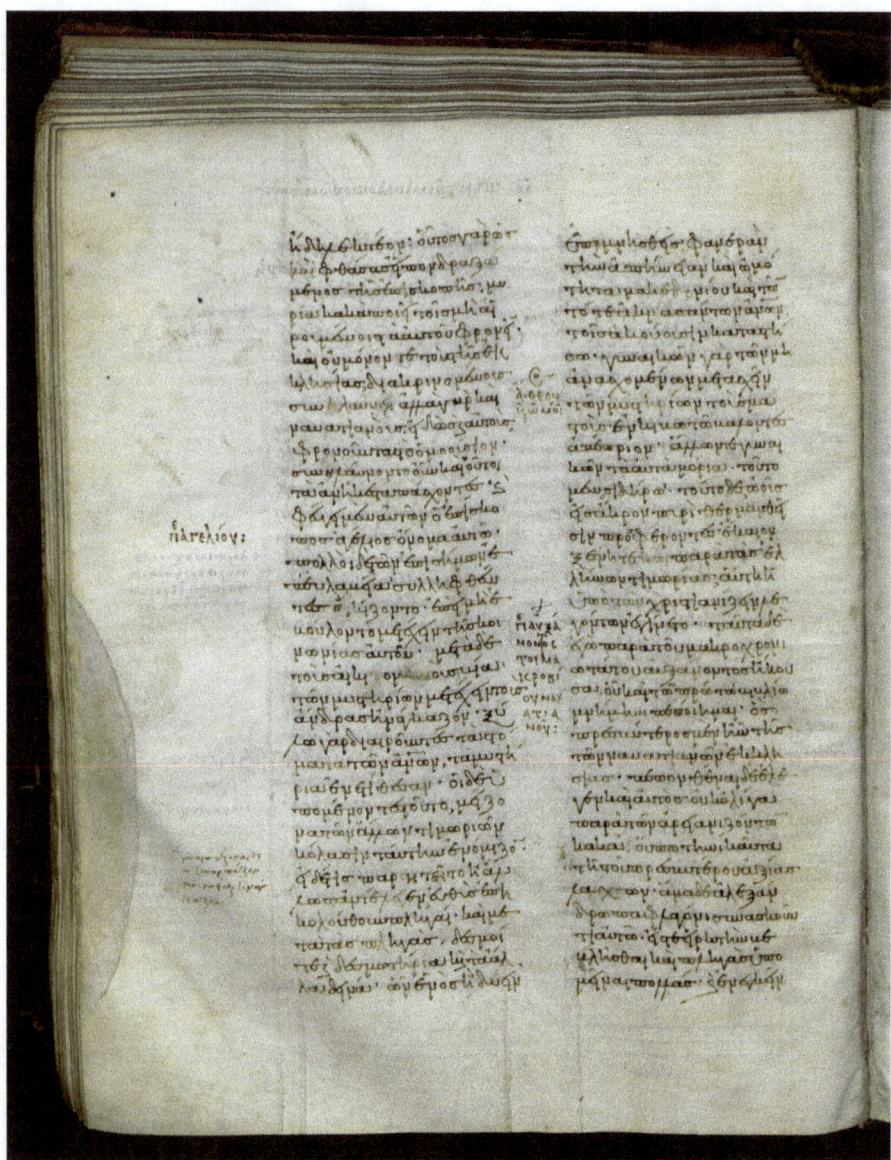

Fig. 3: BML Plut. 70.7, f. 263v.

Nicola Reggiani
Knowledge Construction in Progress: From Paratext to Marginal Annotations in the Greek Medical Papyri

Abstract: This paper deals with the various strategies adopted in the ancient times to construct and transmit medical knowledge in written format. Based on the analysis of Greek papyri from Hellenistic and Roman Egypt, it is possible to uncover the graphical, layout, and textual devices used by the ancient physicians to build, enhance, and improve their ever-changing set of knowledge in the everyday interplay between theoretical knowledge and practical know-how. After an introductory discussion about the concept and the features of paratextual elements, the discourse will focus on the marginal annotations that added further information — often connected to the actual medical practice — to the written content of the medical papyri.

1 Constructing Ancient Medical Knowledge

Hippocrates' famous aphorism "Life is short, art is long" perfectly depicts the nature of medicine as a technical knowledge in continuous progress. Even very recent circumstances — I am referring here to the still ongoing Covid-19 pandemics — warn us about the fact that many centuries of developments and improvements are never sufficient to grant a complete handling of our healthcare. Medicine has always learnt both from the past and from the present and such a set of knowledge, which is consequently characterized by a progressive and ever-growing nature, has always been founded on the expertise boosted by many wisemen through time and continuously updated and fine-tuned thanks

---

This contribution falls within the scopes of the PRIN 2017 project "Greek and Latin Literary Papyri from Graeco-Roman and Late Antique Fayum: Texts, Contexts, Readers" (P.I. Lucio Del Corso, University of Cassino), research unit at the University of Parma (coordinator Nicola Reggiani, http://www.papirologia.unipr.it/ricerca/prin2017.html). Papyri are cited according to the official abbreviations explained in the *Checklist of Editions of Greek, Latin, Demotic, and Coptic Papyri, Ostraca, and Tablets* at https://papyri.info/docs/checklist. I refer to it also for the bibliographical details of the papyrological editions.

to the personal experiences of individual physicians and researchers.[1] Knowledge construction and transmission is accordingly fundamental in the field of ancient medicine and, though it was performed orally at the earliest stages, writing had become an essential aspect of its intellectual process since the times of Hippocrates.[2]

Several ancient medical treatises survived in the manuscript tradition, thanks to European copyists and Arabic translators, but it is from the Greek medical papyri that we get a true glimpse of the actual writing practices of ancient physicians and savants interested in medical topics.[3] The papyri are indeed a direct product of everyday life and activity and allow for what has been defined as "the worm's eye view of history".[4] The Greek papyri from Hellenistic, Roman and Byzantine Egypt (3rd BCE – 7th CE) containing medicine-related texts (treatises, handbooks, prescriptions, and collections of recipes) constitute a very technical corpus, the ca. 350 items of which share common linguistic and scribal features aimed at shaping and conveying their own specialized contents.[5] It is therefore interesting to analyze the strategies adopted to formalize and transmit this specific knowledge.

Beside the corpus-specific technical language, which has already been studied elsewhere,[6] the Greek medical papyri employ a rich network of paratextual or non-textual strategies with the purpose of integrating the very textual information with further meanings that enhanced the technical content of the writings. These strategies thereby contributed to the articulation of an expressive discursive network that was essential to the formulation of the medical writing itself, to its transmission, to its learning, and to its practical use. According to Gérard Genette's textual theory,[7] paratextuality is defined as the relation between a text and what surrounds its own main body — for example: titles,

---

[1] On the transmission of medical knowledge through the time see the very recent collective volume Bovo 2022.
[2] See, e.g., the statement μέγα δὲ μέρος ἡγεῦμαι τῆς τέχνης εἶναι τὸ δύνασθαι κατασκοπέεσθαι περὶ τῶν γεγραμμένων ὀρθῶς. ὁ γὰρ γνοὺς καὶ χρεόμενος τούτοισιν, οὐκ ἄν μοι δοκέῃ μέγα σφάλλεσθαι ἐν τῇ τέχνῃ (Hippoc. *Epid.* III 3, 16, 1–4) "I consider the ability of evaluating correctly what has been written as an important part of the art. He who has knowledge of it and knows how to use it will not commit, in my opinion, serious errors in the professional practice."
[3] On the circulation of medical writings among professionals and laymen in Graeco-Roman Egypt (in the test case of the Arsinoite district), see Reggiani 2019b and Reggiani 2022.
[4] Parsons 1981, 11.
[5] A good introduction to the Greek medical papyri is provided by Andorlini 1993.
[6] Maravela 2018; Bonati 2018a; 2018b; 2019a; 2019c.
[7] Genette 1992, 83–84, as later developed in Genette 1997, 1–7.

headings, and so on. I usually understand this concept in a broader way, including all the voluntary non-linguistic or paralinguistic strategies that enhance the text and add further meaning to its comprehension, that is all the graphical and layout devices that stand between the mere materiality of the act of writing and the linguistic content of the papyri: layout devices such as line displacements or any further spatial distribution of the script; graphical marks such as punctuation, critical and diacritical signs; symbols and abbreviations; and the like.[8]

I have already investigated the ways in which common scribal practices — shared with other literary and even documentary papyri — could be modulated and adapted to special text genres, which are in turn deeply rooted in the typical dichotomy between theory and practice that shapes the medical art. My discourse has focused in particular on two peculiar text typologies, which I will resume here as an introduction to the matter.

The first text typology is constituted by the prescriptions and the collections of recipes (i.e., the so-called 'receptaria'), where the main scribal concerns were to keep each recipe separated from the others by preserving its textual integrity and to articulate its very content in its main conceptual components: title heading, therapeutic scope, list of ingredients and their quantities, instructions for preparation and use. Textual integrity was usually maintained by means of structural indicators, such as horizontal lines (*paragraphoi*) between two consecutive recipes or the displacement of the first line of each new recipe to the left (*ekthesis*), not infrequently starting with the formulaic word ἄλλο "another one" (i.e., another recipe of the same type as above). The internal articulation of the prescriptions was often highlighted with particular layout strategies (e.g., the ingredients columned in single rows) or with special monograms aimed at catching the user's attention: the most frequent were ⟨⟩ for πρός ("against" or "for" a particular disease) at the beginning of the heading section, in order to clarify the therapeutic scope, and ⟨⟩ for χρῶ (imperative "use") in the final section.[9]

The second typology groups the questionnaires or question-and-answer catechisms — i.e., explanatory manuals providing theoretical definitions or practical descriptions in the format of a question followed by an answer —, where the main scribal concern was to outline a particular paging structure aimed at highlighting its didactic and/or reference purposes. Line displace-

---

[8] A general survey of paratext in the Greek medical papyri has been presented by Ricciardetto 2019.
[9] Reggiani 2019a.

ments to the left (*ekthesis*) or to the right (*eisthesis*), blank spaces that stand out in the *scriptio continua* (the uninterrupted writing typical of the Greek papyri), particular graphical marks were frequently deployed to highlight the question-phrase and to keep it separated from the answer-block.[10]

Beside such conscious strategies to construct knowledge with the help of paratextual information, there was a clear trend in enriching the main textual information with marginal annotations, which perfectly represent the fluid nature of the medical knowledge process. Notes and comments, added into the unwritten margins of the writing surface or between the lines of the main text, produced either by the original copyists of such texts or by their subsequent owners, are perhaps the best example of the ancient scholarly and/or personal use of the texts, and they contributed to make them interact with their readers/users. Therefore, they attest to an even more direct and lively process of knowledge construction and transmission.

The appearance, content, and context of the marginal annotations in the Greek literary and paraliterary papyri have been masterfully examined by Kathleen McNamee in her ground-breaking research published in 2007. Though further instances have been retrieved since then, this remains a fundamental milestone on the topic, which is still being addressed by the same scholar in more recent contributions. The medical papyri are not absent from McNamee's discussion, which naturally considers them within the overall frame of the written phenomenon analyzed.[11] A more focused analysis may enhance the understanding of such a practice from the viewpoint of knowledge construction. I will organize the following discussion with MacNamee's categorization of marginal writings in my mind.[12]

---

10 Reggiani 2020.
11 McNamee 2007, 113–114 and 123–124.
12 Of the many possible categories of *marginalia* as categorized by McNamee, the medical annotations fall within six main classes: (a) textual variants (= A3 "Attributed variant" in McNamee's classification); (b) marginal commentaries (= McNamee's B2 "Interpretations and explanations"); (c) notes on the structure of the text (= C1d "Notes on specific topics / The organization of the work"); (d) references to external commentaries (= C1f "References to commentaries"); (e) personal indications of useful passages (= D1 "Indications of useful passages"); (f) personal additions (which can fall into McNamee's generic class D2 "Quasi-personal notes / Other"). I leave the marginal references to external commentaries out of the present discussion because they limit themselves to critical marks of sometimes uncertain interpretation.

2 Marginal Variants

This is the category that most directly pertains to a 'philological' attitude towards the textual content of a medical writing and finds a wonderful witness in Galen's descriptions of his own critical efforts and of the different circulating versions of the relevant literature.[13] Marginal notes containing divergent arrangements of the main text always imply a critical consideration of the text and a comparison with other manuscripts preserving different contents. Whether this proper philological collation was done by the original copyist or by a later user can usually be ascertained by checking the handwriting, though the same person could write in different ways, depending on whether he was copying from a library model or annotating a personal comment.

Undoubtedly did the same informal hand copy both the main text and the marginal additions of P.Oxy. IX 1184, a papyrus fragment from Oxyrhynchus, dated to the first half of the first century CE and containing some pseudo-Hippocratic epistles, copied on the verso of a tax register. All the letters transmitted in this papyrus deal with Hippocrates' alleged invitation to Persia by the Great King Artaxerxes, which he self-confidently refuses — an *exemplum* of Hellenic pride that was certainly used for the sake of ethics. For this reason, we should not assume the medical significance of this papyrus beyond any doubt; nevertheless, it is very important as to the mechanics of transmission of the Hippocratic corpus. The papyrus preserves different versions of letters 3, 4, 4a, 5, and 6a (ed. Smith), separated from one another by *ekthesis* of the beginning line and *paragraphoi* between the individual epistles. [*Ep.*] 3 was shortened at the end, the ordinary termination being appended as an adscript, which starts in the narrow interlinear space between ll. 8 and 9 and continues in the right-hand margin, where it develops into two further, narrower lines, parallel to but independent from ll. 9 and 10 of the main text. Afterwards, [*Ep.*] 4 is transcribed twice, as a compressed version of the long form in the main text, and in a short form (= [*Ep.*] 4a), lacking the introductory salutation, added in the right margin, and separated from the main body of letter 4 with an irregular vertical line that frames ll. 11–17 to the right, following the profile of longer ll. 16–17 but cutting out the last letter of l. 14.

It is impossible to state whether the variants were added at the same time of the copying of the main text or later. However, a stronger textual correction, at ll. 11–12, where former transcription ἀπὸ δὲ Ἀσκλη|πιοῦ γεγονότος was corrected

---

13 See, e.g., Roselli 2012.

into Ἀϲκλη|πιαδέῳ[ν ὄ]ντι ἐγγόνωι by deleting the incorrect letters and replacing them over the line, seems to suggest a later stage of revision, perhaps the same as the interlinear insertions of τέχνης at l. 4 and of Κώωι at l. 11, and as the expunction of δέ by means of two overdots at l. 3 (ἀπὸ δ⟨ὲ⟩ Ἀϲ|κληπιοῦ, see below). It is very possible that the private copyist of the text compared it with another copy, or with more than one copy, and then intervened on his own text by deleting words, which most likely belonged to non-canonical or corrupted versions of the text, sometimes replacing them with the reputedly correct ones, and by simply juxtaposing variant but equally acceptable passages.

A comment inserted between letters 4 and 5 (ll. 17–19), preceded by a *paragraphos* and in slight *ekthesis* — but shorter than the beginning lines of each epistle, to mark its independence — makes us think of a marginal note of the original rolls, later dropped into the main text: ὁ δὲ γενναῖοϲ τηρήϲαϲ τὸ τῆϲ τέχνηϲ ἀξίω|μα καὶ τὸ πρὸϲ τοὺϲ Ἕλληναϲ φιλόϲτοργον | ἀντεφώνηϲεν γράψαϲ τὸν τρόπον τοῦτον "Indeed the well-born, defending the honor of the art and the affection towards the Hellenes, replied writing in such manner." Indeed, this is not attested elsewhere in the Hippocratic epistolary tradition and looks like some marginal comments that we will be discussing below. It is impossible to state whether the copyist already found the text as it is or whether he inserted an extra comment in the main body.[14]

Other cases of marginal variants equally point to philological phenomena of textual collation. In P.Ryl. I 56v (Hippoc. *Acut.* 24–27; unknown provenance, second century CE) ὁκόϲοι | τοιάδε is added by the same informal hand to the right of l. 9, which is unfortunately broken at the relevant passage. The editors postulate such supplement as ὅϲοι δὲ (*vel* ὡϲ ὅϲοι) τάδε ἔχου]ϲι, while the marginal text is more similar to Hippocrates's manuscript tradition, including Galen's commentary *ad loc.*, bearing ὡϲ οἱ / ὅϲοι τοιάδε ἔχοντεϲ (ὅϲοι δὲ τοιάδε ἔχουϲι, Littré). In P.Oxy. LXXX 5221 (Hippoc. *Mul.* I 1, 8–14; Oxyrhynchus, third century CE), εὐρυϲτό|μῳ added by the same hand to the right of l. 21 allows for a supplement ἐ]ν ἀγ|[γείῳ εὐϲτόμῳ κτλ.] at ll. 20–21, which is an unattested variant, while the marginal word corresponds to the unanimous manuscript tradition of the passage.

With the possible exception of epistle 4a, all these marginal variants seem closer to Hippocrates's manuscript tradition than the main text of the papyrus, so that in each case we can guess a collation of the base copy with one better (closer to the original) text or more. However, there seems to be a difference from a mere replacement, which involves the deletion of the incorrect wordings.

---

14 On this case, see also McNamee 2007, 124.

It is true that in both of the latter cases the original passage is lost, but the fact that the variants were added in the margin rather than over the wrong passage (as in P.Oxy. 1184, 11–12, and many other similar instances in the literary papyri) lets us argue that it was not intended to replace the main text, yet rather to juxtapose an alternative option. Conversely, in the same P.Oxy. 5221, 4, γένητα[ι is very likely corrected to γένοιτο (the form attested in all the manuscripts but one, which records γένηται as in the papyrus) by interlinear addition of the correct characters above the wrong ones (γ̣ενη̂τα[) and a καί is supralinearly added at l. 15 (δύο] ἡμέρας ^καὶ δύο εὐφρόνας) — a simple copying lapse or a corrupted text?

Actually, marginal and interlinear supplements are often just additions of missing passages, forgotten by the scribe while copying from the source text or already lost in the textual transmission. Single words, like the examples in P.Oxy. 1184, or the καί in P.Oxy. 5221, 15, are usually written in the interlinear space, over the point where they should have been, but longer passages can extend into the margins, as again P.Oxy. 1184, or occupy them, as the six short lines added to the left of P.Ant. II 86, fr. a (Hippoc. *Aph.* V 43–68; Antinoupolis, late 6th – early 7th century CE), side B, 13–17, corresponding to an omission between ll. 13–14. It is noticeable that in this case the addition was inserted into the left-hand margin.[15]

Some of the interlinear and marginal additions in the Michigan Medical Codex, which I will discuss further below, relate to further explanations of relevant points of the text. It may be questioned whether they derive from the owner's personal knowledge (in this case, they would fall within another class of *marginalia*, see below) or from his collation with a better copy of the book — a procedure that he certainly accomplished, as is confirmed by the several corrections of mechanical mistakes in the main text. On page B verso, between ll. 1–2, [καὶ τὰς] οὐλάς "and wounds that are scarred over" extends the medicament's scope as expressed in the surrounding lines: θε]ρ̣[απ]εύει [τὰ ἕλκη] | [καὶ τὰ δ]υσεπούλ[ωτα καὶ] | [τὰ παλ]αιὰ καὶ τὰ ῥ[ευμα]|[τικὰ] κ̣[α]ὶ̣ κ̣όλπους ἰᾶτα̣ι "it cures the wounds, those hard to cicatrize as well as the old ones and the effusing ones, and heals the fistulous ulcers." The whole context is developed in a sequence of coordinated objects, so that the insertion may well belong to the original work (after all, this is the editor's impression too). On the same side, πρεc(βυτικὰ) "chronic" is added above l. 7 [ῥεύμ]ατα πυοῦcα (= ποιοῦcα) πρὸc {π} ο̣ὐ|λὰc ἡ [ἀφο]^ἐπο̣υλωτική. The letter *pi*, likely deleted by the original copyist and overwritten with ου, makes us

---

15 In P.Oxy. 5221, 3–4, where the copy suffered from a *saut du même au même*, we cannot know whether the missing text was added to the left, because that part went lost. There is no trace of addition to the preserved right.

think that the word πρεcβυτικὰ appeared in the original version and was omitted for some reason, then restored by the revising hand.

3 Supralinear Corrections

Overdots marking expunctions are a common feature of literary papyri. They are conceptually comparable to the replacement of single characters or words by writing the correct text in the interlinear space above the wrong one: in this case, instead of the correct characters, the dots warned that nothing had to be substituted.

πεφωτ̇ιc[μένον] for πεφωcμένον in P.Dub. 1, 32 (Hippoc. [Ep.]; unknown provenance, 1st – 2nd century CE) is certainly a textual enhancement (the technical verb φώζω "to roast" replaces the obviously nonsensical φωτίζω "to illuminate") like the intervention by overdots in the abovementioned P.Oxy. 1184. Whether it was the original copyist to make the correction, or another person, we cannot really tell, though we might suspect the latter, since the only other corrections in the fragment (supralinear insertions ᵏᵃτά and καʹ at ll. 16 and 31, fixing banal transcription mistakes) seem to have been added in a different hand.

Also τουτ̇ε̇ο[ν] for τοῦ ὄντοc in P.Oxy. LXXX 5220 (1), 17 (Hippoc. Alim.; Oxyrhynchus, 2nd – 3rd century CE) is a textual improvement, agreeing with Hippocratic codices, though syntactically problematic, but the original wording is not too far from Deichgräber's conjecture τοῦ δέοντοc — at any rate, there is certainly some philological work behind this correction. Another hint of philological care in the same fragment is the supralinear insertion]η^κτοι at l. 15, which relates to a divergent reading in the codices (δυcεύτηκτοι vs δυcεκτικοί, δυcέκτηκτοι Cornarius) and the text from which the papyrus was copied may have contained some uncertainty.

A diplography lies behind ἐο]ὐc̣ι̣νέοιcι[ν ἐοῦcιν in P.Köln. I 19, 19 (Hippoc. Aph.; unknown provenance, first half of the third century CE), due to the similar spelling of the two words: was the mistake committed by the scribe while copying the text or did he find it in his *antigraphon*? At any rate, the correction may have been applied by more careful a reviser than the one of P.Strasb. inv. 1187 (anonymous surgical treatise), who left the diplography τ]ῶν cιναρῶν {τῶν cιναρῶν} (l. 14) uncorrected.

Another interesting correction by overdots is αυτοτὀἀ[in P.Oxy. LXXX 5240 (1), 2 (anonymous surgical-ophthalmological treatise; Oxyrhynchus, 1st century CE): according to the fascinating hypothesis by W.B. Henry (*apud ed.pr.*), "the scribe may have begun to write τό ἀγγίςτριον [i.e., ἀγκίςτριον, the surgical hook], present in his exemplar as a (perhaps supralinear, and perhaps incorrect) explanation of an ambiguous αὐτό, before realizing his mistake and cancelling the superfluous letters." We may further wonder whether this supralinear addition had already been mistakenly dropped into the main text of the scribe's exemplar. Hint of philological work can also be πάρ'αιρεῖν (παραιρεῖν corrected into περιαιρεῖν) in the same papyrus, fr. 3, 6, while ποιοῦ͂ντα ibid., 9 looks like a banal transcription mistake.

Of various nature are the corrections by overdots applied to P.Oxy. LXXX 5233 (anonymous treatise on acute diseases; Oxyrhynchus, 2nd – 3rd century CE), including a grammatical issue (fr. 1+2, i 2 ἐνδ˙ιδούςη̣ς̣: aorist participle instead of present participle), a missed elision (ibid., i 4 δέεν for δ' ἐν), a diplography (ibid., i 8–9 κ̇α̇ι̇ἐ̇π̇ι̇τ̇ω̇ν̇ καὶ | [ἐ]πὶ τῶν); a iotacism is fixed by supralinear addition (ibid., i 27 δ'⟦ει⟧εγείροντος; uncorrected iotacisms at ll. i 23–25). This extensive correction (but at ii 4–5 βοη]θή{ι}|ματα escaped), together with the circumflex accent likely added at i 25 εᾶν to signal the infinitive ἐᾶν, shows a thorough revision of a poor-quality copy of a circulating text.[16]

A second-stage revision did perhaps undergo P.Oxy. LXXX 5223 (Hippoc. Progn.; Oxyrhynchus, late 1st century CE) too. Here, some characters are cancelled with strokes. At 5–6 δ[ι]απ[υ]|[ή]ματα̇ι̇ the deletion is further marked with an overdot; at 18 ἔξωι̵ with a single horizontal stroke (does this mean that a different person made the correction?). These may have been superfluous iota's erroneously added by the original copyist while transcribing, since also the other corrected mistakes in this fragment belong to banal transcription errors: 6 χρὴ ᵏρίγ̣[ειν (haplography χρ/κρ) and 17 ἐcτά^λμενα (haplography of a triangular sign λ/μ possibly influenced by common participle endings).

A more interesting instance is 14 ρηγιγνῦηται: the original word was ῥήγνυται, and it was certainly trivialized into γίγνηται; it should have been corrected as ʳ̇ʰγιγνηται in the exemplar transcribed by the copyist of our papyrus, who, however, got confused and thought that ρη was a supralinear insertion and not a replacement of the characters below — forgetting the second supralinear correction. The latest corrector, moreover, failed to notice the wrong initial spelling, probably due to the graphical similarity between η and γι in this script (he possibly read ρηηγνηται and missed the double eta). This is a good example of a multiple chain of corrections from manuscript to manuscript.

---

16 P.Oxy. 5233 preserves a slightly different copy of the same treatise as P.Oxy. LXXX 5234 (Oxyrhynchus, first half of the 2nd century AD). This case is a nice witness of the actual circulation of ancient medical writings.

Equally interesting is what happens at the beginning of l. 8 of the same fragment: a single word, [τ]ρέπεται, is written by a second hand — seemingly the same that authored the other corrections — before a *vacat*, after which the first hand continues. It is apparent that the copyist left a blank space later partially filled by the owner of the papyrus: it can be inferred that the former did transcribe from an exemplar that was damaged or illegible in that point, and the missing text was then recovered from other copies.

4 Variants or Corrections? Uncertain Cases

Both marginal variants and supralinear textual adjustments imply the same phenomenon, namely, the contemporary existence of multiple and partially different copies of the same texts, which were compared to one another in order to establish a seemingly correct version, or to just report the diverging traditions. In fact, there is a couple of uncertain cases that may fall within any of the two categories of annotations.

P.Tebt. II 272v (Tebtunis, late 2nd century CE) is a fragment of Herodotus Medicus' *De remediis*, describing the symptomatology of thirst and its treatment; the text corresponds in part to an excerpt of Herodotus Medicus preserved with Oribasius's treatment of thirst in case of fever (*Coll.med.* V 30,6–7 Raeder = CMG VI 1,1). At l. 5, where the text reads αἰτίαι τῆς προϲφορᾶϲ introducing the different reasons for giving the sick something to drink, the scribe adds two groups of three letters between dots above the line: •τῶν• above τῆc, and •ρῶν• above ρᾶc. At a first sight, this may fall within the case of text replacements, in which the correct characters are written above the *delenda*. Certainly, writing a word between dots can be a way to highlight a correction added later on.[17] However, we cannot be sure of what is going on here because this variant is unattested in the manuscript tradition, i.e., in Oribasius' passages quoting Herodotus Medicus, all of which have the singular form. We would have a scribe correcting the form unanimously preserved by the manuscript tradition and replacing it with an unattested variant. The P.Tebt. editors speak of "correction or alternative reading," Marie-Hélène Marganne of "hésitation."[18]

If we should define it, we ought to call it a 'scribal variant,' and compare it with P.Oxy. LVI 3851 (Oxyrhynchus, 2nd – 3rd century CE), a fragment from a

---

17 See, e.g., the *koppa* in P.Eirene III 25, 3 with comment *ad loc.*
18 Marganne 1981, 76.

copy of Nicander's *Theriaka,* where the same device is used to signal a textual alternative between πρεϲβίϲτατ[ον (l. 12 = Nic. *Ther.* 344) and πρεϲβύϲτατον (•υ• above the *iota*). Both forms do appear in Nicander's manuscript tradition, and it is not clear whether the scribe wanted to juxtapose the two variants or to replace the former with the latter. A replacement occurs indeed without dots at l. 7 (ευαινεται, with a rough breathing added above the supralinear *alpha* and an accent over the following *alpha*: αὐαίνεται edd.) and both interventions look like the work of the same copyist.

In fact, unless the intention of the scribe or of the subsequent owner is clearly a replacement of a patent mistake, the choice of leaving the original text and adding corrections or variants in the surrounding space — either interlinear or marginal — seems to entail a certain habit towards the text, which certainly derives from Alexandrian philology.[19]

5 Marginal Commentaries

This class contains an important piece of evidence of erudite work. McNamee has thoroughly illustrated how marginal comments in literary papyri directly source from extensive or 'continuous' commentaries and glossaries, mainly produced in the environment of Alexandrian scholarship. In most of the cases, the question remains, whether annotations were transcribed from such reference books or taken down in the course of oral presentations or classes. From this viewpoint, it is perhaps significant that the examples of medical marginal commentaries come from the papyrus materials discovered at Antinoupolis. As has already been investigated, the 30 medical texts from Antinoupolis[20] — dating from the third to the seventh century CE but especially concentrated in the sixth, and all redacted on papyrus and parchment codices — are expression of a school and academic practice of considerable level, mostly contemporary to the activity of the most important and renown Alexandrian iatrosophists (mid-sixth to mid-seventh century).[21] Therefore, it is not by chance that many of the papyri

---

19 Alexandrian philologists used to produce annotated editions of circulating copies of literary works, instead of editing completely 'new' and 'clean' texts: see Irigoin 1994 along with Montanari 1994.
20 To the 27 texts originally published in the P.Ant. volumes, add fr. 11 of P.Ant. III 184, identified as a different work in the CPF edition, and two new texts published in Pap.Flor. XLIV.
21 Andorlini 2017, 301. On the Antinoupolis materials, see also Marganne 1984; Corazza 2009; 2018.

from Antinoupolis show traces of editorial work: reading notes like the marginal titles in a copy of Hippocrates' *Aphorisms* (P.Ant. I 28, see below), variants, and even proper marginal comments.

The case of P.Ant. III 183, another fragmentary copy of the *Aphorisms* on a sixth-century papyrus codex, is of particular relevance because it lays a bridge towards the consolidated system of Mediaeval scholia, by suggesting that a similar textual and material organization — the composition of erudite material and its annotation in the margins of manuscripts — was already operating in ancient technical texts.²² In fr. 2, side A, the wide margin (4.5 cm) on the right of the remains of *Aph.* III 24 hosts a marginal addition in a smaller handwriting, with a noticeable centered header cχο = cχό(λιον) followed by a comment about the Hippocratic text: τελέcαc ὁ θ(ε)ιότα[τοc] | Ἱπποκράτηc τὸν π[ε]|ρὶ τῶν ὡρῶν καὶ καταc.[τά]|cεων λόγον ἄρχεται[ι τοῦ] | [π]ε[ρ]ὶ τῶν ἡλικιῶν τ[μή]|[ματοc] "Having the most divine Hippocrates concluded the discourse about the seasons and their constitutions, the section about the ages starts." The information given is few more than the titles of the relevant sections (see below, P.Ant. I 28), yet the wording structure and especially the header make us think of an explanatory note that originated in a school context. Indeed, the annotation does not relate to the titles of single aphorisms, nor to the canonical articulation in seven books, already established at Galen's times, but to a different internal subdivision. The note does not belong to the known scholiastic tradition, just as the other extant annotation from the same text, preserved in the lower margin of fr. 3, side B. Here, after a line of the main text identified with *Aph.* IV 5, in a space of about 6 cm a thick text of 10 lines has been compressed in a small and quick handwriting of uneasy decoding, but certainly containing explicatory comments referred to *Aph.* IV 4 (ll. 1–6) and 5 (ll. 7–10), the latter being introduced by the related lemma (πρὸ κυνὸ]c ἐργώδεεc αἱ φαρμακεῖαι, that is the same text as reported in the last extant line of the main text of the fragment), separated from the following explanation by a sort of sinusoid. The lemmatic structure makes it clear that a systematic glossary was the actual source of the note. Other similar marginal commentaries appear in the lower margin of fr. 3, side A (*ad Aph.* III 27?), and in the left margin of fr. 2, side B (*ad Aph.* III 31? and IV 1).²³

Marginal glosses to the Hippocratic texts had existed since centuries: they are attested in literature by Galen and in the papyri by particularly longer versions of some Hippocratic passages, which most likely betray the inclusion in the text of original glosses (P.Oxy. LXXIV 4969, a second/third-century papyrus

---

22 See McNamee 2007, 79–81.
23 See also McNamee 2007, 262–264 (#543.3).

codex with *Articulations*; P.Köln. I 19, the already mentioned early-third century papyrus roll with *Aphorisms*). However, the rise of the codex format implemented the practice of marginal commentaries very much. In particular, as McNamee noticed, a new design of a codex with wide margins developed from around the fourth century to accommodate commented law books, and the trend soon spread to literature.[24]

6 Notes on the Structure of the Text

This category mainly comprises one medical example: the marginal section titles added to the copy of the Hippocratic *Aphorisms* preserved on P.Ant. I 28, side B (*Aph.* I 1–3; Antinoupolis, 5th century CE). This is in fact a peculiar case, because the marginal headings were added — in a smaller size and a less formalized style — by the same hand that copied the main text in an elegant Alexandrian majuscule. The structural indications, therefore, are part of the original layout, not a later addition; it is however significant that they were not inserted within the text column (as in other cases of section headers attested in the papyri) but in the margins. This was certainly due to the codex format of the artefact.

The original book was of good quality (if coming from the school environments of Antinoupolis, we ought to think of a teacher's erudite reference copy, not of a manual), and a paratextual apparatus (*paragraphoi*, inline high dots, inline blanks, enlarged initials) is carefully disposed so to articulate the internal structure of the aphorisms, not only to separate each aphorism from the others, but also to signal discourse breaks within single aphorisms. An elegantly framed title marks the beginning of the new book, Ἱπποκρά[τουϲ ἀφορ]ιϲμοί, after *Prognostics*, which was copied in the preceding pages of the codex and the end of which is preserved on side A of the extant leaf.

The two marginal titles contain few words acting as a summary track of the contents of the related aphorisms and seem to imply the knowledge of more extensive commentaries to the Hippocratic text.[25] The marginal note to *Aph.* I 2 — [πε]ρὶ τῆϲ αὐ|[το]μάτου τα|[ρα]χῆϲ τῆϲ γαϲ|[τρό]ϲ "about stomach's spontaneous evacuation" — recalls the heading of the same aphorism as it appears on an early Medieval manuscript (Paris. Suppl. Gr. 446, 10th cent.) and is built around the keyword ταραχή "agitation," which does appear in the Hippocratic original

---

24 McNamee 2007, 79.
25 See Andorlini 2017, 302–304.

text, while Hippocratic κοιλία is glossed as γαςτήρ, just as some commentators explained that here 'stomach' is meant as 'receptacle of food' (e.g., Steph. *In Hippoc. Aph. ad loc.* = CMG XI 1.3.1, p. 50, 10 ff.). The other original Hippocratic word extracted from the main text is αὐτόματος, which provides the essential information that here the author is dealing with the quality of evacuation. The marginal heading to *Aph.* I 3 — [πε]ρὶ τῆς τῶν | [γυ]μναςτικῶν | [λύς]ε̣ω̣ς καὶ κενώ|[ςι]ο̣ς "about the purification and evacuation of athletes" — is unparalleled but follows the same setting as the previous one: summarizing the content of the aphorism — the peril of an excessive good shape (εὐεξία) for athletes, to be evacuated properly —, it is based on its essential keywords. Traces of characters to the left of P.Ant. III 183 (see above), fr. 2, side B, 4 (δα) are a numerical indicator of the Hippocratic aphorism starting at that line, i.e., IV 1. They are traced in the same hand as the main text.

Marginal titles do appear also in P.Oxy. LXXX 5247 (Oxyrhynchus, 2nd — 3rd century CE) and II P.Ant. II 64 (Antinoupolis, 6th century CE), but their context and meaning are completely different from what discussed above. Both texts are recipe collections. In the former, a short title is added by a second hand to a prescription, in the usual form π̅ + therapeutic scope (ii 12, almost illegible; for the monogram see above). The position (the left margin instead of the right one) and the context speak for the later addition of an original omission (similarly structured headers appear at ll. ii 4 and 7 as parts of the main body of the text) rather than an extra personal annotation like those discussed below. Its purpose, however, was to clarify the content of the prescription, which indeed starts with the mention of the first ingredient (ii 11 ἔφεδρον "horsetail"). Other recipes of this collection do not exhibit the standard π̅-heading, but they nevertheless start with a reference to the therapeutic indications (ii 9 κωφοὺς παῦςαι "stops deaf persons", ii 14 ὧςαι ῥιγοπυρετο["thrusts out shivering fever"). An omission is also behind the marginal addition in Antinoupolis papyrus codex P.Ant. II 64, where μαςτιχάτο[υ "of mastic-wine" is appended to the right of the original indented heading ςκευαςία χ[υλ]ο̣ῦ "preparation of the decoction" (side B, 19; for indention and the other paratext of this papyrus see above). Again, the addition is made by a second hand, more cursive and in a black ink, the main text being copied by a semilibrary hand in brownish ink. Whether it was the fix of an original omission, or an extra personal indication is impossible to state. The same second hand authored a supralinear addition or correction at side A, 1, now illegible.

7 Personal Indications of Useful Passages

This class defines marginal annotations connected not to the production of the copy of the text but to its practical use by its owner. Particularly effective medicaments in recipe collections like P.Oxy. VIII 1088 (Oxyrhynchus, first century CE) and the Michigan Medical Codex (see below) are highlighted on the left margin by means of the monogram ⚹ / ⳨ χρ(ηςτόc) "useful". Similar small comments may be recognized in the addition ἀδυνάτως "powerless" (adverbial) in the lower margin of P.Ant. III 125 (anonymous treatise on diet; Antinoupolis, 6th century CE), fr. 2, side A — a seemingly negative piece of advice, though in the previous traces it could be possible to recover] ̣υ, thus supporting a possible ο̣ὐ̣ ἀδυνάτως with an opposite meaning. ε̣υ[added in the right margin of P.Ant. III 186 (Gal. Comp. med. gen.; Antinoupolis, 6th century CE), fr. 12, side B, 4 can conceal a similar indication of effectiveness, but also something else (another type of comment, a variant; it can be read also ς̣υ[ ).

The same role of highlighting a relevant passage is likely to be attributed to the word μάραθο(ν) added to the left of P.Oxy. XIX 2221r + P.Köln. V 206r (commentary to Nicander's *Theriaka*; Oxyrhynchus, 1st century CE), ii 26, in correspondence to a passage where "fennel" (*marathon*) is dealt with. For reasons unknown to us but certainly connected to his own practice or intellectual interest, the owner wanted to record that key-term:

> Si tratta di un reperto importante per la storia del commentario e dell'ambito di fruizione del 'libro tecnico': infatti, poiché il frammento reca scritte sul verso due colonne di ricette mediche, possiamo pensare di avere oggi di fronte quel che resta di un libro utilizzato e riutilizzato in un contesto professionale. A suggerire l'ipotesi di avere in mano i resti di una cosiddetta 'copia di studio' è anche la presenza di un elemento 'marginale', una parola inserita nell'intercolunnio in scrittura più piccola, formalmente non dissimile dalla mano che ha vergato il testo principale, e in forma abbreviata: esso consiste nel vocabolo μάραθο(ν) (*Foeniculum vulgare*), un termine botanico chiave per la lettura di testo-commento. L'isolata postilla potrebbe essere l'indizio di una possibile utilizzazione selettiva del materiale lessicale di commento ad opera di un fruitore colto concentrato sulla definizione del lessico specialistico. Per quel che riguarda poi la predisposizione del manufatto, osserviamo che la compresenza di testo originale di Nicandro e del commento è così articolata per cui l'occhio del lettore è in grado di seguire il testo continuo di Nicandro 'esposto' (in *ekthesis*) nell'intercolunnio e copiato in sequenza prosastica: l'occhio si sposta con facilità da un lemma all'altro, proprio come Galeno immagina che facessero i lettori del suo commentario al *Prognostico* di Ippocrate i quali, volendo 'saltare' alcune digressioni iniziali, sono invitati a riavvolgere il rotolo fino al punto in cui incontreranno il successivo lemma ippocratico (ῥῆςιc). L'accorgimento dell'*ekthesis* permetteva una 'lettu-

ra selettiva' dell'originale, limitata a ciò che emergeva in posizione di evidenza rispetto alla colonna base di scrittura.[26]

We find another similar case in the Michigan Medical Codex (see below), page H verso, in the right-hand margin of which the second hand added a couple of notes, marking the content of the text: ξ| for ξ(ερόν) or ξ(ερίον) "powder" and πληρ̞ for πληρ(οῖ) "fills," stressing the ulcer-filling power of the powdered medicament.

8 Personal Additions

The practice of adding further material to the texts already copied in the medical papyri is among the best material pieces of evidence of the medical knowledge construction and transmission in a constantly updated flux. It refers to passages supplied by the books' owners — either the authors of the original copy or subsequent users —, all of which not surprisingly consist of medical recipes. As noted since paragraph 1, recipes are the most fluid and customizable typology of medical texts: they rise from individual practice and are continuously enhanced and updated from the personal experience of the next generations. Whole rolls like P.Berl.Möller 13,[27] as well as parchment notebooks and other

---

[26] Andorlini 2017, 299–300 ["It is an important finding for the history of the commentary and of the fruition of the 'technical book.' Indeed, since the fragment preserves two columns of medical recipes on its verso, we can assume to have to do with what survives of a book used and reused in a professional context. The hypothesis that we are dealing with the remains of a so-called 'study copy' is further supported by a 'marginal' element, a word inserted in the intercolumnium in a smaller size, similar in its shape to the hand that wrote the main text, and in an abbreviated form. It is the noun μάραθο(ν) (*Foeniculum vulgare*), a botanical term that is a key to the reading of text and commentary. This isolated note may hint to a possible selection of the lexical content operated by an educated user, who focused on the definition of the specialized vocabulary. Moreover, as regards the layout of the artifact, we notice that the compresence of Nicander's original text and its commentary is so articulated that the readers' eye can follow Nicander's continuous text, protruded (in *ekthesis*) in the intercolumnium and copied in prose sequence. The eye easily moves from one lemma to the other, just as Galen imagines that the readers of his commentary to Hippocrates' *Prognosticum* do — should they wish to skip some initial digressions, they are invited to re-wrap the roll up to the point where they will find the next Hippocratic term (ῥῆcιc). The device of *ekthesis* allowed for a 'selective reading' of the original, limited to what emerged in highlighted position with respect to the writing column"]; see also McNamee 2007, 113–114, 117, 300 (# 1327).
[27] See Marganne 1980; Corazza 2016; Reggiani 2019, 180–182.

such formats, compiled by single physicians and exchanged among colleagues, are one important side of this fundamental aspect. The other side is indeed represented by marginal annotations, which extend the main text with personal contributions, with the purpose of building a reference archive to keep at hand (and perhaps to pass down to colleagues or disciples).

In the case of the late-Ptolemaic *receptarium* PSI Congr.XXI 3v (Tebtunis, 1st century BCE), a fragment of a personal copy redacted on the verso of a Demotic astrological treatise in an uneven informal handwriting, the fact that two of the three extant columns protrude sensibly into the lower margin might be a possible hint of personal additions by the same hand. In the same papyrus, further additions by the same hand (the medicament's type ἡ ψωρ⟦ω⟧ική "the psoriatic" above l. ii, 1 and the extra instruction ὅπου γε καὶ ἄφες "when you believe, you can even remove it [i.e., from the container?]" below l. ii, 4) apparently come from the compiler's own experience, ameliorating the existent references.

Another short annotation directly connected with the physicians' individual experience is the supralinear word ψαῖε in P.Oxy. 1088, above l. ii 39, according to a new reading by John Lundon. In his acute opinion, this would mean the imperative instruction "grind, crush" and would refer to the ingredient κωνήο(υ) "hemlock" (ii 39) of the current prescription, because "la nota tossicità della pianta, soprattutto se assunta in pozione come nel caso della ricetta del papiro (rr. 38–47)" could have suggested "l'aggiunta prudente che si prescrive di sminuzzarne una piccola dose."[28]

A possible personal addition is found also in P.Oxy. LXXIV 4977 (Oxyrhynchus, late 2nd–3rd century CE), written in the wide left-hand margin on three lines perpendicular with respect to the main text, thus against the fibres. The papyrus is a single sheet with multiple prescriptions and the material feature just described is coherent with the customary practice of letter and document writing. The left margin remained empty and even, while the writing lines tended to extend towards the right, often filling the available surface and sometimes squeezing at the end. This strategy was mainly intended to favor the composition of *tomoi sunkollesimoi*,[29] and allowed to accommodate the continuation of the writing, *post scripta* or later additions in that space, after conveniently rotat-

---

28 Lundon 2004, 127–128 ["the well-known toxic power of the plant, above all if taken in potion as in the case of the recipe on the papyrus ... the cautious addition that it is prescribed to grind a small dose of it"].
29 The term refers to 'secondary' papyrus rolls, produced with single written sheets joined and glued together, which was the most common way of archiving files in public and private environments. See Sarri 2018, 106.

ing the papyrus of 90 degrees.[30] Since the bottom of P.Oxy. LXXIV 4977 is lost, it is impossible to state whether the marginal writing is just a continuation of the main text, or a new recipe added there. However, the fact that in the marginal text some ingredients are readable can suggest that it was the beginning of a new prescription.

The most remarkable examples of this category of marginal writings (and of marginal annotations *tout court*) are certainly the extensive additions to P.Mich. XVII 758 and P.Ant. III 126.

The former, the so-called Michigan Medical Codex, is a *receptarium* compiled on a small-format papyrus codex in the 4th century CE, of which thirteen leaves survive to an amount of twenty-six pages, in which numerous recipes are collected — seemingly — according to type of medication (pills and lozenges, followed by wet and dry plasters, at least in the surviving portions). Many prescriptions are ascribed to famous doctors, and "the presence of plasters from a variety of different physicians suggests that the basic text of the codex was combining and taking its shape over considerable time."[31] A characteristic feature is the constant intervention by the owner of the codex, certainly a practicing physician himself:

> not only did he intervene in the text by correcting a few of the scribe's obvious errors of copying, but he also squeezed into the copious bottom margins some twenty additional recipes on related topics, doubling the number of recipes in the preserved sections. Because empty space was limited, he emphasized separation between recipes through lines and marginal markers,[32]

providing one of the most striking pieces of evidence of personal work on technical texts. It is not actually possible to ascertain whether the newly added compositions had been invented by himself or taken from other physicians' collections, but this does not really matter, since the knowledge construction mechanics are the very same in either case.[33] I just recall the central role played by the codex format in the development of marginal writings, as mentioned above.

---

30 Sarri 2018, 112–113.
31 Hanson 1997, 303.
32 Hanson 1997, 303.
33 On the marginal additions of the Michigan Medical Codex, beside naturally its edition by Louise C. Youtie, then collected and introduced by Ann E. Hanson, see also McNamee 2007, 123 and 464–469 (# 2407.01).

A comparable situation is shown by the papyrus codex P.Ant. III 126 (Antinoupolis, 6th – 7th century CE), a medical compilation — an encyclopedia, as it is sometimes called, exhibiting loose resemblance with Aetius and tentatively identified by Fridolf Kudlien with a lost chapter of Oribasius' *Medical Collections* (*ap. ed.pr.*) — with further text broadly added in the lower margins by a small and cursive hand which may be the same as the main text, copied in a sloping informal script. These marginal integrations are not easy to decipher, but they seem to add pharmacological information related to the topics dealt with by the main text.[34]

In this category, we can take into consideration also a sort of personal addition to be found in P.Ryl. III 531 (unknown provenance, mid-3rd – mid-2nd century BCE), a Ptolemaic collection of medical recipes partially and loosely taken from Hippocrates' *Female diseases*. The compositions transcribed in the second column of the recto do indeed find parallels with Hippoc. *Mul.* II 200–201, with original updates consisting in the replacement of an ingredient (beaver's oil) with another one (otter's dried kidneys) that was easiest to find in Egypt, and in the attachment of a statement intended to add more details to the description of the medicament: τοῦτο καὶ πρὸϲ τοὺϲ τῶν διδύμων πό|νου(ϲ) βο{ι}ήθει καὶ κλυϲτήριον ἔϲτιν ὑϲτέρων (rr. 5–6) "This also helps against the pains at the testicles and is a washing for the uterus."[35] This sentence does not appear in the Hippocratic treatise; it is not a marginal addition, since it is part of the main body of the text, but it is separated from what precedes by means of a short blank space: a supplement, which had already become part of the transmission of the main text.

9 Conclusion

The general reconsideration of marginal annotations in the Greek medical papyri as presented and discussed above, in connection with the considerations about the conscious use of paratext and other writing strategies, demonstrates how much the construction and the transmission of ancient medical knowledge was entrusted to the materiality of the written texts, which was consequently a substantial and inalienable share of the entire intellectual process. The 'text' in its material existence, and not in its virtual essence, was at the center of knowledge

---

34 See also McNamee 2007, 123–124 and 463–464 (# 2362.3).
35 See Roselli 2019, 83–85.

construction and transmission, and well represents the point of contact between the two inseparable aspects of medicine: theoretical knowledge and practical know-how.

Bibliography

Andorlini, I. (1993), "L'apporto dei papiri alla conoscenza della scienza medica antica", in: H. Temporini/W. Haase (eds.), *Aufstieg und Niedergang der römischen Welt*, Berlin/New York, 458–562.

Andorlini, I. (2017), *πολλὰ ἰατρῶν ἐστι συγγράμματα. Scritti sui papiri e la medicina antica*, N. Reggiani (ed.), Florence.

Bonati, I. (2018a), "Tra composti, suffissi e neologismi nella microlingua della medicina: alcuni *specimina* tratti dai papiri", in: N. Reggiani (ed.), *Parlare la medicina: fra lingue e culture, nello spazio e nel tempo*, Florence, 30–52.

Bonati, I. (2018b), "Tra *verba* e *res*: alcuni contenitori d'uso medico nei papiri greci d'Egitto", *Quaderni del Museo del Papiro* 15, 65–87.

Bonati, I. (2019a), "*Medicalia Online*: tecnicismi medici tra passato e presente", in: N. Reggiani (ed.), *Greek Medical Papyri: Text, Context, Hypertext*, Berlin/Boston, 257–276.

Bonati, I. (2019b), "La parola delle cose: nuove voci dal passato dei papiri", in: N. Reggiani/ A. Bovo (eds.), *Papiri, medicina antica e cultura materiale. Contributi in ricordo di Isabella Andorlini*, Parma, 129–141.

Bonati, I. (2019c), "*Medicalia Online*: A Lexical Database of Technical Terms in Medical Papyri", in: A. Nodar/S. Torallas Tovar (eds.), *Proceedings of the 28th Congress of Papyrology (Barcelona, 1–6 August 2016)*, Barcelona, 683–689.

Bovo, A. (ed.) (2022), *La trasmissione del sapere medico: linguaggi e idee dai papiri ad oggi*, Parma.

Corazza, F. (2009), *The Antinoopolis Medical Papyri: A Case Study in Late Antique Medicine*, PhD Diss., Berlin.

Corazza, F. (2016), "New Recipes by Heras in P.Berol.Möller 13", *Zeitschrift für Papyrologie und Epigraphik* 198, 39–48.

Corazza, F. (2018), "Il rapporto tra medicina templare e tradizionale nella testimonianza dei papiri greci di Antinoupolis", in: N. Reggiani (ed.), *Parlare la medicina: fra lingue e culture, nello spazio e nel tempo*, Florence, 80–88.

Genette, G. (1992), *The Architext: An Introduction*, Berkeley [*Introduction à l'architexte*, Paris, 1979].

Genette, G. (1997), *Palimpsests. Literature in the Second Degree*, Lincoln [*Palimpsestes: la littérature au second degré*, Paris, 1982].

Hanson, A.E. (1997), "Fragmentation and the Greek Medical Writers", in: G.W. Most (ed.), *Collecting Fragments / Fragmente sammeln*, Göttingen, 289–231.

Irigoin, J. (1994), "Les éditions de textes", in: F. Montanari (ed.), *La philologie grecque à l'époque hellénistique et romaine*, Vandoeuvres/Genève, 39–82.

Lundon, J. (2004), "POxy VIII 1088: problemi e proposte", in: I. Andorlini (ed.), *Testi medici su papiro. Atti del Seminario di studio (Firenze, 3–4 giugno 2002)*, Florence, 119–130.

Maravela, A. (2018), "Medical Micro-Language in the Greek Papyri", in: N. Reggiani (ed.), *Parlare la medicina: fra lingue e culture, nello spazio e nel tempo*, Florence, 12–29.

Marganne, M.-H. (1980), "Une étape dans la transmission d'une prescription médicale: P. Berl. Möller 13", in: R. Pintaudi (ed.), *Miscellanea Papyrologica*, Florence, 179–183.

Marganne, M.-H. (1981), "Un fragment du médecin Hérodote: P. Tebt. II 272", in: *Proceedings of the Sixteenth International Congress of Papyrology (New York, 24–31 July 1980)*, Chico, 73–78.

Marganne, M.-H. (1984), "La 'Collection Médicale' d'Antinoopolis", *Zeitschrift für Papyrologie und Epigraphik* 56, 117–121.

McNamee, K. (2007), *Annotations in Greek and Latin Texts from Egypt*, Oakville.

Montanari, F. (1994), "Discussion", in: F. Montanari (ed.), *La philologie grecque à l'époque hellénistique et romaine*, Vandoeuvres/Genève, 83–94.

Parsons, P.J. (1981), "Background: The Papyrus Letter", in: J. Veremans/E. Decreus (eds.), *Acta Colloquii Didactici Classici Octavi (Amstelodami, 8–11 apr. 1980)*, Gent, 3–19.

Reggiani, N. (2019a), "Transmission of Recipes and Receptaria in Greek Medical Writings on Papyrus Between Ancient Text Production and Modern Digital Representation", in: R. Berardi/N. Bruno/M. Filosa/L. Fizzarotti (eds.), *On the Track of Books: Scribes, Libraries and Textual Transmission*, Berlin/Boston, 167–188.

Reggiani, N. (2019b), "Ancient Doctor's Literacies and the Digital Edition of Papyri of Medical Content", in: *Classics@* 17, http://nrs.harvard.edu/urn-3:hlnc.essay: ReggianiN.Ancient_Doctors_Literacies.2019 [last accessed 12 December 2022].

Reggiani, N. (2020), "Digitizing Medical Papyri in Question-and-Answer Format", in: M. Meeusen (ed.), *Ancient Greek Medicine in Questions and Answers. Diagnostics, Didactics, Dialectics*, Leiden/Boston, 181–212.

Reggiani, N. (2022), "Medical Literary and Documentary Culture in Graeco-Roman Fayum", in: A. Jacob/S. Schiødt (eds.), *Scientific Traditions in the Ancient Mediterranean and Near East*, New York, in press.

Ricciardetto, A. (2019), "La ponctuation dans les papyrus grecs de médecine", in: *Eruditio Antiqua* 11, 121–160.

Roselli, A. (2012), "Galeno e la filologia del II secolo", in: E. Bona/C. Lévy/G. Magnaldi (eds.), *Vestigia notitiai: scritti in memoria di Michelangelo Giusta*, Alessandria, 63–79.

Roselli, A. (2019), "Un corpo che prende forma (*addendum*): papiri ippocratici e dintorni", in: N. Reggiani (ed.), *Greek Medical Papyri: Text, Context, Hypertext*, Berlin/Boston, 75–88.

Sarri, A. (2018), *Material Aspects of Letter Writing in the Graeco-Roman World*, Berlin/Boston.

Courtney A. Roby
Learning from Mistakes: Constructing Knowledge in Late Antique Mathematical Texts

Abstract: This paper analyzes problems in practical mathematics compiled in late antiquity from two sources: the newly published *P. Math.* (Bagnall/Jones 2019) and the *Stereometrica* associated with Hero of Alexandria. These texts are often far from orderly, and often far from innovative at a first glance: tangles of algorithmic problem-solving techniques, most of uncertain authorship, and often plagued by scribal, mathematical, and conceptual errors. Yet the very features that make these texts so difficult to assess cleanly also mean they are fascinating windows onto a rougher stage of "knowledge construction."

1 Introduction

The surviving corpus of metrological texts (i.e., mathematical texts containing problems on measuring areas and volumes of objects and unit conversions, often practically oriented) takes a marginal role in the study of Greek mathematics, edged out of the spotlight by the justifiably intense focus by most scholars on geometry. Euclid's orderly, rigorous cascades of proofs and Archimedes' dazzling innovations are indeed a compelling field of study. The metrological texts, on the other hand, are far from orderly, and often far from innovative at a first glance: tangles of algorithmic techniques for solving measuring problems, most of uncertain authorship, and often plagued by scribal, mathematical, and conceptual errors. Unlike geometrical texts like Euclid's, where later proofs often rely explicitly on earlier ones and so tend to preserve the wholeness of the work, the metrological texts are by nature much more "discrete" (to use Markus Asper's term), and in the surviving texts their problems are mixed and matched with abandon.[1] Yet the very features that make these texts so difficult to assess cleanly also mean they are fascinating windows onto a rougher stage of "knowledge construction." The manuscript codices of problem-sets assembled and reassembled in late antiquity, the pedagogical papyri that preserve students' errors among their efforts to learn by imitation — these show us

---
1 Asper 2007, 198.

knowledge in the making at the level of the discipline and the individual. In what follows I will use recent scholarship on mathematics pedagogy to show how the very errors found in these texts can open up that learning process for analysis.

Perhaps "corpus" is not quite the right term here: this term suggests something more cohesive than the actual state of affairs. Metrological texts survive as problem collections in papyri and manuscript codices, texts often accompanied (or meant to be supplemented) by diagrams, tables of fractions and unit conversions, and other aids to visualization and calculation. Several of the texts compiled into Byzantine manuscripts are associated with the name of Hero of Alexandria, but most should not be attributed to the historical Hero, a figure likely from the 1st or 2nd century CE who composed works on geometry, theoretical mechanics, and practical applications of mechanics like catapult design or the construction of automatic puppet theaters.[2]

Hero did compose a *Metrica* whose three books include one on geometrical and arithmetical techniques for calculating surface areas of a wide range of geometrical objects, one on calculating their volumes, and a third on methods for dividing up those objects in set proportions. The *Metrica* is a fascinating text in its own right for the way it blends the techniques and language associated with geometrical methods (usually abstract, general, and highly privileged) and those characteristic of arithmetical calculation methods (which by contrast are typically focused on specific concrete problems and are less privileged). It also served as the foundation for a centuries-long tradition of Greek metrological texts, many associated with Hero's name, like the *Geometrica*, *Geodaisia*, and *Stereometrica*. These texts incorporate some problems and techniques from the *Metrica* alongside a host of new types of problems, many of them creatively reworked and reorganized in the texts' several recensions.

Vitrac has made a detailed codicological study of the resulting "corpus" of metrological texts, updating previous studies by Hultsch and Heiberg, focusing more on the complexities of their collection and propagation rather than trying to establish a single authoritative text, as Heiberg of necessity did in pursuit of a definitive edition.[3] Amid the variations in structure, content, and apparent audience between the various texts of the metrological corpus, Vitrac nevertheless identifies some common features, like the inclusion of Euclidean-style defini-

---

[2] For an excellent overview of these metrological texts with detailed consideration of questions about authorship, see Hero 2014, 429–533. On Hero's works more generally, see Cuomo 2002; Tybjerg 2003; 2004.
[3] Vitrac 2010.

tions of the objects under study, tables of metrical units and equivalences including a wide range of geographical variations, and the assimilation of real-world objects to geometrical objects and diagrams. Vitrac notes further that the problems in the metrological texts other than the *Metrica* draw almost exclusively on the "algorithmic" tradition of practical mathematics rather than the demonstrative tradition of geometrical texts. And indeed, Hero's persistent focus on the practical applications of science and mathematics, even as he continues to engage with the "demonstrative" tradition in his own texts, probably encouraged his association with the metrological texts, which are overwhelmingly practical in their focus.

The practicality of the metrological texts might seem pedestrian compared to Archimedes' flights of logic or Apollonius's elegant curves, but the mathematics of the "real world" has its own kind of beauty. Gregory of Nazianzus eloquently praised the hexagonal precision of honeycombs, the complex webs woven by spiders, and the effortless flying formations of cranes, contrasting them with Euclid, whom he characterizes as "finding philosophy in nonexistent lines and exhausting himself in his demonstrations."[4] He critiques the efforts of geometers and tactical theorists as empty labor that blinds them to the order already present in the natural world. The metrological authors are, to be sure, concerned with the study of human artifacts like granaries, theaters, and taxation systems rather than the natural world. But one can imagine a comparable frustration with Euclid's "nonexistent lines" fueling their commitment to developing techniques to apprehend the concrete, the measurable, and the marketable. Metrological texts often bridge the gap between geometry and the "real world" representations featured in many technical texts by blending problems dealing with measuring purely geometrical objects with problems in measuring objects, like buildings or wells, that can be approximated by geometrical objects like cylinders or rectangular prisms. These problems can take various forms, from proofs to algorithmic problem-solving routines, with accompanying variations in their formal characteristics like forms of address, use of letter labels and numerical quantities, and the way the text interacts with visual elements like diagrams and tables.

But it is not only human artifacts as objects of study, but humans as learning *subjects*, that the metrological texts illuminate with particular clarity. Their focus on algorithmic problem-solving is in some ways conceptually rigid: one identifies the problem-type, chooses an appropriate algorithm for the type, and follows the steps of calculation. In practice, however, the surviving texts offer

---

4 Gregorius Nazianzenus, *De theologia* 25.

glimpses into the human behind the algorithm: their selection of problem-solving techniques, the diagrams, calculations, and other aids used to help them along the way, and even the errors and missteps that the journey to a solution may entail. Some of these errors are simple scribal or arithmetic errors, but others are conceptual errors that can, from a perspective focused on mathematical pedagogy, illuminate some aspects of the processes of learning in antiquity that are otherwise so difficult to piece together from the surviving evidence.

Those learning processes are captured still more vividly in the mathematical papyri, another class of texts dealing with practical mathematics. A long Egyptian tradition of mathematical papyri written first in hieroglyphics and later in demotic Egyptian were eventually augmented by Greek mathematical papyri beginning in the Hellenistic period. While the Greek papyri do include some fragments of geometrical texts like Euclid's *Elements*, both the Egyptian and Greek papyri more commonly featured problems familiar from the long Egyptian and Mesopotamian traditions of arithmetical problems focused on techniques for measuring and manipulating real-world objects.[5] Quite often these problems are framed as "model" problems for a technique, including a formulaic statement that similar problems may be solved with the same method. The whole population of mathematical papyri is of course quite diverse, including formal geometrical and algebraic texts, astronomical texts, and less formal problem collections that seem to have served a pedagogical purpose.[6] Most interesting here will be the tradition of papyri that seem for various reasons to have been designed for a teaching context.

In this paper I will compare the collections of metrological problems edited by Heiberg as the pseudo-Heronian *Stereometrica* to the problem-solving approaches taken in *P. Math.*, a mathematical papyrus recently published by Bagnall and Jones, likely dating from 4th-century Oxyrhynchus.[7] Diverse as these texts are, they are linked by common threads of problem types and algorithms, so I will begin by sketching out these links, emphasizing in particular their situations within particular cultures. I will then explore a few case studies of missteps in problem-solving in *P. Math.*, including conceptual and algorithmic errors with mentally assembling complex objects, and related struggles on the solver's part to visualize and diagram elements of his problems in a way that facilitates correct solution.

---

[5] For wide-ranging analyses of these traditions, see Høyrup 1994; Imhausen 2016. For an excellent review of the papyrus evidence for Greek geometrical texts, see Fowler 1999, 204–217.
[6] An overview of the mathematical papyri is found in Jones 2009.
[7] Bagnall/Jones 2019.

Given that we know so little about the details of pedagogy of any kind in antiquity, but especially technical education such as the *P. Math.* solver seems to have been engaged in, it might seem fruitless to understand these errors as anything but the random vagaries of a novice student. However, I hope that I can extract some insight into the solver's experience both by comparing his missteps to more successful solutions of comparable problems in the differently organized *Stereometrica*, and also by engaging with contemporary scholarship on cognition and mathematics learning. Here I will give particular attention to the importance of what Davis calls problem-solving "frames" and the conceptual "framing errors" that manifest in some of the solutions in *P. Math.* and other texts.[8] Both the correct solutions and errors open up a picture of what Lave calls "cognition in practice," mathematics performed in and on a real world that offers pedagogical and conceptual opportunities quite different from "pure" mathematical exercises like those we associate in antiquity with Greek geometrical texts.[9]

2 Learning Mathematics

The aims and practices of ancient education remain, for the most part, tantalizingly out of reach, all the more so for the specific case of education in technical or scientific subjects. Cribiore touches on numeracy in her foundational study of ancient education, while Fowler considers the mathematics curriculum suggested by Plato's *Republic* alongside some surviving material evidence for geometry teaching in antiquity.[10] Nevertheless, more questions than answers remain about how mathematics was taught in antiquity and the differences that might have separated the teaching of geometry from "practical" mathematics education. The metrological texts in the "Heronian" corpus and several of the surviving mathematical papyri do seem to have been composed with pedagogical aims in mind, though the signals of these aims differ considerably between the two types of text.

The *Metrica* is a model for many of the later compilations of metrological problems, and it is structured quite rigorously in a way that facilitates learning from the ground up, not unlike Euclid's *Elements*. For example, the first book of

---

8 Davis 1984.
9 Lave 1988.
10 Cribiore 2001, 180–183; Fowler 1999, 103–151.

the *Metrica* is dedicated to techniques for measuring plane figures. Hero begins with the trivial case of the rectangle, and indeed this first passage seems to be as much a continuation of the argument from the preface in favor of the use of abstract "units" (*monades*) rather than concrete units like cubits or feet as it is about the rectangle itself. As the book proceeds, Hero goes on to deliver a series of highly standardized problems in finding the areas of equilateral polygons from the triangle to the dodecagon. Each of these problems is structured in the same way, beginning with the same formulaic language stipulating that each side of every polygon is 10 units. Each begins its solution with a geometrical construction that closely follows the "prototypical" Euclidean linguistic form.[11] Indeed, each of those constructions proceeds through steps familiar from Euclid, locating the center of the polygon's circumscribed circle (compare *Elements* III.1) and using that point to launch the triangles between center and edge that will allow Hero to demonstrate the proportional relationships between them (or, in the case of the enneagon and hendecagon, the diameters that define the right triangles used for that purpose).[12] All three books of the *Metrica* proceed similarly, beginning with simpler problems in each domain (plane geometry for book 1, solid geometry for book 2, and proportional division for book 3) and working toward more complex problems.

The later compilations of metrological problems adopt some of the same organizational strategies as the *Metrica*. The *Stereometrica*, at least in Heiberg's recension, often builds up stretches of problems based on the same basic geometric form, starting with simpler cases and working up to more complex variations. So, for example, a string of problems in the second book (which we will examine in more detail later) begins with a semicircular arch inscribed in a rectangular wall, goes on to a free-standing arch where the reader needs to consider the relationship between its inner and outer semicircular peripheries, and then combines those two forms of arch into a single construction. Other connections between problems are more complex; the series of problems above continues with a structure where arches made specifically of bricks are combined with rubble into a construction element, then moves on to a shell-shaped form (*konchē*) made of bricks, and eventually to a house whose roof has to be

---

[11] On the formulaic language of Greek geometry, see especially Netz 1999, 9–11, 127–167. Further discussion of the stylistic features of this genre of text may be found at Asper 2001, 75–76.

[12] The equilateral triangle is an exception to this pattern as Hero does not circumscribe a circle, but he does make use of another Euclidean mainstay, the "Pythagorean theorem" of *Elements* I.47.

covered in tiles. The internal structures of these later metrological compilations thus hint strongly at a context blending familiarity with the basics of the Euclidean "elements" with a strong emphasis on practical tasks. Vitrac suggests that while the metrological texts associated with Hero's name certainly suggest associations with technical education such as surveyors and architects may have received, they may also have drawn on a tradition of elementary geometrical education, perhaps offering a kind of geometrical analogue to Nicomachus's *Introduction to Arithmetic*.[13]

Yet the caveat above about reference to Heiberg's recension is an important one. The metrological texts associated with Hero's name (and to a lesser extent with Euclid's, as well as other figures like Didymus of Alexandria) reflect a dizzying codicological history of textual blending and reshuffling. The works constructed by modern editors Hultsch and Heiberg as the *Geometrica, De mensuris,* and *Stereometrica* in fact emerge from an array of manuscripts that collect various subsets of problems and tables of metrological conversions under different titles. To be sure, these manuscripts are far from being random assortments of individual problems; in many cases relatively stable clusters of problems and tables are found in multiple manuscripts, in the same order, and often under the same or similar title. Still, on the scale of the whole work there remains an immense amount of variation between the collections, and Hultsch and Heiberg's editions naturally tend to make sense of the varied problem collections they inherited by grouping similar problems together in the edition, even when this means creating a problem collection that does not entirely match any single manuscript.[14] Vitrac indeed views these editions effectively as novel creations by their editors, and so emphasizes the importance of analyzing the contents and entitled collections found in individual manuscripts.[15]

While it is difficult to assign a particular date to the formation of the collections found in this wealth of manuscripts, there are some indicators that in most cases this process took place sometime in the first few centuries CE. The *De mensuris*, for example, was already collected by the 9th century, as it appears in a branch of the Archimedean manuscript tradition whose earliest known witness dates from then.[16] Heiberg observes that the problems from the *Stereomet-*

---

13 Vitrac 2010.
14 Comparisons of the lists of problems in the texts I discuss here in the editions assembled by Hultsch and Heiberg can be found at Hero 1976, vii–viii.
15 Hero 2014, 430–448; Vitrac 2010.
16 Hero 2014, 435 n. 16. The manuscript in question is known to have been in the possession of Giorgio Valla in the fifteenth century, and went missing by the sixteenth, but not before having yielded several copies, many of which feature the *De mensuris*.

rica on vaults and arches, which will be a topic of particular interest here, seem to correspond to a work attributed to Hero for which Isidorus of Miletus composed a commentary in the 6th century.[17] Corcoran further suggests a tentative dating of the *Stereometrica* to the first half of the 5th century, based on a reference to a particular praetorian prefect's having fixed the weights per volume of commodities like bacon.[18] While other collections appear somewhat more unruly and resistant to dating, then, we can at least say that the work of constructing these compilations of practically-focused metrological problems was well underway in late antiquity. The resulting corpus, loose-limbed though it may be, is a rich store of practical problem-solving techniques, squarely located in the domain of the marketplace and construction site both by the kinds of problems the texts solve and by the metrological conversion tables themselves.

While the surviving Byzantine manuscripts reflect one set of processes of mathematical knowledge-construction dating at least partially to late antiquity, the mathematical papyri reflect another side of those construction processes. The majority of the surviving mathematical papyri draw on contexts of practical problem-solving comparable to those found in the "Heronian" metrological texts, and many seem to have functioned as tools for teaching and learning. Cuomo gives the example of a demotic papyrus from Hermopolis dating to the 3rd century BCE, which features a selection of arithmetical and geometrical problems framed largely as practical problems about measuring land or cloth, as well as some practice problems with common techniques like finding square roots. Cuomo argues that "a teaching context is suggested by direct appeals to the reader and by statements such as this: 'When another [add-fraction-to-them] (problem) is stated to you, it will be successful according to the model.'"[19] So while the problems in these papyri are solved for the specific case of the given sample numbers rather than in the entirely general manner characteristic of Greek geometry, those sample solutions are meant to serve as templates for solving similar problems encountered later.

Imhausen's comprehensive examination of Egyptian mathematical papyri suggests some similar conclusions. Her study of the major demotic mathematical papyri (Cairo, BM 10399, BM 10520, BM 10794, Carlsberg 30, Griffith I E7, and Heidelberg 663) explores both the mathematical techniques they exemplify and the way these problem collections are contextualized against a backdrop of "practical" problems. The scare quotes here reflect the complication that as

---

17 Hero 1976, xxxi.
18 Corcoran 1995, 380.
19 Cuomo 2001, 72.

Imhausen points out, several problems that appear quite practical at first glance turn out to be what she calls "suprautilitarian." This term refers to problems designed to showcase a mathematical technique rather than an actual guide to the physical processes one would undertake in carrying out the task described in the problem. For example, problem 8 in *P. Cairo* purports to deal with measuring out a piece of cloth of a given area and cutting it, preserving the total area while reducing the height by one cubit and increasing the width.[20] However, as Imhausen notes, the cut-off strip vanishes from the problem almost immediately, as the problem is actually focused on determining how broad the strip added to the width dimension would have to be in order to keep the area the same once a one-cubit strip was removed from the height. Obviously that same one-cubit strip cannot just be stuck back onto the width dimension; the answer to the problem tells you the required width of the addition, but not how to make it from the existing cut-off strip. So the problem is less practical than it might first have appeared, geared rather for the pedagogical exercise of calculating rectangular areas.

Among the likely Greek "pedagogical" papyri is *P. Mich.* [inv.] 4966, written on one side of a papyrus dated to the second century CE.[21] This document features a table of fractions (all with prime numbers as denominators) expressed as the sum of unit fractions, combined with a series of practical problems: arithmetical calculations framed as being about quantities of wheat, problems asking the reader to convert different amounts of money to copper or silver drachmai, calculations on areas of land, and so on. Smyly conjectured that the Akhmim mathematical papyrus (*P. Cair.* [inv.] 10758) dated to the seventh century CE and edited by Baillet was a school exercise book, as it consists of a set of division tables and a collection of "disconnected problems, with no method in their arrangement" whose solutions often include conceptual and methodological errors, to say nothing of frequent errors in Greek.[22]

P. Math. combines model business contracts, tables of metrological conversions, and a very diverse group of mathematical problems including calculations of areas of land, volume calculations on excavations and buildings, arithmetical problems about the total wages of different classes of workers working for various amounts of time, and several other kinds of problems. These are very often framed as "model" problems with a formulaic note ("this way for similar problems"), similar to the formula Cuomo observed in the Hermopolis papyrus.

---

20 Imhausen 2016, 193.
21 Boyaval 1976.
22 Baillet 1892; Smyly 1920.

Bagnall and Jones note that many of the *P. Math.* problems appear to reflect a formulaic "dialogue" of question and answer between teacher and student.[23] This "dialogue" was far from fluent in *P. Math.*, however; they note numerous orthographical and mathematical errors, leading them to conclude that "the codex belonged to a student in a school devoted to training business agents and similar professionals."[24] These pedagogical mathematical papyri seem to have aimed at teaching a quite different skill set from the "scribal" education more typically associated with grammarians' schools. Instead of grammar and orthography, *P. Math.* reflects an education focused on algorithms for making calculations and unit conversions, models for calculating daily wages, and drafting contracts.

A key skill set in this educational model was fluency with visual "information technologies" ranging from geometrical diagrams to tables of numbers meant to aid in calculation with fractions, multiplication, division, and so forth (indeed, some of the mathematical papyri consist solely of such tables).[25] The papyri that seem to have served a principally pedagogical function are particularly interesting because they include diagrams that played a role in the learning process. A fragmentary metrological text in a papyrus dated to the second century CE (*P. Corn.* inv. 69) features diagrams of two trapezoidal figures, one dissected into several polygons, whose sides are labeled with numbers given in the problems.[26]

P. Math. includes diagrams for most problems with a spatial component, usually labeled with numbers corresponding to quantities given in the problem, and often the result as well. The images in *P. Math.* are of several kinds; some are "diagrams" in the sense of spatially representing objects or quantities, while several of the problems are additionally separated from one another by decorative borders and drawings of palm fronds and ankhs. Diagrams of the first type will be of most interest here, and they too take several forms. Some depict bird's-eye views of geometrical forms representing problem topics like the dimensions of fields, granaries, or holes in the ground. Others are slightly more complex representations of three-dimensional objects. A few tabulate step-by-step results of an arithmetic process or conceptual elements in another kind of problem-solving process. Finally, a few are simply baffling, like a curvilinear

---

23 Bagnall/Jones 2019, 23.
24 Bagnall/Jones 2019, 55.
25 On the broader history of tables of information in the Roman world (and in particular their relative rarity in most contexts), see Riggsby 2019, 42–82.
26 Taisbak/Bülow-Jacobsen 2003.

shape surmounted by a scribbled line that seems to represent a vaulted granary in problem *o1* (fig. 4).

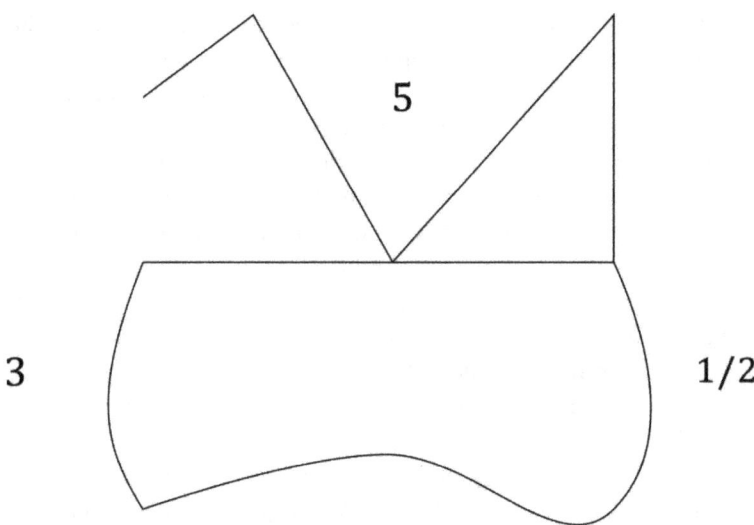

Fig. 4: "Granary" diagram from *P. Math.*, problem 01 (after Bagnall/Jones 2019).

Some medieval manuscripts also include informal diagrams added by readers at later stages of the composition process, but the papyri are particularly rich sources of these diagrams, which largely appear to have been produced spontaneously as part of the solving process, rather than being copied from formal exemplars. This latter feature in particular makes the diagrams in the papyri witnesses to a live learning process that is otherwise difficult to capture. Indeed, the importance of diagrams to Greek mathematics can hardly be overstated.[27] Geometrical proofs are linked at every stage to a letter-labeled diagram depicting every component referenced in the proof. In cases where formal geometrical proof is no longer the principal objective, diagrams take on a variety of other roles and forms. When technical texts in other genres like mechanics or surveying call upon them to represent objects in the world rather than purely geomet-

---

27 The foundational work on diagrams in Greek geometry is Netz 1999. Further studies that focus on the manuscript traditions of these diagrams include Saito 2012; 2018.

rical ones, they may adapt the systems of spatial representation and letter labeling to new ends.

Several different skills are involved in producing a mathematical diagram. Some amount of scribal skill and draftsmanship, possibly involving the use of compass and straightedge, is necessary to produce a clearly drawn diagram. Provided the diagram is not simply copied from an exemplar, competence in the "graphical languages" that might come into play is also required. For a table, this might mean an ability to distinguish headers from data in individual cells, and to keep the rows and columns properly aligned; for a geometrical diagram, this might include an understanding of the relative placement of letter-labeled points in the diagram. However, as Netz, Carman, and others have pointed out, manuscript diagrams are "underdetermined" with respect to the problem statement and do not reliably reflect relative lengths of line segments or arcs (so a triangle specified as isosceles might be represented as scalene), or even preserve easily assumed features such as line segments bounding a polygon (e.g., polygons in some manuscripts are represented as bounded by arcs or spiked triangles instead of straight lines).[28]

In addition to the skills required to produce *some* diagram of a polygon, a circle, and so forth, another set of skills serves to produce a "correct," or at any rate heuristically useful, diagram for the problem at hand. Van Garderen, Scheuermann, and Poch enumerate a set of "strands of diagram proficiency" for modern mathematics students. These include a conceptual understanding of how to use a diagram to solve a given problem, the procedural skill to generate an accurate diagrammatic representation of the situation in the problem, and the strategic ability to engage the diagram as a problem-solving tool.[29] Additionally, van Garderen et al. identify proficiencies in students' ability to explain how the diagram was used to solve the problem, and their belief in their ability to use the diagram appropriately. These latter two are obviously impossible to extract from the surviving ancient evidence, but clues to the first three can be found, and can yield some insight into the process of mathematical learning at play in the papyrus.

Cases where students of mathematics are not told what a diagram should look like are particularly revealing in this sense. Van Garderen, Scheuermann, and Jackson record the results of several experiments where students of different ability levels were asked to solve word problems with diagrams, but not told

---

28 On these features see Carman 2018; Netz 2020, 512, 521.
29 Van Garderen/Scheuermann/Poch 2014, 137.

what type of diagram to use.[30] The example below (fig. 5) shows two very different approaches, along with interviews that illuminate the reasoning process the students used. The second student's carefully counted divisions of the sandwich, and the accompanying strategy of making further subdivisions and counting those up, are worlds apart from the iconic depiction of several stick-figure students next to an assortment of sandwiches drawn by the first student, who ultimately resorts to guesswork when that graphical strategy fails.

Fig. 5a: Figures 5a and 5b: Two different approaches to diagrammatic problem-solving, author's drawing after van Garderen *et al.* 2013.

Interview a:
I: All right, how did you get that answer? Tell me about that.
S: I don't know.
I: Where did the 10 come from?
S: People.
I: How did you use this picture then to help solve it? Tell me about that.
S: I don't know.
I: Tell me about what's this and what's this.
S: Those are the students and those are the sandwiches.
I: OK, and then what were you counting to get to 10?
S: I just guessed on the 10.

---

30 Van Garderen/Scheuermann/Jackson 2013.

Fig. 5b: Figures 5a and 5b: Two different approaches to diagrammatic problem-solving; author's drawing, after van Garderen *et al.* 2013.

Interview b:
I: How did you solve this one?
S: I drew the sandwich. Then I divided it up into 12 ¾ feet long. I drew little lines above it and counted all the little fourths, all the way up to 17 sets of 3's.

The practically oriented problems found in *P. Math.* and other metrological texts are in many ways close analogues to the kinds of problems students were asked to solve in studies like van Garderen's. They engage the diagram in a very different way from geometrical texts, where the construction of the diagram is typically explained in the course of the proof. The metrological problems do not specify the drawing process in this way. Some are phrased in such a way that the appropriate diagram is obvious, like problem *f6* from *P. Math.*: "A right-angled (triangle) whose hypotenuse is 17. To find the other sides." Others allow for more latitude in selecting a diagram, like *o2*, which specifies the length of each side of a quadrilateral plot of land but does not call it a quadrilateral, accompanied by a diagram that is just a horizontal line with the measurements marked above, below, and on either side. Such a diagram might be viewed as incorrect for the analogous geometrical problem carried out on an abstract quadrilateral, but the simplified line diagram includes all the information needed to carry out the calculation. As it happens, the example dimensions given to carry out the calculation turn out to refer to a quadrilateral which is actually impossible to construct, a problem that could have been illuminated by a more faithful diagram. However, the same kind of breakdown between the problem's sample numbers and the geometrical object depicted also occurs elsewhere in the papyrus even where the diagrams are more robust.

Papyri like *P. Math* and problem collections like the metrological problems associated with Hero's name can thus be construed as valuable witnesses to how education in "practical mathematics" might have been constructed in late antiquity. Yet on their own the ancient texts leave many gaps in our understanding of how mathematical concepts might have been inculcated and practiced, and how this education might have worked on the learner's side. In addressing these mysteries we can call not only on scholarship on ancient pedagogy, where mathematics education is not particularly strongly represented, but also on investigations of modern mathematics pedagogy exploring how students grapple with a growing corpus of mathematical concepts, some more successfully than others.

A particularly lucid and influential study of mathematics learning is Davis's *Learning Mathematics*, which largely focuses on errors as evidence for how students learn mathematics. Davis argues that student errors often follow distinctive and regular patterns of their own, and explains many of these common errors as the result of selecting the wrong conceptual "frame" from the collection of frames students acquire in the course of their mathematics education. Davis uses the term "frame" flexibly to refer to different types of "knowledge representation structures."[31] While his particular approach takes an information-processing view of how the mind handles those structures, the principles of mathematics learning he invokes are flexible enough to suit other cognitive models as well, such as more embodiment or enaction-focused approaches.[32]

A second source of comparisons that will prove particularly useful here is Lave's *Cognition in Practice*, a groundbreaking study of how non-mathematicians perform mathematical tasks in everyday environments like the grocery store. Lave found that her experimental subjects typically performed quite poorly on a written test of their ability to make calculations. However, when they were observed doing everyday tasks like grocery shopping and meal preparation demanding those very same calculations, they performed with a very high degree of confidence and accuracy. Lave concludes that there is an important distinction between contextualized "math-in-practice" and "math conceived as a system of propositions and relations (a 'knowledge domain')."[33] In what follows, I will focus on three main lines of investigation: the ways mathematics learners seem to acquire mathematical concepts and apply them to new problems (appropriately or inappropriately), the relationship between abstract mathematical concepts and what Lave calls "cognition in practice," and the uses of diagrams in mathematics learning.

---

31 Davis 1984, 107.
32 On the role of embodiment and gesture in mathematics education, see for example Alibali/Nathan 2012; de Freitas/Sinclair 2012.
33 Lave 1988, 97.

3 Problems with Problem-Solving

Papyri like *P. Math.* contain a rich variety of types of errors. Some are simple scribal errors or departures from Greek orthographical conventions, which these papyri of course have in common with papyri of every genre. Some are the numerical equivalent of scribal errors: mistakes in the modified alphabetic system used to represent numbers in Greek mathematics. Other types of errors are more interesting, since conceptual errors offer another window into the student's learning process. The solver of *P. Math.*, while highly competent in some respects like unit conversions and arithmetical calculations, stumbles into a range of conceptual errors. These include failures to match up a problem with a diagram that illustrates features of the structure under investigation in a sensible way, inappropriate selection of algorithms for calculation, and confusion about the elements of a geometrical object. Other "errors" are not mathematical mistakes in and of themselves but rather common-sense breakdowns in choices of dimensions, yielding improbably tiny vineyards or granaries, or worse, structures that turn out to be impossible given the specified dimensions, e.g., of outer and inner perimeters and wall thickness. Even though these are not exactly errors, they do seem to be "precursors" to errors in the sense that they often lead to mistakes in constructing diagrams and performing calculations. That is, a breakdown between the solver's mental conception of the problem and a real-world object that can actually be pictured does seem to lead him into errors that he otherwise might not make.

Case study 1: Faults with Vaults

A particularly interesting conceptual error plagues two problems in *P. Math* with the same basic aim: to calculate the volume of a granary shaped as a rectangular building surmounted by a vaulted (*kamarōtos*) roof. In neither case is the form of the vault specified, though the default form (at least in mathematical teaching problems in the metrological collections) is the relatively mathematically simple case where the vault is a section of a circle. However, this is the least of the troubles the *P. Math.* solver encounters. In the first of these problems (*n4*), the solver multiplies the granary's length times its breadth, which yields the floor area. So far so good, but then he multiplies the depth by a dimension he calls the "vault (*kamara*)," and finally multiplies the two products by one another. The resulting product of the four dimensions is then converted from solid-cubit volume to grain measure in artabas using the standard conversion figure. But of course, the four-dimensional product of lengths in cubits is no longer in solid cubits: Bagnall and Jones delightfully suggest "hypercubits" as a name for this newly coined unit of measure.[34] The numerical result is an impossibly large 364,500 artabas.[35]

Perhaps the solver realized he had gone astray upon revealing this answer, because the next problem is framed just the same, though the dimensions are reduced: the length from 25 cubits in $n4$ to 5 cubits in $o1$, the breadth from 15 cubits to 3, the depth from 16 cubits to 2, and the "vault" from 18 to 2. The problem-solving process is close to identical, but a little more deliberate: instead of multiplying the two pairs of numbers and then finding their product, the author first multiplies the length (misnamed "breadth") by the depth, then the result by the breadth, and finally that result by the "vault." Of course the result is once again nonsense, even after this second attempt with smaller (and thus perhaps more tractable) numbers: this tiny granary is calculated to hold 60 solid cubits, or about 9 cubic meters. This repetition of the initial error is common in problem-solvers even today; Davis notes from a study of student mathematical errors carried out by Erlwanger that "the malfunction occurs, as it were, at the same location in the cognitive machinery. *In nearly every case, a super-procedure selects the wrong sub-procedure.*"[36] As in Erlwanger's study, the solver of *P. Math.* is stuck in the same faulty routine the second time he attempts the problem.

The solver's inappropriate introduction of the "vault" dimension thus renders the problem completely intractable. What was so appealing about that framework for solution that the solver attempted it not once, but twice? Bagnall and Jones consider that the solver may have had in mind the formula for calculating the area of a half-oval using the formula $A = 3w/4h$, but since the ¾ coefficient (or its unit-fraction equivalent) doesn't appear here, he certainly did not get far if that was his intent. To better understand where the solver of *P. Math* went wrong, we might search the metrological corpus for models of correct solutions. Hero's *Metrica* does discuss the measurement of vaults, but only briefly. *Metrica* II.12 proposes a method for measuring a washtub (or bathtub?) conceptualized as a slice of a spherical shell: a figure consisting of the space between two concentric spheres is sliced by two parallel planes, one defining the top of the tub, and the other the flat surface upon which it rests. Hero intro-

---

[34] Bagnall/Jones 2019, 149.
[35] Converting this result to more familiar units is tricky as the value of the *artabē* could vary, but converting directly from the result in solid cubits, this volume would be around 15,500 cubic meters!
[36] Davis 1984, 98. Italics in original.

duces II.13 with a retrospective look back at II.12, saying that now that the reader has encountered strategies for measuring conical, cylindrical, and spherical shapes, he can use the "tub" example as a model for how to perform calculations on vaults having any of those forms. However, he does not go on to calculate the space inside a cylindrical vault (or any other form), but rather proceeds with the process of measuring the torus. He mentions vaults again in II.15, where the topic is a cube containing two cylinders intersecting perpendicularly to yield a form which he says is useful for designing baths with windows or doors on all sides, or "places difficult to roof over with wood." He does not follow up further on this tantalizingly opaque description, however, and Acerbi and Vitrac note that while a comparable figure is mentioned in the preface to Archimedes' *Method*, the solution does not survive.[37]

The connection between vaults and tori at first appears contextual rather than mathematical, since Hero refers explicitly to the use of segments of tori as decorative elements on architectural columns. However, in measuring the volume of the torus (II.13, fig. 6) he appeals to a result relating a torus to a cylinder, which he credits to a lost work *On the torus* by a certain Dionysodorus. The torus in Dionysodorus's result is generated by translating the circle BΓΔE around the circle formed by looping the line segment AB to connect to itself. The cylinder he relates to this torus has axis HΘ and base radius EΘ. Finally, the proportional relationship Dionysidoros discovered is that the circle BΓΔE has the same ratio to half ΔEHΘ as the torus and cylinder defined above have to one another. A neat result indeed, but the *Metrica* then takes a puzzling turn. As is often the case in this text, the numerical "synthesis" where the dimensions and proportions are actually calculated follows the demonstrative "analysis" where they were introduced. The synthesis in this case does involve a cylinder, but the cylinder turns out to be not the one defined by Dionysodorus, but the one produced by unfurling the torus so that AB becomes a straight line rather than a circle. Vitrac and Acerbi suggest that the metrical procedure here is likely to be a later insertion, though it is not incorrect. Whatever the particular textual history of this proposition, the close association between tori and cylinders is clear.

---

[37] Hero 2014, 293 n. 145. On the different ways this form is treated by Archimedes and the Chinese mathematician Liu Hui, see Netz 2018.

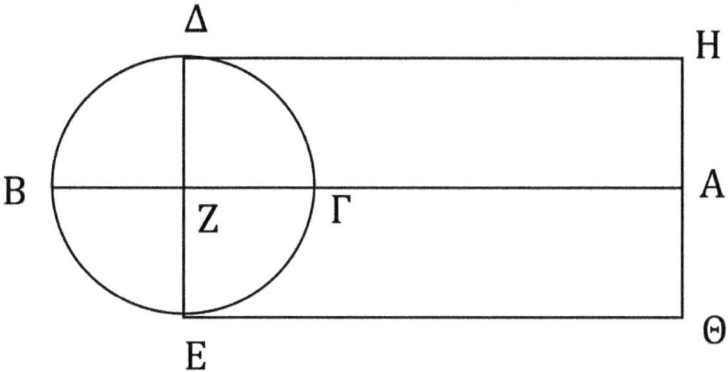

Fig. 6: Schematic depiction of the features of a torus from Hero *Metrica* II.13.

The next section of the *Metrica* (II.14) gets us one final step closer to the connection between the vault and the cylinder. This proposition offers a method for measuring the volume of a segment of a cylinder sliced by a plane through the center of its base, citing a result from Archimedes' *Method* that this segment will be one-sixth the volume of the rectangular prism with cross-section defined by the square circumscribing the cylinder's base and the same height (maybe more easily conceived of as length) as the cylinder. The diagram associated with this problem shows the cylinder mounted on the circumscribing square, in a way that immediately summons the image of a structure with a cylindrical vaulted roof. So in a roundabout way, Hero does relate the torus to the cylinder, a form that could be related to a vault, but the application to problems like the vaulted granary in *P. Math.* is hardly obvious.

However, in the texts of the metrological corpus compiled in the centuries following Hero, problems having to do with the measurement of vaults became more common as the focus on real-world objects grew stronger. Heiberg's edition of the *Stereometrica* includes two clusters of problems related to the calculation of the area or volume enclosed by vaults and arches. The more obviously relevant of these is found in the collection edited by Heiberg as the second book of the *Stereometrica*. Given the cautions mentioned above about the difficulties of creating an edition of the *Stereometrica*, I should begin with a word about how the problems I discuss here fit into that complicated manuscript tradition. All are found in the manuscript denoted S (*Codex Seragliensis* G.I.1 or *Constantinopolitanus Palatii Veteris* 1), which likely dates to the early tenth century, making it the earliest of the metrological manuscripts, and the only one to contain Hero's own *Metrica*.³⁸ Some are also found in the other major manuscripts that contained material found in Heiberg's edition of the work, and for the most part appear in the same order in all manuscripts.³⁹ This problem series is thus built on relatively firm foundations by the standards of the metrological corpus.

This cluster (2.28–45) begins by telling the reader how to construct a semicircular arch within a square framework, then how to find the area enclosed by the outer and inner semicircular perimeters of a free-standing arch, then combines the two structures in the form of a square framework enclosing an interior semicircular arch and surmounted by another. The next problem (32) introduces a new method for calculating the area under a semicircular arch, and then proceeds to describe a comparable process for finding the area under a "disproportionate (*apeulogos*)" arch, which is not clearly described in the problem (itself beset with scribal errors). Returning to more readily comprehensible objects, the author next integrates the method from the first part of problem 32 into a problem involving arches made of bricks which border the exterior of a segment of rubble wall. The next few problems continue with the now-established context of architectural construction while introducing a new shape, the "conch (*konchē*)": first constructed of bricks, then covered in mosaic tiles. Next the author returns to the vault. Let us study this problem more closely:

> To measure a vault whose enclosure is less than a semicircle, of which the base of the interior space is 14 feet, and the "front-wedges" [πρωτοσφῆνες; this term seems to refer to the thickness of the wall] on each side 2 feet, whose perpendicular in the interior space is 6 feet, and whose length is 15 feet. Do it like this: add the 14 feet of the interior space and the 6 of the perpendicular; the result is 20. Of this [take] the half; the result is 10. [Multiply] this by the 6; the result is 60. Again, add the 14 feet of the interior space and the "front-wedges" of 2 feet on each side; the result is 18. To these add the 6 of perpendicular of the interior space and the 2 feet; the result is 26. Of these [take] half; the result is 13. [Multiply] these by the whole height/extension (*anatasis*), by 8; the result is 104. Divide this by the 60 feet of the interior space; the remainder of the framework/foundation is 44 feet. Multiply this by the 15 feet of the length; the result is 660 feet. So large is the vault.⁴⁰

We may immediately note how the author here has gone about calculating the cross-section of the vault: the formula $(d + h)/2 \times H$ (in this case, $(18 + 6)/2 \times 8$). Just as in *P. Math.*, an incorrect formula has again been engaged to find this area. However, the erroneous formula here may point the way to the

---

38 For more details on this manuscript, see Hero 2014, 85–97; Lévy/Vitrac 2018, 190–192.
39 For a detailed discussion of how the problems are ordered in the manuscripts, see Hero 2014, 471–474.
40 [Hero] *Stereometrica* 2.37.

reasoning behind the error in *P. Math*, since the error here is slight — the author has forgotten to include a corrective factor of (1 + 1/21), which was previously introduced in problem 28. The same formula, or variants of it meant to apply to different cross-sections, is used several times on problems of this type in the *Stereometrica*, and it is plausible that it was a common formula for this kind of calculation in late antiquity.[41] The solver of *P. Math.* could have recalled that there was a formula for calculating the volume under a roughly semicircular vault that involved combining three different dimensions of the cross-section, including the height of the space under the vault, and multiplying those by the length to produce a volume. In Davis's terms, however, he inappropriately retrieved the "multiplication" rather than the "addition" frame in the course of carrying out that calculation, hence ending up with a granary occupying four dimensions rather than the more conventional three. The additional errors of failing to divide by half and omitting the (1 + 1/21) corrective here seem trivial by comparison.

Of course it is impossible actually to reconstruct the thought process of the *P. Math.* solver, particularly given the lack of a parallel, correctly solved problem in that text. But, in a sense, that lack is precisely the point: the structure and scale of the *Stereometrica* are such that the author can introduce new geometrical forms gradually, starting from simple shapes and building up to more complex variations and combinations. The reader of manuscript S has by this point been led carefully along a path where each step usually involves a fairly minor variation on what has come before. The same would have been true for readers of other sequences of problems in other versions of the manuscript, which typically group similar problems together, even if the particular groupings change from one manuscript to the next. The steps of the path are by no means flawlessly laid; the *Stereometrica*, including this sequence of chapters, contains a great many erroneous formulas. However, unlike the case of the comparatively short *P. Math.*, the lengthy Byzantine codices of metrological problems afford the opportunity to check a formula against a similar problem, and if a variation occurs (as in this case), the reader is provoked to compare the two and select what appears to be the correct algorithm rather than doubling down on an incorrect formula as in *P. Math.*

---

41 Other ancient pedagogical contexts may furnish some comparable examples. Monika Amsler suggested in her comments to this paper that the remarkable stability of the exemplary rhetorical progymnasmata described by Theon, Aphthonius, Nicolaus, and other authors might reflect a similar case. On the pedagogical context and sources of these examples, see Webb 2009, 39–49.

The process of gradually accumulating related problem-solving techniques invites comparisons between recently acquired techniques and new ones, and provides opportunities for self-correction not unlike the problem-solving dialogues between students and teachers (or researchers) common to contemporary studies of mathematical problem-solving. Davis notes that in the studies he analyzes, when a teacher intervened by following up a student's retrieval of an incorrect procedural frame (e.g., "4*4=8," where the "addition" frame is inappropriately retrieved) by asking them the question that would have generated the wrong answer (in this case "what is 4+4?"), the student nearly always immediately corrected the previous wrong answer rather than simply answering the new question. Even though many of the problems in *P. Math.* are framed as though they represented a question-and-answer dialogue between teacher and student, the actual learning process does not seem to have involved a similar one-on-one dialogue where the student could have been alerted to his incorrect problem-solving "frames." While the *Stereometrica* is clearly even further removed from the classroom context of genuine question-and-answer dialogue, its more robust structure, with a greater number of similar problems gathered together, could have facilitated a cognitive process in the reader more like what Davis posits for the contemporary student who corrects her response thanks to an "interesting phenomenon of perception, control or short-term memory" fostered by the dialogue with the teacher.[42]

Besides the greater availability of "checks" on incorrect formulas and problem-solving techniques in the *Stereometrica* compared to *P. Math.*, we should not neglect to mention the value of the *Stereometrica*'s chains of problems related to a particular context, in this case the construction of buildings. *P. Math.* is one of the largest collections of mathematical problems in a papyrus, but even so it is a short text relative to the Heronian metrological works. Within a span of relatively few problems which aim to address a very wide-range of problem-solving techniques, it is simply not possible to follow the *Stereometrica*'s strategy of gathering together a large number of problems focused on vaults and arches and incrementally building complications onto a relatively firm problem-solving foundation. By the time the reader works through a series of problems like Heiberg's *Stereometrica* 2.28–44, she has built up a fairly solid mental picture of the walls, archways, peristyles, and roofs in those problems. Those images may not be elegantly drawn, as is the case for the Vatican manuscript (fig. 7), but simply seeing how the geometrical objects fit into the more complex structures allows the reader to anchor their problem-solving process in their

---

[42] Davis 1984, 100.

lived experience. By mentally constructing the more complex structures step by step, the reader is less likely to make a grave conceptual error like the extra dimension attributed to the granary by the *P. Math.* solver. As we will see, this kind of mental slippage in picturing the object under study is a recurrent problem in *P. Math.*

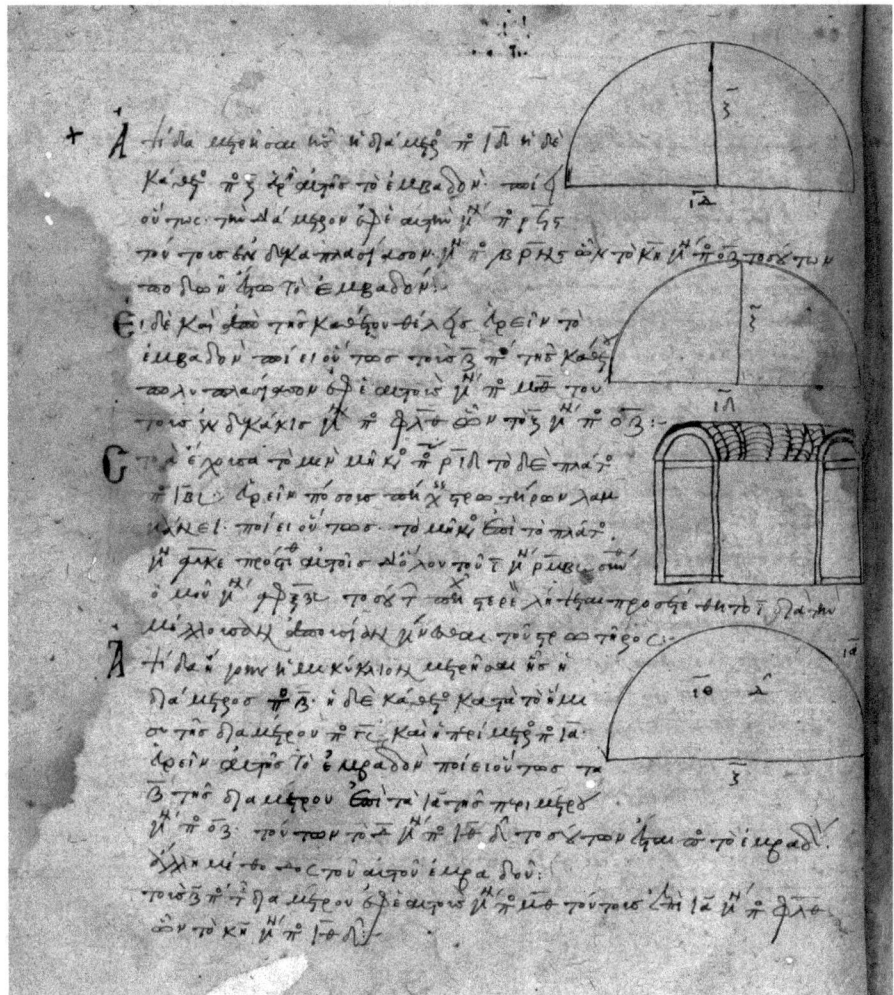

Fig. 7: Stereometrica text and images from Vat. gr. 215, fol. 9r.

Case study 2: Reality Breaks

Some of the "errors" in *P. Math.* are not really mathematical errors at all, but rather involve a breakdown between the numerical values stipulated in the problem and the real-world objects they allegedly correspond to. The vagueness of some of the problem statements can make this assessment difficult, as when problem *b5* calculates the volume of a form called a "quadrangular trapezoid," an odd nomenclature that turns out to refer to an extremely elongated trapezoidal prism. Certainly it is true that a trapezoidal prism (like any polygonal prism) has quadrangular sides, but this is an odd way to frame the shape given that prisms are usually just identified by their cross section. The trouble the solver seems to have giving the shape a name appears to mirror a difficulty in visualizing its dimensions; Bagnall and Jones point out the improbability of a "rod-like object" 48 cubits in length, just 10 cubits wide, and only 5 fingers and 2 fingers on the parallel trapezoidal surfaces. Other forms are improbably small rather than too large; the vaulted granary with a 5x3x2-cubit rectangular base surmounted by a 2-cubit high vault was already mentioned above. Trivial as these errors may seem, they suggest a breakdown in common sense at some point in the process from devising the problem in the first place, to copying it down, to attempting a solution, which makes it difficult for the solver to perform a "reality check" on whether the numbers make sense. In the case of problem *b5* (the "quadrangular trapezoid"), the solver has so much trouble envisioning the object under consideration that he fails to perform the necessary unit conversion from cubits to fingers, a rare mistake for him.

Problem *b3* demands the solver picture a more complicated object: a tower (*porgos*) with "substructures (*krēpidai*)," where the aim is to calculate how many bricks the tower contains. This kind of calculation has a long tradition in both the Mesopotamian and Egyptian traditions.[43] In this case, the tower is described in an unnecessarily confusing way and is quite difficult to picture. First, the tower: we are given the outer and inner perimeters, as well as the thickness of the walls, but not the shape. In fact, the given dimensions (where the thickness of the wall is equal to the difference between the two perimeters) render the tower impossible to construct, whatever its form (in the likely event it was a rectangle, for example, the wall's thickness would be ¼ the difference between the perimeters). Still, the solver chooses an appropriate frame for this calculation, recognizing that the wall's cross-section can be dissected into four trape-

---

[43] On "brick numbers" in Babylonian mathematics, see Friberg 2007, 89, 93–95, 169–174.

zoids and calculating the walls' volume using the algorithm for calculating the volume of a trapezoidal prism.

So far so good, but what about the "substructures"? One might reasonably imagine that the tower would be supported on some kind of rectangular prism, likely hollow on the inside like the tower. The solver seems to have had this idea in mind in stating the problem: "the length of the rectangle 10 [cubits], breadth 8 cubits." However, alert readers will already have noticed that the substructure does not have enough given dimensions, and the solver runs into trouble because of this later in the problem when he goes to calculate the number of bricks it is made of.

Recognizing the missing dimension of thickness, he spontaneously introduces a factor of 2 cubits into his calculations on the substructures, likely importing it from the "tower" section of the problem and assuming incorrectly that they have the same thickness as the tower walls. However, rather than calculating as though he were picturing an 8x10x2 cubit rectangular prism (which would be a rickety support indeed for the tower but at least makes some sense spatially), he lets the plural "substructures" in the problem statement lead him to satisfy the "rectangular prism" schema in a different way. He posits two "substructures" of 8x2 and 10x2 cubits respectively, and then adds together the size of these two-dimensional bases. But since the brick calculations require a three-dimensional structure, the schema is lacking a dimension. The seeds of the solver's catastrophic response to this lack have already been sown in the form of a numerical error at the very start of the 10*8 multiplication: "Likewise also of the rectangle, [the length, 10] times 60. The result is 20." Obviously, 60 is an error for 2, given that the result is 20. But that 2 itself has just been introduced by the solver's need to fill in one missing element in the dimensional schema, and his decision to import it from the "tower" frame. And now at this later point in the problem, he repeats the strategy: he again draws the missing dimension from the "tower" frame, this time multiplying the two bases each by the height of the *tower* (60 cubits), rather than any given measure corresponding to the "substructures." The solver then adds up the volumes of the two tower-height "substructure" sheets, finding the sum slightly larger than the volume of the tower. He then converts the solid cubits to bricks with a factor of 48, yielding the answer 213,120 bricks.

As is often the case in *P. Math.*, the solver's arithmetic is unproblematic, but this tower is built on the shakiest of conceptual foundations. The solver is not disturbed by the fact that the "substructures" represent the bulk of the construction because he has not visualized the tower-substructure complex in enough detail to have a sense for whether this should be the case. The diagram, drawn on the verso of B, emphasizes this confusion: it has suffered considerable damage but appears to have consisted simply of a trapezoid with some horizontal lines across it, marked with "8" at the bottom (the length of one of the "substructures"), "60" at the side (the height of the tower) and a "54" that figures nowhere in the problem, like the trapezoidal shape itself. However, a trapezoid marked with a "54" dimension *did* feature in the problem illustrated at the top of the recto of B. Given the conceptual confusion the solver experienced with the basic task of picturing the tower/substructure complex, it would not be surprising if he borrowed the last stable conceptual image he had of a mathematical object, the trapezoid from problem *b1* (= *a5*), to fill the gap.

As in the case of the vaults described above, the total collapse of the solver's mental image of the tower/substructure complex seems likely to stem in part from the structure of the text itself. Problem *b3* occurs early in the text, following a series of problems on trapezoids and trapezoidal solids. The only exceptions to this pattern are a unit-fractions exercise and the problem that immediately precedes it, a trivially simple calculation of the area of a square field. It would not be surprising, then, if the solver carried the "trapezoid" conceptual frame from these prior problems into problem *b3*. Moreover, he used the "trapezoid" frame correctly in dissecting the tower's cross-section into four trapezoids to find its area. It is only when he attempts to determine the volume of the pathologically underdetermined "substructures" that the strength with which this conceptual frame has been lodged in his mind leads him astray, producing the incorrectly visualized "substructures" and the nonsensical diagram. Had problem *b3* been preceded instead by a series of problems on rectangular prisms, the solver might have performed better even if the tower's structure was still underdetermined in the problem. Much like the case of the vaults, a text like the *Stereometrica* creates a hedge against these lapses in visual comprehension by building up the components of more complex structures more gradually.

Students attempting to solve mathematical problems today often indicate comparable difficulties with common-sense checks on numerical calculations. Davis ascribes several such errors to inappropriate retrieval of mathematical "frames." One student, asked to divide 6 into 3606, arrived at the incorrect answer of 61.[44] When the interviewer, attempting to spark a self-correction, then asked the student to divide 6 into 366 (which would in fact yield 61), the student was not surprised, but accepted the identity of the answers as correct, since she had learned that "adding zero doesn't change [the answer]" and "zero means

---

44 Davis 1984, 199–200.

nothing." The student's inappropriate retrieval of the "addition" frame for the 0 in the division problem, coupled with the semantic drift in the phrase "zero means nothing," overwhelmed what should have been their common-sense reaction that these very different dividends should not yield the same quotient.

Davis explores another kind of "framing" error that speaks more specifically to the breakdown between numerical and real-world objects, centered on problems of the following type.[45] When students (even engineering, physics, or math students) asked to put a phrase like "there are six times as many students as professors" into the form of an equation involving the variables S and P, they overwhelmingly wrote the equation erroneously as "6S=P." The error (called the Rosnick-Clement phenomenon after the psychologists who first studied it) affects people regardless of their level of mathematical skill and experience, and even trumps real-world experience with the objects named in the problem. One might think that the error simply stems from writing the S and P in the order in which "students" and "professors" were encountered in the problem statement, but switching the word order had no perceptible effect on the results. The students, familiar with the fact that students outnumber professors (usually by a factor of considerably more than 6) should have been able to perform the common-sense check that multiplying the number of students by 6 should not yield the number of professors.

The very same error persisted in different formulations of the problem. A student familiar with the recipe for vinaigrette (which calls for more oil than vinegar), who was even given the correct formula 3V = O for the proportions, still managed to talk herself into reversing the proportions, drawing pictures with the reversed proportions, and finally insisting that the formula meant the dressing contained more vinegar than oil. Even a mathematically adept physics major, given a formula describing the proportions of people in England and China, persuaded himself to reverse the meanings of "E" and "C" in the formula rather than renounce his incorrect problem-solving frame. These students are not unlike the *P. Math.* solver, who finds the "trapezoid" frame so firmly lodged in mind after several repetitions that it is difficult to break even when encountering the apparently trapezoid-free tower-complex problem. Like the students Davis describes, the *P. Math.* solver seems to talk himself into a mindset where an absurd fusion of a tower supported by thin rectangular sheets as tall as the tower itself seems like a plausible construction. Davis makes the key point that solvers were not plugging in sample numbers to check that their formulas made

---

45 Davis 1984, 111–123.

sense, which would have called attention to the breakdown between reality and number here.

How can Davis's characterization of these errors help us better understand what is going on in *P. Math.*? Let us consider a few more troubled mappings from reality onto mathematical problems in the text. Problem *f2* posits three granaries containing various amounts of wheat (200, 300, and 400 artabas respectively). The problem's drama begins when "someone came in and mixed them up. To find 630 artabas. We proceed as follows." But proceed with what, exactly — what is this mysterious "630 artabas" about, and why did someone come and mix up the grain from different granaries? One might surmise that they came not only to mix up the grain, but also to steal it, and took 630 artabas out of the original 900. And indeed that is quite correct, as Bagnall and Jones point out a parallel in *P.Cair. cat* 19758 (problems 47–49), where someone came along, mixed up the grain from each granary, and then stole some grain, so the problem is to determine how much of the stolen wheat originally came from each granary. So in this case, rather than failing to correctly picture a realistic *object*, as in the case of the very long "quadrangular trapezoid" of *b5*, here the solver has failed to imagine a plausible *process* for the grain-theft.

A comparable case occurs at *c2*, where "someone loaded on a boat, from the granary half, and for the taxes one-third, and for the pay of the donkey-driver one twelfth, and there remained on the boat 50 artabas of wheat." Now, as Bagnall and Jones note, the activities described in the problem make sense in the context of *unloading* a boat rather than loading one. The problem continues: we must find the solution to this indeterminate equation by adding the fractions listed, finding that their sum is 1/12 less than a unit, and calculating that since the 50 artabas remaining are 1/12 of the original amount, the original amount on the boat (before unloading) was 600 artabas. Yet the solver frames the solution as "the boat will hold 600 artabas of wheat" — again, suggesting he has a framework of loading rather than unloading in mind. Still, even though the "loading" frame does not make sense with the tax calculation and so forth, the solver seems to have in mind a robust and stable context of activity within that framework, and carries it out correctly. So this case differs from *f2* in that the solver is able to picture the process correctly, implausible though that process may be in a strictly real-world context.

Lave warns that typical studies of mathematical cognition presuppose that all action is preceded by a separate "structuring" step, which leads to a misunderstanding of the relationship between experience and strategic thought:

> The view is consistent with an emphasis on thought distanced from experience as the canonical form of human experience to be investigated, but it is not compatible with the everyday math practices just described, nor with a theory of practice.[46]

Lave's experimental study of ordinary people (referred to in the text as "just plain folks" or "jpfs") involved first giving them a formal mathematical test, and then following them around the grocery store, watching and questioning them as they select, buy, and prepare food. Most of the people in her study performed quite poorly on the math test but extremely well on practical tasks like determining which size jar of mayonnaise was the better buy (averaging 98% accuracy). As she points out, "98% accuracy in the supermarket is practically error-free arithmetic, and belies the image of the hapless jpf failing cognitive challenges in an everyday world."[47] Lave's study found

> not a single significant correlation between frequency of calculation in supermarket, and scores on math test, multiple choice test, or number facts. There is a significant correlation between weight and volume facts (but not length) and frequency of calculation in the supermarket.[48]

The high correlation between shoppers' mastery of facts helping them make weight or volume conversions and their fluency of calculation in the supermarket is of particular interest in the context of the ancient metrological texts. *P. Math.* and other mathematical papyri, as well as texts like the *Stereometrica*, provide the reader with an astonishing array of conversion mechanisms for length, area, volume, and weight. These include universal conversions that could work for any substance as well as more specific conversions. For example, *Stereometrica* 2.54 includes standards set by a praetorian prefect named Modestus for converting fresh or stored barley from *xestai* to cubic feet, bacon from cubic feet to *litrai*, and so on.

And in fact the writer of *P. Math.* functions very fluidly with those conversions, nearly always performing them correctly. His fluency with conversions and other arithmetical tasks suggests an orientation much like Lave's jpfs. He is really very competent within a known framework of mathematical action, but he often struggles to retrieve and apply the correct problem-solving frame for new kinds of problems. These problems are exacerbated by the relative lack of problem-solving supports in the text such as are found in the *Stereometrica*,

---

[46] Lave 1988, 130.
[47] Lave 1988, 58.
[48] Lave 1988, 57.

notably chains of problems on similar geometric forms, generally built up from simpler to the more complex. Crucially, in the *Stereometrica* these chains are often focused on a common real-world application like buildings (or vessels containing water, ships, theaters full of seats, etc.), encouraging the reader to build up a relatively robust mental picture of the object in question that may help them perform a "reality check" on the results. Lave's study offers an important intervention in conventional studies of mathematical problem-solving as divorced from the "real world":

> I propose to address cognition and culture and their various entailments at different levels of social analysis. Among other things, this requires a broadening of the terms of analysis to reflect the claim that the 'person,' including the person thinking, is constituted in relation with other aspects of the lived-in world.[49]

These texts (*P. Math.* and other papyri focused on practical problem-solving, as well as the "Heronian" metrological texts) make their meaning not merely from recording the arithmetical structures of calculating algorithms, but more profoundly from fitting those algorithms into a concrete and populated world. Crucially, the *Stereometrica* constructs knowledge by arranging problems into clusters that replicate the construction of objects in the world itself: from abstract arches to arches of bricks, to walls, to roofed-over buildings. These clusters would seem to constitute a pedagogical process in their own right, affording the reader a familiar and grounded problem-solving environment more like the grocery store where Lave's subjects thrived than the abstract math test she administered her "hapless jpfs" beforehand.

4 Conclusion

The corpus of Greek metrological texts developed after the *Metrica*, like the *Geometrica* and *Stereometrica* as well as papyri containing related "practical mathematics" problems, owe a great deal to the much older Egyptian and Mesopotamian traditions of arithmetical problems focused on techniques for measuring and manipulating real-world objects. Not only do the techniques and content of the problems differ between the "demonstrative" geometrical and "algorithmic" arithmetic traditions, but so does the very language in which those problems are couched. Greek geometers in general hewed remarkably

---

[49] Lave 1988, 180.

closely to a canonical model of proof-writing. In this model, proofs proceed through a series of formulaic steps couched in equally formulaic language: from enunciation (*protasis*) to conclusion (*sumperasma*), all progress evidently made not by the author's own hand but a shadowy entity adumbrated by the third-person passive imperatives that are such a peculiar verbal marker of these texts. Fowler and Taisbak memorably characterize this mysterious actor as the "Helping Hand," which "is always there first to see that things are done and to keep the operations free from contamination by our mortal fingers."[50] The "Helping Hand" is an effective rhetorical tool, suggesting that the work of mathematical proof happens in a domain far removed from human fallibility. The geometrical proof comes prepackaged and sanitized, as it were, without any indication of the trials and errors the text's author doubtless experienced in its discovery.[51] By contrast, texts in the arithmetical tradition typically frame the mathematical activities they recount as direct instructions to the reader, as an active account of steps being taken by the author, or both.

This difference results from the different generic expectations of the two traditions, to be sure, but it also resonates powerfully with questions of "knowledge construction." Texts in the geometrical tradition, with their impersonal, passive constructions mediated by the "Helping Hand," are worlds away from the first- and second-person constructions of the arithmetical tradition. The difference between a problem framed as being solved through an impersonal and permanently valid demonstrative act on the one hand, and a problem framed as being solved through a person's selecting an algorithm, carrying it out, and inviting the reader to do the same (explicitly or implicitly) on the other, also reframes the meaning of "error." An error in a geometrical demonstration might be seen as a fatal flaw because of the impression of impersonal eternity the generically imposed form of the solution creates. But in a problem framed as a personal adventure in problem-solving, errors and other idiosyncrasies have a value of their own as witnesses to that peculiar personal experience.

When the *P. Math.* solver accidentally imagines a four-dimensional granary, or collapses the area diagram of a field down to just one dimension, those choices open up a window — however hazy — into a living process of "knowledge con-

---

50 Fowler and Taisbak 1999, 362.
51 This is not to say that Greek geometrical texts are devoid of personality, of course; Netz describes some of the authorial personae developed in Greek geometrical texts at Netz 2013. Still, he describes a textual tradition where "the mathematician's results cannot be otherwise" (225) even if the writing style varies from author to author, which is clearly not the case here. For additional considerations of authorial personae in mathematical commentaries, see Asper 2019.

struction" that works by fits and starts as students of different ability levels grapple with mathematical concepts and their real-world analogues. The same may be said for the compilers of the metrological problems that crystallized into the *Stereometrica* and related texts: their choices to bring a certain set of problems and tables together represent a form of "knowledge construction" in its own right. That construction process roots the invariant principles of mathematics in a gloriously varied world, where the mathematical system's users navigate a complex landscape of culturally determined units of measurement and assemble geometrical forms into concrete constructions, building meaning from the progress from a semicircular arch to a roofed building every bit as much as they build meaning from a growing collection of algorithms for calculation.

Bibliography

Alibali, M.W./Nathan, M.J. (2012), "Embodiment in Mathematics Teaching and Learning: Evidence from Learners' and Teachers' Gestures", *Journal of the Learning Sciences* 21, 247–286.

Asper, M. (2001), "Stoicheia und Gesetze: Spekulationen zur Entstehung mathematischer Textformen in Griechenland", *Antike Naturwissenschaft und ihre Rezeption* 11, 73–106.

Asper, M. (2007), *Griechische Wissenschaftstexte: Formen, Funktionen, Differenzierungsgeschichten*, Stuttgart.

Bagnall, R.S./Jones, A. (2019), *Mathematics, Metrology, and Model Contracts: A Codex from Late Antique Business Education (P. Math.)*, New York.

Baillet, J. (1892), *Le papyrus mathématique d'Akhmim*, Paris.

Boyaval, B. (1976), "P. Mich. III 145", *Zeitschrift für Papyrologie und Epigraphik* 23, 196.

Carman, C.C. (2018), "Accounting for Overspecification and Indifference to Visual Accuracy in Manuscript Diagrams: A Tentative Explanation Based on Transmission", *Historia Mathematica* 45, 217–236.

Corcoran, S. (1995), "The Praetorian Prefect Modestus and Hero of Alexandria's 'Stereometrica'", *Latomus* 54, 377–384.

Cribiore, R. (2001), *Gymnastics of the Mind: Greek Education in Hellenistic and Roman Egypt*, Princeton.

Cuomo, S. (2001), *Ancient Mathematics*, London.

Cuomo, S. (2002), "The machine and the city: Hero of Alexandria's Belopoeica", in: C. Tuplin/T.E. Rihll (eds.), *Science and Mathematics in Ancient Greek Culture*, Oxford, 165–177.

Davis, R.B. (1984), *Learning Mathematics: The Cognitive Science Approach to Mathematics Education*, Norwood.

Fowler, D. (1999), *The Mathematics of Plato's Academy: A New Reconstruction*, 2nd ed., Oxford.

Fowler, D./Taisbak, C. (1999), "Did Euclid's Circles Have Two Kinds of Radius?", *Historia Mathematica* 26, 361–364.

de Freitas, E./Sinclair, N. (2012), "Diagram, Gesture, Agency: Theorizing Embodiment in the Mathematics Classroom", *Educational Studies in Mathematics* 80, 133–152.

Friberg, J. (2007), *A Remarkable Collection of Babylonian Mathematical Texts*, New York.
Hero (1976), *Heronis Alexandrini opera quae supersunt omnia*, Vol. 5, J.L. Heiberg (ed.), Stuttgart.
Hero (2014), *Metrica*. F. Acerbi/B. Vitrac (eds.), Pisa.
Høyrup, J. (1994), *In Measure, Number, and Weight: Studies in Mathematics and Culture*, Albany.
Imhausen, A. (2016), *Mathematics in Ancient Egypt: A Contextual History*, Princeton.
Jones, A. (2009), "Mathematics, science, and medicine in the papyri", in: R.S. Bagnall (ed.), *The Oxford Handbook of Papyrology Oxford Handbooks*, Oxford, 338–357.
Lave, J. (1988), *Cognition in Practice: Mind, Mathematics, and Culture in Everyday Life*, New York.
Lévy, T./Vitrac, B. (2018), "Hero of Alexandria and Mordekhai Komtino: The Encounter between Mathematics in Hebrew and the Greek Metrological Corpus in Fifteenth-Century Constantinople", *Aleph: Historical Studies in Science & Judaism* 18, 181–262.
Netz, R. (1999), *The Shaping of Deduction in Greek Mathematics: A Study in Cognitive History*, New York.
Netz, R. (2013), "Authorial presence in the ancient exact sciences", in: M. Asper/A.-M. Kanthak (eds.), *Writing science: medical and mathematical authorship in ancient Greece*, Berlin, 217–253.
Netz, R. (2018), "Divisions, big and small: Comparing Archimedes and Liu Hui", in: G.E.R. Lloyd/ J.J. Zhao/Q. Dong (eds.), *Ancient Greece and China compared*, Cambridge, 259–289.
Netz, R. (2020), "Why Were Greek Mathematical Diagrams Schematic?", *Nuncius: Journal of the History of Science* 35, 506–535.
Riggsby, A. (2019), *Mosaics of Knowledge: Representing Information in the Roman World*, Oxford.
Saito, K. (2012), "Traditions of the Diagram, Tradition of the Text: A Case Study", *Synthese* 186, 7–20.
Saito, K. (2018), "Diagrams and Traces of Oral Teaching in Euclid's Elements: Labels and References", *ZDM* 50, 921–936.
Smyly, J.G. (1920), "Some Examples of Greek Arithmetic", *Hermathena* 19, 105–114.
Taisbak, C.M./Bülow-Jacobsen, A. (2003), "P. Cornell inv. 69: fragment of a handbook in geometry", in: A. Piltz (ed.), *For Particular Reasons: Studies in Honour of Jerker Blomqvist*, Lund, 54–70.
Tybjerg, K. (2003), "Wonder-Making and Philosophical Wonder in Hero of Alexandria", *Studies in the History and Philosophy of Science* 34, 443–466.
Tybjerg, K. (2004), "Hero of Alexandria's Mechanical Geometry", *Apeiron* 37, 29–56.
van Garderen, D./Scheuermann, A./Jackson, C. (2013), "Examining how Students with Diverse Abilities Use Diagrams to Solve Mathematics Word Problems", *Learning Disability Quarterly* 36, 145–160.
van Garderen, D./Scheuermann, A./Poch, A. (2014), "Challenges Students Identified with a Learning Disability and as High-Achieving Experience When Using Diagrams as a Visualization Tool to Solve Mathematics Word Problems", *ZDM* 46, 135–149.
Vitrac, B. (2010), Héron d'Alexandrie et le corpus métrologique: état des lieux, Paris. Published in HAL archives-ouvertes, accessible online under https://hal.science/hal-00473981/PDF/ Heron_d_Alexandrie_et_le_corpus_metrologique.pdf, last accessed February 6, 2023.
Webb, R. (2009), *Ekphrasis, Imagination and Persuasion in Ancient Rhetorical Theory and Practice*, Farnham.

Monika Amsler

The "Poetic Itch" and Numerical Maxims in the Talmud: An Inquiry into Factors of Knowledge Construction

Abstract: This paper explores possible factors responsible for knowledge presented as numerical maxims found in the Babylonian Talmud. Written in a late Hebrew, the maxims follow the pattern "X 'things' do/are..." and have previously been analyzed in the context of mnemotechnical strategies and pedagogy. Yet the sheer number of these maxims — 54 sayings alone on "threes" — appears to contradict at least a straightforward connection with pedagogy. Indeed, the circumstances that produce a certain stock of knowledge are not necessarily identical with its future use. To trace the maxim's possible origins, Ausonius's "poetic itch," according to himself responsible for his *Riddle of the Number Three*, will serve as a starting point for an investigation into social and intellectual factors involved in the construction of this condensed form of knowledge: poetic contests, numerology, and the concept and place of pastimes in late-antique society. The paper will thereby show that incentives for accumulating knowledge were as multi-faceted as occasions to implement knowledge.

1 The Final Construct: Numerical Maxims in the Babylonian Talmud

Late-antique literature is characterized by its use of unattributed and attributed maxims.[1] Reason for the prevalence of the use of maxims (*gnomai*) as compared to antiquity was, complemented by other factors, the Greco-Roman curriculum and its exercises, the so-called *progymnasmata*. This curriculum acquainted the alphabetized pupil with the art of writing and argument-building. It introduced the simple maxim; its attributed form, which turns the maxim into a *chreia*; or the maxim that recalls someone's deed and hence becomes a reminiscence (*apomnemoneuma*).[2] The maxim is thereby presented to the student not as

---

1 See Formisano 2007; Roberts 1988; Fontaine 1977.
2 This was especially the case in the *progymnasmata* by Aelius Theon 3.96; see Kennedy 2003, 15. The other *progymnasmata* translated by Kennedy introduce the *chreia*, a trope that builds

something static but, rather, as a trope that can be used in different contexts and for different purposes. Indeed, the different *progymnasmata*, throughout all their stages, continue to make recourse to maxims, e.g., as a concluding moral to a fable or a proof in an inquiry (*thesis*). Yet the *progymnasmata* are conspicuously quiet about how one should *compose* a maxim. Rather, the maxim is conceived of as a fixed entity, a brick that serves the late-antique art of "narrative bricolage," to borrow a term used by Reuven Kiperwasser to describe this very feature, which applies to Talmudic narratives as well.[3]

Many of the used maxims are quotes from ancient authors, brilliant lines that speak for themselves. There are whole compilations of maxims, however, that are attributed to otherwise unknown authors and incompatible with any known work.[4] These collections testify to the fact that maxims were not only intentionally collected but also likely purposefully composed. The collections of sayings were, among other things, certainly useful for teachers, who used them to craft model exercises for their students, while students may have used them to embellish their literary creations according to the previously described exercises. That maxims relate a timeless truth that makes them fit for education, does not, however, necessarily imply that they were originally intended to be used in schools or other instructional settings. Rather, they might have had their inception in educated vanity, intellectual competition, playfulness, leisure — maybe even a sort of productive boredom, a "poetic itch".

I would like to illustrate how such factors may have led to the composition of maxims by looking at the numerical maxims dispersed throughout the Babylonian Talmud (henceforth Talmud). It may well be that these numerical maxims once constituted distinct collections, which were then disassembled for the purpose of compiling the Talmud, in which process the maxims would have been detached from each other and inserted associatively to similar thematic threads. The numerical sayings in the Talmud have traditionally, and for fairly obvious reasons, been placed in the context of the biblical numerical sayings, which, in turn, are also attested in other literatures of the ancient Near East.[5] Wayne S. Towner and, more recently, Ariel-Ram Pasternak and Shamir Yona,

---

on maxims, after fable and narrative, but likewise continue recommending its use throughout the subsequent exercises.

3 Kiperwasser 2018.

4 E.g., the Mishanic tractate Avot ("Sayings of the Fathers"), the *Apophthegmata Patrum*, or the late-antique and Byzantine collections of the *paroimographoi* or the *Gnomai of the Council of Nicaea*. Morgan 2007, 257, further mentions collections by Didymus Chalkenterus (Alexandria) and Lucillus of Tarrha (Crete).

5 See Pasternak/Yona 2016, 209.

have pointed to significant differences between this ancient "graded numerical parallelism" and the numerical maxims that appear in rabbinic literature.[6] The biblical graded parallelism is structured according to the formula *X and X+1*, as in the following example:

> *Three* things are beyond me; *Four* I cannot fathom: How an eagle makes its way over the sky; How a snake makes its way over a rock; How a ship makes its way through the high seas; How a man has his way with a maiden. (Prov. 30:18–20)[7]

The numerical maxim in rabbinic literature may also appear as graded parallelism, but it "separates the pair of numbers, and each number is situated in different stiches,"[8] e.g.:

> *Five* things in a burnt-offering can combine with one another: the flesh, the fat, the fine flour, the wine and the oil. And *six* in a thanksgiving-offering: the flesh, the fat, the fine flour, the wine, the oil and the bread. (m. Me'il. 4:2)[9]

The present paper will focus on such lists of "X 'things' do/are..." that appear — graded like this example, or ungraded — in every tractate of the Babylonian Talmud (except for b. Meg. and b. B. Metz.).[10] It is noteworthy that they are always in Hebrew and mostly use numbers 3, 4, 5, 6, 7, 8, and 10.[11] The fact that

---

6 See Pasternak/Yona 2016; Towner 1973, esp. 12.
7 Quoted according to Pasternak/Yona 2016, 212.
8 Pasternak/Yona 2016, 225–226; see also Towner, 1973, 5–7.
9 Pasternak/Yona 2016, 226. The X+1 pattern is rare and always attributed to Ben Sira (Pasternak/Yona 2016, 237–238). Pasternak/Yona also draw attention to the rhetorical device of "gaping" (*hamshakhah*), used in the second verse, which omits the subject "things," thereby contributing to a more appealing syntax (Pasternak/Yona 2016, 237–238).
10 My research was based on the compound "X *things*." Yet, even the Vilna standard edition does not conclude with "things" (דברים) in every case. The results presented here are likely to be incomplete (but certainly not exaggerated) and may explain the absence of numerical sayings in b. Meg. and b. B. Metz. It is also noteworthy that the five talmudic tractates that differ in terms of technical language from the rest (b. Ned.; b. Naz.; b. Me'il.; b. Ker.; b. Tamid) also contain such lists.
11 *Lists of three:* b. Ber. 3a (2x), 7a, 42a (3x), 51a, 54b (4x), 55a (3x), 62a (2x the same); b. Shabb. 34a (3x), 75b, 87a; b. Eruv. 87b; b. Pesah. 42a (3x), 112b (2x), 113a (2x), 116b; b. Rosh Hash. 16b; b. Yoma 9b, 84a; b. Betzah 11b, 15b, 21b, 23a; b. Mo'ed Qat. 18a; b. Yevam. 16a, 62a; b. Ketub. 10b, 39a, 42a; b. Sotah 25a; b. Git. 6b, 28b, 70a (2x); b. B. Bat. 147a; b. Sanh. 11b, 37b, 88a; b. Mak. 19a, 23a (2x); b. Zevah. 64a; b. Menah. 29a; b. Nid. 51a. *Lists of four:* b. Ber. 50b; b. Eruv. 17a; b. Pesah. 111a, 112b; b. Sukkah 29a (4x); b. Rosh Hash. 16b, 18b; b. Shabb. 23a; b. B. Qam. 4a, 4b, 26a, 26b, 53b, 55b (2x), 84a; b. Sotah 42b; b. Nid. 8a (only Soncino Print), 16b, 17a (only Ms. Vatican 111); b. Me'il. 15b (2x). *Lists of five:* b. Shabb. 129b; b. Betzah 39a; b. Ber. 10a,

the maxims are in Hebrew and not in Aramaic may point to an archaizing feature or an early date. At least in the case of sayings using *hapax legomena*, we may surmise that they reflect somewhat older material. Indeed, although these maxims are quite similar to each other in makeup, it does not seem that they are all products of just one author or stem from a single compilation, since they are also found in the five talmudic tractates that differ from the other tractates in their use of technical language (b. Ned.; b. Naz.; b. Me'il.; b. Ker.; b. Tamid). The sayings seem, therefore, to have been part of an established genre, rather than the signature style of a certain author. Here is an example of an agglutination of such maxims in tractate Gittin:

> **Three things** wither the strength[12] of man, and they are these: fear, the road [i.e., travelling], and sin.
> Fear, as it is written: "My heart is palpitating, my strength has left me" (Ps. 38:11); travelling, as it is written: "On the way my strength..." (Ps. 102:24); sin, as it is written: "My strength wavered because of my iniquities" (Ps. 31:11).
>
> **Three things** tear down the body of man, and they are these: eating while standing, drinking while standing, and having intercourse while standing.
>
> **Five** draw [man] closer to death than to life, and these are they: to eat and to stand up [immediately]; to drink and to stand up [immediately]; to sleep and to stand up [immediately]; to let blood and to stand up [immediately]; to have intercourse and to stand up [immediately].
>
> **Six** – the one who does them will die immediately: One who comes back from a journey exhausted, lets blood, enters the bathhouse, drinks and becomes intoxicated, sleeps on the ground, and has intercourse.
>
> **Eight things** are harmful in abundance but beneficial in moderation, and they are these: travel, "the way of the world" [i.e., conjugal relations], wealth,[13] labor, wine, sleep, warmth, and bloodletting.

12b, 27a, 56b; b. Pesah. 76b, 77b, 112a, 113b, 118a; b. Yoma 18a, 21b (2x), 83b; b. Betzah 3b, 32b; b. Ta'an. 26a, 28b; b. Hag. 13a; b. Git. 70a; b. B. Qam. 82a, 83b, 85a, 91a; b. B. Bat. 145a; b. Avod Zar. 17b; b. Hor. 13b; b. Ker. 16a. *Lists of six:* b. Ber. 10b, 43b, 44b, 51a, 57b (2x); b. Pesah. 55b; b. Pesah. 49b, 56a (2x), 113b; b. Shabb. 77a, 127a; b. Hag. 16a (2x); b. Yevam. 81b; b. Naz. 52a (2x); b. Git. 70a, 70b. Avod. Zar. 29a; b. Zevah. 2b, 46b, 72b; b. Menah. 71a, 104a; b. Hul. 104b. *Lists of seven:* b. Pesah. 54a, 54b, 112a; b. Shevu. 8a; b. Ketub. 109a (3x); b. Ned. 39b; b. Sotah 15a; b. Ker. 26a (only Venice Print and Mss.); b. Menah. 51b, 73b; b. Arakh. 16a. *Lists of eight:* b. Git. 70a (2x); b. Tem. 28b. *Lists of ten:* b. Ber. 51a, 55a, 57b; b. Hag. 12a; b. Yoma 23a; b. Pesah. 54a; b. Shabb. 81a; b. B. Bat. 10a; b. B. Qam. 82a (ten regulations of Ezra); b. B. Qam. 82b; b. Hor. 13b; b. Avod. Zar. 29a; b. Qidd. 82a; b. Arakh. 32b; b. Tamid 31b.

12 Ms. Munich 95 reads "the body," as in the next numerical saying.

Eight things diminish the semen, and they are these: salt, hunger, to be "torn,"[14] crying, sleeping on the ground, *gadgadnyut*,[15] dodder which is not in due season, and bloodletting below is like doing it two times. (b. Git. 70a)[16]

The array of subjects treated in these numerical sayings is very wide, as the above examples and those in tractate Berakhot demonstrate. They address decency (e.g., "Three things about the correct behavior in the privy," b. Ber. 62a); prolongation of life (e.g., b. Ber 42a, or b. Git. 70a above); theology (e.g., "Three things that God prompts," b. Ber. 62a, or: "Three things that make heaven recall one's sin," b. Ber. 54); and social interactions (e.g., "Three people who need protection," b. Ber. 54b). The maxims, with their style and content, were obviously appealing beyond Talmudic times. Several anthologies have been transmitted that include these lists (sometimes in a modified form) together with other prominent proverbs from the Talmud and other rabbinic literature.[17] Fragments of such anthologies have been found in the Cairo Genizah.[18]

Scholars have concluded that the purpose of the maxim lays in the realm of mnemotechnics.[19] This claim is reinforced by the observation that the maxims hardly move beyond numbers that can be counted on one's fingers.[20] Still, the large number in which they appear reduces their value as mnemotechnical devices (i.e., 54 maxims alone on "threes"). This does not mean to say that people did not know some by heart — the example below in which such a maxim is used as proof may reflect such an instance of memorization. Or, alternatively, may hint at the systematic organization of maxims (these and others) according to topic from where suitable proof could be retrieved. At least, the large number of numerical maxims indicates that their form was considerably popular.

---

13 This is missing in Ms. Munich 95, which thus only enumerates seven of the eight.
14 נתק; the same root was used several times in the preceding maxims in the formula "seized and torn."
15 גדגדניות; *hapax legomenon*, maybe cherries. See Josephus 1834, 42.
16 Unless otherwise noted, the translations are mine and follow Ms. Munich 95.
17 See Lehmhaus 2015, 66–83, for a discussion of the structure of three 9th-century Midrashim consisting entirely of lists of such numerical sayings, i.e., the Midrash Ma'asseh Torah-tradition: Ḥuppat Eliyahu (The Canopy of Elijah), Midrash Shloshah ve-'arba' (Midrash of 'Three and Four'), and Pirqe Rabbenu Ha-Qaddosh (Lectures of Our Holy Teacher). The works "can most likely be dated to the 9th century" (Lehmhaus 2015, 71). See Judith Olszowy-Schlanger 2014, 26 n. 2, for a summary of the texts' history and editions.
18 See Olszowy-Schlanger 2014, 28.
19 Towner 1973, 4, also cited in Lehmhaus, 2015, 83. See also Valler, 1995, 184; Pasternak/Yona, 2016, 244; Olszowy-Schlanger 2014, 27.
20 The use of fingers for counting is mentioned in b. Yoma 22a/b; see Executive Committee of the Editorial Board/Levias, 1906.

> Cabbage for sustenance and beet for health [=quote from the baraita]. Is then cabbage only for sustenance and not for healing? Was it not taught: "Six things *heal a sick person from his disease and his health will be 'healthy,' and they are these: cabbage, water from bran, honey, maw/rennet, keeping the law, and the large lobe of the liver.*" This is to say that cabbage, like beet, is beneficial and not only good for a meal! (b. Ber. 44b)[21]

That the sayings were remembered and quoted may have been at least part of the intention of their original authors. We can assume that ancient creative minds felt the same pleasure as we do today when their creations "went viral," i.e., were quoted by others, or appeared scribbled on a public wall. However, the sheer ubiquity of these maxims, and their controversial content, which is, as in the above example, even in the Talmud often disputed and supplemented by some commentary, prevents us from drawing a straightforward conclusion regarding memorization. Although memorization remains a possible incentive for the creation/emergence of a numerical maxim, the conclusion has been, perhaps, too quickly drawn.

Although they are creative and even ingenious, talmudic numerical maxims obviously focus less on poetic style than did those in biblical and other Ancient Near Eastern literature, and more on packing content into the format of the numbered list.[22] They look less like neat literary creations and more like a display of knowledge, such as structured notes taken while reading, or a spontaneous creation made while musing. By investigating the different factors that might have originally helped generate these maxims, I would like to show that late-antique knowledge construction had various causes, which were neither more straightforward (i.e., to teach students), nor less complicated, biased, and selfish, than factors involved in contemporary knowledge construction, despite the different contexts.

The focus on pedagogical relevance alone ignores that the artistry of literary communication is driven by public attention. In addition, the numerical maxims seem too ingenious for the classroom alone.[23] This is particularly evident in their expression of the idea that everything can be pressed into, and conveyed by, numbers and letters, that is, the signs of the Hebrew alphabet. As will be shown, numerological structures were conceived of as inherent in every matter, with the intellectual challenge consisting in finding and understanding these

---

21 Translation follows Ms. Munich 95. In the second cent. BCE through the first cent. CE, cabbage, *brassica*, was highly esteemed, e.g., Cato the Elder's "Praise of the Cabbage" in *On Agriculture*, 156–157.
22 See Pasternak/Yona 2016, 244.
23 See Helmut Krasser 2019, 159–174.

correspondences: an often unattributed and unconscious Pythagorean idea. The production of such an intellectual project necessitates time and certain intellectual predispositions and ambitions. These aspects will be addressed in the reminder of this paper.

The Talmud is not descriptive literature but, rather, an elaborate compilation of previously constructed knowledge. Clues for understanding the actual social setting, the intellectual views and educational principles, that gave birth to the texts collected in the Talmud have to be deduced from the broader geographical and chronological surroundings. Subsequent comparison will then show to what extent the clues gained from cultural contexts in the Roman Empire may be applied to the rabbinic setting in Sasanid Mesopotamia, if indeed we were to place the origin of the Hebrew maxims into the latter geographical context.

2 Social Incentives: Erudition and Competition – Some Scenarios

Riddles

The production of maxims requires some basic education, time, a material surface, and an incentive or occasion. Recent scholarship's consideration of data that included previously neglected or unavailable traces of writing, such as graffiti and ostraca, showed that literacy was more widespread than previously assumed and penetrated social classes beyond the elites.[24] In particular, concise compositions, such as sayings, riddles, and jokes circulated and were sometimes even composed collaboratively on walls.[25] Some of the numerical maxims under discussion may indeed have been the result of such a group "chain enumeration," if we imagine a first person writing on a public wall, "Eight things diminish the semen," and maybe adding a first example. Passersby would then have continued the list.[26] At least the Palestinian Talmud mentions in one case information that was gathered from the wall in the house of a particular sage.[27]

---

24 See Baird 2016; Benefiel 2012; Lougovaya 2018; Stern 2018, 141–168.
25 See Benefiel 2012.
26 Graffiti generally tended to accumulate and to interact thematically with each other, see Lohmann 2017, esp. 108–109.
27 See y. Kil. 1:1, 27a.

Maxims may have been the result of systematic summaries of texts and hence were dependent on a more formal workspace. Although we do not have direct evidence that "summarizing" was systematically taught by late-antique curricula, summarizing seems to have become the fashion, which is visible in the general "condensation of literature" in late antiquity.[28] Summaries of prior volumes, for example, became common in introductions (e.g., by the historians Polybius, Diodorus of Sicily, or Dionysius of Halicarnassus).[29] Aulus Gellius wrote summaries of the content of the very book that was to follow and thus provided a digest. Indeed, the first example in the above-quoted list from tractate Gittin seems to hint that some of the numerical maxims may have been summaries as this maxim extracts its information from the biblical text, which it references.

Some of the numerical maxims may have summarized sources that were not subject to talmudic exegesis and hence not worth quoting or referencing (as in "Rabbi X said…"). These sources may have presented knowledge similar to the content of the plays attributed to Euripides, e.g., fragment 907: "(Heracles) was eating green figs along with portions of oxflesh, howling unmusically enough for a barbarian to notice it;"[30] fragment 853: "There are three virtues you should practise, child: to honour the gods, the parents who begot you, and the common laws of Greece. If you do these things, you will always have good repute, the fairest of crowns;"[31] and fragment 906: "Cold is most hostile to a delicate skin."[32] Such information can easily be contracted and listed numerically. Yet, as in the example of continuing another's musings on walls, the creation of numerical sayings may often have been a more playful and sociable activity than the production of summaries in seclusion. Indeed, as Laura Lieber pointed out after an analysis of late-antique Jewish Aramaic poetry, the "consideration of performance can and should be applied more widely."[33]

Ausonius's *Riddle of the Number Three* (*Griphus ternarii numeri*) presents an appealing case for comparison within the genre of "wisdom cast in numbers" and writes the following about the occasion that stimulated his writing:

---

28 On the phenomenon of condensation in late antiquity, see Dusil/Schwedler/Schwitter 2017, 1–22.
29 See Jacob 2000, 107.
30 Euripides 2009, 504–505.
31 Euripides 2009, 478-479.
32 Euripides 2009, 502–503.
33 Lieber 2014, 563.

> The occasion of this bit of foolery was as follows. When I was on active service — a season which, as you know, is one of military freedom — at my mess a challenge was issued to drink, not in Greek fashion — as at the banquet of Rubrius, but after the manner described by Flaccus in that piece of his where by reason of "midnight" and the "new moon" and "Muraena's augurship" "the bard inspired calls for thrice three cups." At this subject of the triple number that poetic itch (*poetica scabies*) of mine at once began scratching away... (Ausonius, *A Riddle of the Number Three*, prologue)[34]

The military campaign to which Ausonius refers might have been the one against the Alamanni (368/9).[35] The immediate occasion to write the little booklet on the number three, however, had been a drinking game.[36] Ausonius's poem consists of a "thrice triple tenfold" of lines and enumerates things that come in threes, making use of poetic license and a number of self-quotations.[37] The poem uses hexameter, a meter divisible by three and, of course, six:[38]

> Everything follows that law of three, or three threes:
>
> The shaping of a man, his full gestation period,
> And his life-span's final end at nine times nine years. (*Riddle*, lines 4–6)[39]

Although Ausonius's composition is called *Gryphos* (Riddle), there is nothing left to be solved for the audience: Ausonius has already completed the task and found the number three wherever it appears in his surroundings. The sympotic *Aenigmata* (Riddles) by a certain Symphosius differ in that regard from the *Gryphos* but share a considerable amount of numerical and other features with the latter.[40] Both works and authors embrace the symposium and especially drinking as their creative stimulus.[41] And like the *Gryphos*, the *Aenigmata* favor the number three through the choice of three hexameters, or multiples of three, per

---

34 Ausonius, trans. Evelyn White 1919, 354–355.
35 See Lowe, 2013, 338.
36 "And that you may know me for a boaster — I began these bits of verses during tiffin and finished them before messtime, that is to say, (again)." Ausonius, trans. Evelyn White 1919, 355–357 (prologue).
37 Lowe 2013, 343–344.
38 Lowe 2013, 342.
39 Translated by Lowe 2013, 335.
40 On the question of whether the attribution *symphosii* refers to a person or to the locus of the riddles, or maybe even to both (with the name's being a pun to the latter), see Leary 2015, 1–2. The composition is most likely to be dated to the late-fourth/early-fifth century (ibid. 4).
41 These claims might also have been influenced by Martial, who clearly influenced both the *Gryphos* and the *Aenigmata*, see Leary 2015, 6.

riddle.⁴² Yet, although Symphosius's riddles ask to be answered, one of his habits distinguishes his composition from contemporary puzzle books: he renders the solution to the riddle as its lemma. This rendering of the solution as a title probably aimed at provoking a reaction in the reader, that is, to stimulate their admiration for the cleverness of the composer, an intention that Ausonius's "riddle" seems to share.⁴³ A similar game with the audience appears to be at play in the talmudic numerical maxims as well. The audience is first informed about what is to come and is given a short amount of time to start thinking about the topic on their own — just enough to be deeply impressed by the speed with which the riddler then adds the solution. Although the members of the audience did not have sufficient time to devise a decent solution themselves, they could assess and determine whether the riddler was to be admired or criticized, or both.

Yet, the social contexts of riddles involved not only performance, but also the exchange of parting gifts (*apophoreta*) by lottery at banquets, for example. The tickets (*pittacia*) may have contained a poetic description of the gift to be received — some of Martial's epigrams (books 13 and 14) seem to render the content of such tickets. Sometimes, the guests also had to guess the gift based on the description.⁴⁴ Petronius (56.7–10) preserves a funny version of this tradition, in which the ticket seemed to refer to a traditional gift but then turned out to be just a pun for the real one.⁴⁵ In a different context, such ticket-slats were used by pilgrims at Christian shrines to ask questions and receive oracular answers.⁴⁶ *Pittacia* (פיתקא), in the sense of small, very thin wooden slats, are also mentioned in the Talmud.⁴⁷ The numerical sayings on such slats could easily be imagined as little riddling summaries of gifts, dedicatory notes, or "cheat sheets."

Intellectual Games

Another platform for riddles and maxims were symposia like, for example, the one in honor of the Roman festival Saturnalia. At symposia, riddles were used in

---

42 For a summary of parallels between the two works, and for the reference, see Leary 2015, 5.
43 See Leary 2015, 12–13; and further Sebo 2012, 184–195, and esp. 192–195, for references to examples of riddles with multiple or additional solutions.
44 See Leary 2015, 9.
45 See Ullman 1941.
46 See Luijendijk 2014, 49–50.
47 E.g., b. Sanh. 26a, 96b; b. Bekh. 8b; b. B. Metz. 86a; b. Sanh. 64a; b. Yoma 69b; b. Hor. 13b.

the context of intellectual challenges. Gellius provides a nice account of the procedure of such intellectual games:

> *The kinds of questions we used to discuss when spending the Saturnalia at Athens; and some amusing sophistries and riddles.*
>
> We used to spend the Saturnalia at Athens very merrily yet temperately, not "relaxing our minds," as the saying is — for, as Musonius asserts, to relax the mind is like losing it — but diverting our minds a little and relieving them by the delights of pleasant and improving conversation. Accordingly, a number of us Romans who had come to Greece, and who attended the same lectures and devoted ourselves to the same teachers, met at the same dinner-table. Then the one who was giving the entertainment in his turn, offered as a prize for solving a problem in the work of some old Greek or Roman writer and a crown woven from laurel, and put to us as many questions as there were guests present. But when he had put them all, the question which each was to discuss and the order of speaking were determined by lot. Then, when a question was correctly answered, the reward was a crown and a prize; if it was not correctly answered, it was passed on to the next in the allotment, and this process was repeated throughout the circle. If no one could answer a particular question, the crown was dedicated to the god in whose honour the festival was held. Now the questions that were proposed were of this kind: an obscure saying of some early poet, amusing rather than perplexing; some point in ancient history; the correction of some tenet of philosophy which was commonly misinterpreted, the solution of some sophistical catch, the investigation of a rare and unusual word, or of an obscure use of the tense of a verb of plain meaning. (*Attic Nights* 18.2.1–6)[48]

Other sources report that those who lost at such intellectual games had to drink wine mixed with saltwater or perform sconcing (excessive drinking).[49] The pressure seems to have been quite high, and guests are described as having resorted to hiding notes in their garments to avoid public embarrassment.[50]

Although Symphosius's riddles for the symposium have a completely different form than the talmudic numerical maxims, they share their outlook. Thus, like the maxims, the *Aenigmata* show an "erudite concern … with word

---

48 Aulus Gellius, trans. Rolfe 1927, 296–299, slightly adapted. In the sequel, Gellius offers seven such questions.
49 Leary 2015, 10 and n. 72 for references.
50 E.g., Lucian, *On Salaried Posts*, 27. The term used for "note" here is γραμματίδια, "small tablet," "memorandum,"; see Liddell/Scott 1968, s.v. γραμμᾰτείδιον. Since such games could challenge the integrity of guests, Suetonius writes approvingly of Ceasar Augustus, "He gave dinner parties frequently, but they were always formal and showed great regard for social status and the individuals concerned. […] For he would encourage the silent or those who talked quietly to share in the general conversation. He would intersperse entertainments and actors or even street-players from the circus and more frequently story-tellers" (*Vita divi Augusti* 74). Translation follows Suetonius, trans. Wardle 2014, 68.

play and etymology, their literary debts and the astronomical, mythological, geographical, medicinal and botanical knowledge they display."⁵¹ The numerical sayings in the Talmud could, in fact, have started out as riddles in need of completion by attendees at a symposium. We could even imagine a die involved in the determination of the number of items to be enumerated. Throughout late antiquity, not only dinner parties occasioned by festivals, but also gatherings more generally, could serve as platforms for agonistic displays of knowledge, whether anticipated or spontaneously.⁵² Philostratus (2nd to 3rd century CE), for example, "describes a sympotic group known as the *Klepsydrion* (the 'water-clock group'), a selection of ten "star pupils" who would gather to listen to Herodes Atticus offer his interpretations of 100 lines of poetry during a period limited by a water-clock."⁵³

The *skolion* — or variants thereof — is a noteworthy game that can quite easily be imagined having stimulated numerical verses. The meaning of the term *skolion* is not entirely clear, but it has been related to both σκολιός, "crooked," and δύσκολος/δυσκολία, which could refer to "difficult" as well as "riddling."⁵⁴ The tenth-century Byzantine encyclopedia *Suda* notes the following about the *skolion* game: "*Skolion*: the drinking song, as Dicaearchus says in his *On Musical Contests*, because there were three types of songs: one was sung by all, another by each person one after the other, a third by the most educated since the order was random. It is called *skolion* (because of the order)."⁵⁵ The second and third variant of this game seem to be the most interesting for the present purpose, since the song was composed on the spot by the symposiasts, who took turns, each trying to cap the previous contribution. Thus, we can imagine a game like the *skolion* — maybe sung, maybe not — being started with someone calling "x 'things' that do/are...". Participants were challenged to think of a suitable "thing" until the number x was completed. A servant or student may have been instructed to write noteworthy outcomes down. Imagined as such a *skolion* game, a numerical maxim may have come about like this (talmudic text in italics):

---

51 Leary 2015, 12. On the encyclopedic outlook of Macrobius's symposiac work, see Olmos 2012.
52 Krasser 2019, 159–160, traces the emergence of the literary agon back to the early Empire. See also Krasser 2005, 374.
53 *Lives of the Sophists*, 2.10, 585–586; see König 2012, 16.
54 See Collins 2004.
55 Collins 2004. Indeed, the fact that the song was composed spontaneously obviously contributed to its being crooked (Scholia Aristoph., *Wasps*, 1222).

> The gamemaster calls the game: "Three whom the Holy One, Blessed Be He, proclaims every day:"
>
> First participant (who happened to be a bachelor): *The bachelor who walks around in a city and does not sin!* (Laughter in the audience and cheers.)
> Second participant, sitting right next to him (a first-time attendee who was invited spontaneously upon returning the host's missing lamb): *The poor person who returns a lost item to its owner!* (People clap, one calls out the host and shouts, "Give him money!")
> Third person in the row: *The rich person who tithes his produce in secret!* (Awkward silence until someone says: "Wow, you just spoiled *your* proclamation in heaven!" Laughter.)

Similar contexts can be imagined for the following two rounds of the game. Since someone had been assigned to record the answers, the playful setting produced a total of three clever maxims. These are the other two:

> Three [whom] the Holy One, Blessed Be He, loves: The one who does not get angry; the one who does not get drunk; and the one who does not insist on his principles.
>
> Three [whom] the Holy One, Blessed Be He, hates: The one who says something different with his mouth and something different in his heart; the one who knows of evidence in favor of his friend and does not testify on his behalf; the one who sees something shameful in his friend and testifies alone against him. (b. Pesah. 113a/b)

Athenaeus describes a game called *gryphos* (γρῖφος), perhaps the one that inspired the title of Ausonius's poem. It was yet another game designed to test the knowledge and grammatical aptitude of the guests. Like the *skolion*, the *gryphos* could take different forms. It could request that participants name words starting with, or omitting, a given letter; that they would find names that did or did not contain the name of a particular or any god; or to state words starting or ending with a given syllable. Yet, a *gryphos* could also be a quiz testing the player's versatility in adapting meter, answering questions about literature or grammar, or solving riddles.[56] Here, we could again imagine that contestants had to enumerate a requested number of "things" that do/are a certain something.

In sum, we see that a lot of learned and creative work was going on at dinner parties or in intellectual associations such as the *Klepsydrion*. It seems not unwarranted to place the talmudic numerical maxims within the setting of a banquet or gathering. Not only is their scope very broad, covering all kinds of topics that may come up on such occasions and by different people, but they also build on each other, taking a starting point and evolving from there.

---

56 See Luz 2010, 139–146, for a discussion and examples.

A Playful Talmud?

As I argue elsewhere at some length, the Talmud is arranged like a symposiac work, that is, it presents the listener/reader with a symposiac setting into which they are drawn as silent (or not-so-silent) participants.[57] The intellectual activity of discussion and argument-building, the presentation of knowledge, and engagement with the insights of others is thereby placed at the center and set before the audience as a model for imitation. While the Talmud does not describe the gatherings that led to the composition of its content, it arranges the output of these gatherings, some of which was probably produced for or within symposiac settings, into an impeccable rhetorical discussion. Similarly, although the rabbinic movement is best explained as having emerged from organized associations that gradually became more uniform and institutionalized, we find only implicit evidence for such structures in the writings they left to posterity.[58]

The Mesopotamian plain was heavily influenced by Greco-Roman customs, due to its proximity and fluid border lines, but also on account of prior Seleucid rule. There is not, however, much archaeological proof of Judean life in Sasanid Mesopotamia. Arguments for symposiac and collective activity derived from the Greco-Roman context are corroborated by the fact that, from the first century onwards, there is increasing physical evidence for communal dining in synagogues, which, for this purpose, provided a kitchen and a *triclinium*.[59] "(M)eals," Lee I. Levine concludes, "were a familiar feature of ancient synagogue life. This was true of the diaspora as well as Palestine, and throughout all of Late Antiquity."[60] Moreover, as Gil Klein has pointed out, the architecture of a dining room, whether furnished in the old-fashioned Greek style (*andron*), which seated people against the walls of a square room, leaving an "arena-like structure with a

---

[57] See Amsler (forthcoming), chapter 1.
[58] See Lapin 2012, esp. 64–97.
[59] See Williams 2013, 165, and further references there. Persian or "oriental" symposiac traditions have been discussed by Burkert 1991; Eliav 2015, 165–172, albeit with a focus on the purported lavish aspects of symposia. In the wake of a general rectification of the economic system in late antiquity that focuses on the actual working force of society, i.e., the craftsmen, who organized themselves in associations, the elitist focus on the banquet needs to change as well: Not everyone, and not all associations, had the means to sponsor lavish meals. But such festivities nonetheless remained important for cohesion and trust within the group; see Venticinque 2016, esp. 99–132.
[60] Levine 2005, 394, and see further 316–319 for references (mostly) from the Palestinian Talmud to such practices.

defined empty space at the center," or in the manner of the Roman *triclinium*, with its three couches facing each other in "a Pi-shaped (Π) arrangement," seems suited for rabbinic Torah study.[61] Given the Persian habit of using pillows rather than fixed furniture, one can imagine more flexible structures that would have been equally supportive of joint discussion, study, and intellectual games.[62]

There is, however, only rare, if distinct, evidence for sympotic activity among members of the rabbinic association. As Philip A. Harland and David Instone-Brewer have discussed, the structures of associations manifest themselves mostly in the organization of festive meals (pre-registration, seclusion) or distinct vocabulary with which fellow associates are addressed (e.g., *chaver*, colleague, associate).[63] Harland is certainly right that the talmudic discussion of certain passages from the Mishna show that measures suggested by the earlier work were no longer relevant. In other talmudic passages, however, we find that similar rulings were still issued in talmudic times. The order in which people should wash their hands at banquets, say grace, and open the meal, for example, is an issue of discussion (b. Ber. 46b–47a). Scattered clues describe occasions that could possibly give rise to a banquet: if a colleague recovered from a disease (b. Ber. 46a), if a student completed the study of a mishnaic tractate (b. Shabb. 118b–119a), or simply if one wanted to invite colleagues (b. Git. 55a).[64] Talmudic texts, therefore, clearly associate the banquet with the context of learning and other learned men with whom they shared tight bonds. Not surprisingly, then, the Talmud also cites a critique of those who abandon study in favor of banquets (b. Shabb. 151b).

Wine was clearly used to stimulate productivity and to turn gatherings into even more enjoyable moments. At least one story finds it quite feasible that a teacher would get so drunk with his students that, after their meeting, they needed a cure for their intoxication (b. Shabb. 66b).[65] Thus, whether the numerical maxims in question originated in Palestine or Babylonia, it remains feasible that at least some of them were the product of games played at leisurely gatherings in a private dining room between teachers and students or among equals, or that they resulted from officially organized dinners according to the habits of

---

61 Klein 2012, 332.
62 On Persian interior furnishing, see Simpson 2015, 15.
63 See Harland/Instone-Brewer 2008. It is interesting to note here that agricultural managers in Kellis refer to their fellow managers as "brothers" (*adelphoi*); see Bagnall/Hope 1997, 70.
64 The Aramaic terms for festive days or banquets are יומא טבא and סעודתא.
65 Knowledge about wine was quite substantial (e.g., b. Git. 70a), although Babylonia seems to have favored beer; see Rosenblum 2020, esp. 180–182.

associations. Games, it has been amply pointed out, contributed, and continue to contribute, to the stability and cohesion of societies in general and of smaller groups.[66]

Late antiquity perceived learning and playing games or adulthood and playing as much less of a dichotomy than they appear today.[67] Even physical games or games with objects such as ball games, wrestling, hide-and-seek, or knucklebones remained a part of adult entertainment.[68] Like physical games, intellectual games were an occasion to divert the mind, to show off, and build social reputation with wit and knowledge.[69] Such games caused people to be prepared with a stock of maxims, riddles, and jokes, which thus travelled widely. A wall in Pompeii apparently prompted the guests of the house to write something memorable — a sort of an intellectual guest book.[70] Much more than a serious activity like, for example, the creation of a teacher for his students, the numerical maxims may have risen out of such playful contexts or were crafted in preparation for them. They have the potential to display the erudition of their author by combining quick-wittedness with common knowledge. Additionally, the structure reveals also certain algorithmic competences and insights. These will be the subject of the next section.

3 Intellectual Mannerism: Numerology

In the Greek, Hebrew, Aramaic, and Syriac alphabets, letters also carried numerical values. Consequently, the semantic and numeric value of letters were intrinsically entwined: words could also be read as numbers. This implied that, "People who were literate were as a rule also numerate," which, to some extent, included their ability "to perform the basic arithmetical operations."[71] This seems even more true for people who used the talmudic numerical system,

---

[66] See Schwartz 2010, 641–642, and further references there.
[67] Although in many ways outdated and racist, the work of Ariès 1996, 60–97, demonstrates this quite nicely.
[68] On such physical games in and out of rabbinic literature, see the overview article by Schwartz 2010.
[69] Similarly, lighthearted games of divination are a more recent appropriation, dating to the end of the fifteenth century. In late antiquity, they are used as an earnest means for finding answers to pressing questions; see Luijendijk 2014, 8 and n. 31.
[70] See Benefiel 2012, 68.
[71] Cuomo 1998, 46. Mathematical knowledge pops up repeatedly for exegetical purposes (48–51). On the simultaneous study of letters and numbers, see, further, Cribiore 2001, 181.

which, after reaching 400 with the last letter (*tav*), combines numbers to move beyond 400, thereby imposing arithmetic competences (e.g., 500 = 400 + 100). Playful or strategic ciphers alike were often based on the exchange of letters that together added up to a certain number.[72]

The people who composed the talmudic maxims under discussion may have enjoyed an education that went beyond the stage of basic alphabetization and "numeralization." Advanced education, however, did not diminish the sense of an intrinsic connection between the numeric and semantic value of letters. To the contrary: the more advanced students were, the more they became aware of these conflating values. The engagement with the subject was prevalent throughout late antiquity: numerology was not a distinct, liminal theory, but a broad one, applicable to many different subjects. The virtue of a "broader explanation" renders such theories likely to enter the common sense of their time.[73]

This sweeping persuasiveness of numerical structures is also confirmed by Latin authors, whose numerical system involved only, or, rather, precisely, seven letters. The importance of numbers in the writings of Roman authors is mostly due to the prevalence of Stoic thought among the Roman elite because of its emphasis on public and private duty.[74] In Stoic thought, numbers constitute the most fundamental "bricks of the universe," since not even a god can change the fact that 2 x 10 equals 20.[75] Ausonius had made the connection between number and his physical surroundings ("nature" in the modern paradigm), but also between number and language, the subject of his *Riddle of the Number Three*. Other authors also used such numerical arrangements, but in less obvious ways. Symmachus, the recipient of Ausonius's riddle, seems to have intended to compose a seven-book letter collection.[76] Therein, he may have followed Varro's example of the *Hebdomades*, a collection of 700 painted portraits of famous people, each appended with an epigram.[77] Varro, in fact, wrote a now-lost treatise entitled *On the Beginnings of Numbers* (*De principiis numerorum*). Ausonius refers to this work in his introduction as among the things "the uninitiated herd wots not of."[78] In an epitome of the introduction to the *Hebdomades* preserved in Gellius's *Attic Nights*, Varro highlights the importance of

---

[72] Paz/Weiss, 2015.
[73] Lehoux 2012, 176–199, esp. 192.
[74] Beagon 1992, 27.
[75] Beagon 1992, 29 n. 7.
[76] Sogno 2017, esp. 181–182.
[77] Salzman 2018, 92–93, and see Pliny, *NH* 35, 2.11.
[78] Ausonius, trans. Evelyn White 1919, 356–357.

the number seven in cosmological correlations, down to human gestation periods and critical days in the course of a disease.[79] Along with similar cosmological information, scholars have also observed numerical arrangements within talmudic lists of arguments or as underlying literary devices.[80] The privileged numbers are mostly congruent with those used in the numerical maxims, namely three, four, five, seven, ten, and fourteen (i.e., 2x7).

Exegetes used numerology to interpret numbers in their base texts, be they the Bible or Plato. Philo of Alexandria, for instance, employed it to explain underlying numerical structures in the Bible. For him, the method is so evident that he thinks Moses must have used it, too:

> They [the animals permitted for consumption according to Deut. 14:4] are the calf, the lamb, the kid, the hart, the gazelle, the buffalo, the wild goat, the pygarg, the antelope, and the giraffe, ten in all. For as he [Moses] always adhered to the principle of numerical science (ἀριθμητικῆς θεωρίας), which he knew by close observance to be a paramount factor in all that exists, he never enacted any law great or small without calling to his aid and as it were accommodating in his enactment its appropriate number. But from all the numbers from the unit (μονάδος) upwards ten is the most perfect, and, as Moses says, most holy and sacred, and with this he seals his list of clean animals when he wishes to appoint them for the use of members of his commonwealth. (*On Special Laws* 4.18)[81]

In other instances, Philo used numerology to interpret actual numbers that appear in the text, such as the seven days of creation, the forty days of the flood, and so on.[82] This concern was also shared by Christian exegetes such as Augustine and the Syriac author Gabriel Qatraya.[83] The latter wrote a commentary on the Liturgical Offices (around 600 CE in present-day Qatar) in which he made use of Pythagoras's number science to explain the perfect creation by the perfect creator:[84]

---

79 *Attic Nights* 3.10, 1–17. Similarly, see Macrobius in his commentary on the *Dream of Scipio*; see Lehoux 2012, 190–191.
80 See Simon-Shoshan 2008, and, on numerical structures, e.g., Jacobs 1983; Pasternak/Yona 2017; Valler 1995. A hemerology preserved in tractate Shabbat 129b is a good example of the correlation between a particular action and the auspiciousness of the day as a number in the week or the month (e.g., On the first day of the week do not do X). A section on astrology in b. Shabb. 156a-b is obviously crafted around the numbers seven and three; see Rubenstein 2007, 118.
81 Philo, trans. Colson 1939, 70–73.
82 See Cuomo 2001, 180–181, and 250.
83 E.g., Augustine *De doctrina christiana* 2.16.25, and Cuomo 2001, 251–254.
84 Brock 2014, 155.

He defines everything by number, and by means of certain numerical symbols he used to transmit the mystery/secret of his teaching to his disciples ... He handed down that the number one is the equivalent of the Maker, whom he in truth confesses as being one. The number two (symbolizes) matter, and three species, and four the elements, providing four equivalents. And just as the numbers 1, 2, 3 and 4 make up the number 10, so, by the power of the Creator, who is one in the simplicity of his nature, this whole world came into being with the number of the elements and the (full) number of its natural constituents (lit. natures), bearing the equivalence of the perfect number of ten.[85]

Pythagorean ideas similarly seem to have influenced rabbinic hermeneutics, which, although revolving around the most frequently used numbers in the Hebrew Bible, become increasingly conscious of their mathematical qualities. The analysis of the numerical value of words (Gematria/Isopsephy) and number symbolism ultimately became part of the catalogue of the thirty-two hermeneutic rules by Rabbi Jose the Galilean.[86]

The reason behind this preoccupation with numbers was not just the entanglement of number and letter. Rather, these authors drew on a concept of numbers that differed considerably from the modern one, which treats numbers exclusively as quantitative entities.[87] For late-antique mathematicians such as Boethius, Nikomachos of Gerasa, Philoponos, and Neoplatonist thinkers, by contrast, numbers were compounds of units adding up to even or uneven numbers.[88] In this system, three was considered to be the first actual number, since one (the monad) is not a composite, and two (the dyad) is a composite of two monades.[89] The resulting quantitative numbers were seen as only the reflection of the intelligible numbers through which "the One"/God created the world.[90] They are therefore inherent in the creation, just like the four seasons, the five elements (including ether), or the seven vowels and planets (the latter number including the sun and the moon). Ten was considered the perfect number be-

---

85 Brock 2014, 162. Brock further notes that, "A Discourse by Pythagoras and a collection of his sayings in Syriac translations are known from other sources, but Gabriel must have derived this information from somewhere different" Brock 2014, 162).
86 See Executive Committee of the Editorial Board/Levias 1906.
87 See Heilmann 2007, 140.
88 See Heilmann 2007, 130–131.
89 See Heilmann 2007, 134. Moreover, in Pythagorean thought, the dyad was considered to be a number that challenged the uniqueness and goodness of "the One"; see Kate Hobgood (undated), Pythagoras and the Mystery of Numbers, accessed under http://jwilson.coe.uga.edu/EMAT6680Fa06/Hobgood/Pythagoras.html, February 6, 2023.
90 Heilmann 2007, 136–137, 140. The most direct reflection of these intelligible numbers was considered to be the soul, which is why the study of the *quadrivium* begins with an examination of the soul (Heilmann 2007, 143).

cause 4+3+2+1=10.[91] More individual interpretations were also possible. Thus, Iamblichus described the number five as the fulcrum of a balance, with numbers 1–4 on one side and numbers 6–9 on the other.[92] Julius Africanus extols the numbers 6 and 4.[93] Africanus further used pentagons, and probably also hexagons, with pictures and musical notations, from which one could infer ingredients for his medical recipes.[94] Here, geometry and harmony are distinctly linked to therapy. Late-ancient mathematics was essentially a study in the "harmonic faculty" of the cosmos.[95]

These considerations shed a different light on the use of numbers in the numerical maxims under investigation. The numbers were likely used not just for enumeration or summary; they also point to an intrinsic connection between the threes, fives, eights, and so on. Organizing principles according to number instead of subject can be observed in compilations of sayings such as Mishna tractate Avot or the Pirqa de-Rabbenu ha-Qadosh.[96] The categorization according to number reveals the cosmological connection of and between these subjects, just as do the threes in Ausonius's Riddle.

4 Essential Factors: Space and Leisure

I would like to end this paper about factors that may have contributed to the creation of numerical maxims now found in the Talmud by considering first the geographical, and finally the temporal space in which adult learning took place. This will provide a platform to address issues connected to learning that will further help situate the numerical maxims within a learning culture that was, in many ways, different from ours. For example, we tend to focus on the urban space as the driving force behind intellectual creativity. Surely, we reason, the density of intellectuals in a city provided more opportunities to network and to increase the audience for one's ideas.[97] Just because cities hosted some famous

---

[91] See Hunger 1978, 222–223.
[92] Theologia Arithmetica 35.6ff; see Cuomo 2001, 254 n. 19.
[93] See Cesti 24–25.
[94] See Africanus, trans. Wallraff/Scardino/Mecella/Guignard/Adler 2012, XXX–XXXI. For examples of such recipes see, e.g., F12, 45, Seventh Cestus or F12, 5, Seventh Cestus.
[95] See Nathan Sidoli 2014, 17 n. 8.
[96] See Executive Committee of the Editorial Board/Levias 1906, "Numbers and Numerals;" and Olszowy-Schlanger 2014, respectively.
[97] See Stenger 2019, 6–11.

schools, however, does not mean that the countryside was inhabited by illiterate ignoramuses.⁹⁸ Recent excavations in rural Egypt, for example, have pointed to a rich culture of learning.⁹⁹ Rather than as a peripheral space where, occasionally and rather accidentally, a bit of learning occurred or a piece of knowledge ended up, I suggest seeing the countryside as an equal partner in knowledge production. This approach can be justified if we look, for example, at mathematics.

Contrary to ancient mathematics, which appears primarily theoretical, late-antique mathematics becomes mostly feasible to us as implemented: sophisticated bookkeeping records from big estates attest to the work of meticulous accountants; complicated tax systems necessitated land surveyors who were well-versed in geometry, as they measured, counted, calculated, and projected the harvest.¹⁰⁰ Mathematical capability was clearly needed in the countryside, by owners of estates but even more so by those whom they employed, and by self-employed farmers and craftsmen. The mathematics used in the Talmud similarly exhibits applied mathematical knowledge that draws mostly from planimetry, stereometry, and (applied) arithmetic operation.¹⁰¹ No matter where we situate the rabbinic scholars in Babylonia, whether in the megalopolis of the Sasanid capital Ctesiphon (Mahoza), in smaller towns such as Sura or Pumbedita, or in one of the above-mentioned villages, they had to be in a position to carry out appropriate mathematical operations.¹⁰² This was probably even more true in rural areas, since it was harder to procure a specialist.

---

98 This idea seems to have been imported into the study of history via its conflation with anthropology and a distinct evolutionary paradigm of civilization. Cohn 1980, 203–205, points to a way of analyzing areas starting in the 1930s that framed the indigenuous village as a primordial "bound entity" vis-à-vis the modern and progressive city. "The village was not only the site of 'the before' in terms of its 'backwardness,' but the assumed locus of the traditional civilization, practices and beliefs" (Cohn 1980, 205).
99 E.g., Kellis in the Dakhleh Oasis or Tebtunis; see Bagnall 2018 and Hanson 2005, respectively. Many of the highly sophisticated papyri collected under the name of Papyri Graecae Magicae have similarly been found in rural spaces.
100 See Serafina Cuomo 2001, 212–218; for an example, see Rathbone 1991, 331–369.
101 Zuckermann 1878, 1. He further mentions that the decimal system is referred to in b. Bekh. 60a, and that b. Naz. 8b and b. B. Bat. 164b mention several geometrical figures also by their arithmetical value (idem. 1n1). Other examples include b. Pesah. 109a/b (the space people need in the *sukka*) or b. Eruv. 14a (Pi). The most exhaustive treatment of the issue is still Zuckermann. Feldman 1913, relies heavily on Zuckermann. The subject would benefit from a more exhaustive research project in conversation with recent work on late-antique mathematics.
102 These villages often appear in connection to names, i.e., "Ravin from Nares" or "Rav Aha from Difti" (both in b. Git. 69b). Aharon Oppenheimer attempted to locate these places on the

The Talmud also participates in what might be termed "literary mathematics," that is, riddles describing a mathematical problem cast in "fictional situations" that were either "historical, mythological, or just everyday."[103] Some of these types of mathematical riddles, which may be "attributed to the fourth-century grammarian Metrodorus," have been collected in the *Palatine* (or *Greek Anthology*).[104] Here are two examples:

> Croesus the king dedicated six bowls weighing six minae [= 600 drachms] each one drachm heavier than the other.
> Solution: The weight of the first is 97 1/2 drachm, and so on.[105]

> Demochares lived for a quarter of his whole life as a boy, for a fifth part of it as a young man, and for a third as a man, and when he reached grey old age, he lived thirteen years more on the threshold of eld.
> Solution: He lived 15 years as a boy, 12 as a young man, 20 as a man, and 13 years as an old man; in all 60.[106]

The Talmud preserves similar problems that were adapted to the talmudic world and its protagonists.[107] For the less trained eye, they are not recognizable as mathematical riddles, but, rather, appear as puzzling, exaggerated stories, like the following example:

> Rav Pappa and Rav Huna the son of Rav Joshua once dined together, and Rav Pappa ate 4 times as much as Rav Huna .... On another occasion Rav Huna and Ravina dined together, and Ravina ate 8 times as much as Rav Huna. Then, said Rav Huna: "I would rather dine with 100 people like R. Pappa than with one Ravina." (b. Pesah. 89b)[108]
> Solution: After dining with 100 other guests eating like Rav Pappa, Huna and the other guests are charged for 401 helpings. Since there are 101 guests with Rav Huna, each one pays for 401/101. When dining with Ravina, Rav Huna's share costs 9/2.[109]

Mesopotamian map. According to him, Nares may be located in the "hilly district" southeast of Sura, while he was unable to identify Difti/Difte; see Aharon Oppenheimer 1983, 264, with map on 549, and 113 and esp. n. 12, respectively.
103 Cuomo 2001, 245.
104 See Cuomo 2001, 245.
105 Translated by Paton 1918, 33.
106 Translated by Paton 1918, 95.
107 E.g., in b. Avod. Zar. 9b, the instructions on how to calculate the Sabbatical year (attributed to R. Huna, son of R. Joshua); see Zuckermann 1878, 62–63, or Feldman 1931, 20, for more examples.
108 Translation follows Feldman 1931, 20.
109 See Zuckermann 1878, 50.

These mathematical problems may, again, have served as entertainment or for teaching purposes and maybe both, although it does not seem that teachers were concerned about the entertaining factor of their teaching. Much like the riddles, which these mathematical problems in fact are, the problems appear to have been used to intellectually challenge other learned men while also enjoying a decent meal together.

Placed in this setting, the following somewhat puzzling story appears to be a tricky mathematical riddle, which starts considerably easy with comparison and estimation and ends with a complicated punch line:

> Said Rabbi Yohanan, "Rabbi Ishmael the son of Yose's member was like a wineskin of nine *kav* [approximately five gallons]; Rabbi Elazar the son of Rabbi Shimon's member was like a wineskin of seven *kav*." Rav Pappa said, "Rabbi Yohanan's member was like a wineskin of three *kav*." And there are those who say: like a wineskin of five *kav*. Rav Pappa himself had a member which was like the baskets of Hipparenum. (b. B. Metz. 84b)[110]

The first two statements about the size of Rabbi Ishmael and Rabbi Elazar's member suggest that the member of the next Rabbi is again two *kav* smaller, which would result in five *kav* for Rabbi Yohanan's member. Alternatively, it may be four *kav* smaller since the decrease might double from member to member. This would result in three *kav* for Rabbi Yohanan's member. Both answers seem valid according to the solutions attributed to Rav Pappa and "others." After this tricky but still considerably easy start, the puzzle ventures into geometry. The volume of Rav Pappa's member must be calculated based on the radius of the basket. The radius needs to be squared, then multiplied by the height of the basket and the result again multiplied by Pi. Pi appears with the value of 3.0 in rabbinic literature, and the radius of the particular "basket of Hipparenum" is not rendered here but might have been common knowledge.[111]

Life in the countryside was busy, but it was also less disturbed by regular social performances and obligations than life in the city. It thus offered the necessary peace and quiet for intellectual productivity, but also other forms of entertainment. Martial muses somewhat romanticizing:

> Could but you and I, dear Martialis, enjoy carefree days [*tempus otiosum*] and dispose our time in idleness, and both alike have leisure for true living, we should know nothing of the halls and mansions of the mighty, nor sour lawsuits and the gloomy Forum, nor haughty deathmasks: but riding, chatting, books, the Field, the colonnade, the shade, the

---

110 Translation follows Boyarin 2009, 182.
111 On the use of Pi in rabbinic literature, see Zuckermann 1878, 23; Feldman 1931, 22–23.

Virgin [aqueduct], the baths—these should be our daily haunts, these our labors (Martial, *Epigrams* 5.20).[112]

Reference to spare time or leisure in late-antique sources does not, of course, imply the daily intervals of work and leisure to which post-industrial human beings are accustomed. Rather, the Latin *otium* (free time/leisure) and its opposite, *negotium* (busyness), alternated in longer intervals. Rainy seasons and winter, for example, caused *otium*.[113] The life of intellectuals and passionate literati was organized according to these intervals: "Since leisure was a prerequisite for literary interests, whether active or passive, men like Cicero waited for the time and place when the Roman conscience could relax. It could be a national holiday, or springtime in Campania, or high summer in the Alban hills — when the Senate and courts are adjourned, and gentlemen have settled into their villas, bringing their secretaries and readers, and perhaps a visiting philosopher, to keep them company."[114] Similarly, Aulus Gellius wrote in the introduction to his work, "And since, as I have said, I began to amuse myself by assembling these notes *during the long winter nights which I spent on a country-place in the land of Attica*, I have therefore given them the title of Attic Nights."[115] This quote from Gellius completes the above list of possible leisure by adding a season (winter) and a particular time of the day (the night) as *otium*. Gellius is quite consistent with his emphasis on nights and writes elsewhere that, after having bought a number of books, he "ran through all of them hastily in the course of the next two nights (9.4.3)."[116] Late-antique schools in Mesopotamia, both Judean and Christian, similarly profited from times freed of labor and engaged with students seasonally, a month in winter and a month in summer.[117]

Of course, rich people could afford to engage in recreation in a manner that may be described in the modern sense as "leisure," in that it established "a feeling of freedom and pleasure by formulating a sense of choice and desire."[118] Considering the importance of education in the social life of late antiquity, but

---

112 Martial, trans. Shackleton Bailey 1993, 346–347.
113 See Macrobius, *Saturnalia* VI.12; or Gellius, *Attic Nights*, Praef. 10. The Aramaic term usually translated with "to idle" (בטל) refers similarly not to voluntary idling, but to the opposite of busyness; see Sokoloff 2002, s.v. בטל(3). "Idlers" (בטלני) stand at the marketplace and wait for somebody to give them a job; see, e.g., b. Pesah. 51b and 55a; b. Ber. 17b; b. Ta'an. 29b; and b. B. Metz. 32b.
114 Fantham 1996, 41.
115 From the preface of Aulus Gellius, trans. Rolfe 1927), xxvii, emphasis mine.
116 Gellius, trans. Rolfe 1927, 163.
117 See Goodblatt 1975, 164.
118 Toner 1995, 17.

also the entertaining quality attributed to it, spending one's free time studying books was to a certain extent also imperative. This imperative to know, together with the limited amount of time available for this purpose, contributed to the time's preference for short and condensed texts such as handy summaries. The latter were much appreciated gifts since they spared laborious research.[119]

Different ethical aspirations were attached to how one spent free time and even eventually became decisive for the term's mainly negative connotation in the middle ages.[120] The cenobite monks, for example, interpreted *acedia* ("sloth") to be equal to the "noontide demon of the Psalms [Ps. 91:5–6], which attacked the cenobites most frequently between the hours of ten and two."[121] At the same time the sun reaches its zenith, the monk's spirit is at its weakest, and he is most likely to do nothing, to become careless, indifferent. *Acedia* was therefore considered a sin among the monks.[122] Similarly, the Talmud assigns times and even periods to demons, during which people should not go out and, in fact, should stay at home.[123] Moreover, the distinction between *otium* and *negotium* is captured with Torah study on the one hand and public obligation and "action" (*derekh erets* and *ma'aseh*) on the other.[124] The numerical maxims under discussion were mostly the product of *otium*/Torah: As the result of time spent with friends and family, associates, or even strangers they were conceived in the dining room of a private house, the synagogue, or even the marketplace.[125]

5 Conclusion

This brief investigation into the factors responsible for the generation and construction of the numerical maxims scattered over the Talmud has essentially shown that learning itself, as well as the occasions for implementing knowledge, was multi-faceted. Although a clear-cut division between *otium* and

---

119 E.g., *The Birthday Book*, a summary of the astrology of the time by Censorinus, which he offered to Quintus Carellius on his, well, birthday.
120 Fischler 2001, 178.
121 Kuhn 1976, 43.
122 Kuhn 1976, 43–45.
123 See Harari 2017, 395–396.
124 Klein 2012, 359–362.
125 As Gil Klein noted regarding the relationship between the road and the triclinium: "This pair [road/triclinium] represents the divide separating inside and outside, private and public, academy and city, but also functions as a contact zone where insiders and outsiders, household members and guests, sages and commoners may meet," Klein 2012, 362.

negotium was (and is) not possible, the framing of talmudic texts as the product of leisure gives some liberty to juggle the material and move its formation beyond the study house and into the dining hall of the synagogue or a villa. Conversely, we may also start thinking of the study house as a place that could turn into a location for a banquet.[126]

Knowledge production needs incentives. In the case of the numerical maxims, these were the popularity of small significant units such as maxims and sayings and the social approval gained for outstanding performance, whether smart, witty, sharp, or wise. The maxims could serve all these functions, depending on their content, and they were always attractive due to their organization around numbers. The construction of these maxims needed participants, occasion, location, time, and material. The content of the maxims is so varied that everybody was able to compose them or at least to contributed to its construction by adding one or more elements. Occasions that may have stirred people to compose such maxims may have been public performances, games, the production of witty gift tags or dedications, or even the empty space on public walls.

Locations would have been the above-mentioned dining hall, the synagogue, the study house, or the marketplace, that is, places in which people celebrated or gathered for entertainment. I concluded that entertainment that engaged the attendees, rather than professional entertainers, was more likely to have produced numerical maxims, especially in rural settings. The time when some of these maxims were composed were times reserved for study, when the hustle and bustle of the busy times came to a halt: the night, winter and summer, the Sabbath, the holidays. Others may have emerged just because of the creative hustle and bustle, especially when we think of graffiti. As suitable material support served the already-mentioned wall, small leaf tablets (*pittacia*/פיתקא) or ostraca. Memory may have helped in the composition of these maxims, although retaining more than one maxim per finger or several numerical maxims on the same subject may have been confusing. Moreover, ancient mnemotechnical theory does not build on numbers but on places.[127]

The maxims' mnemotechnical value is only brought forward in the way the Talmud presents them associatively during a symposiac discussion. By so doing, the composers of the Talmud naturalize these crafty little units while actually repurposing them.

---

126 This approach ties in with recent suggestions to think of a "study city" instead of a study house (Klein 2012, 341) or a "marketplace of ... education" (Marks 2021, 307).
127 Small 1997, 83.

Bibliography

Africanus, S.J. (2012), *Cesti: The Extant Fragments*, M. Wallraff/C. Scardino/L. Mecella/ C. Guignard/W. Adler (trans.), Berlin.
Amsler, M. (forthcoming), *The Babylonian Talmud and Late Antique Book Culture*, Cambridge.
Ariès, P. (1996), *Centuries of Childhood* (with an introduction by Adam Philips), London.
Ausonius (1919), *Volume I: Books 1-17*, H.G. Evelyn White (trans.), Cambridge, MA.
Bagnall, R. (2018), "The Educational and Cultural Background of Egyptian Monks", in: L.I. Larsen/S. Rubenson (eds.), *Monastic Education in Late Antiquity*, Cambridge, 75–100.
Bagnall, R.S./Hope, C.A. (1997), *The Kellis agricultural account book: (P. Kell. IV Gr. 96)*, Oxford.
Baird, J.A. (2016), "Private Graffiti? Scratching the Walls of Houses in Dura-Europos", in: R.R. Benefiel/P. Keegan (eds.), *Inscriptions in the Private Sphere in the Greco-Roman World*, Leiden, 13–31.
Beagon, M. (1992), *Roman Nature: The Thought of Pliny the Elder*, Oxford.
Benefiel, R.R. (2012), "Magic Squares, Alphabet Jumbles, Riddles and More: The Culture of Word-Games among the Graffiti of Pompeii", in: J. Kwapisz/D. Petrain/M. Szymanski (eds.), *The Muse at Play. Riddles and Wordplay in Greek and Latin Poetry*, Berlin, 65–80.
Boyarin, D. (2009), *Socrates and the Fat Rabbis*, Chicago.
Brock, S.P. (2014), "Gabriel of Beth Qatraye as a Witness to Syriac Intellectual Life c. 600 CE", in: M. Kozah/A. Abu-Husayn/S.S. Al-Murikhi/H. Al Thani (eds.), *The Syriac Writers of Qatar in the Seventh Century*, Piscataway, 155–167.
Burkert, W. (1991), "Oriental Symposia: Contrasts and Parallels", in: W.J. Slater (ed.), *Dining in a Classical Context*, Ann Arbor, 7–24.
Cohn, B.S. (1980), "History and Anthropology: The State of Play", *Comparative Studies in Society and History* 22, 198–220.
Collins, D. (2004), *Master of the Game: Competition and Performance in Greek Poetry*, Washington D.C. [https://archive.chs.harvard.edu/CHS/article/display/6738, last accessed 11 October 2022].
Cribiore, R. (2001), *Gymnastics of the Mind. Greek Education in Hellenistic and Roman Egypt*, Princeton.
Cuomo, S. (1998), *Pappus of Alexandria and the Mathematics of Late Antiquity*, Cambridge.
Cuomo, S. (2001), *Ancient Mathematics*, London.
Dusil, S./Schwedler, G./Schwitter, R. (2017), "Transformationen des Wissens zwischen Spätantike und Frühmittelalter", in: *Millennium-Studien / Millennium Studies 64. Exzerpieren - Kompilieren - Tradieren. Transformationen des Wissens zwischen Spätantike und Frühmittelalter*, Berlin, 1–22.
Eliav, Y.Z. (2015), "The Material World of Babylonia as Seen from Roman Palestine: Some Preliminary Observations", in: M.J. Geller (ed.), *The Archaeology and Material Culture of the Babylonian Talmud*, Leiden, 153–185.
Euripides (2009), *Fragments: Oedipus-Chrysippus. Other Fragments*, C. Collard (ed. and trans.), Cambridge.
Executive Committee of the Editorial Board/Levias, C. (1906), "Numbers and Numerals", in: *Jewish Encyclopedia.com: The unedited full-text of the 1906 Jewish Encyclopedia*. Retrieved from https://www.jewishencyclopedia.com/articles/11619-numbers-and-numerals, last accessed February 6, 2023.

Fantham, E. (1996), *Roman Literary Culture. From Cicero to Apuleius*, Baltimore.
Feldman, W.M. (1931), *Rabbinical Mathematics and Astronomy*, New York.
Fischler, B.-Z. (2001), "Ten Batlanim (= Ten Men of Leisure)", in: W. Moskovich (ed.), *Festschrift Professor Allerhand: Judaeo-Slavica et Judaeo-Germanica*, Jerusalem, 178–184.
Fontaine, J. (1977), "Unité et diversité du mélange des genres et des tons chez quelques écrivains latins de la fin du Ive siècle : Ausone, Ambroise, Ammien", *Entretiens sur l'Antiquité Classique* 23, 425–482.
Formisano, M. (2007), "Towards an aesthetic paradigm of Late Antiquity", *Antiquite Tardive*, 277–284.
Gellius, A. (1927a), *Attic Nights, Volume I: Books 1-5*, J.C. Rolfe (trans.), Cambridge.
Gellius, A. (1927b), *Attic Nights, Volume III: Books 14-20*, J.C. Rolfe (trans.), Cambridge.
Gellius, A. (1927c), *The attic nights, Volume II: Books 6-13*, J.C. Rolfe (trans.), Cambridge.
Goodblatt, D.M. (1975), *Rabbinic Instruction in Sasanian Babylonia*, Leiden.
Hanson, A.E. (2005), "Greek Medical Papyri from the Fayum Village of Tebtunis: Patient Involvement in a Local Health-Care System?", in: P.J. van der Eijk (ed.), *Hippocrates in Context: Papers Read at the XIth International Hippocrates Colloquium University of Newcastle upon Tyne, 27-31 August 2002*, Leiden, 387–402.
Harari, Y. (2017), *Jewish Magic before the Rise of Kabbalah*, Detroit.
Harland, P.A./Instone-Brewer, D. (2008), "Jewish Associations in Roman Palestine: Evidence from the Mishna", *Journal of Greco-Roman Christianity and Judaism* 5, 200–221.
Heilmann, A. (2007), *Boethius' Musiktheorie und das Quadrivium. Eine Einführung in den neuplatonischen Hintergrund von "De Institutione Musica"*, Göttingen.
Hobgood, K. (undated), "Pythagoras and the Mystery of Numbers," accessed online under http://jwilson.coe.uga.edu/EMAT6680Fa06/Hobgood/Pythagoras.html, February 6, 2023.
Hunger, H. et al. (1978), *Die Hochsprachliche Profane Literatur der Byzantiner*, Munich.
Jacob, C. (2000), "Athenaeus the Librarian", in: D. Braud/J. Wilkins (eds.), *Athenaeus and his World: Reading Greek Culture in the Roman Empire*, Exeter, 85–110.
Jacobs, L. (1983), "The Numbered Sequence as a Literary Device in the Babylonian Talmud", *Hebrew Annual Review* 7, 137–149.
Kennedy, G.A. (2003), *Progymnasmata: Greek Textbooks of Prose Composition and Rhetoric*, Leiden.
Kiperwasser, R. (2018), "Narrative Bricolage and Cultural Hybrids in Rabbinic Babylonia: On the Narratives of Seduction and the Topos of Light", in: G. Herman/J.L. Rubenstein (eds.), *The Aggada of the Bavli and Its Cultural World*, Providence RI, 23–45.
Klein, G.P. (2012), "Torah in Triclinia: The Rabbinic Banquet and the Significance of Architecture", *The Jewish Quarterly Review* 102, 325–370.
König, J. (2012), *Saints and Syposiasts: The Literature of Food and the Symposium in Greco-Roman and Early Christian Culture*, Cambridge.
Krasser, H. (2005), "Universalisierung und Identitätskonstruktion. Formen und Funktionen der Wissenskodifikation im kaiserzeitlichen Rom", in: G. Oesterle (ed.), *Erinnerung, Gedächtnis, Wissen: Studien zur kulturwissenschaftlichen Gedächtnisforschung*, Göttingen, 357–376.
Krasser, H. (2019), "Me manus una capit: Von kleinen Büchern und ihren Lesern in Martials Epigrammen", in: C. Ritter-Schmalz/R. Schwitter (eds.), *Antike Texte und ihre Materialität: Alltägliche Präsenz, mediale Semantik, literarische Reflexion*, Berlin, 159–174.
Kuhn, R. (1976), *The Demon of Noontide: Ennui in Western Literature*, Princeton.
Lapin, H. (2012), *Rabbis as Romans: The Rabbinic Movement in Palestine, 100-400 CE*, New York.

Leary, T.J. (2015), *Symphosius, the Aenigmata: an Introduction, Text and Commentary*, London.
Lehmhaus, L. (2015), "Listenwissenschaft and the Encyclopedic Hermeneutics of Knowledge in Talmud and Midrash", in: J.C. Johnson (ed.), *In the Wake of the Compendia: Infrastructural Contexts and the Licensing of Empiricism in Ancient and Medieval Mesopotamia*, Berlin, 59–100.
Lehoux, D. (2012), *What Did the Romans Know? An Inquiry into Science and Worldmaking*, Chicago.
Levine, L.I. (2005), *The Ancient Synagogue: The First Thousand Years* (2nd ed.), New Haven.
Liddell, H.G./Scott, R. (1968), *A Greek-English Lexicon*, Oxford.
Lieber, L.S. (2014), "Setting the Stage: The Theatricality of Jewish Aramaic Poetry from Late Antiquity", *The Jewish Quarterly Review* 104, 537–572.
Lohmann, P. (2017), *Grafitti als Interaktionsform. Geritzte Inschriften an den Wohnhäusern Pompejis*, Materiale Textkulturen 16, Berlin.
Lowe, D. (2013), "Triple Tipple: Ausonius' Griphus ternarii numeri", in: J. Kwapisz/D. Petrain/M. Szymanski (eds.), *The Muse at Play Riddles and Wordplay in Greek and Latin Poetry*, Berlin, 335–352.
Luijendijk, A. (2014), *Forbidden Oracles? The Gospel of the Lots of Mary*, Tübingen.
Lougovaya, J. (2018), "Writing on Ostraca: Considerations of Material Aspects", in: F.A. Hoogendijk/S.M. van Gompel (eds.), *The Materiality of Texts from Ancient Egypt: New Approaches to the Study of Textual Material from the Early Pharaonic to the Late Antique Period*, Leiden, 52–61.
Luz, C. (2010), *Technopaignia: Formspiele in der griechischen Dichtung*, Leiden.
Marks, S. (2021), "Who Studied at the Beit Midrash?: Funding Palestinian Amoraic Education", *Journal of Ancient Judaism* 12, 281–312.
Martial (1993), *Epigrams, Volume I: Spectacles, Books 1-5*, D.R. Shackleton Bailey (trans.), Cambridge.
Morgan, T. (2007), *Popular Morality in the Early Roman Empire*, Cambridge.
Olmos, P. (2012), "Two Literary Encyclopaedias from Late Antiquity", *Studies in the History and Philosophy of Science* 43, 384–392.
Olszowy-Schlanger, J. (2014), "Un rotulus du midrash Pirqa de-Rabbenu ha-Qadosh de la Geniza du Caire", *Annuaire de l'École Pratique Des Hautes Études (EPHE), Section Des Sciences Historiques et Philologiques* 145, 26–40.
Oppenheimer, A. (1983), *Babylonia Judaica in the Talmudic Period*, Wiesbaden.
Pasternak, A.-R./Yona, S. (2016), "Numerical Sayings in the Literature of the Ancient Near East, in the Bible, in the Book of Ben-Sira and in Rabbinic Literature", *The Review of Rabbinic Judaism* 19, 202–244.
Pasternak, A.-R./Yona, S. (2017), "The Use of Numbers as an Editing Device in Rabbinic Literature", *The Review of Rabbinic Judaism* 20, 193–234.
Paton, W.R. (trans.) (1918), *The Greek Anthology, Volume V: Book 13: Epigrams in Various Metres. Book 14: Arithmetical Problems, Riddles, Oracles. Book 15: Miscellanea. Book 16: Epigrams of the Planudean Anthology Not in the Palatine Manuscript*, Cambridge.
Paz, Y./Weiss, T. (2015), "From Encoding to Decoding: The AṬBḤ of R. Hiyya in Light of a Syriac, Greek and Coptic Cipher", *Journal of Near Eastern Studies* 74, 45–65.
Philo (1939), *On the Special Laws, Book 4. On the Virtues. On Rewards and Punishments*, F.H. Colson (trans.), Cambridge.
Rathbone, D. (1991), *Economic rationalism and rural society in third-century A.D. Egypt: The Heroninus archive and the Appianus estate*, New York.

Relihan, J.C. (1992), "Rethinking the History of the Literary Symposium", *Illinois Classical Studies* 17, 213–244.
Roberts, M. (1988), "The Treatment of Narrative in Late Antique Literature: Ammianus Marcellinus (16.10), Rutilius Namatianus and Paulinus of Pella", *Philologus* 132, 181–195.
Rosenblum, J.D. (2020), *Rabbinic Drinking: What Beverages Teach Us About Rabbinic Literature*, Oakland.
Rubenstein, J.L. (2007), "Talmudic Astrology: Bavli Šabbat 156a-b", *Hebrew Union College Annual* 78, 109–148.
Salzman, M.R. (2018), "Symmachus' Varro: Latin Letters in Late Antiquity", *Bulletin of the Institute of Classical Studies* 61, 92–105.
Schwartz, J. (2010), "Play and Games", in: C. Hezser (ed.), *The Oxford Handbook of Jewish Daily Life in Roman Palestine*, Oxford, 641–653.
Sebo, E. (2012), "In scirpo nodum: Symphosius' Reworking of the Riddle Form", in: J. Kwapisz/ D. Petrain/M. Szymanski (eds.), *The Muse at Play: Riddles and Wordplay in Greek and Latin Poetry*, Berlin, 184–195.
Sidoli, N. (2014), "Mathematical tables in Ptolemy's Almagest", *Historia Mathematica* 41, 13–37.
Simon-Shoshan, M. (2008), "The heavens proclaim the glory of God...": a study in rabbinic cosmology, *Journal of Torah and Scholarship* 20, 67–96.
Simpson, S.J. (2015), "The Land Behind Ctesiphon: The Archaeology of Babylonia During the Period of the Babylonian Talmud", in: M. Geller (ed.), *The Archaeology and Material Culture of the Babylonian Talmud*, Leiden, 6–38.
Small, J.P. (1997), *Wax Tablets of the Mind. Cognitive Studies of Memory and Literacy in Classical Antiquity*, London.
Sogno, C. (2017), "The Letter Collection of Quintus Aurelius Symmachus", in: C. Sogno/ B.K. Storin/E.J. Watts (eds.), *Late Antique Letter Collections: A Critical Introduction and Reference Guide*, Oakland, 175–189.
Sokoloff, M. (2002), *Dictionary of Jewish Babylonian Aramaic of the Talmudic and Geonic Periods*, Jerusalem.
Stenger, J.R. (2019), "Learning Cities: A Novel Approach to Ancient paideia", in: J.R. Stenger (ed.), *Learning Cities in Late Antiquity: The Local Dimension of Education*, London, 1–23.
Stern, K.B. (2018), *Writing on the Wall: Graffiti and the Forgotten Jews of Antiquity*, Princeton.
Suetonius (2014), *Life of Augusts (Vita divi Augusti). Translated, with Introduction and Historical Commentary*, D. Wardle (trans.), Oxford.
Toner, J.P. (1995), *Leisure and Ancient Rome*, Cambridge.
Towner, S.W. (1973), *The Rabbinic "Enumeration of Scriptural Examples." A Study of a Rabbinic Pattern of Discourse with Special Reference to Mekhilta d' R. Ishmael*, Leiden.
Ullman, B.L. (1941), "Apophoreta in Petronius and Martial", *Classical Philology* 36, 346–355.
Valler, S. (1995), "The Number Fourteen as a Literary Device in the Babylonian Talmud", *Journal for the Study of Judaism in the Persian, Hellenistic, and Roman Period* 26, 169–184.
Venticinque, P.F. (2016), *Honor among Thieves: Craftsmen, Merchants, and Associations in Roman and Late Roman Egypt*, Ann Arbor.
Williams, M.H. (2013), "Alexander, bubularus de macello - Humble Sausage Seller or Europe's First Identifiable Purveyor of Kosher Meat", in: M.H. Williams, *Jews in a Graeco-Roman Environment* Tübingen, 155–166.
Zuckermann, B. (1878), *Das Mathematische im Talmud. Beleuchtung und Erläuterung der Talmudstellen mathematischen Inhalts*, Breslau.

Lillian I. Larsen
Re-scaffolding a 'Missing Chapter'

Abstract: The interpretive scaffolding that supports caricatured discussions of monasticism in Henri-Irénée Marrou's *History of Ancient Education* (Rappe 2001; cf. Marrrou 1956), richly elucidates Vincent Wimbush's assessment that "all historical interpretive efforts ... their methods and approaches illuminate some things, cast shadows over others ... they foreground some things, render into the background certain others" (Wimbush 1997, 1). Ironically, however, it is Marrou's *History* that simultaneously supplies a pedagogical toolkit to re-scaffold his interpretive efforts. Re-directing Marrou's methods and approaches, the present essay mines the rich interpretive shadows shaped by larger-than-life caricature. After identifying the foundational fissures that destabilize Marrou's "totalizing narrative" (Too 2001), it re-reads Marrou's pedagogical blueprints, so as to more securely re-assemble his evidentiary building blocks. The aim is not solely to re-scaffold what has been named a "missing chapter" in the history of education (Rappe 2001), but also to re-write what remains a missing chapter in the history of monasticism.

1 Introduction

Henri-Irénée Marrou's *History of Education in Antiquity*, introduces discussion of "the monastic school in the East" with the premise that the earliest monks would have received "a kind of training that was ascetic and moral, spiritual

---

Thanks to Dr. Monika Amsler for the invitation to present at the 'Knowledge Construction' workshop, from which this volume derives. Thanks, likewise, to Prof. Hayim Lapin and the Meyerhoff Center for Jewish Studies at University of Maryland, College Park, for their generosity in hosting this venture. Over the course of two days of rich conversation, engagement with each of the conference participants was truly a delight. The more explicit response offered by Dr. Daniel Picus was, likewise, joyfully generative.

rather than intellectual."¹ By selectively parsing an otherwise rich evidentiary base, his mid-twentieth century analysis names rejection of "intellectual" pursuits "one of the most characteristic features of 'Eastern' monasticism."² More explicitly, Marrou asserts that a "fundamental feature of Eastern monasticism" was its emphasis not on "learning … [but] forgetting … poetry and secular knowledge."[3]

In recent examination of the "influence of French colonial humanism on the study of late antiquity,"[4] Thomas Hunt demonstrates that Marrou's assessments are not unlike those readily encountered across a broader mid twentieth-century landscape.[5] The present essay documents the degree to which the subsequent geo-textual trajectory of Marrou's work has, in turn, rendered these assertions singularly influential.[6] First published in Paris in 1948, Marrou's recounting of the *Histoire de l'éducation dans l'antiquité*, saw five further editions in French. Between 1950 and 1969, it was translated into Italian (1950), English (1956), German (1957), Greek (1961), Spanish (1965), Polish (1969), and Portuguese (1969).[7] Given the scope of the text's geographical and chronological footprint, it is sobering — but perhaps not surprising — that one finds Marrou's interpretive scaffolding still mirrored in a 'commemorative' anthology published in 2001. Albeit aimed at "rethinking of Marrou's totalizing narrative,"[8] half a century post-publication, this North American iteration, serves rather to underscore the stubborn tenacity of Marrou's colonialist constructs.

As Marrou's *History* has structured knowledge of monastic education — across now three quarters of a century,[9] repairing the fissures that destabilize

---

1 In introducing this portion of the *History*, Marrou 1956, 330, writes: "St. Antony, the great founder of monasticism, was an illiterate Coptic peasant who was able to get on quite well without any books, as he soon proved to any philosophers who came and argued with him. This was a fundamental feature of Eastern monasticism and it was never lost: these desert people were less concerned with learning than with forgetting the poetry and secular knowledge they had picked up in the schools before conversion. Monasticism brought back into the Christian tradition the virtues of the simple and unlettered, as against the intellectual pride fostered by the old culture, which, as is clear from the Gnostics and the Alexandrians, was in the third century threatening to destroy the original simplicity of the Gospels".
2 Marrou 1956, 333.
3 Marrou 1956, 330.
4 Hunt 2018, 255–278, richly complexifies Marrou's overarching influence.
5 See discussion in Larsen 2007, 4–24; cf. Mack 1988; Clark 1999, 19–20.
6 Cf. Larsen 2001, 2007, 2013a, 2016, 2017, 2018a, 2018b, 2021.
7 As summarized by Riché 1977, 491–515, 493.
8 Y.L. Too 2001.
9 See, for example, relatively recent echoes in Wilken 2012, 99–108.

his interpretive foundations has grown ever more urgent. Ironically, however, it is Marrou's *History* that simultaneously supplies a pedagogical toolkit to re-structure his interpretive efforts. Re-directing Marrou's methods and approaches, the present essay mines the rich interpretive shadows shaped by larger-than-life caricature. After identifying the foundational fissures that destabilize Marrou's "totalizing narrative" (Too 2001), it re-reads Marrou's pedagogical blueprints, so as to more securely re-assemble his evidentiary building blocks. The aim is not solely to re-scaffold what has been named a "missing chapter" in the history of education (Rappe 2001), but also to re-write what remains a missing chapter in the history of monasticism.

2 Foundations

It is the case that sizable segments of the complex corpus of stories and sayings associated with emergent Christian monasticism merit closer investigation. However, among scholars (and even armchair *afficionadi*), one would be hard put to find even one reader of late-antique sources who is unfamiliar with narrative portrayals of the monks Antony, Arsenius and Evagrius, as a- and/or begrudgingly literate.[10]

In the most frequently referenced accounts, Antony is depicted as not only ἀγράμματος, but explicitly uninterested in "learn[ing] letters":

> Καὶ παιδίον μὲν ὢν, ἐτρέφετο παρὰ τοῖς γονεῦσι, πλέον αὐτῶν καὶ τοῦ οἴκου μηδὲν ἕτερον γινώσκων· ἐπειδὴ δὲ καὶ αὐξήσας ἐγένετο παῖς, καὶ προέκοπτε τῇ ἡλικίᾳ, γράμματα μὲν μαθεῖν οὐκ ἠνέσχετο, βουλόμενος ἐκτὸς εἶναι καὶ τῆς πρὸς τοὺς παῖδας συνηθείας· τὴν δὲ ἐπιθυμίαν πᾶσαν εἶχε ... ὡς ἄπλαστος οἰκεῖν ἐν τῇ οἰκίᾳ αὐτοῦ.
>
> [Antony was] cognizant of little else besides [his parents] and his home. As he grew and became a boy, and was advancing in years, he could not bear to learn letters, wishing also to stand apart from friendship with other children. All his yearning ... was for living, an unaffected person, in his home.[11]

---

10 The most notable early testimony to the *Vita*'s influence is Augustine's *Confessions* (8.6.15); cf. Gemeinhardt 2013.
11 Athanasius, *Vit. Ant.* 1 (PG 26: 841) in Gregg (transl.) 1980, 30.

With similar effect, the monks Arsenius and Evagrius are fashioned as 'begrudgingly' literate. In the first of two oft cited *apophthegmata*,[12] Evagrius queries Arsenius:

> *Quomodo nos excitati eruditione et scientia nullas virtutes habemus, hi autem rustici in Aegypto habitantes tantas virtutes possident?*
>
> How is it that we educated and learned men have no goodness, and the Egyptian peasants have a great deal?

Arsenius responds:

> *Nos quia mundanae eruditionis disciplinis intenti sumus, nihil habemus; hi autem rustici Aegyptii ex propriis laboribus acquisierunt virtutes.*
>
> We have nothing because we go chasing after worldly knowledge. These Egyptian peasants have got their goodness by hard work.[13]

---

12 Because they have long served as the conduit via which individuals encounter the 'Sayings of the Desert Fathers [and Mothers]' — and 'desert' monasticism, more generally, the present essay draws from the most readily accessible collections of 'sayings'. In English language editions, this includes the Greek Alphabetic collection (*AP/G*) translated by B. Ward and published as *The Sayings of the Desert Fathers: The Alphabetic Collection* (1975), and the topically organized Latin Systematic Collection (AP/Syst), also translated by Ward and published as *The Desert Fathers: Sayings of the Early Christian Monks* (2003). Until quite recently, Ward's inexpensive volumes were the loci where both critical scholars and lay readers became acquainted with the monastic *apophthegmata*. Over the past decade, J. Wortley's translations have likewise gained currency. However, the interpretive overlays that attend Wortley's renderings, commend Ward's more straightforward, and less theologically laden, prose.

13 AP/Syst 10.5 (Ward); cf. Πῶς ἡμεῖς ἀπὸ τοσαύτης παιδεύσεως καὶ σοφίας οὐδὲν ἔχομεν, οὗτοι δὲ οἱ ἀγροῖκοι καὶ Αἰγύπτιοι τοσαύτας ἀρετὰς κέκτηνται; Ἡμεῖς ἀπὸ τῆς τοῦ κόσμου παιδεύσεως οὐδὲν ἔχομεν· οὗτοι δὲ οἱ ἀγροῖκοι καὶ Αἰγύπτιοι ἀπὸ τῶν ἰδίων πόνων ἐκτήσαντο τὰς ἀρετάς (AP/G Arsenius 5). The chronology of particular sayings collections is a topic of wide debate. However, in contemporary scholarship, the work of Ch. Faraggiana is seminal. Faraggiana raises foundational questions about the conventional dating of this material, as well as the trajectories assumed in defining its transmission. As significant is Faraggiana's emphasis on the inherent instability of the *apophthegmatic* content included in extant collections. Faraggiana 1997 describes the underlying manuscript evidence for the most frequently cited alphabetic and systematic compilations, as "a stew of sources." Her assessment, in turn, troubles the ready availability that has rendered these compilations the 'go-to' material for 'authoritative' witness to normative 'desert'/monastic praxis. The studies of Dahlman 2018 and Holmberg 2013 are fundamentally informed by Faraggiana's scholarship, affirming and extending Faraggiana's groundbreaking insight.

In a second exchange, an unnamed protagonist challenges Arsenius while the latter is consulting an Egyptian γέρων about his thoughts. As reported, the interlocutor queries:

Ἀββᾶ Ἀρσένιε, πῶς τοσαύτην παίδευσιν Ῥωμαϊκὴν καὶ Ἑλληνικὴν ἐπιστάμενος, τοῦτον τὸν ἀγροῖκον περὶ τῶν σῶν λογισμῶν ἐρωτᾷς;

Abba Arsenius, how is it that you with such a good Latin and Greek education, ask this peasant about your thoughts?

Arsenius replies:

Τὴν μὲν Ῥωμαϊκὴν καὶ Ἑλληνικὴν ἐπίσταμαι παίδευσιν· τὸν δὲ ἀλφάβητον τοῦ ἀγροίκου τούτου οὔπω μεμάθηκα.

I have indeed been taught Latin and Greek, but I do not know even the alphabet of this peasant.[14]

Across generations, these foundational caricatures have been iteratively restated. Simultaneously, the interpretive fissures that de-stabilize Marrou's structural scaffolding have largely gone unnoticed.[15]

Re-scaffolding

Marrou's parsing of Antony, "the great founder of monasticism" as "an illiterate Coptic peasant who was able to get on quite well without any books,"[16] takes no account of the *Vita*'s later depictions, which complexify such assessment. His allusive portrayal of the classically educated Arsenius and Evagrius is similarly reductive. In broader monastic history, Arsenius is introduced as a tutor, formerly employed in the imperial household. In turn, Evagrius is best known for producing a synthetic corpus of monastic erudition — while living as a monk in Egypt.[17] Marrou's *History*, instead, designates these figures "desert" people, "less concerned with learning" than with rejecting and/or "forgetting [any] poetry and secular knowledge they had picked up in the schools before their conversion."[18]

---

14 AP/G Arsenius 6 (Ward).
15 See discussion in Larsen 2016.
16 Marrou 1956, 330.
17 See discussion in Larsen 2021, 313–332.
18 Marrou 1956, 330.

The caricatured, a- and begrudging literacies assigned Antony, Arsenius and Evagrius are foundational to Marrou's broader scaffolding of both 'eastern' and 'western' monasticism.[19] In turn, one might build an entire library of subsequent historical studies that remain firmly rooted in Marrou's caricatured refractions.[20] In re-scaffolding this *History*, however, it is important to note that later in Antony's *Vita*, Marrou's "illiterate peasant" is depicted counseling his disciples to "write down their thoughts ... as if reporting them to each other." Elsewhere, the *Vita* names "reading" a primary pastime in Antony's desert πόλις.[21] In the broader *apophthegmatic* record, Evagrius similarly commends reading to his disciples, "to strengthen a wandering mind."[22] In turn, a disciple of Arsenius is praised for his exemplary "fortitude" as he alternates between plaiting palm leaves and reading in his cell.[23]

3 Blueprints

Even as Marrou names rejection of literate pursuits a characteristic feature of emergent monastic life,[24] it is striking that in selectively scaffolding his *History*, he also identifies a subset of 'blueprints', which seek to regulate — and inadvertently document — persistent monastic investment in pedagogical pursuits.[25] As identified by Marrou, one is found in the earliest of two regulatory canons,

---

19 See Brakke 1995, for a more sanguine reading of Athanasius' prose.
20 Cf. Wilken 2012, 99–108.
21 *Vit. Ant.* 55 (Gregg): ... οὕτως, ἐὰν ὡς ἀπαγγέλλοντες ἀλλήλοις τοὺς λογισμοὺς γράφωμεν, μᾶλλον τηρήσομεν ἑαυτοὺς ἀπὸ λογισμῶν ῥυπαρῶν, αἰσχυνόμενοι γνωσθῆναι. Ἔστω οὖν ἡμῖν τὸ γράμμα ἀντὶ ὀφθαλμῶν τῶν συνασκητῶν· ἵνα, ἐρυθριῶντες γράφειν ὡς τὸ βλέπεσθαι, μήθ' ὅλως ἐνθυμηθῶμεν τὰ φαῦλα; cf. Rousseau 2000, 89–109. The practice — here attributed to Antony — surfaces earlier in the writings of Plato. It forms a recurring motif in subsequent philosophical discourse, and finds further echo in monastic sources. For example, in Step Four of John Climacus' sixth century *Ladder of Divine Ascent*, a monk/cellarer is depicted wearing a small notebook on his belt to keep track of his thoughts.
22 AP/Syst. 10.20 (Ward): *Dixit abbas Evagrius: Mentem nutantem vel errantem solidat lectio, et vigiliæ, et oratio.*
23 AP/Syst. 7.27 (Ward).
24 See preliminary discussion in Larsen 2007, 4–24. Hunt's examination of "The influence of French colonial humanism on the study of late antiquity" (2018) invites consideration of the degree to which such echoes can be traced to Marrou's influence.
25 See Larsen 2017, 147–174.

attributed to Basil of Caesarea;[26] a second, in Jerome's letter to a wealthy female householder in Rome.[27] A third, is included in John Chrysostom's apologetic, addressing "opponents of the monastic life."[28] A fourth appears in a collection of regulatory *Praecepta*, attributed to Pachomius.[29]

Basil (Caesarea, 329–379 CE)

The *Longer* of Basil's two regulatory corpora is generally numbered among the earliest monastic *Rules*. It is likewise in this primary, *Longer Rule*, that monastic pedagogy is most explicitly addressed. Here, Basil mandates that children held in common by the community should be educated according to a monastic "ideal." He recommends that both children and adults meet together for prayer, but that the groups be kept separate with respect to houses and meals. His rationale is straightforward. This is to insure that "the house of the monks ... not be disturbed by ... repetition of lessons necessary for the young."[30] Conceiving what may be most accurately regarded as an emergent monastic curriculum, Basil suggests that lessons include the "language of Scripture" and "maxims drawn from the Proverbs."[31] In place of "myths," he advises that instruction incorporate stories of wonderful deeds "so [that] ... [children's] soul[s] may be led to [practice] good immediately and from the outset, while [they are] still plastic and soft, pliable as wax, and easily molded by the shapes pressed upon [them]."[32] This is to insure that "when [with maturity] reason is added, and the

---

26 Basil, *Regula Fusius Tractate* (*Reg. Fus.*) 15 in *The Ascetic Works of Saint Basil*, Clarke (transl.) 1925, 175–178 [PG 31.952–957].
27 Jerome, *Epistle* (*Epist.*) 107 in *Select Letters of Jerome*, Wright (transl.) 1933, 338–370. Jerome's emergent 'Christian' curriculum likewise exhibits rich confluence with the *Institutio Oratoria* (*Inst.*) of Quintilian, penned in the 1st century CE.
28 John Chrysostom, *Adversus oppugnatores vitae monasticae* (*Adv. Opp.*) III (PG 47: 319–392) in Hunter (transl.) 1988.
29 Pachomius' *Praecepta* (*Praec.*) 139–140 in *Pachomiana Latina*, Boon (ed.) 1932, 50–51; *Pachomian Koininia 2: Chronicles and Rules*, Vielleux (ed. and transl.) 1981, 166.
30 καὶ ἅμα οὐδὲ θόρυβον ἕξει ὁ οἶκος τῶν ἀσκητῶν ἐν τῇ μελέτῃ τῶν διδαγμάτων ἀναγκαίᾳ οὔσῃ τοῖς νέοις (*Reg. Fus.* 15 [PG 31: 953; Clarke 1925, 176]).
31 ὥστε καὶ ὀνόμασιν αὐτοὺς τοῖς ἐκ τῶν Γραφῶν κεχρῆσθαι ... καὶ γνώμαις παιδεύειν ταῖς ἐκ τῶν Παροιμιῶν, καὶ ἆθλα μνήμης ὀνομάτων τε καὶ πραγμάτων αὐτοῖς προτιθέναι (*Reg. Fus.* 15 [PG 31: 953; Clarke 1925, 176–177]); cf. Gregory of Nyssa, *Vita Macrina* 962D.
32 καὶ ἀντὶ μύθων τὰς τῶν παραδόξων ἔργων ἱστορίας αὐτοῖς διηγεῖσθαι ... εὔπλαστον οὖν ἔτι οὖσαν καὶ ἀπαλὴν τὴν ψυχήν, καὶ ὡς κηρὸν εὔεικτον, ταῖς τῶν ἐπιβαλλομένων μορφαῖς ῥαδίως ἐκτυπουμένην, πρὸς πᾶσαν ἀγαθῶν ἄσκησιν εὐθὺς καὶ ἐξ ἀρχῆς ἐνάγεσθαι χρή (*Reg. Fus.* 15 [PG 31: 953–956; Clarke 1925, 177]).

power of discrimination, [early training will] run its course ... [and] habit will make success easy."³³

Jerome (Palestine, 347–420 CE)

The pedagogical blueprint included in a relatively contemporary letter, penned by Jerome, is still more explicit. Written in Palestine, this missive is addressed to Laeta — an elite Roman householder. The letter's primary focus, however, is the education of Laeta's young daughter, Paula.³⁴ Echoing broader Graeco-Roman practice, Jerome recommends that Laeta have "a set of letters made ... of boxwood or of ivory," so that young Paula may learn to call each by its proper name.³⁵ In order to know them by sight as well as by sound, he suggests that the child be made to grasp "not only ... the right order of the letters and remember their names in a simple song, but also frequently upset their order and mix the last letters with the middle ones, the middle with the first."³⁶

Moving from letters to syllables to words, Jerome advises that the very names (*ipse nomina*) Paula uses in forming sentences not be assigned haphazardly, but "chosen and arranged on purpose."³⁷ To aid in training both tongue and memory, he suggests wordlists include "the names of the prophets and the apostles, and the whole list of patriarchs from Adam downward, as [given by] Matthew and Luke."³⁸ Progressing to sentences and short passages, Jerome advises that Paula recite portions of Scripture, as a fixed daily task. These "verses" should be learned first in Greek, then in Latin. He recommends that the

---

33 ὥστε τοῦ λόγου προσγενομένου, καὶ τῆς διακριτικῆς ἕξεως προσελθούσης δρόμον ὑπάρχειν ... ἐκ τῶν ἐξ ἀρχῆς στοιχείων, καὶ τῶν παραδοθέντων τῆς εὐσεβείας τύπων, τοῦ μὲν λόγου τὸ χρήσιμον ὑποβάλλοντος, τοῦ δὲ ἔθους εὐμάρειαν πρὸς τὸ κατορθοῦν ἐμποιοῦντος (*Reg. Fus.* 15 [PG 31: 956; Clarke 1925, 177]); cf. Quintilian, *Inst.* 1.1.4.
34 *Ep.* 107 (Wright 1933, 338–371); cf. Quintilian, *Inst.* 1.1.1–37.
35 *Fiant ei litterae vel buxeae vel eburneae et suis nominibus appellentur* (*Ep.* 107 [Wright 1933, 344–347]).
36 ... *et non solum ordinem teneat litterarum, ut memoria nominum in canticum transeat, sed ipse inter se crebro ordo turbetur et mediis ultima, primis media misceantur ut eas non sonu tantum, sed et visu noverit* (*Ep.* 107 [Wright 1933, 346–347]); cf. Quintilian, *Inst.* 1.1.27.
37 *Ipsa nomina, per quae consuescet verba contexere, non sint fortuita, sed certa et coacervata de industria* (*Ep.* 107 [Wright 1933, 346–347]); cf. Quintilian, *Inst.* 1.1.30–5.
38 ... *prophetarum videlicet atque apostolorum, et omnis ab Adam patriarcharum series de Matheo Lucaque descendat, ut, dum aliud agit, futurae memoriae praeparetur* (*Ep.* 107 [Wright 1933, 346–347]); cf. Quintilian, *Inst.* 1.1.30–5.

child begin "with the sweet music of the Psalms,"[39] then (echoing Basil) turn to "lessons of life [found] in the proverbs of Solomon."[40]

Although ostensibly outlining an ideal 'home schooling' curriculum, Jerome concludes by emphasizing the difficulties implicit in Laeta's prioritizing such instructional goals amidst her broader household duties. He urges, rather, that young Paula be sent to Bethlehem, to be educated in a monastery. Here, in an establishment run by the child's grandmother (Paula, the elder), and aunt (Eustochium), he offers his own services as tutor. As Paula's ideal instructor, a man of "approved years, life, and learning," he likens his role to that of Aristotle — teaching Alexander "his first letters."[41]

John Chrysostom (Antioch, 347–407 CE)

Complementary commendations texture the writings of John Chrysostom. In his apologetic *Against Opponents of the Monastic Life*, Chrysostom likewise encourages Antiochene parents to send their children to be educated by local monks. Expanding the descriptive detail provided by Basil and Jerome, he suggests that instruction begin once boys have reached the age of ten and continue for at least ten years.[42] Like Basil and Jerome, he emphasizes the value of being tutored by spiritually approved masters, who will encourage students to develop both intellectual and moral strength.[43]

---

39 ... *adhuc tenera lingua psalmis dulcibus inbuator* (*Ep.* 107 [Wright 1933, 344–345]).
40 *Discat primum Psalterium ... et in Proverbiis Salomonis erudiatur ad vitam* (*Ep.* 107 [Wright 1933, 364–365]).
41 ... *magister probae aetatis et vitae atque eruditionis ... initia ei traderet litterarum*. In fact, Jerome offers to serve young Paula as "both her tutor and her foster-father." Carrying her on his shoulders, he will "train her stammering lips ... tak[ing] more pride in [his] task than ... the worldly philosopher; for ... [rather than] teaching a Macedonian king, destined to die by poison in Babylon, [he will instruct] the handmaid and bride of Christ who one day [will] be presented to the heavenly throne". *Ipse, si Paulam miseris, balbutientia senex verba formabo multo gloriosior mundi philosopho, qui non regem Macedonum Babylonio periturum veneno, sed ancillam et sponsam Christi erudiam regnis caelestibus offerendam* (*Ep.* 107 [Wright 1933, 368–371]). Elsewhere, Jerome's contemporary (and sometimes rival) Rufinus also depicts Jerome as a teacher — in this instance, charged with the education of young boys (*Apol.* II, 8, 592A; cf. *Hist. Mon.* 332–333). Rufinus reports that after Jerome "had settled in the monastery at Bethlehem, he took the office of a teacher in grammar." Rufinus additionally critiques Jerome for not limiting his instructional resources to biblical texts, but also introducing "the comedians ... lyrical and historical writers to the young boys who had been entrusted to him" (*Apol.* II 8 [NPNF²]).
42 Chrysostom, *Adv. Opp.* III 17–18.
43 Chrysostom, *Adv. Opp.* III 11–13; cf. Marrou 1956, 332.

Pachomius (Egypt, 320–340/340–404 CE; 292–346 CE)

Implicit to Marrou's caricatured depictions of Antony, Arsenius, and Evagrius, is scaffolding that frames Egyptian monasticism as trenchantly 'rustic'. However, early regulations attributed to Pachomius — often identified as the 'founder' of coenobitic monasticism in Egypt — are akin to those attributed to Basil, Chrysostom and Jerome.

Mirroring education as a fixed facet of emergent communal life,[44] the Pachomian *Praecepta* mandate that each newly entering monk, if unformed, should be given "twenty psalms or two of the Apostle's epistles, or some other part of the Scripture."[45] As explicitly, anyone who is illiterate (*litteras ignorabit*), is directed to go at the first, third and sixth hour

> ... *hora prima et tertia et sexta uadet ad eum qui docere potest et qui ei fuerit delegatus, et stabit ante illum, et discet studiosissime cum omni gratiarum actione. Postea uero scribentur ei elementa syllabae, uerba ac nomina, et etiam nolens legere compelletur.*

> ... to someone who can teach and has been appointed for him. He shall stand before him and learn very studiously with all gratitude. Then the fundamentals of a syllable, the verbs, and nouns shall be written for him, and even if he does not want to, he shall be compelled to read.[46]

An accompanying 'Precept' makes the aim of this instruction clear: "There shall be no one ... in the monastery who does not learn to read and does not memorize something of the Scriptures."[47]

Re-scaffolding

In addressing the complementary emphases that link these pedagogical 'blueprints', Marrou dismisses any details which might destabilize the interpretive

---

[44] That these injunctions may well address an alternate demographic, adds critical valence to depictions of tensive encounters between elite and 'garden variety' monks; see Larsen 2012a, 245–260; Larsen 2012b, 307–328.

[45] ... *dabunt ei uiginti psalmos uel duas epistulas apostoli, aut alterius scripturae partem* (Praec. 139 [Boon 1932, 49–50; Vielleux 1980, 2.166]).

[46] *Praec.* 139 (Boon 1932, 49–50; Vielleux 1980, 2.166). In later redaction, Caesarius of Arles echoes this Pachomian mandate in legislation addressed to a community of female monastics. See further discussion in Larsen, forthcoming.

[47] ... *et omnino nullus erit in monasterio qui non discat litteras et de scripturis aliquid teneat* (Praec. 140 [Boon 1932, 50; Vielleux 1980, 2.166]).

scaffolding which buttresses his *History*. For example, when discussing Basil's regulatory prescriptions, Marrou reduces the *Longer Rule's* detailed instructions to the simple question of whether such lessons would have been aimed at "young monks" or "children of the world."[48] In turn, he reframes the curricular commendations included in Jerome's letter *ad Laeta* as a singular instance of service to a close family friend.[49] Marrou also downplays the pedagogical parameters included in John Chrysostom's *Opponents of the Monastic Life*,[50] noting that in later writing, Chrysostom appears to limit the scope of 'Christian' education to the household.[51] Finally, although Marrou affirms the pedagogical priorities explicitly articulated in the Pachomian *Praecepta*, he shifts the focus of included mandates to remedial reading and rote recitation of scripture.[52]

Inversely incongruous with foundational caricatures of Antony, Arsenius and Evagrius, is Marrou's suggestion that 'western' monasticism reflects an "utterly different state of affairs."[53] Here, he identifies "the reading of Holy Scripture, and above all [recitation of] the Office" as "essential to any full monastic life."[54] In fact, he argues that in "western" communal structures, "there was a kind of automatic association between monks and the written word."[55] Astutely observing that this was the case "even in an environment as utterly remote from classical culture as Ireland,"[56] he inadvertently mirrors the patent precedents that link 'eastern' and 'western' practice. In short, when "adopting a boy … to become a monk," Patrick first "baptized [the child] and then gave him an alphabet."[57]

---

48 Marrou 1956, 332.
49 As noted above, notwithstanding, Rufinus — Jerome's contemporary, likewise situates him within a monastic pedagogical setting — as instructor to a group of young boys.
50 Chrysostom, *Adv. Opp.* III 11–13.
51 Marrou 1956, 332. There is, simultaneously, good evidence to suggest that a diversity of positions, even within the writings of a single author, reflects wider debate. See, for example, Thomas of Marga, *Book of Governors* I 74.3–10, 75.1–14, as discussed in Becker 2006, 169–171.
52 Marrou 1956, 330–331.
53 Marrou 1956, 333.
54 Marrou 1956, 333.
55 Marrou 1956, 333.
56 Marrou 1956, 333.
57 As cited in Marrou 1956, 333; cf. *Vit. Pat.* II. Countering Marrou's constructs, Patrick's practice appears akin to that delineated in 'eastern' monastic legislation attributed to Basil, Jerome, Chrysostom and Pachomius.

4 Building Blocks

Across Marrou's geographic and interpretive binaries, what emerges from extant 'blueprints' is a monastic instructional curriculum, uniformly comprised of discrete components. These 'building blocks' of letters and alphabets, syllables, words, sentences, and passages, likewise align with Marrou's overarching summary of broader pedagogical scaffolding:

> The master began by teaching the child to draw the letters one by one... Once the child had learned how to do it he would go on practicing (*sic*), repeating the same letter for a line or a page at a time. After the letters came the syllables ... then ... single words ... then short sentences... But from the second century A.D. onwards ... short passages ... were used—aphorisms—*chreiai*—commonly attributed to Diogenes, and a whole stock of short maxims—*gnomoi monostichoi*—supposedly the work of Menander.[58]

Given Marrou's foundational premise that a "fundamental feature of Eastern monasticism" was its emphasis not on "learning ... [but] forgetting ... secular knowledge,"[59] broad discussion of these 'building blocks' is notably absent from any address of an 'eastern' monastic frame. However, by virtue of climate, it is the case that a sizable portion of the 'building blocks' Marrou uses to derive and elucidate the 'classical' precedents of 'western' classroom forms are not only Egyptian, but monastic in provenance.[60]

Letters and Alphabets

Marrou reports that in the ancient world — as in the contemporary — conventional classroom instruction began with "teaching ... child[ren] to draw the letters one by one."[61] The monastic 'blueprints' sketched by Basil, Jerome, Chrysostom, Pachomius (and Patrick), likewise identify letters and alphabets as primary pedagogical building blocks. In turn, each echoes established commendation of "giving [children] ... letters to play with" in order to stimu-

---

58 Marrou 1956, 156; cf. *History of Education* 400 (8).
59 Marrou 1956, 330.
60 Cribiore 2001 offers a useful case in point. Cribiore's seminal reconstruction of Graeco-Roman pedagogical practice takes Egypt as its primary focus. See also, Cribiore 1996; Morgan 1998; Cf. See Larsen 2018a, 101–124; cf. Larsen 2013b, 1–34; Larsen 2017, 147–174.
61 Marrou 1956, 156.

late learning.⁶² Once the letters had been sufficiently fixed in a child's mind in "their usual order," both conventional and monastic curricula advise "revers[ing] that order or rearrang[ing] it in every kind of combination," so that young pupils "learn to know the letters by their appearance and not from the order in which they occur."⁶³

Four alphabetic exercises — respectively associated with three Egyptian monastic sites — usefully concretize this descriptive scaffolding. The first, provenanced to the Monastery of Epiphanius in Thebes, preserves a Greek alphabet in "the right order" (Jerome, *Epist.* 107). Penned in an informal, but practiced hand, the alphabet's twenty-four characters are spread over four horizontal lines and formed to fit the shape of an irregular ostracon. Affirming monastic, if not explicitly pedagogical purpose, the alphabet is followed by a brief line of text: θεοφιλεστατοι μοναχοι ("...monks most beloved of God") (fig. 8).⁶⁴

---

62 Quintilian, *Inst.* 1.1.26 (Russell 2001); *Non excludo autem, id quod est inventum irritandae ad discendum infantiae gratia eburneas etiam litterarum formas in lusum offerre.*
63 Quintilian, *Inst.* 1.1.25 (Russell 2001); *Quae causa est praecipientibus, ut etiam, cum satiss adfixisse eas pueris recto illo quo primum scribi solent contextu videntur, retro agant rursus et varia permutatione turbent, donec litteras qui instituuntur facie norint non ordine*; cf. Jerome, *Ep.* 107; Pachomius, *Praec.* 138–139.
64 O.MMA. 12.180.107; *ed. pr.* Crum/Winlock/Evelyn White (eds.) 1926, 136 and 322 no. 620; cf. Cribiore 1996, 189 no. 67. Although such an alphabet would routinely be designated as a 'school' artifact, when discussing monastic remains, assignation of pedagogical purpose is less consistent. Here debates often hinge on differentiating scribal from school practice. However, per Quintilian (*Inst.* 1.1.27–8) and Jerome (*Epist.* 107.4), it is clear that both pre-suppose pedagogical investment; cf. Amsler, this volume; Marks 2021, 281–312. Alternately diverse perspectives on this question are respectively captured in the essays of Bagnall, Larsen, Maravela, and Lundhaug/Jenott in Larsen/Rubenson 2018; cf. Bucking 2007.

Fig. 8: Greek Alphabet, Monastery of Epiphanius (O.MMA. 12.180.107).

A second artifact — also provenanced to the Monastery of Epiphanius — survives only in fragments.[65] Re-assembled, these preserve patterned letters organized in successive horizontal rows. Each re-constructed row is comprised of nine letters. The four initial and the four final characters are *betas*. These precede and follow an alphabetically sequenced central character, thus: ΒΒΒΒΑΒΒΒΒ / ΒΒΒΒΒΒΒΒΒ /

---

65 O.MMA. 14.1.188; *ed pr.* Crum/Evelyn White 1926, Vol. 2, 118 and 298 no. 576; O.BM. Inv 19082, 18816, 18798, 18972; *ed. pr.* Hall 1905, 36 pl. 29, no. 2; cf. Cribiore 1996, 181 no. 34, pl. I; Hasitzka 1990, 42 no. 39; Larsen 2013b, 17 and 26. Although respective sherds have been variously categorized, there is good evidence to support both pedagogical purpose and monastic provenance; cf. Larsen 2018a, 101–124.

ᴃᴃᴃᴃΓᴃᴃᴃᴃ / ᴃᴃᴃᴃΔᴃᴃᴃᴃ, etc. Careful iteration concretizes Marrou's suggestion that "once [a] child had learned how to [form a letter s/]he would go on practicing (*sic*), repeating the same letter for a line or a page at a time."⁶⁶ In turn, both patterned content, and rough execution suggest practice aimed not only at building alphabetic knowledge, but also forming letters with "frequency," and eventually, "speed" (Quintilian, *Inst.* 1.1.28; Cf. Jerome, *Ep.* 107.4) (fig. 9).⁶⁷

Fig. 9: Writing Exercise, Monastery of Epiphanius (O.MMA.14.1.188).

---

66 Marrou 1956, 156.

67 In emphasizing the importance of fluency in writing the alphabet, Jerome echoes Quintilian, who notes that while some might deem "the art of writing well and quickly ... unimportant," learning to efficiently shape letters is essential to later study because "a sluggish pen delays thoughts" Quintilian, *Inst.* 1.1.28 (Russell 2001); *Non est aliena res, quae fere ab honestis negligi solet, cura bene ac velociter scribendi ... tardior stilus cogitationem moratur*[!] Quintilian commends practice be structured so that students develop a steady hand by following "fixed outlines" with increasing "frequency and speed" (Quintilian, *Inst.* 1.1.27; Russell 2001); *... et celerius ac saepius sequendo certa vestigia firmabit articulos*. Jerome's instructions are less detailed, but commensurate. He suggests that when young Paula "begins with uncertain hand to use the pen," her fingers should be guided to "follow outlines" until she is able to form the letters on her own "without straying away" (*Epist.* 107.4; Wright 1933); *Cum vero coeperit trementi manu stilum in cera ducere, vel alterius superposita manu teneri regantur articuli vel in tabella sculpantur elementa, ut per eosdem sulcos inclusa marginibus trahantur vestigia et foras non queant evagari.*

An exercise preserved on both sides of a third ostracon is as interesting. Generally provenanced to Thebes, and provisionally associated with the Monastery of Phoibammon, the ostracon's included content consists of five alphabets. Penned in a less than practiced hand, the exercise is organized in horizontal lines. As transcribed by Anneliese Biedenkopf-Ziehner, the ostracon's first and third alphabets — two of three included on the *recto* — follow conventional alphabetic order. The second alphabet variously "reverse[s] that order." In turn, a fourth alphabet — the first of two preserved on the *verso* face — presents a "rearranged" sequence of letters (Quintilian, *Inst.* 1.1.25; cf. Jerome, *Epist.* 107.4). The first letter of this alphabet is paired with the last, the second with the second to last, the third with third to last, thus: ⲁ ⲱ, ⲃ ⲯ, ⲅ ⲭ ... ⲙ ⲛ.

The ostracon's fifth alphabet is incomplete. Adhering to an overall pattern of interspersed sequencing, however, like the first and third, the fifth alphabet appears to follow the "usual order." Four of the five alphabets begin with a chrism, a symbol which additionally serves to separate one iteration from the next. In turn, both content and execution concretize classroom practice that insured "not only ... grasp[ing] the right order of ... letters" but also routinely "upset[ting] their order and mix[ing] the last letters with the middle ones, the middle with the first" (Jerome, *Epist.* 107.4; cf. Quintilian, *Inst.* 1.1.25) (tab. 1).[68]

Tab. 1: Mixed Alphabets, Thebes AM 21 (C.O. 16).

(V) ☧	ⲁ ⲃ ⲅ ⲇ ⲉ ⲍ ⲏ ⲑ ⲓ ⲕ ⲗ
	ⲙ ⲛ ⳉ ⲟ ⲡ ⲣ ⲥ ⲧ ⲩ ⲫ ⲭ
	ⲯ ⲱ
☧	ⲱ ⲯ ⲭ ⲫ ⲩ ⲧ ⲥ ⲣ ⲡ ⲟ
	ⳉ ⲟ ⲡ ⲣ ⲥ ⲧ ⲩ ⲫ ⲭ ⲯ ⲱ
[☧]	ⲁ ⲃ ⲅ ⲇ ⲉ ⲍ ⲏ ⲑ ⲓ ⲕ ⲗ
	ⲙ ⲛ ⳉ ⲟ ⲡ ⲣ ⲥ
(R) ☧	ⲁ ⲱ ⲃ ⲯ ⲅ
	ⲭ ⲇ ⲫ ⲉ ⲩ ⲍ
	ⲧ ⲏ ⲥ ⲑ ⲣ ⲓ ⲡ
	ⲕ ⲟ ⲗ ⳉ ⲙ ⲛ
☧	ⲁ ⲃ ⲅ ⲇ ⲉ

---

68 AM 21 (C.O. 16); As published in Biedenkopf-Ziehner 2000, 137–144, Taf. 17.

A fourth example is preserved, not on an ostracon, but rather the plastered wall of a re-used tomb. It is provenanced not to Thebes, but to the middle-Egyptian Pharaonic site of Beni Hasan.[69]

Faintly visible — in a space variously identified by its use as a pedagogical locus,[70] and/or occupation by late ancient monks[71] — it is comprised of a series of three alphabets arranged in squarish sectors.[72] Like the interspersed, iterative sequences preserved in the student exercise examined above (tab. 1), the first sector includes an alphabet sequenced in conventional order; the second, an alphabet in reverse order; the third, an alphabet of mixed sequencing (tab. 2; cf. fig. 10). The three iterations, as a unit, appear to be aimed at facilitating practice with "learn[ing] to know letters by their appearance and not [solely] from the order in which they occur" (Quintilian, *Inst.* 1.1.25; cf. Jerome, *Epist.* 107.4).[73]

Tab. 2: Mixed Alphabets, Beni Hasan.

ⲁ ⲃ ⲅ ⲇ ⲉ ⲍ	ⲱ ⲯ ⲭ ⲫ ⲩ ⲧ	ⲁ ⲱ ⲃ ⲯ ⲅ ⲭ
ⲏ ⲑ ⲓ ⲕ ⲗ ⲙ	ⲥ ⲣ ⲡ ⲟ ⲝ ⲛ	ⲇ ⲫ ⲉ ⲩ ⲍ ⲧ
ⲛ ⲝ ⲟ ⲡ ⲣ ⲥ	ⲙ ⲗ ⲕ ⲓ ⲑ ⲏ	ⲏ ⲣ ⲫ ⲡ ⲓ ⲟ ⲥ
ⲧ ⲩ ⲫ ⲭ ⲯ ⲱ	ⲑ ⲉ ⲇ ⲅ ⲃ ⲁ	ⲕ ⲝ ⲗ ⲛ ⲙ

---

69 See Larsen 2017, 153 fig. 10 for photo.
70 Cribiore 2001, 23–24.
71 Bucking 2007, 40.
72 The recurring classroom detail that textures monastic *apophthegmatic* sources invites new appreciation for the 'apt' wit that characterizes assertions like that attributed to Arsenius, who with all his "Latin and Greek education" does not yet "know the "alphabet" of an Egyptian ἀγροῖκος (AP/G Arsenius 6). As noteworthy is the implicit irony of precisely these 'sayings' being used to argue against monastic investment in literate pursuits. See additional discussion in Larsen 2008, 21–30; cf. Larsen 2013b, 1–30.
73 Cf. Newberry 1893 (Vol. 2), 76–77, pl. XXV. The alphabets are not included in J.F. Champollion's initial publication of the site, *Monuments de l'Égypte et de la Nubie*, 1889. Instead, the three sectors are simply described as "Composé des Lettres de l'alphabet, voyelles et consonnes melées sans ordre" (459). Perhaps derivatively, the alphabets have remained peripheral to broader scholarly discussion of this body of school evidence. While Newberry's 1893 publication includes the alphabets, their distinctive character is not mentioned; cf. Larsen 2018a, 101–124.

Syllables

The attention Marrou accords syllables is relatively cursory. In his brief summary of the ancient curriculum, he simply notes that "after the letters came the syllables."[74] Here again, however, there is little in 'eastern' monastic curricular 'blueprints' that suggests alternate pedagogical protocol. The Pachomian *Praecepta* explicitly mandate that each newly entering monk, if "ignorant of letters," should with all gratitude "go at the first, third and sixth hour to someone who can teach" in addition to letters, "the fundamentals of a syllable."[75] In turn, the role of repetition is emphasized in both monastic and Graeco-Roman classroom protocol. In particular, Quintilian notes that with respect to syllables "no short cut is possible: they must all be [thoroughly] learnt." He additionally warns that "there is no good in putting off … the most difficult … [for] the sole result is bad spelling."[76] Urging caution in "placing … blind confidence in a child's memory," he commends both repetition, and adjusting the pace while reading — so that "clear and obvious sequence[s] of letters can suggest [themselves] without [it] being necessary for [a] child to stop to think."[77] What is known of the auditory dimension of such practice, in turn, adds meaningful resonance to Basil's suggestion that the living quarters of adults and children be kept separate, so that "the house of the monks … not be disturbed by … repetition of lessons necessary for the young."[78]

---

[74] Marrou 1956, 156.
[75] *Praec.* 139 (Boon; Vielleux).
[76] Quintilian, *Inst.* 1.1.30–31 (Russell 2001); *Syllabis nullum compendium est; perdiscendae omnes nec, ut fit plerumque, difficillima quaeque earum differenda, ut in nominibus scribendis deprehendantur.*
[77] Quintilian, *Inst.* 1.1.31 (Russell 2001); *Quin immo ne primae quidem memoriae temere credendum; repetere et diu inculcare fuerit utilius, et in lectione quoque non properare ad continuandam eam vel accelerandam, nisi cum inoffensa atque indubitata litterarum inter se coniunctio suppeditare sine ulla cogitandi saltem mora poterit.*
[78] Basil, *Reg. Fus.* 15 (PG 31.953; Clarke); καὶ ἅμα οὐδὲ θόρυβον ἕξει ὁ οἶκος τῶν ἀσκητῶν ἐν τῇ μελέτῃ τῶν διδαγμάτων ἀναγκαίᾳ οὔσῃ τοῖς νέοις; cf. Cribiore 2001, 23–24; discussion of Basil, above.

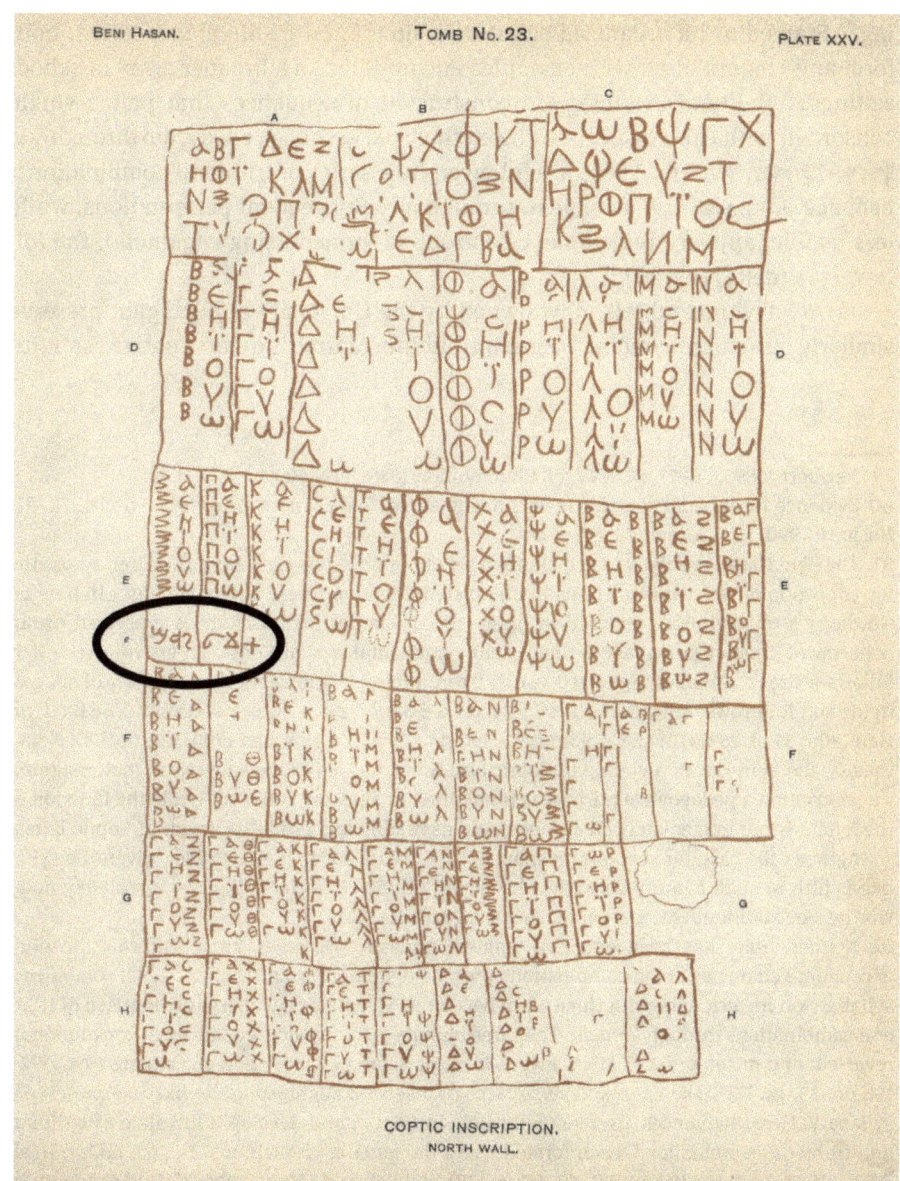

Fig. 10: Alphabets and Syllabary, Beni Hasan (Newberry 1893, Pl. XXV) © Universitätsbibliothek Heidelberg.

The rough chart of syllabic combinations, penned below the mixed Beni Hasan alphabets (fig. 10) are 'building blocks' that concretize this descriptive scaffolding.⁷⁹ Framed as an organized series of bi-literal and tri-literal sequences, both form and content align with examples encountered in a broader array of school settings.⁸⁰ Bi-literal syllables are constructed of sequences that pair a single consonant with each respective vowel, thus: ⲃⲁ, ⲃⲉ, ⲃⲏ, ⲃⲓ, ⲃⲟ, ⲃⲩ, ⲃⲱ through ⲯⲁ, ⲯⲉ, ⲯⲏ, ⲯⲓ, ⲯⲟ, ⲯⲩ, ⲯⲱ. These are followed by a series of tri-literal combinations: ⲃⲁⲃ, ⲃⲉⲃ, ⲃⲏⲃ, ⲃⲓⲃ, ⲃⲟⲃ, ⲃⲩⲃ, ⲃⲱⲃ, through ⲃⲁⳉ. Subsequent permutations, while less legible, appear predictable. One group is formed using ⲅ (gamma), the following, ⲇ (delta) (fig. 10).⁸¹

Two Fayyumic tablets, now owned by the University of Michigan, preserve similarly structured content.⁸² Again, troubling Marrou's determinative scaffold-

---

79 Newberry 1893, 76–77, pl. XXV; cf. Champollion 1889, 459–460.
80 Evidence for broader practice is well documented. See Cribiore 1996, 191–196 nos. 78–97; Hasitzka 1990, 1.55–63 nos. 73–82; et al.
81 The Beni Hasan syllabary also includes a set of Coptic letters (ϣ ϧ ⲍ ⳉ ⳋ ϯ) written across the lower portion of two segments of its bi-literal combinations. These letters are offset in blue on Newberry's transcription, pictured in figure 10c. A similar juxtaposition is preserved on an ostracon of Theban provenance. Here, a fifth horizontal row of Coptic letters (ϣ ϧ ⲍ ⳉ ⳋ ϯ) follows a Greek alphabet organized vertically in a regular arrangement comprised of six columns and four rows: α β γ δ / ε ζ η θ / ι κ λ μ / ν ξ ο π / ρ σ τ υ / φ ψ χ ω (O.BM. 31663; ed. pr. Hall 1905, 35 pl. 28 no. 4; cf. Cribiore 1996, 190 no. 72, pl. VI; Hasitzka 1990, 1.51 no. 64). Nonetheless, the Beni Hasan blending of Coptic and Greek has led to the suggestion that assigning the inscription a pedagogical purpose is premature; cf. Bucking 2007, 40. While the function of the letters is not immediately clear, one could as readily argue that inclusion of Coptic letters strengthens the case for school provenance; cf. Cribiore 2001, 24–25. In fact, given the syllabary's fifth to sixth century date, the absence of Coptic characters might be alternately noteworthy. See additional discussion in Larsen 2018a, 101–124.
82 Neither tablet has been explicitly named monastic. However, each reaffirms the nonexceptional character of the combinations preserved at Beni Hasan. The first tablet combines a syllabary on its *recto* face with three alphabets on its *verso*. The syllabary is comprised of triliteral combinations through *lambda*. The three alphabets are, again, sequenced in conventional, reversed, and mixed order (T.Mich. inv. 763; ed. pr. Boak 1921, 189–194; cf. Cribiore 1996, 192–193 no. 83, pl. VII). The *recto* and *verso* faces of a second Michigan tablet likewise preserve a syllabary. Here, sequences are rendered solely in Coptic, and develop a full slate of bi-literal and tri-literal combinations, each formed using the letter ⲱ (T.Mich. inv. N. 765; *Ed. pr.* Boak 1923, 296–297; cf. Hasitzka 1990, 59–60 no. 78). Published by Husselman, a third syllabary in the Michigan collection is preserved within a classroom codex, which contains a range of school related content (P. Mich. Inv. 926; *ed. pr.* Husselman 1947; cf. Hasitzka 1990, 133–138 no. 207 Fol. 1v–5r). Husselman identifies the syllabary's combination of Greek and Bohairic as particularly significant. While, again, no secure monastic provenance is claimed, in passing, Husselman suggests possible links to "a [monastic] settlement on the edge of the desert to the south of Theadelphia" (129). As interesting are the extensive syllabaries included in two relatively late Egyptian grammars used by Arabic speaking monks, tasked with learning Coptic.

ing (and countering long tradition of privileging Greek over Coptic, when identifying classroom media),[83] both the *recto* and *verso* of the second of these tablets preserves content comprised of syllabic combinations which begin with (ϣ) *shai* (tab. 3):[84]

Tab. 3: Coptic Syllabary, The Fayyum (T.Mich. inv. N. 765).

Recto											
ϣⲁ	[ϣⲁⲃ]	[ϣⲁ]ⲅ	ϣ[ⲁ]ⲇ	[ϣⲁz]	ϣⲁⲑ	ϣⲁⲓ	ϣⲁⲕ	ϣⲁⲗ	ϣⲁⲙ	ϣⲁⲛ	ϣⲁϫ	ϣⲁⲡ
ϣⲉ	ϣⲉⲃ	ϣⲉⲅ	ϣⲉⲇ	ϣ[ⲉz]	ϣⲉⲑ	ϣⲉⲓ	ϣⲉⲕ	ϣⲉⲗ	ϣⲉⲙ	ϣⲉⲛ	ϣⲉϫ	ϣⲉⲡ
ϣⲏ	ϣⲏⲃ	ϣⲏⲅ	ϣⲏⲇ	ϣⲏ[z]	ϣⲏⲑ	ϣⲏⲓ	ϣⲏⲕ	ϣⲏⲗ	ϣⲏⲙ	ϣⲏⲛ	ϣⲏϫ	ϣⲏⲡ
ϣⲓ	ϣⲓⲃ	ϣⲓⲅ	ϣⲓⲇ	ϣⲓz	ϣⲓⲑ	ϣⲓⲓ	ϣⲓⲕ	ϣⲓⲗ	ϣⲓⲙ	ϣⲓⲛ	ϣⲓϫ	ϣⲓⲡ
[ϣⲟ]	ϣⲟⲃ	ϣⲟⲣ	ϣⲟⲇ	ϣⲟz	ϣⲟⲑ	ϣⲟⲓ	ϣⲟⲕ	ϣⲟⲗ	ϣⲟⲙ	ϣⲟⲛ	ϣⲟϫ	ϣⲟⲡ
[ϣⲩ]	ϣⲩⲃ	ϣⲩⲅ	ϣⲩⲇ	ϣ[ⲩz]	ϣⲩⲑ	ϣⲩⲓ	ϣⲩⲕ	ϣⲩ[ⲗ]	ϣⲩⲙ	ϣⲩⲛ	ϣⲩϫ	ϣⲩⲡ
[ϣⲱ]	ϣⲱⲃ	ϣⲱⲣ	ϣⲱⲇ	[ϣⲱz]	ϣⲱⲑ	ϣⲱⲓ	ϣⲱⲕ	ϣⲱ[ⲗ]	ϣⲱⲙ	ϣⲱⲛ	ϣⲱϫ	[ϣ]ⲱ[ⲡ]

Words

When introducing work with "single words," Marrou suggests that the "master would draw initials in alphabetical order on an ostracon and the child would add the rest of the word."[85] In parallel delineation, Quintilian suggests that after learning the syllables, it is important that "students begin to construct words with them."[86] Jerome, again, follows Quintilian, who cautions against "wast[ing] … labour in writing out common words of everyday occurrence." In mirrored prose, each instead commends "learn[ing] … more obscure words" (with attendant explanations), in order to "acquire [knowledge that] would otherwise demand special time … be devoted to it" later on.[87] Pachomius abbre-

---

(Thanks to H. Takla for calling these texts to my attention, and to J. Fahim for his work in addressing included Arabic content).
83 Cf. Larsen 2017; 2018a.
84 A.E.R. Boak, "A Coptic Syllabary at the University of Michigan," *Aegyptus* 4 (1923), 296–297; cf. Hasitzka, nr. 78.
85 Marrou 1956, 156.
86 Quintilian, *Inst.* 1.1.31 (Russell 2001); *Tunc ipsis syllabis verba complecti …*
87 Quintilian, Inst. 1.1.34–35 (Russell 2001); *Illud non poenitebit curasse, cum scribere nomina puer (quemadmodum moris est) coeperit, ne hanc operam in vocabulis vulgaribus et forte occurrentibus perdat. Protinus enim potest interpretationem linguae secretioris … dum aliud agitur,*

viates more detailed instruction into a cryptic progression of working from the "fundamentals of a syllable, [to] verbs, [then] nouns."⁸⁸

Although not explicitly identified as a school exercise, it is interesting to consider whether a mundane word list, provenanced to the Monastery of Epiphanius and preserved on a papyrus fragment (not pictured), depicts routine classroom practice. Comprised of a simple list of bird names, these are enumerated in Greek with Coptic equivalents.⁸⁹ A second Epiphanian list includes days of the week, in various combinations of Christian and/or "planetary" nomenclature (fig. 11).⁹⁰

Alternately elucidating are the sequences included in a set of 'word lists', preserved *in situ* at Beni Hasan.⁹¹ Arranged in small clusters, and in variously dispersed combinations, these are comprised of biblical (and/or monastic) names: ⲛⲱⲉ[ⲉ] (Noah), ⲁⲃⲣⲁⲍⲁⲙ (Abraham), ⲓ[ⲥⲁ]ⲕ (Isaac), [ⲓⲁⲕⲱ]ⲃ (Jacob), ⲓⲱⲥⲏⲫ (Joseph) … ⲓⲱⲍⲁⲛⲛⲏⲥ (John), ⲇⲁⲛⲓⲏⲗ (Daniel), ⲁⲛⲁⲛⲓⲁⲥ (Ananias), ⲙⲓⲥⲁ[ⲏⲗ] (Michael), and ⲁⲍ[ⲁ]ⲣⲓⲁⲥ (Azarias).⁹²

---

ediscere et inter prima elementa consequi rem postea proprium tempus desideraturam; cf. Jerome, *Epist.* 107.4 (Wright 1933); Basil, *Reg. Fus.* 15 (PG 31.953); Pachomius, *Praec.* 139 (Boon; Vielleux); Marrrou 1956, 156.

88 *Praec.* 138–139; See additional discussion, above.
89 O.MMA. 14.1.549; *ed. pr.* Crum/Winlock/Evelyn White 1926, 2: 137 and 323 no. 621. As originally published in the excavation's catalogue, this piece is categorized as "miscellaneous." Attendant commentary suggests that it may have functioned as a Greek-Coptic "glossary" of which the Greek is preserved, but "the presumed Coptic equivalents [have] broken away" (323); cf. Hasitzka 1990, 173 no. 247. Cribiore names the list "an exercise, not a glossary" (1996, 202 no. 123, pl. XI).
90 O.MMA. 14.1.214; Crum/Winlock/Evelyn White 1926, 2:136 and 322 no. 618, pl. XIV; cf. Hasitzka 1990, 178–179 no. 252; Cribiore 1996, 202 no. 122; Cribiore 2012. It is not unusual to encounter similar content in broader classroom archives. In fact, extant school artifacts readily attest commensurate practice across a range of school settings (cf. Hasitzka 1990, 63–74 nos. 83–107; Cribiore 1996, 196–203 nos. 98–128). Bucking suggests the juxtaposition of Greek and Coptic in the first wordlist invites consideration of what subset of monastic instruction may have been aimed at facilitating fluency across languages (Bucking, "Scribes and Schoolmasters," 23ff). In turn, the inclusion of both 'Christian' and 'planetary' nomenclature, raises interesting questions about the degree to which extant artifacts mark, and bridge, the melding of disparate cultures and source material.
91 Newberry 1893, 2:65–68.
92 The lists were first transcribed by Champollion 1889, 384; then re-published by Newberry 1893, 2:68 no. 75; cf. Larsen 2018a, 101–124. Elsewhere, one encounters iterative rehearsal of the monastic commonplace "ⲁⲡⲁ," repeated ten times (Newberry 1893, 2:67 no. 69), see Larsen 2017, 153 fig. 14 for photo.

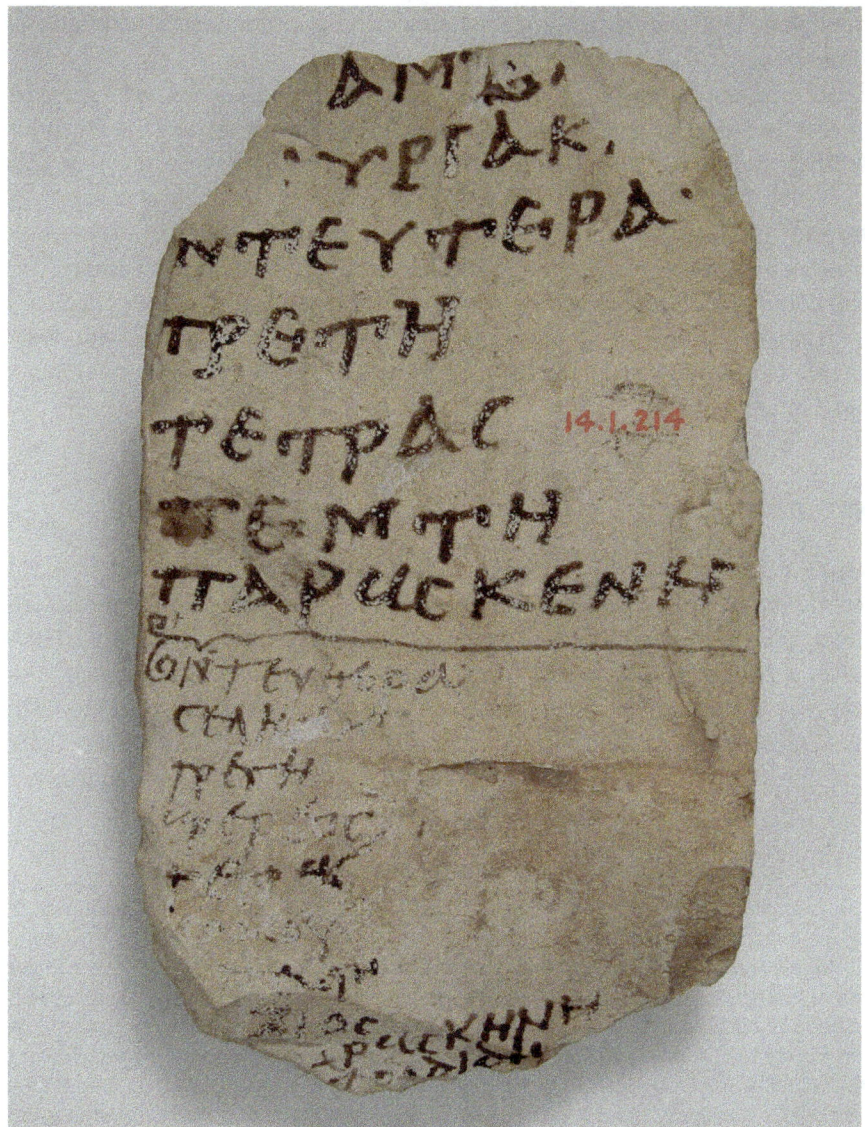

Fig. 11: Days of the Week, Monastery of Epiphanius (O.MMA. 14.1.214).

Each brings to mind Jerome's enjoinder that Paula practice pronouncing names of the "prophets ... apostles ... [and] patriarchs ... from Adam downwards" (*Epist*. 107.4). In turn, placement proximate with linked alphabets and a syllabary, lends interesting context to Pachomius' cryptic injunction that with the letters, and "the fundamentals of a syllable ... verbs and nouns" should also be written (*Praec.* 139).[93]

An alternate ostracon of monastic provenance preserves complementary content. As described by Marrou, it is one of a number of ostraca that "contain word-lists full of Christian names;"[94] in this instance, "a list of all the proper names that occur in the story of Pentecost in the Acts [of the Apostles]."[95] By virtue of its biblical character, Marrou discounts the merits of this piece as school related. However, like the word clusters preserved at Beni Hasan, the small collection preserved on this 'building block' can perhaps more effectively be parsed as a concretization of recurrent suggestions that students work with excerpted vocabulary so as to offset spending additional time to gain familiarity, at a later point.

Sentences

Marrou melds his summary of "short sentences" with classroom use "from the second century A.D. onwards [of] short passages" comprised of "aphorisms—*chreiai*—commonly attributed to Diogenes, and a whole stock of short maxims—*gnomoi monostichoi*—supposedly the work of Menander."[96] Once again, one finds commensurate content in the 'building blocks' commended in monastic pedagogical 'blueprints'. The cryptic injunctions of Pachomius, loosely echo those offered by Quintilian, who suggests that once syllables have been learned,

---

93 On comparative grounds, a wordlist included in the Greek-Bohairic codex published by Husselman is particularly interesting (P.Mich. Inv. 926). The list appears on the *verso* of the fifth folio — following the lengthy Greek-Bohairic syllabary, discussed above. Constituted solely of biblical names, the wordlist begins with ⲃⲁⲣⲛⲁⲃⲟⲥ (Barnabus), then turns to a broader range of biblical characters: ... ⲁⲛⲁⲣⲉⲁⲥ (Andreas), ⲥⲟⲗⲟⲙⲟⲛ (Solomon), ⲁⲇⲁⲙ (Adam), ⲛⲟⲉ (Noah), ⲁⲃⲣⲁϩⲁⲙ (Abraham), ⲓⲥⲁⲕ (Isaac), ⲓⲁⲕⲱⲃ (Jacob), ⲙⲱⲩⲥⲏⲥ (Moses), ⲇⲁⲩⲓⲇ (David), ⲥⲉⲧⲣⲁⲕ (Shadrach), ⲙⲉⲥⲁⲕ (Meshak), ⲉⲃⲑⲉ-ⲛⲁⲅⲅⲱ (Abednego), ⲇⲁⲛⲓⲏⲗ (Daniel). It is positioned adjacent to a copying exercise, comprised of the greetings that introduce Paul's letter to the Romans, and in close proximity to a pronunciation exercise using Paul's name (Husselman 1947, 129–135, 147–148; cf. Hasitzka 1990, 138–139 no. 207 fol. 5v–6r). One of the two school tablets published by Boak likewise combines practice with syllables and words. Here, the included wordlist is comprised of both biblical and monastic names (Boak 1923, 296–297; cf. Hasitzka 1990, 59–60 no. 78).
94 Marrou 1956, 331.
95 Marrou 1956, 331; cf. O.Lond.Hall 26210 = O.BM.inv. 26210+26211+26215; Hasitzka 1990, 174–176, no. 248; Cribiore 1996, 203 no. 127. See Cribiore 1996, pl. VI no. 127 for photos.
96 Marrou 1956, 156.

students "begin construct[ing] words with them and sentences with the words."[97] In turn, both Basil and Quintilian link sentences with 'sayings' (*chreiai*), which report the names, words and actions of illustrious individuals.[98]

Whether copying, constructing, or iteratively re-framing gnomic maxims into sayings and stories, all agree that the long-term usefulness of work with such content was implicit. Rehearsal and composition was aimed not only at attaining fluid command of established compositional forms, but also insuring "that the soul ... be lead to practise (*sic*) good immediately and from the outset, [and] while ... still plastic and soft, pliable as wax, [be] ... molded by the shapes pressed upon it."[99]

---

[97] Quintilian, *Inst.* 1.1.31–32 (Russell 2001); *Tunc ipsis syllabis verba complecti et his sermonem connectere incipiat.*

[98] *Reg. Fus.* 15 (PG 31.953; Clarke); ...καὶ ἆθλα μνήμης ὀνομάτων τε καὶ πραγμάτων αὐτοῖς προτιθέναι; cf. Larsen, "On Learning a New Alphabet," 59–77; *et al.* Both Quintilian and Basil likewise commend the use of games and rewards as enticement to enhance the pleasurable value of such practice; counting "entertainment" an immediate impetus for core competency in "learning the sayings of famous men [as well as] ... selections from the poets." Quintilian, *Inst.* 1.1.36 (Russell 2001); *Etiam dicta clarorum virorum et electos ex poetis maxime (namque eorum cognitio parvis gratior est) locos ediscere inter lusum licet.*

[99] Basil, *Reg. Fus.* 15 (PG 31.956; Clarke); Εὔπλαστον οὖν ἔτι οὖσαν καὶ ἀπαλὴν τὴν ψυχήν, καὶ ὡς κηρὸν εὔεικτον, ταῖς τῶν ἐπιβαλλομένων μορφαῖς ῥᾳδίως ἐκτυπουμένην, πρὸς πᾶσαν ἀγαθῶν ἄσκησιν εὐθὺς καὶ ἐξ ἀρχῆς ἐνάργεσθαι χρή; Here Basil is echoing not only Quintilian, but a constructive principle that recurs across generations of school curricula. This is the premise that each iteration of a gnomic extract retained implicit capacity to promote virtue and shape character. Writing in the fourth century BCE, Plato recommends that the end result of "compil[ing] anthologies of the poets and mak[ing] collections of whole passages, which ... must be committed to memory" is not only that a student gain wide familiarity with literature, but "to make [one] a good and wise [individual]" (*Leg.* 810e–812a [Bury]; οἱ δὲ ἐκ πάντων κεφάλαια ἐκλέξαντες καί τινας ὅλας ῥήσεις εἰς ταὐτὸν συναγαγόντες, ἐκμανθάνειν φασὶ δεῖν εἰς μνήμην τιθεμένους, εἰ μέλλει τις ἀγαθὸς ἡμῖν καὶ σοφὸς ἐκ πολυπειρίας καὶ πολυμαθίας γενέσθαι). In his pedagogical treatise *ad Demonicum*, Pseudo-Isocrates suggests that noble behavior results from a mind " ... fraught with many noble maxims; for, as it is the nature of the body to be developed by appropriate exercises, it is the nature of the soul to be developed by moral precepts" (*Ad Demonicum* 12 [Norlin]; Οὕτω δὲ τὴν γνώμην οὐ δυνατὸν διατεθῆναι τὸν μὴ πολλῶν καὶ καλῶν ἀκουσμάτων πεπληρωμένον· τὰ μὲν γὰρ σώματα τοῖς συμμέτροις πόνοις, ἡ δὲ ψυχὴ τοῖς σπουδαίοις λόγοις αὔξεσθαι πέφυκε). Plutarch premises that teachers be selected by virtue of their ability to set "precepts and exhortations beside the young, in order that [children's] characters [might] grow to be upright" (*De liberis educandis* 4C [Babbitt]; οἱ νόμιμοι τῶν διδασκάλων ἐμμελεῖς τὰς ὑποθήκας καὶ παραινέσεις παραπηγνύουσι τοῖς νέοις, ἵν'ὀρθὰ τούτων βλαστάνῃ τὰ ἤθη); cf. Morgan 2007; Carr 2005; Larsen 2013a, 67–69; Larsen 2013b, 1–34; Larsen 2016, 13–33; Larsen 2018, 471–490.

Derivatively, as with wordlists, both mainstream and monastic pedagogues urge caution in choosing content. Even at the early stage of copying texts, it is advised that the lines set before young students "should not express thoughts of no significance but convey some sound moral lesson."[100] The rationale is simple. At a later point in life, such subject matter might still be remembered, "and the impression made upon [an] unformed mind [also] contribute to the formation of ... character."[101]

Once again, 'eastern' monastic 'sentences' can be identified by the same classroom characteristics as those used to classify school texts of 'classical' or 'western' provenance. For example, four of the ten artifacts categorized as "school pieces" in Crum, Winlock and Evelyn White's catalogue of excavations undertaken at the Monastery of Epiphanius, preserve lines drawn from Homer.[102] These extracts are rendered in Greek, and like the mixed alphabets discussed above (Tab. 1), each is introduced by Christian symbolism – in this instance, a cross (fig. 12).[103]

---

100 Quintilian, *Inst.* 1.1.35-6 (Russell 2001); ... *ii quoque versus, qui ad imitationem scribendi proponentur, non otiosas velim sententias habeant, sed honestum aliquid monentis*.
101 Quintilian, *Inst. Or.* 1.1.36 (Russell 2001); *Prosequitur haec memoria in senectutem et impressa animo rudi usque ad mores proficient*; Cf. Jerome, *Epist.* 107.4 (Wright 1933); Basil, *Reg. Fus.* 15 (PG 31.953; Clarke); Pachomius, *Praecepta* 139 (Boon; Vielleux); Marrou 1956, 156.
102 The first is O.MMA. 14.1.139; *ed. pr.* Crum/Winlock/Evelyn White 1926, 2: 135 and 320 no. 612, pl. XIV; cf. Cribiore 1996, 225 no. 225; Larsen 2013b, 17 and 27 fig. 4; the second, O.MMA. 14.1.140; *ed. pr.* Crum/Winlock/Evelyn White 1926, 2: 135 and 320 no. 611, pl. XIV; cf. Cribore 1926, 213 no. 168. The third preserves *Iliad* 1.201: "And to him speaking he addressed winged words" (και μιν φων- / ησας επεα π- / τεροεντα π- / ροσηυδα); *ed. pr.* Crum/Winlock/Evelyn White 1926, 2: 135 and 320 no. 613; cf. Cribiore 1996, 225 no. 226; the fourth, *Iliad* 1.22: "Then indeed all the others..." (ενθ αλλοι μ[εν] / παντες); *ed. pr.* Crum and Evelyn White, *Monastery of Epiphanius* 2, 135 and 320 nos. 614; cf. Cribiore 1996, 226 no. 227.
103 Whether the four ostraca should be broadly classified as school related, solely "scribal," or both, remains a topic of debate (cf. Bucking 2007, 21–47; Maravela 2018, 125–149). It is noteworthy, however, that *sans* a monastic frame, the inclusion of Homeric content is routinely named a traditional marker of pedagogical provenance.

Fig. 12: *Iliad* 1.1–2 Monastery of Epiphanius (O.MMA 14.1.139).

As pedagogically consonant with the 'building blocks' Marrou proposes, is a large Epiphanian ostracon that preserves a sizable collection of Menandrian "*gnomoi monostichoi*" (fig. 13).[104]

---

104 O.MMA 14.1.210; *ed. pr.* Crum/Winlock/Evelyn White 1926, 2: 135 and 320–321 no. 615; cf. Cribiore 1996, 252 no. 319, Pl. XLIV; Larsen 2007, 67–69; Larsen 2013a, 59–77; Larsen 2013b, 18 and 34, fig. 7; Larsen 2016, 13–33. (For an alternate reading, see Maravela 2018, 140ff.) Again, a broader array of classroom examples is well documented. Particularly interesting, however, is

Fig. 13: Sentences of Menander, Monastery of Epiphanius (O.MMA. 14.1.210).

Like the structures Marrou commends for building wordlists, these are loosely organized alphabetically, from α (*alpha*) through φ (*phi*).[105] Akin to more familiar collections of Menandrian maxims,[106] the first, partially legible line enjoins "fear of God" ([...]φοβὸς θεοῦ); the second assigns "the beginning [of great wisdom" to "learning] letters" (Ἀρχὴ μ[εγίστη τοῦ φρονεῖν τὰ] γράμματα). Subsequent sentences meld classical and biblical content; each suggestive of practice with lines that "convey some sound moral lesson".[107]

---

a lengthy Greek-Coptic codex included in Hasitzka 1990, 1.202–210 no. 269, 2.95–96; cf. Hagedorn/Weber 1968, 15–50.

105 Again, a broader array of classroom examples is well documented. Particularly interesting, however, is a lengthy Greek-Coptic codex included in Hasitzka 1990, 1.202–210 no. 269, 2.95–96; cf. Hagedorn/Weber 1968, 15–50.
106 Cribiore 2001, 178–179; Morgan 1998, 120–122; cf. Carr 2005.
107 Quintilian 1.1.35; cf. Jerome, *Ep.* 107; Basil, *Reg. Fus.* 15.

Sayings

Monastic material (and textual) remains likewise align with Marrou's observation that from the second century onward, school texts were increasingly distinguished by transformation of "short sentences" and "maxims" into "short passages" comprised of "aphorisms" and "*chreiai*" (sayings).[108] Again, extant monastic 'building blocks' serve to illustrate 'blueprinted' forms.

Content preserved on two-sides of an ostracon provenanced to the Monastery of Epiphanius (in Thebes) offers a particularly rich lens for re-scripting monastic manifestations of broader classroom convention (fig. 14a-b). Faintly visible on the ostracon's *verso* and *recto* faces, one meets excerpts extracted from both biblical and monastic texts (and contexts). Examined in conversation, respective components appear functionally akin to the "simple sentences" and "*chreiai*" (or sayings) that played a well-documented, central role in late-ancient classroom practice.

Fig. 14a-b: Proverbs and Saying, Monastery of Epiphanius (Cairo 44674.118 verso/recto; Photo Courtesy of K. Brown).

---

108 Marrou 1956, 156.

As identified in Crum and Evelyn White's early transcription, the ostracon's *verso* face preserves two 'lines from Proverbs'. The first is Proverbs 13.7:

ογν νετειρε μμοογ νρμμαο εμντογ λααγ αγω ογν νε[τ]θββιο μμοογ εγενογννοб μμντρ[μμαο].

There are those who make themselves rich, having nothing, and there are those who humble themselves, while being very [wealthy] (fig. 14a).

This is followed by Proverbs 13.13:

πετκαταφρονει νογεωβ σεναкαταφρονε μμοϥ πετρεωβ δε εητς ντεντολη [παι] πε ετογχ [μ]νλααγ ναгαθο[ν] ναϣωπ[ε.

He who despises a matter, he will be despised; the one who acts according to the commandment, [this one] is safe; nothing good will happen [(to a deceitful son)] (fig. 14a).[109]

The *recto* contains what appears to be a paraphrase of this content; here, re-framed as a 'saying'/*chreia*, attributed to Basil:

βασιλιος νιμ гαρ ενεε πενταγμακαριζε μμοϥ χεογντϥ χρημα η νιμ πενταϥογχαι εϥενογμτον νςωμα.

Apa Basilios [said:] For who has ever been blessed because he had property, or who has been saved while in bodily rest (fig. 14b).[110]

By virtue of traditional cataloguing, this artifact has long escaped categorization as school related. However, examined in light of the pedagogical 'blueprints' provided by Jerome and Basil, the ostracon's juxtaposed content is suggestive. The combination of two "moral maxims" — gleaned from Proverbs, re-worked as a "saying" — attributed to a famous philosopher (and monk), effectively mirrors the pedagogical models that both Marrou, and his ancient/late-ancient predecessors define as increasingly characteristic of foundational pedagogical practice.[111]

---

109 Cairo 44674.118 (*verso*); *ed. pr.* Crum/Winlock/Evelyn White 1926, 2: 5 and 157 no. 22.
110 Cairo 44674.118 (*recto*); *ed. pr.* Crum/Winlock/Evelyn White 1926, 2: 12 and 163 no. 52. In attendant commentary, Crum and Evelyn White classify the 'saying' as elsewhere "unattested." Cf. Larsen 2013b, 18–19, 32; 2016, 13–33; 2018a, 101–124.
111 Marrou 1956, 156; In introducing his compendium of *Progymnasmata*, Kennedy suggests that the classroom forms which governed such re-formulation were as ubiquitous as the "structural features of classical architecture" (ix); cf. Hock/O'Neil 1986.

Passages

A final classroom 'building block' is as provocative. Published by Raffaella Cribiore in 1997, its content — preserved on a sizable pottery sherd, usefully elucidates Marrou's emphasis on the classroom links that connect "short sentences" with longer "passages."[112] Although the ostracon is again provenanced to the Egyptian desert, the passage is drawn from a homily, likewise attributed to the urbane, Basil of Caesarea.[113] Per Cribiore's re-construction, the lines read as follows:

> (1a) [τοῦτό σοι τὸ ῥῆμα καὶ λαμπρῶς εὐημεροῦντί ποτε καὶ παντὸς τοῦ βίου κατὰ]
> (1) [ῥοῦν φερομέ]νου χρησ[ίμως παραστήσεται ὥσπερ τις ἀγαθὸς σύμβουλος] [ὑπόμνησ]ιν φέρων [ἀνθρωπίνων. Καὶ μέντοι καὶ ὑπὸ περιστά-]
> σεως πιεζομένω εν [καιρῷ ἂν γένοιτο τῇ καρδίᾳ κατεπᾳδόμενον ὡς μήτε τυφω προς αλ[αζονείαν ὑπέρογκον ἐπαρθῆναι μήτε ἀπο-]
> (5) [ν]
> ὡς μήτε τυφω προς αλ[αζονείαν ὑπέρογκον ἐπαρθῆναι μήτε ἀπο-]
> (5) [ν]γνωσει προς αγενν[η δυσθυμίαν καταπεσεῖν. Πλούτω κο-] μᾶς καὶ προγόνοις μ[έγα φρονεῖς; καὶ ἐπαγάλλη πατρίδι καὶ κάλ-] λει σώματος καὶ ταῖς [παρὰ πάντων τιμαῖς; Πρό- σεχε σεαυτῷ]
> ὅτι θνητος εἶ ὅτι γῆ εἶ κ[αὶ εἰς γῆν ἀπελεύσῃ. Περίβλεψαι τοὺς] προ σοῦ εν ταῖς ομολίαις περιφανείαις ἐξετασθέντας.]
> (10) ποῦ οι τας πολιτικα[ς δυναστείας περιβεβλημένοι;] που οι δυ[σ]μ[αχώ]τατοι [ῥήτορες; ποῦ οἱ τὰς πανηγύρεις] δ[ι]ατιθέντες] οἱ λαμπ[ροὶ ἱπποτρόφοι οἱ στρατηγοί.]
> οἱ σατραπ[αι] οἱ τυρανν [οι οὐ πάντα κόνις; οὐ παν-] τα μῦθο[ς; οὐκ ἐν ὀλίγοις ὀστέοις τὰ μνη-] (15) μ[όσυνα] τ[ῆ]ς [ζωῆς αὐτῶν;]

"Give heed to yourself": This admonition, like a good counselor who reminds you of human things will be useful to you when you are enjoying brilliant success and your whole life goes with the stream. And even when you are cast down by crisis it might profitably be recited again and again by your heart that you may not fall into boastful pride because of vanity nor for desperation become ignobly disheartened. Is wealth your boast? Are you proud of your ancestors? Do you find cause for glory in your fatherland, in physical beauty, in the honors universally given to you? Give heed to yourself for you are mortal, "for dust you are and unto dust you shall return." Pass in review those persons who have enjoyed positions of eminence before you. Where are those who held the exercise of political power? Where the peerless orators? Where are they who had charge of the national assemblies — the famous breeders of horses, the generals, the governors, the sovereigns? Are not they all dust? Are not they all legend? Is it not true that a few bones are the memorial to the life of these men?

---

112 Marrou 1956, 156.
113 O.Col. inv. 766; *ed. pr.* Cribiore 1997, 187–193; cf. Basil, *Homilia in illud: "Attende tibi ipsi"* (*CPG* 2847). See Cribiore 1997 and Larsen 2017, 170 fig. 18 for photos.

Cribiore argues that the text's awkward nomenclature, haphazard punctuation, and the nature of the topic itself, suggests a document that served as a classroom copying exercise, perhaps a 'building block' used to practice lexical signs and accents.[114]

The passage simultaneously illustrates the static 'blueprints' and malleable content 'blocks' endemic to classroom work. While the excerpt is framed as a pithy paragraph, its focal point is a simple maxim: πρόσεχε σεαυτῷ ("Give heed to yourself").[115] Traditionally attributed to one (or more) of the 'seven sages' of classical antiquity — not unlike the elastic *gnomoi monostochoi* loosely collected as 'Sentences of Menander' — the short aphorism is drawn from a core of conventional source material, routinely deployed with pedagogical goals in mind.[116] Serving as a 'textbook' example of constructive classroom habits, its 'elaboration' richly illustrates the "structural features" of classic reformulations; and at a later stage, the compositional "habits" of literate elites.[117]

As significant, however, is the degree to which Basil's well practiced parsing of a simple sentence, at once, elucidates and de-stabilizes Marrou's interpretive frame.[118] Qua copying exercise, Basil's homily elegantly illustrates the "structural forms" that bind "short maxims" with "short sentences" and ultimately, longer "passages."[119] Simultaneously, this building block's melding of classical, Christian and monastic content — not to mention its Egyptian provenance — insistently challenges the colonialist constructs, which Marrou has selectively scaffolded. Belying the binaries of simple or sophisticated, spiritual or pedagogical, monastic or urbane, Basil's elaboration showcases deft manipulation of the 'elementary exercises'/*progymnasmata* which defined a broad range of classroom composition.[120] Per George Kennedy, like the "structural

---

114 Cribiore 1997, 192; Cribiore notes that a similar text was translated into Latin by Rufinus in 398 CE, and is preserved in a number of medieval manuscripts (187); cf. Rudberg 1962, 152. Simultaneously, she observes that the looseness of applied translation techniques "does not help in determining the correct text of the homily" (187); cf. Brock 1979, 69–87.
115 When encountered nested in a lengthy treatise of substantive proportion, it is easy to overlook the classroom contexts in which such content would have found its form.
116 In discussing *Literate Education in the Hellenistic and Roman Worlds*, Morgan 1998 notes that "more gnomic [sentences] survive [in schoolhands], than fragments of any other literature or any other exercise" 122. As demonstrated here, such content is derivatively manifested in the treatises, sermons and stories that more advanced application facilitated; cf. Larsen 2001, 1–11; 2013b, 1–32.
117 Cf. Kennedy 2003; Hock/O'Neil 1986; *et al.*
118 Marrou 1956, 156.
119 Kennedy 2003, ix.
120 Cf. Larsen 2018b, 471–490; Amsler, this volume.

features of classical architecture," these forms governed the construction of all ancient literature (east and west), from the Hellenistic period, through late antiquity, into Byzantium, and beyond.[121]

5 Conclusions

In his brief essay, "Reading Resistance, Resisting Interpretation," Vincent Wimbush premises that "all historical interpretive efforts and their methods and approaches illuminate some things, cast shadows over others ... they foreground some things, render into the background certain others."[122] The interpretive emphases that define discussions of monastic pedagogy in Henri-Irénée Marrou's *History of Ancient Education*, might serve as a case study of Wimbush's assessment. While examples abound, the stubborn imprint of Marrou's influence in "constructing knowledge" of monastic late antiquity is perhaps nowhere more apparent than in Yun Lee Too's early twenty-first century, commemorative anthology — aimed at "rethinking of [Marrou's] totalizing history."[123]

The volume's rich range of studies features an impressive cast of scholars, tasked with re-assessing almost every aspect of Marrou's chronicle. Topics range from the question of 'Public' and 'Private' in early Greek institutions of education,[124] to 'Schools of Platonic Philosophy' in the Late Roman Empire.[125] A penultimate treatise, authored by Sara Rappe, addresses the inclusion and subtraction of "Pagan Elements in Christian Education."[126] The bulk of Rappe's essay traces a trajectory defined by the writings of early Church Fathers. However, a final segment additionally takes up the question of monastic education. Here, Rappe astutely identifies monasticism as "a kind of absent chapter" in the history of education. Simultaneously, her re-assessment remains reliant on Marrou's broader scaffolding; that monasticism remained a type of Christian

---

121 Kennedy 2003, ix; Re-working a maxim/'saying', elsewhere attributed to the Delphic sages (and identified by Plato as the "essence of true education"), the elaboration moves from statement, to paraphrase, to cause, contrary, comparison, example and recapitulation; Cf. Larsen 2018b, 471–490; Amsler, this volume.
122 Wimbush 1997, 1.
123 Too 2001.
124 Griffith 2001.
125 Lamberton 2001.
126 Rappe 2001.

school "wholly devoted to religion and had none of the features of the old classical school."[127]

Per Marrou, Rappe's "re-thinking" begins with immediate reference to the *Life of Antony*. It then moves to the well-worn *apophthegmatic* dismissal of literate education attributed to Evagrius and Arsenius (cited above). Re-framing Marrou, Rappe identifies the 'classically' educated Evagrius as "one of the most original thinkers and radical teachers in the tradition."[128] However, her broader parsing of Evagrius' pedagogical preoccupations remains reliant on Marrou's colonialist foundations. Privy to the same 'blueprints' commended by his peers, there is good evidence to suggest that Evagrius fostered complex networks of pedagogical exchange — both within and beyond the Egyptian desert.[129] Following Marrou, however, Rappe's essay leaves the literate Evagrius "pitted against the fathers," an urban intellectual "facing off" with "desert wisdom."[130]

Inadvertently, Rappe's mirrored reiteration of Marrou's mid-century analyses usefully registers the cumulative weight of Marrou's interpretive scaffolding. As readily, it elucidates Tom Hunt's recent investigation of the "influence of French colonial[ism] on the study of late antiquity" in general, and the work of Henri-Irénée Marrou, in particular.[131] Hunt premises that the frameworks which define emergent conceptualizations of "late antiquity" were cast in the crucible of French "colonial humanism" and, as such, remain dependent on colonial ideals in their "constitution."[132] The re-scaffolding proposed in this essay documents the degree to which the same colonial ideals have derivatively defined discussions of monastic education.

The residual binaries rendered patent in re-scaffolding the "missing chapter" that is monastic education, underscore the degree to which recognizing the constructed character of all knowledge, retains the potential to re-shape broader history — both ancient and contemporary. In turn, as elite institutions grapple with the powerful challenges implicit to listening to (and for) long silenced voices, the contemporary urgency of 'inspecting' the interpretive presuppositions used in scaffolding notions of knowledge, grows ever more acute. When testing the integrity of colonialist foundations, re-reading pedagogical blueprints, and re-assessing the arrangement of primary building blocks — the deep

---

127 Marrou 1956, 330.
128 Rappe 2001, 423.
129 Larsen 2021, 313–332.
130 Rappe 2001, 423, 430.
131 Hunt 2018, 255–278.
132 Hunt 2018, 255.

roots that anchor historical systems (and notions) of 'elite' and 'less elite' learning are impossible to ignore. That they can be traced to the delimiting influence of a singular individual, and/or school of thought is, at once, sobering and liberating. As importantly, however, it is a mandate to explore further.

Bibliography

Amsler, M. (2023), "'The Poetic Itch' and Numerical Maxims in the Talmud — An Inquiry into Factors of Knowledge Construction" (this volume).
Babbitt, F. (1927), *Plutarch: Moralia* 1, Cambridge, MA.
Bagnall, R. (2018), "The Educational and Cultural Background of Egyptian Monks", in: L.I. Larsen/S. Rubenson (eds.), *Monastic Education in Late Antiquity*, Cambridge, 75–100.
Becker, A.H. (2006), *Fear of God and the Beginning of Wisdom: The School of Nisibis and Christian Scholastic Culture in Late Antique Mesopotamia*, Philadelphia.
Biedenkopf-Ziehner, A. (2000), *Koptische Ostraka: Ostraka aus dem Ashmolean Museum in Oxford*, Wiesbaden.
Boak, A.E.R. (1921), "Greek and Coptic School Tablets at the University of Michigan", *Classical Philology* 16, 189–194.
Boak, A.E.R. (1923), "A Coptic Syllabary at the University of Michigan", *Aegyptus* 4, 296–297.
Brakke, D. (1995), *Athanasius and Asceticism*, Baltimore.
Bucking, S. (2007), "Scribes and Schoolmasters? On Contextualizing Coptic and Greek Ostraca Found at the Monastery of Epiphanius", *Journal of Coptic Studies* 9, 21–47.
Bury, R.G. (1926), *Plato: Legates (Leg.)*, Cambridge, MA.
Carr, D. (2005), *Writing on the Tablet of the Heart: Origins of Scripture and Literature*, New York.
Clark, E.A. (1999), *Reading Renunciation: Asceticism and Scripture in Early Christianity*, Princeton.
Clarke, W.K.L. (1925), *The Ascetic Works of Saint Basil*, New York.
Champollion, J.F. (1889), *Monuments de l'Égypte et de la Nubie*, vol. 2, Paris.
Cribiore, R. (1996), *Writing, Teachers and Students in Graeco-Roman Egypt*, Atlanta.
Cribiore, R. (1997), "A Fragment of Basilius of Caesarea", in: B. Kramer/W. Luppe/H. Maehler/ G. Poethke (eds.), *Akten des 21. Internationalen Papyrologenkongresses, Berlin, 13.-19. 8.1995*, Stuttgart, 187–193.
Cribiore, R. (2001), *Gymnastics of the Mind: Greek Education in Hellenistic and Roman Egypt*, Princeton.
Cribiore, R. (2012), "A list of Words of Christian Origin from the Kelsey Museum", in: R. Ast *et al.* (eds.), *Papyrological Texts in Honor of Roger S. Bagnall*, Durham, NC, 61–66.
Crum, W.E./Winlock, H.E./Evelyn White, H.G. (1926), *The Monastery of Epiphanius at Thebes*, 2 vols., New York.
Dahlman, B. (2018), "Textual Fluidity and Authorial Revisio: The Case of Cassian and Palladius", in: L.I. Larsen/S. Rubenson (eds.), *Monastic Education in Late Antiquity*, Cambridge, 281–305.
Faraggiana di Sarzana, Ch. (1997), "*Apophthegmata Patrum*: Some Crucial Points of Their Textual Transmission and the Problem of a Critical Edition", *Studia Patristica* 29, 455–467.

Gemeinhardt, P. (2013), *Antonius Der erste Mönch: Leben, Lehre, Legende*, Munich.
Gregg, R.C. (1980), *The Life of Antony and the Letter to* Marcellinus, Mahwah.
Griffith, M. (2001), "'Public' and 'Private' in Early Greek Institutions of Education", in: L. Too (ed.), *Education in Greek and Roman Antiquity*, Leiden, 23–84.
Hagedorn, D./Weber, M. (1968), "Die griechisch-koptische Rezension der Menandersentenzen", *Zeitschrift für Papyrologie und Epigraphik* 3, 15–50.
Hall, H.R. (1905), *Coptic and Greek Texts of the Christian Period from Ostraka, Stelae, etc. in the British Museum*, London.
Hasitzka, M.R. (1990), *Neue Texte und Dokumentation zum Koptisch-Unterricht. Mitteilungen aus der Papyrussammlung der Österreichischen Nationalbibliothek (Papyrus Erzherzog Rainer)*, Vienna.
Hock, R.F./O'Neil, E.N. (eds.) (1986), *The Chreia in Ancient Rhetoric: The Progymnasmata*, Atlanta.
Holmberg, B. (2013), "The Syriac Collection of *Apophthegmata Patrum* in MS Sin. syr. 46", *Studia Patristica* 55, 35–57.
Hunt, T. (2018), "The influence of French colonial humanism on the study of late antiquity: Braudel, Marrou, Brown", *International Journal of Francophone Studies* 21, 255–278.
Hunter, D.G. (1988), *Comparison Between a King and a Monk/Against the Opponents of the Monastic Life*, Lewiston.
Husselman, E.M. (1947), "A Bohairic School Text on Papyrus", *Journal of Near Eastern Studies* 6, 129–151.
Kennedy, G.A. (2003), *Progymnasmata: Greek Textbooks of Prose Composition and Rhetoric*, Atlanta.
Lamberton, R. (2001), "The Schools of Platonic Philosophy of the Roman Empire: The Evidence of the Biographies", in: Y.L. Too (ed.), *Education in Greek and Roman Antiquity*, 433–458.
Larsen, L.I. (2001), "Ørkenfedrenes *Apophthegmata*", *Meddelanden från Collegium Patristicum Lundense* 16, 26–35.
Larsen, L.I. (2006), "The Apophthegmata Patrum and the Classical Rhetorical Tradition", *Studia Patristica* 39, 409–415.
Larsen, L.I. (2007), "Pedagogical Parallels: Re-reading the Apophthegmata Patrum", Ph.D. diss., Columbia University.
Larsen, L.I. (2008), "The Apophthegmata Patrum: Rustic Rumination or Rhetorical Recitation", *Meddelanden från Collegium Patristicum Lundense* 22, 21–30.
Larsen, L.I. (2012a), "Monastic Meals: Resisting a Reclining Culture", in: D.E. Smith/H.E. Taussig (eds.), *Meals in the Early Christian World: Social Formation, Experimentation, and Conflict at the Table*, New York, 245–260.
Larsen, L.I. (2012b), "Meals and Monastic Identity", in: M. Klinghardt/H. Taussig (eds.), *Mahl und religiöse Identität*, Tübingen, 307–328.
Larsen, L.I. (2013a), "'On Learning a New Alphabet': The Sayings of the Desert Fathers and the Monostichs of Menander", *Studia Patristica* 55, 59–77.
Larsen, L.I. (2013b), "Re-drawing the Interpretive Map: Monastic Education as Civic Formation in the *Apophthegmata Patrum*", *Coptica* 12, 1–34.
Larsen, L.I. (2016), "Early Monasticism and the Rhetorical Tradition: Sayings and Stories as Schooltexts", in: P. Gemeinhardt/L. Van Hoof/P. Van Nuffelen (eds.), *Education and Religion in Late Antiquity*, Farnham, 13–33.

Larsen, L.I. (2017), "Monastic Paideia: Textual Fluidity in the Classroom", in: L.I. Lied/
    H. Lundhaug (eds.), *Snapshots of Evolving Traditions: Jewish and Christian Manuscript
    Culture, Textual Fluidity, and New* Philology, Berlin, 147–174.
Larsen, L.I. (2018a), "Excavating the Excavations of Early Monastic Education", in: L.I. Larsen/
    S. Rubenson (eds.), *Monastic Education in Late Antiquity*, Cambridge, 101–124.
Larsen, L.I. (2018b), "School Texts", in: S. McGill/E.J. Watts (eds.), *A Companion to Late Antique Literature*, New York, 471–490.
Larsen, L.I. (2021), "Evagrius in the Classroom", *Studia Patristica* 115, 313–332.
Larsen, L.I. (Forthcoming), "On Teaching a New Alphabet".
Lundhaug, H./Jenott, L. (2018), "Production, Distribution, and Ownership of Books in the Monasteries of Upper Egypt: The Evidence of the Nag Hammadi Colophons", in: L.I. Larsen/
    S. Rubenson (eds.), *Monastic Education in Late Antiquity*, Cambridge, 306–325.
Mack, B. (1988), *A Myth of Innocence: Mark and Christian Origins*, Minneapolis.
Maravela, A. (2018), "Homer and Menandri Sententiae in Upper Egyptian Monasticism", in:
    L.I. Larsen/S. Rubenson (eds.), *Monastic Education in Late Antiquity*, Cambridge, 125–149.
Marks, S. (2021), "Who Studied at the Beit Midrash? Funding Palestinian Amoraic Education",
    Journal of Ancient Judaism 12, 281–312.
Marrou, H.-I. (1956), *A History of Education in Antiquity*, translated by G. Lamb, Madison.
Morgan, T. (1998), *Literate Education in the Hellenistic and Roman Worlds*, Cambridge.
Morgan, T. (2007), *Popular Morality in the Early Roman Empire*, Cambridge.
Newberry, P.E. (1893–1900), *Beni Hasan*, 4 vols., Archaeological Survey of Egypt, London.
Norlin, G. (1928), *Isocrates* 1, Cambridge, MA.
Rappe, S. (2001), "The New Math: How to Add and to Subtract Pagan Elements in Christian
    Education", in: Y.L. Too (ed.), *Education in Greek and Roman Antiquity*, 405–432.
Riché, P. (1977), "In Memoriam Professeur Henri-Irénée Marrou", *Pedagogica Historica* 17,
    491–515.
Rousseau, P. (2000), "Antony as Teacher in the Greek Life", in: T. Hägg/P. Rousseau (eds.),
    Greek Biography and Panegyric in Late Antiquity, Berkeley, 89–109.
Russell, D.A. (2001), *Quintilian. Institutio Oratorio (Inst)*, Cambridge, MA.
Too, Y.L. (ed.) (2001), *Education in Greek and Roman Antiquity*, Leiden.
Veilleux, A. (1980–82), *Pachomian Koinonia 2: The Lives, Rules, and Other Writings of Saint
    Pachomius and His Disciples*, Kalamazoo.
Ward, B. (1975), *The Sayings of the Desert Fathers: The Alphabetical Collection*, Kalamazoo.
Ward, B. (2003), *The Desert Fathers: Sayings of the Early Christian Monks*, London.
Wilken, R.L. (2012), *The First Thousand Years: A Global History of Christianity*, New Haven.
Wimbush, V.L. (1997), "Interpreting Resistance, Resisting Interpretations", *Semeia* 79, 1–27.
Wright, F.A. (1933), *Jerome: Select Letters*, Cambridge, MA.

Robert Edwards
Grammar in the School of Diodore of Tarsus: An Institutional Context for the Transfer of Exegetical Knowledge

Abstract: This essay offers a description of the production of exegetical knowledge in the school of Diodore of Tarsus, a Christian school which was active in Syrian Antioch in the latter half of the fourth century. Against a background of scholarship which has attempted to extract an exegetical "method" from Diodore's biblical commentaries, and in which Diodore and his students were "influenced" by their grammatical education, it argues that the extant commentaries of Diodore and his student Theodore of Mopsuestia actually derive from the context of grammatical instruction. The larger institutional context of this grammatical instruction and of the commentaries produced therefrom are also described: the school, which also included higher instruction in theology (at the level of philosophy or rhetoric) was likely connected to the hierarchy of the pro-Nicene diocese in Antioch. This institutional context provided for the social and economic means for these commentaries to be produced and disseminated.

1 Introduction

Writing in the middle of the sixth century CE, Cassiodorus stated that his school — which would go on to shape the medieval European liberal arts curriculum — was influenced by the schools of Syria: "I strove (to see to it) that in Rome ... the Christian schools, more than others, be able to acquire acknowledged professors, as is reported was for a long time a custom in Alexandria and as we are told is zealously displayed even now by the Hebrews at Nisibis, city of the Syrians."[1] Despite the mention of "Hebrews," it is widely accepted that the latter school refers to the *Christian* school of Nisibis: Cassiodorus had likely

---

1 Cassiodorus, *Inst. praef.* 1 (Bürsgens 2003, 92): *Nisus sum cum beatissimo Agapito papa urbis Romae ut, sicut in Alexandria multo tempore fuisse traditur institutum, nunc etiam in Nisibi civitate Syrorum Hebraeis dedulo fertur exponi, collatis expensis in urbe professos doctores scholae potius acciperent Christianae.* My translation is adapted slightly from Fiaccadori 1985, 135.

Open Access. © 2023 Robert Edwards, published by De Gruyter. This work is licensed under the Creative Commons Attribution 4.0 International License.
https://doi.org/10.1515/9783111010311-010

heard of these schools from the works of Junillus Africanus, who was himself familiar with the exegetical works of the school of Nisibis.² In the school of Nisibis itself were produced multiple texts which tell of the school's founding, and the student-teacher genealogies provided usually begin with Antiochene teachers, among whom are Diodore of Tarsus and Theodore of Mopsuestia.³ Although there is a mythological flavor to these genealogies, it remains that the Syrian "scholastic culture" (as Adam Becker has termed it) did make extensive use of the biblical commentaries of Theodore of Mopesuestia, and, to a lesser extent, those of Diodore.⁴ Thus, there is a pedagogical lineage which can be traced from Diodore of Tarsus — whose work is the subject of this essay — to the medieval university. However, more than simply demonstrating the importance of Diodore, this lineage (from Antioch to Nisibis to Constantinople to southern Italy) shows the close relationship that exists in late antiquity between institutional contexts and the production of texts, which together contribute to the creation and propagation of exegetical knowledge. This paper describes Diodore's school as one of these institutional contexts in which exegetical knowledge was constructed and propagated through grammar teaching and the writing of grammatical biblical commentaries.

My description of this school has two starting points, one less controversial than the other. The first is the existence of some sort of Christian school in Syrian Antioch in the latter half of the fourth century, which was led by Diodore of Tarsus. We know a little about this school from sources which were written not too long after the existence of the school itself. Socrates of Constantinople, writing his *Ecclesiastical History* sometime in the 440s, mentions that John Chrysostom and Theodore of Mopsuestia — among others — "became pupils in monastic exercises with Diodore and Carterius, who then directed a monastery. After this Diodore became bishop of Tarsus and composed many books, attending to the simple letter of the divine Scriptures and refraining from contemplation (*theōria*)."⁵ Shortly thereafter Sozomen largely copied Socrates' account.⁶ In the first half of the fifth century, Theodoret of Cyrrhus — himself from Antioch — also mentions Diodore's teaching role in several different contexts: first, as the

---

2 See Fiaccadori 1985; Barnish 1989; O'Donnell 1979, 133–134; Halporn 2004, 25.
3 These sources are conveniently translated in Becker 2008.
4 Becker 2006a; 2006b.
5 Socrates, *Hist. eccl.* 6.3.6–7 (Périchon-Maraval 2006, 264–266): μαθητεύουσιν εἰς τὰ ἀσκητικὰ Διοδώρῳ καὶ Καρτερίῳ, οἵτινες τότε μὲν ἀσκητηρίων προΐσταντο, Διόδωρος δὲ αὐτῶν ὕστερον ἐπίσκοπος Ταρσοῦ γενόμενος πολλὰ βιβλία συνέγραψεν, ψιλῷ τῷ γράμματι τῶν θείων προσέχων γραφῶν, τὰς θεωρίας αὐτῶν ἐκτρεπόμενος.
6 Sozomen, *Hist. eccl.* 8.2.5–6.

teacher of Theodore of Mopsuestia and John Chrysostom and, second, as one who educated Antioch's clergy in theology and polemics.[7]

The second, more controversial starting point is that there is some kind of coherence to the exegesis of Christians who have, for the last two centuries, usually been labelled "Antiochenes," belonging to the "Antiochene school."[8] Although the idea that there is a common Antiochene exegetical method has come under increasing scrutiny in recent years — especially with the breakdown of the Alexandria-Antioch dichotomy — several scholars have shown that there are genuine textual relationships among the exegetical works of many of the figures usually associated with the school.[9] It is not only a vague exegetical "method" that connects the figures of the school (as has so often been assumed), but common textual interpretations of obscure passages — interpretations which are exceedingly unlikely to have been arrived at independently of one another. For example, Hagit Amirav, focusing on select passages from Genesis, showed that Antiochene interpretations — including the proof texts which exegetes employed to interpret problem passages — are highly consistent among those exegetes usually identified as Antiochene: Diodore, Theodore, Chrysostom, of course, but also the earlier Eusebius of Emesa, and the later Theodoret of Cyrrhus and Gennadius of Constantinople.[10] In his work on Adrian the Exegete's *Introduction to the Divine Scriptures,* Peter Martens has shown that Adrian belongs to a group of exegetes who share (as he rightly says) "striking similarities" in their specific interpretations of various prophetic verses. In addition to those just mentioned, to this group belong Polychronius of Apamea (Theodore's brother), Adrian himself, Junillus Africanus, Olympiodorus of Alexandria ("the Deacon"), and Cosmas Indicopleustes.[11] The similarities among these interpreters demonstrate something more significant than that they share exegetical methods: they show that from the middle of the fourth century "Antiochene" interpreters were reading and recycling earlier exegetical texts, and thus placing themselves within a certain interpretative tradition.

In this paper, I put these two observations together: namely that Diodore's school existed as one of the places where this Antiochene interpretative tradi-

---

7 Theodoret, *Hist. eccl.* 4.25.4; 5.39.
8 There are too many to count, but the first appear to have been Münter 1811; the most recent monograph treatment of this group of exegetes is Hill 2005.
9 Mitchell 2005; Fairbairn 2007; Martens 2012.
10 Amirav 2001; 2003.
11 Martens 2017, 17–19. Martens also points to ter Haar Romeny 1997, 131–139. For the relationship that Junillus and Cosmas had to the school of Antioch — Theodore of Mopsuestia in particular — see Becker 2006a.

tion was transmitted. I describe the institutional context in which Diodore's Antiochene commentaries were produced, and therefore one historical instance of the transmission of this exegetical tradition. Strangely, scholars have rarely attempted to consider the relationship between Diodore's and Theodore's commentaries and this school mentioned by Socrates and other ancient historians, other than to establish that the Antiochene school — as an intellectual tradition with an exegetical method — had some basis in a historical school as a specific institution. Its institutional character has also been described, but not in relation to the pedagogical program found in the commentaries.[12] I do rather more than this, by describing a plausible, if sometimes speculative, school context in which this concrete Antiochene exegetical knowledge was produced and passed down.

I therefore describe the social and material conditions that allowed this exegetical knowledge to be transmitted — where and how the propagation and transmission of this exegetical knowledge took place. Such a description is crucial because, as I elaborate on below, Antiochene exegesis has often been abstracted into an intellectual "method" devoid of historical context. However, we know that the reading of old books and the production of new books did not take place in isolation. For example, Diodore would not have read Eusebius of Emesa's commentaries as a lone, *virtuoso* scholar, burning the midnight oil in his study.[13] Rather, as William Johnson has shown, across Greco-Roman antiquity, reading and writing was a social, communal activity.[14] Furthermore, all manner of practices — social, material, textual — of reading and writing contributed to the production not only of an intellectual "method," but also of books: namely, exegetical commentaries. The most plausible context in which

---

12 The most extensive treatment of the institutional character of Diodore's school is Leconte 1957, who critiques Meyer 1933 and Baur 1929–1930. Because the ancient mentions of Diodore's school are usually contained in narrations of John Chrysostom's life, scholarly accounts of the school are also often related to Chrysostom (as Meyer and Baur). However, more recent accounts of Chrysostom's life do not include extensive descriptions (or at least re-assessments) of the school itself (Kelly 1995; Brändle 1999). Many passing comments are also made about the school, but often with little reflection on how Diodore's school might have compared to other schools or what role it might have played in passing down exegetical knowledge (e.g., Liebeschuetz 2011, 127–130).
13 See, e.g., Schäublin 1974, 12, who draws from a statement made by Theodore in his *Commentary on John* to argue that the preacher's (i.e., John Chrysostom's) exegesis is determined by its homiletical context, while Theodore's scholarly commentary contains "pure" intellectual exegesis. For an account of the exegetical and theological differences between Theodore and John Chrysostom, see Edwards 2021.
14 Johnson 2009; 2010.

Diodore passed on his exegetical knowledge, in part through his commentaries, is his school in Antioch.

This paper falls into two parts. The first establishes that the commentaries of Diodore were produced in a school context — specifically in the instruction of grammar. While it has been argued that these figures were "influenced" intellectually by their grammatical and rhetorical educations, this sections shows that the connection is much closer than this: the commentaries derive from a school context in which grammar was taught on the basis of biblical texts. The second considers the larger institutional context in which the transmission of exegetical knowledge was made possible at this particular point in time: what the rest of the school might have looked like, and what hierarchical and economic factors allowed for this institution to flourish — and thus for exegetical knowledge to be propagated and passed on.

2 Diodore's Grammar School and Its Commentaries

Since the publication of Christoph Schäublin's pioneering work on Theodore's and Diodore's exegetical remains and, in the Anglophone world, Frances Young's independent evaluation of the same, it has become very common to claim that the "school of Antioch" is influenced by late ancient grammatical and rhetorical schools.[15] Even if the particulars of their arguments differ, both are concerned to show that these schools have "influenced" Diodore's and Theodore's exegesis. Indeed, "influence" stands in the title of Young's essay, while it is Schäublin's stated goal to come to a new understanding of the school of Antioch's *Einflüsse* and its *Hintergrund*. Likewise, both are concerned with charting continuities and discontinuities in methods (*Methoden*) and exegetical principles (*Grundsätze*). Schäublin amasses a huge amount of material to show that Diodore's and Theodore's exegesis resemble the exegesis of the grammar schools of antiquity — not, of course, in the interpretation of Homer and the Tragedians, but in the interpretation of the Bible.

While Schäublin shows convincingly that there is a relationship between grammatical instruction and the commentaries of Diodore and Theodore, his methodological approach leaves something to be desired. He chooses Diodore and Theodore as paradigms of the school of Antioch because, in contrast to the

---

15 Schäublin 1974; Young 1989.

works of John Chrysostom and Theodoret of Cyrrhus, their extant works are "pure and clear" (*rein und deutlich*) representations of the school's exegesis, before it has been put to pastoral use.¹⁶ However, because Schäublin is so focused on locating exegetical "methods," he ignores a good deal of the evidence even from Diodore – namely, those parts of his *Commentary on the Octateuch* which do not comport methdologically with a "typical 'Antiochene' achievement."¹⁷ Although he shrugs off this material, the evidence calls into question whether Antiochene exegesis, even in its "purest" form, is characterized by a consistent method.

Schäublin himself points towards a new answer to the problem of the coherence of Antiochene commentary. In the same chapter that he laments the loss of the "Antiochene" character of Diodore's exegesis in the *Commentary on the Octateuch*, he shows that the extant fragments of the commentary belong to the genre of questions and answers (*problemata kai luseis*), which was a common school exercise in antiquity.¹⁸ In other words, the commentaries of Diodore, whether or not they are characterized by a common method, are coherent insofar as *they are derivative of a school context*.

It should come as no surprise that these commentaries would come from a school context, since in late antiquity there is plenty of evidence of commentaries coming from a variety of school contexts: philosophical, grammatical, mathematical.¹⁹ Furthermore, the commentaries were produced in different ways, having different relationships to the act of teaching: some were lecture notes taken by students; some were written directly (but, of course, probably with the help of students, slaves, or other clergy) by someone who also taught philosophy; the texts of some were more "closed" based on the authority of the author, while some were more "open" and continued to be revised through successive generations of readers.²⁰ Some of these commentaries were, of course, grammatical. And it is especially these – more so than the philosophi-

---

16 Schäublin 1974, 11–12.
17 Schäublin 1974, 54.
18 Schäublin 1974, 56–57. Naturally, question and answer literature was not produced only within schools, but would leave a lasting impression in the "higher" literature of those educated in various subject areas. For example, within Diodore's circle, John Chrysostom often crafted sermons around *problemata kai luseis* (Mitchell forthcoming). Also see Reggiani 2020, esp. 181–184; Leith 2009.
19 See Taub 2017, esp. 86–90; Cribiore 2001, 142–143; Sharples 1990. Many have simply assumed that commentaries come from pedagogical contexts: Most 1999; Sluiter 1999.
20 Taub 2017, 90. On enslaved persons who were often involved in the production of knowledge in antiquity, see Coogan, in this volume.

cal — which should be classified as school texts; they were often produced in close proximity to teaching. As Raffaella Cribiore notes, the grammarian especially drew on commentaries, which were "geared toward rendering the text more easily approachable. Though learned points from erudite commentaries occasionally crept in, much of that information was omitted in favor of a concentration on notes of grammatical character, brief paraphrases, and glossographical material."[21] As we will see, Cribiore's description of the didactic commentaries of the grammarians, who commented on Homer and the Tragedians, applies also to Diodore's and Theodore's biblical commentaries.

Diodore's and Theodore's commentaries include what Raffaella Cribiore refers to as the "historical" side of grammar: "extracting from a text all of its constitutive elements, dealing not only with *realia* of persons and historical, geographical, and mythological components but also with glosses, figures, and tropes."[22] This included the "elucidation of unfamiliar vocabulary," "expanding on mythological matters," and "provid[ing] explanatory details on persons, places, and events mentioned in a text," as well as often extensive etymologizing.[23] With the exception of etymologies (which the Antiochenes employ less than, say, Philo of Alexandria), Cribiore's descriptions of the "historical" side of grammar — and what Bonner refers to as the "literary"[24] — is exactly what we find in the commentaries of Diodore and Theodore. Because there were different ways of categorizing the parts of grammar in antiquity, below I follow Frances Young, who employs Quintilian's terminology, and divide my discussion into *methodikē* — "analys[ing] a verse into parts of speech, metre, etc., to note linguistic usage, especially commenting on acceptable and unacceptable usage and style, to discuss the different meanings which may be given to each word, to expound unusual words, to elucidate figures of speech or ornamental devices" — and *historikē* — "explain[ing] the stories[,] unpack[ing] allusions to classical myths, gods, heroes, legends, histories."[25]

Under *methodikē* fall a number of the interpretative comments that occur in Diodore's and Theodore's commentaries on the psalms.[26] Both comment on

---

21 Cribiore 2001, 142.
22 Cribiore 2001, 206.
23 Cribiore 2001, 207–210.
24 Bonner 1977.
25 Young 1989, 185, 187.
26 Here I primarily draw upon Diodore's *Commentary on the Psalms*, in order to supplement the evidence identified by Schäublin, who was unable to make use of this commentary, since there was still uncertainty as to its authenticity. It remained unedited until Olivier 1980 — six years after Schäublin's book was published.

instances in which a psalm contains a verbal tense which goes against the sense of the psalm. These comments are plentiful, and occur on almost every page of Theodore's commentary in particular; yet a single example from Diodore will suffice — the first instance of such a comment in his *Commentary,* on Psalm 3: "One tense is used in place of another tense in these lines, and this is found frequently in the psalms."[27] Likewise, Diodore frequently comments on the use of the dative and accusative cases with the verb *krinō*. For example, "It should be noted that if 'Judge me' is used with the dative, it means 'Vindicate me,' as has often been said; but if 'Judge me' or 'Judge them' is used with the accusative, it means 'Condemn them.'"[28] He often offers definitions of terms which are particular to the Psalms, sometimes repeating himself; for example, he defines "ready" (ἕτοιμον) as "firm" (ἑδραῖον) and "solid" (βέβαιον) at least three times in his *Commentary*.[29] Likewise, both he and Theodore define obscure terms, sometimes differently from one another: for example, Diodore takes ὅπλου καὶ θυρεοῦ in Ps 34:2 — the latter being obscure — to refer to a round shield and a rectangular shield respectively, while Theodore takes the first to refer to all the accoutrements of war, and the second to a shield.[30] Both Theodore and Diodore (as well as Chrysostom) comment on Scripture's various linguistic "habits" (*ethē*); both comment time and again on the Psalms' tendency to substitute actions for speech: commenting on Psalm 2, Diodore writes, "[the Psalmist] took 'saying' not as speech but as an event,"[31] and a little further on in his comments on the same Psalm, "Again 'Then he will say' is as an event."[32]

Both Diodore and Theodore comment on multiple Greek versions of the Psalms — as does John Chrysostom — but each in different ways. Theodore is the most exuberant citer of the versions, and they also do the most work in his commentary, where he attempts to look for the version which expresses the

---

27 Diodore, *Comm. Ps.* 3.5 (Olivier 1980, 18): Χρόνος ἀντὶ χρόνου κεῖται ἐν τοῖς στίχοις, καὶ τοῦτο πολλαχοῦ τῶν ψαλμῶν εὑρίσκεται.
28 Diodore, *Comm. Ps.* 25.1b (Olivier 1980, 149): Σημειωτέον τοῦτο ὅτι εἴ ποτε ἐπὶ τῆς δοτικῆς κεῖται τὸ κρῖνόν μοι, δίκασόν μοι λέγει, καθὼς πολλάκις εἴρηται· εἰ δὲ ἐπὶ τῆς αἰτιατικῆς τεθείη τὸ κρῖνόν με ἢ κρῖνον αὐτούς, καταδίκασον αὐτοὺς λέγει. Also see Diodore, *Comm. Ps.* 5.11a (Olivier 1980, 31); *Comm. Ps.* 42.1b (Olivier 1980, 258).
29 Diodore, *Comm. Ps.* 7.13–14a (Olivier 1980, 41); *Comm. Ps.* 32.14a (Olivier 1980, 190); *Comm. Ps.* 37.18 (Olivier 1980, 232).
30 Diodore, *Comm. Ps.* 34.2 (Olivier 1980, 200); Theodore, *Comm. Ps.* 34.26b (Hill 2006, 384).
31 Diodore, *Comm. Ps.* 2.3 (Olivier 1980, 13): Τὸ «λέγοντες» οὐκ ἐπὶ φωνῆς ἔλαβεν, ἀλλ' ἐπὶ πράγματος.
32 Diodore, *Comm. Ps.* 2.5 (Olivier 1980, 14): «Τότε λαλήσει» πάλιν ἐπὶ πράγματος. Also see *Comm. Ps.* 34.3b (Olivier 1980, 201).

thought of the psalm "more clearly" (φανερώτερον).³³ All of them favor Symmachus over the other versions. Similarly, each comments on places where the sense of the Psalm is unclear as a result of the translation from Hebrew, even if they appear not to know Hebrew or ever Syriac.³⁴ Furthermore, although it is unclear exactly where the use of tropes should fall — whether *methodikē* or *historikē* (and different theorists of grammar class these differently) — metaphors and comparisons are especially explained in these commentaries. All of these comments so far mentioned, which occupy a significant part of the commentaries of Diodore and Theodore, are typical of grammar, and fall in Young's category (following Quintilian) of *methodikē*.

Likewise, the commentaries often include comments which fall under *historikē*. For every Psalm Diodore and Theodore interpret, they mention the psalm's *hypothesis* — its theme. These *hypotheseis* often are based on the historical figures and events found in other biblical books (especially Kings and Maccabees), but the commentators sometimes draw on extra-biblical material, as in Theodore's mention of Josephus.³⁵ Therefore, sometimes David is speaking about his own experiences, and sometimes he is prophesying about future events. More striking still are those psalms which have a sort of double persona, where David — one persona (*prosōpon*) — assumes the persona of yet another biblical character (often Hezekiah).³⁶ These *hypotheseis* are sometimes very lengthy, and the commentators often refer to the books from which they have learned of the stories by name. Then, in the verse-by-verse commentary that follows from these historical *hypotheseis*, Diodore and Theodore can be extremely specific with respect to the historical referents of various details in the Psalms.³⁷ For example, Diodore comments, "And again it says 'dog' here in the place of 'Absalom and Ahithophel'";³⁸ "He is talking about the same Assyrians,

---

33 See, for example, Theodore, *Comm. Ps.* 34.8a (Hill 2006, 356).
34 See, for example, Diodore, *Comm. Ps.* 26.6a (Olivier 1980, 155).
35 Theodore, *Comm. Ps.* 34.13b (Hill 2006, 368).
36 For example, as in Diodore's interpretation of Pss 19 and 31.
37 Diodore also thinks some of the Psalms do not have "historical" referents, but are instead "general," for the teaching of doctrine or ethics, for example in his interpretation of Pss 1 and 18.
38 *Comm. Ps.* 21.21 (Olivier 1980, 133): «Κυνὸς» δὲ πάλιν ἐνταῦθα λέγει ἀντὶ τοῦ αὐτοῦ τε τοῦ Ἀβεσαλώμ καὶ τοῦ Ἀχιτόφελ.

but he calls them 'unjust witnesses'";³⁹ "Here he calls the verdict against the Assyrians a 'word.'"⁴⁰

I have outlined these points of Diodore's and Theodore's exegesis, which are fairly well-known, not in order to show that their interpretative method is influenced by grammar, but to show that the commentaries themselves are evidence of schoolroom teaching, namely, grammatical instruction. The exegetical methods cannot be extracted from the form of the work; and indeed both the commentary form and the grammatical content point towards the grammar schoolroom as the historical context of the production and ongoing use of these commentaries.

3 From Schoolroom to Commentary

How exactly classroom instruction related to written commentary in Greco-Roman antiquity is not altogether clear. However, it is doubtful that there was only a single kind of relationship between the two. Some late antique commentaries derive from the notes of students, while philosophical commentaries are often written (i.e., taken down by a scribe) for pedagogical purposes, but less closely resemble classroom instruction. Probably in other cases, we have notes from classroom instruction which a scribe took down, and which the teacher would then edit accordingly — or even unedited transcripts.

In his study of Eusebius of Emesa, ter Haar Romeny assumes that Antiochene commentaries employed the last option, and on the basis of these commentaries — and with the help of a famous essay on grammar by Hermann Usener — describes the activities that he thinks would have taken place within the Antiochene schoolroom.⁴¹ First would come the reading of the text to be interpreted (τὸ ἀναγνωστικόν) — with proper "accentuation, word division, and punctuation."⁴² The next two parts, τὸ ἐξηγητικόν and τὸ διορθωτικόν, can come in either order. The latter is shorter in the Antiochenes than the former, including references to other versions and to the Hebrew, while the former is longer, and entails use of four "tools" (ὄργανα): τὸ γλωττηματικόν, τὸ ἱστορικόν, τὸ μετρι-

---

39 Diodore, *Comm. Ps.* 26.12b (Olivier 1980, 157): Αὐτοὺς λέγει τοὺς Ἀσσυρίους. «Ἀδίκους» δὲ «μάρτυρας» αὐτοὺς καλεῖ.
40 Diodore, *Comm. Ps.* 32.4 (Olivier 1980, 187): «Λόγον» ἐνταῦθα καλεῖ τὴν ἀπόφασιν τὴν κατὰ τῶν Ἀσσυρίων.
41 ter Haar Romeny 1997, 97–100. Usener 1892.
42 ter Haar Romeny 1997, 97.

κόν, τὸ τεχνικόν. The exegetical stuff of these "tools" is largely the same as what we have seen Frances Young describe as ἱστορική and μεθοδική, and Cribiore as the "historical" part of grammar. Finally would come ἡ κρίσις ποιημάτων or τὸ κριτικόν, which ter Haar Romeny identifies with moral or theological teaching, particularly typology (*theōria*). Although I am not as confident as ter Haar Romeny that we can arrive with such precision at the pedagogical process of Diodore's or Theodore's schoolroom, it is possible that this is not far off the mark.[43]

Notably, the commentaries of Diodore and Theodore lack a significant part of what fell under the purview of grammar. For example, there is no evidence in the commentaries of τὸ ἀναγνωστικόν — though this is not the kind of exercise that would lend itself to being written down — nor of the "classification and definition of the various parts of speech," and no review of declensions or conjugations.[44] When Diodore and Theodore do comment on verb tense or the uses of the dative or genitive, they assume that their audiences know these basics well. Likewise, the commentaries do not refer to the "technical" side of grammar — namely "letters, syllables, parts of speech, parsing and scansion, spelling, [and] correct Greek (with analogy, barbarisms, and solecisms)."[45] In other words, although the categories that grammarians used varied, this "technical" and more elementary part of grammatical instruction is mostly excluded from Antiochene commentaries.[46]

If these commentaries really testify to grammatical instruction, then why precisely these elements are excluded is not clear. It was probably not considered useful to record these more elementary aspects of grammar, and indeed there is little written evidence of this more elementary instruction in any of our sources. Furthermore, Diodore's grammatical curriculum could have included

---

43 We have been duly warned: Cribiore 2001, 143: "The transmitted school exercises are precious skeletons of ancient instruction, mere shadows of what went on in the classroom. They reach us as if in a vacuum, almost always deprived of the voice of the teacher..."; Sharples 1990, 83: "trying to establish what happened in that school and how it functioned is comparable to the task we would have if we had to establish what went on in a philosophy department in a modern university on the basis of a selection of books by the professor and a confused collection of his papers, the notes from which he lectured and the essays of his students, with no obvious indication of which were which."
44 Cribiore 1996, 52.
45 Bonner 1977, 52.
46 But, see Young (1989, 184): "Quintilian regrets that many teachers do not pay enough attention to these preliminary mechanical foundations, but rush on to display the more interesting aspects of their act."

different types of classroom instruction, with these commentaries giving access to only one sort; alternatively, these more mundane details might have been edited out of the commentary itself by the selectiveness of the scribe or by the choice of the commentator upon reviewing the transcript.

Fortunately, we also have a close comparandum for Diodore's school, namely that of Didymus the Blind in Alexandria. Didymus and Diodore were teaching at the same time: though Didymus appears to have had a longer teaching career, both were active in the middle to the latter half of the fourth century. In Didymus' case, we have not only some of his biblical commentaries, but also a couple of texts that appear to be lecture notes. It is usually thought that the lecture notes were taken down by stenographers in order to serve as the basis for a more polished, revised commentary. By some accident of history, these were never turned into a more literary commentary, but survive only in this unpolished form.[47] These lecture notes thus give insight into the relationship between the teacher and the exegete — the lectures delivered and the commentaries later produced. Even if there is not a linear development from the one to the other, there is a close relationship, for Didymus' more polished commentaries as well as these notes on the Psalms and Ecclesiastes include grammatical content. In other words, Didymus' commentaries were not produced in a vacuum — he was not a "pure" exegete — but within a specific pedagogical environment. Furthermore, as Blossom Stefaniw has recently argued, it is not just that the lectures — or even the commentaries — were vaguely "influenced" by Greco-Roman grammatical instruction, but instead testify to grammatical instruction on the basis of biblical texts instead of Homeric or tragic ones.[48] Notably, Didymus' commentaries and lecture notes only very occasionally include the more technical, elementary part of grammar. So it is hardly surprising that those of Diodore and Theodore also lack it.

A crucial question for the transmission of exegetical knowledge is the role that past interpretations played in Diodore's classroom. How, materially, does Diodore access older Antiochene exegetical tradition such that he can pass it down to his students and, later, to those who read his commentary? We know

---

[47] Bayliss 2015, 33; Nelson 1995, 17. Stefaniw (2019) disagrees with this assessment, especially given the differences between these lecture notes and the fragments of Didymus' *Commentary on the Psalms* which are extant in the catenae.

[48] Stefaniw 2019. Didymus was not the first of the Alexandrians to teach grammar in a Christian vein, but was preceded by Origen in the previous century: Neuschäfer 1987; Chin 2008, 74–76. Furthermore, Martens 2017 has identified Adrian's *Introduction to the Divine Scriptures* — whatever its relationship to Diodore's school — as a work of grammatical instruction and Adrian as doing the work of a *grammaticus* (52–55).

that one of the marks of many late ancient commentaries is that they engage closely with previous interpretations;[49] Porphyry, in his *Life of Plotinus*, gives us a precious (and famous) example of the use that earlier commentaries play in Plotinus' schoolroom: "In the meetings, commentaries would be read aloud to him"; then naming various Platonists and Aristotelians, Porphyry continues: "Nothing from these commentaries was spoken with absolute authority, but was peculiar to him and different in theory, and bore the sense of Ammonius in its insights. He would finish quickly and would briefly give the meaning of a profound theory, and move on."[50] It is not necessary that Diodore used other commentaries in a similar way; indeed the commentaries that come down to us would lead us to believe that he did not operate in this way. Nevertheless, his commentaries are derivative of earlier Antiochene commentary. Ter Haar Romeny has shown that Diodore is indebted to Eusebius of Emesa's interpretation.[51] So even if he did not make use of the physical books of Eusebius or others in the classroom, he has made substantial use of them at another time. Because we have less of the earlier Antiochene exegetical tradition, it is harder to trace the transmission of knowledge from his predecessors to Diodore than it is to trace from Diodore to those who follow him. And we have already seen that the commentaries of Diodore's students — those of Theodore and Chrysostom, and slightly later, Theodoret — were highly derivative of Diodore's exegesis. And, likewise, even if they did not carry Diodore's book into their own classrooms, they were deeply familiar with his teachings, whether from reading his commentaries or from recalling his grammar lessons (though, as we will see below, it was likely the former). In any case, the locus of the transmission of exegetical knowledge was the grammar classroom; closely linked to this classroom are the commentaries themselves, which then become loci of transmission of exegetical knowledge in their own right.

Although these grammatical commentaries — whether those of Diodore or Didymus — do not include everything that falls under the purview of the *grammatikos*, there is a relationship between grammatical instruction and these commentaries that goes beyond mere "influence." The commentaries *are* grammar. Although the exact process of production of these texts is lost to us

---

49 See, e.g., Sharples 1990.
50 Porphyry, *Life of Plotinus* 14.10–18 (Henry/Schwyzer 1964, 17–18): Ἐν δὲ ταῖς συνουσίαις ἀνεγινώσκετο μὲν αὐτῷ τὰ ὑπομνήματα, ... Ἐλέγετο δὲ ἐκ τούτων οὐδὲν καθάπαξ, ἀλλ' ἴδιος ἦν καὶ ἐξηλλαγμένος ἐν τῇ θεωρίᾳ καὶ τὸν Ἀμμωνίου φέρων νοῦν ἐν ταῖς ἐξετάσεσιν. Ἐπληροῦτο δὲ ταχέως καὶ δι' ὀλίγων δοὺς νοῦν βαθέος θεωρήματος ἀνίστατο.
51 ter Haar Romeny 1997, 131–135.

(even if we might guess at it), there appears to be a real relationship between grammar instruction through the psalms and the commentaries themselves, which together work to transmit the Antiochene exegetical tradition.

4 Higher Education in Diodore's *Asketerion*

The pedagogical nature of these commentaries coincides with the information that ancient historical sources provide: that Diodore was actively teaching at an institution in Antioch. For the sake of better understanding the context in which Antiochene exegetical knowledge was passed down, I attempt a broader reconstruction of the school. This reconstruction is necessarily speculative, but is nevertheless based upon ancient comparanda, accounts of the late ancient ecclesiastical historians, and the literary remains of Diodore and his students.

Whether Diodore's and Carterius' school was a "day school" or a "boarding school" of a monastic type is impossible to know, and scholars have often disagreed — which is easy to do, given the limited evidence of the institutional school itself. However, it is unlikely that it was as informal as has sometimes posited of other late ancient religious schools.[52] Rather, given its close relationship to grammatical and rhetorical education, it probably had an extensive curriculum which was designed by the teachers themselves and which could fluctuate somewhat (something especially likely given the novelty of Christian education in the middle of the fourth century). There were likely regular days and hours of instruction and the instruction in the Psalms and Genesis would have been integral to this curriculum.[53] Diodore's important role within the ("moderate" pro-Nicene) Antiochene church lends further credence to the idea that there was some formal, if not institutional, character to the school. As a priest, Diodore was close to the bishop Meletius and his successor Flavian. The school itself was probably endorsed by the Antiochene bishop as means of educating the clergy, and several of its students ended up as prominent bishops. Since Diodore was a priest of the diocese, it also seems likely that the school was supported financially by the same (with personnel, even more so than in

---

[52] On the Manichees: Han 2021; on Palestinian Rabbinic Judaism: Hezser 1997, 195–214, on rabbinic Judaism in Sasanian Babylonia: Goodblatt 1975, 263–285.
[53] Stefaniw 2019 suggests this with respect to Didymus' school (86); compare with the schedule of the law school in Berytus, on which study was six days per week (excluding Sundays): Harries 2016, 160. Also see Bonner 1977, 139–140.

the modern world, being the major expense).⁵⁴ Unfortunately much else — for example, where this school met and what other instructors there might have been — is lost to us. Nevertheless, based on the commentaries which come down to us from members of this school (Diodore, Theodore, and John Chrysostom) it is clear that part of what went on at this school was grammatical instruction.

When we survey the other evidence for the school, it begins to seem unlikely that grammar was the only subject taught at Diodore's school. There are several reasons for thinking that instruction went beyond grammar. First, Theodoret of Cyrrhus, in his *Ecclesiastical History*, comments that Diodore's business as a priest in Antioch was not preaching, but teaching polemical theology:

> Like a trainer, the excellent Flavian anointed the great Diodore as an athlete for the pentathlon. For at that time [Diodore] didn't preach at church services, but provided those who did serve with a great abundance of arguments and scriptural concepts. While the former thus stretched their bows against the blasphemy of Arius, he offered them arrows from his mind, as if from a quiver. And discoursing at home and abroad, he easily tore asunder the net of the heretics.⁵⁵

This description of Diodore's teaching does not sound like the grammatical instruction of his commentaries. Rather, Diodore seems to have taught *polemics* — in other words, a higher level of theological argumentation. Additionally, when Theodoret of Cyrrhus relates that Theodore of Mopsuestia and John Chrysostom studied with Diodore, he mentions not the interpretation of Scripture, but the combatting of heresy.⁵⁶ Admittedly, Theodoret, who was in the midst of having his own orthodoxy questioned, has good reason for maintaining that those from whose writings he had benefited — Theodore and Diodore — spent their time combatting heretics. However, Theodoret is also consistent

---

54 This is in constrast, apparently, to the later school of Nisibis. See Possekel 2020b.
55 Theodoret, *Hist. eccl.* 4.25.4 (GCS 19, p. 264, lines 5–14): Φλαβιανὸς δὲ ὁ ἄριστος ... οἷόν τις παιδοτρίβης τὸν μέγαν Διόδωρον καθάπερ τινὰ πένταθλον ἤλειφεν ἀθλητήν. κατ᾽ ἐκεῖνον γὰρ τὸν καιρὸν ἐν μὲν τοῖς ἐκκλησιαστικοῖς οὐκ ἐδημηγόρει συλλόγοις, τοῖς δὲ τοῦτο δρῶσι πολλὴν παρεῖχεν ἀφθονίαν ἐνθυμημάτων τε καὶ γραφικῶν νοημάτων. καὶ οἱ μὲν ἔτεινον κατὰ τῆς Ἀρείου βλασφημίας τὰ τόξα, οὗτος δὲ καθάπερ ἔκ τινος ὁπλοθήκης, ἐκ τῆς διανοίας τὰ βέλη προσέφερεν· οἴκοι μέντοι καὶ δημοσίᾳ διαλεγόμενος, τῶν αἱρετικῶν τὰς ἄρκυς ῥᾳδίως διέσπα. There are also many ancient and medieval sources that report that Diodore wrote theological treatises, which are now almost entirely lost to us. For a discussion of these fragments, see Ambramowski 1931, esp. 247–253; additionally, a fragment of his treatise *Against the Manichees* was discovered (Malavasi 2015). For a compilation of the theological fragments of Diodore (and Theodore), see Behr 2011.
56 Theodoret, *Hist. eccl.* 5.39.

enough in mentioning Diodore's role in teaching polemics that Diodore was likely teaching at a level above the grammatical instruction that we have already seen.

It is also doubtful that John Chrysostom and Theodore attended Diodore's school merely for grammar lessons. These two — and undoubtedly other prominent students — had already received their grammatical education long ago. Chrysostom in particular had received a thoroughgoing education in the art of rhetoric from the famous Libanius. If Diodore was only teaching grammar, and not higher theological instruction, then we should not expect Theodore or John Chrysostom to have studied with him at all — not to mention his other well-educated student Maximus, who later became bishop of Isaurian Seleucia, and perhaps also Evagrius of Pontus.[57] It is much more likely that John and Theodore, along with others who were being prepared for high office in the church, were educated in the higher studies that Theodoret suggests: theology and polemics.

There are also hints in Diodore's extant works that he is reserving certain theological or exegetical teachings for those capable of them, at a more advanced pedagogical stage, and for this reason excludes them from his grammatical instruction and, thus, his commentary. For example, in the prologue to Diodore's *Commentary on Psalm* 118, he writes, "But it is necessary to leave such contemplation (*theōria*) for those who have a greater gift to consider, and we shall speak about the answer according to history."[58] Likewise, in Diodore's *Commentary on the Psalms* there are multiple instances in which the commentator approves of a psalm being interpreted christologically, but declines to do so himself, at least in the context of his current *grammatical* interpretation. In one of these instances he writes, "If someone were to call the weapons and foes and nations, metaphorically, demons, and say that the coming of Christ is liberation from them, such a person would perhaps be interpreting in a contemplative manner. And we do not keep them from doing so, but we prefer nothing to the facts themselves and truth itself."[59] Throughout the commentary Diodore thus sets the "ground rules" for higher interpretation. Remarkably, in John Chrysos-

---

[57] Bunge 2018.
[58] Mariès 1919, 98: Ἀλλὰ τὴν μὲν τοιαύτην θεωρίαν τοῖς πλείονος τυχοῦσι χαρίσματος καταλειπτέον νοεῖν, ἡμεῖς δὲ τὴν καθ' ἱστορίαν αἴτησιν.
[59] Diodore, *Comm. Ps.* 9.1 (Olivier 1980, 51): Εἰ δέ τις μεταφορικῶς ὅπλα καὶ ἐχθροὺς καὶ ἔθνη τοὺς δαίμονας ὀνομάζει, καὶ ἀπαλλαγὴν τούτων εἶναι φησὶ τὴν τοῦ Χριστοῦ παρουσίαν, θεωρηματικώτερον μὲν ὁ τοιοῦτος ἴσως ἐξηγήσεται, καὶ οὐ κωλύομεν, ἡμεῖς δὲ αὐτῶν τῶν πραγμάτων καὶ αὐτῆς τῆς ἀληθείας οὐδὲν προτιμῶμεν. Also see his comments at *Comm. Ps.* 15.11c (Olivier 1980, 84) and *Comm. Ps.* 23.10b (Olivier 1980, 142).

tom's *Commentary on the Psalms*, as he interprets the same psalm, he almost entirely follows Diodore in suggesting the possibility — even importance — of a higher interpretation, while declining to do so himself: "If it is necessary to say something according to a higher interpretation, it shouldn't be rejected."[60] Then, having discussed the value of interpreting according to this higher sense, he writes, "But we leave these considerations for the learned to apply."[61] Thus while Diodore's and Theodore's commentaries instruct in grammar, they are also meant to be propaideutic for higher interpretation, which Diodore calls *theōria* and Chrysostom, *anagōgē*. This aspect of Diodore's commentaries might reflect the reality of the biblical and theological instruction within this school.

It is also possible that students such as Theodore and John Chrysostom were "apprenticed" to Diodore as exegetes, and that as part of this education they composed their own commentaries in imitation of Diodore's *Commentary on the Psalms*.[62] Indeed, both Theodore's and John Chrysostom's commentaries on the psalms are derivative of Diodore's. What remains of Chrysostom's *Commentary on the Psalms* is not typical of the exegesis found in his sermons or even in his other commentaries: for example, in many of his interpretation of the Psalms he states first — like Diodore and Theodore — what the *hypothesis* of the Psalm is before going into more detail verse-by-verse. This is also Chrysostom's only exegetical work where he comments with any frequency and in any detail on different levels of interpretation: *kata lexin* and *kat' anagōgēn*. He also sometimes follows Diodore's interpretations very closely. Chrysostom's *Commentary* might therefore be among his earlier works.[63] We can say with more certainty, though, that Theodore's *Commentary on the Psalms* was written in his youth: Facundus of Hermiane, in his work defending the "Antiochenes" against the accusations of Justinian's *Three Chapters*, reports that Theodore himself was unhappy with his *Commentary on the Psalms*, as it was written when he was still immature.[64] It is thus a distinct possibility that both of these figures, early in

---

60 John Chrysostom, *Exp. Ps.* 9.3 (PG 55, 126, 44–46): Εἰ δὲ χρή τι καὶ κατὰ ἀναγωγὴν εἰπεῖν, οὐ παραιτητέον. Τὰ μὲν γὰρ ἔστι καὶ θεωρῆσαι· τὰ δὲ οὕτω δεῖ νοεῖν, ὡς εἴρηται μόνον.
61 John Chrysostom, *Exp. Ps.* 9.3 (PG 55, 127, 16–17): Ἀλλὰ ταῦτα τοῖς φιλομαθέσι καταλιπόντες ἁρμόζειν.
62 Although by this time legal training had changed, earlier Roman legal education through apprenticeship serves as a good parallel (Crook 1995, 42).
63 See Hill 1998, 4–5.
64 Facundus of Hermiane, *Pro defensione* 3.6, apparently quoting Theodore's own reflections on his *Commentary on the Psalms* which is found in a fragment of Theodore's *Contra allegoricos*. On the other side of the controversy from Facundus, however, is Hesychius of Jerusalem,

their ecclesiastical careers, wrote these works under the supervision of Diodore, the master grammarian and exegete. As I will note below, however, given the great expense of book production and the length of their commentaries, these figures were no *mere* apprentices, but had ascended to the summit of biblical and theological education, perhaps even teaching at the school under the watchful eye of Diodore.[65]

Although here we are primarily concerned with Diodore's school in Antioch, it is worth noting the potential contexts for Theodore's commentaries, since they closely resemble the grammatical nature of Diodore's commentaries. Although scholars have often repeated the claim that Theodore succeeded Diodore as the head of the school of Antioch, the evidence for this is late.[66] It seems more likely that he remained in Antioch for only a short time after Diodore was ordained bishop of Tarsus, and shortly thereafter left for Tarsus himself; after his arrival in Tarsus he was ordained to the subsidiary bishopric of Mopsuestia, which was near Tarsus.[67] Nevertheless, there are two plausible school contexts for Theodore's grammatical commentaries. As already mentioned, it is likely that he was already teaching as a biblical grammarian at the school in Antioch while Diodore presided over the school. However, it is also possible that in addition to his episcopal duties in Mopsuestia, he also taught grammar there — or even in nearby Tarsus. (He hardly would have been as busy as Diodore in the metropolis of Tarsus.) Again, grammar instruction was not always as formal as what we have described with respect to the school of Antioch. Theodore could have served as bishop, grammarian, and teacher of theology in Mopsuestia with some ease, and with the help of a priest or two.

Much of this account of this school is speculative. Nevertheless, I have ventured to fill out the picture of Diodore's school because there is some historical context in which these commentaries were produced. This pedagogical context is the most compelling explanation for the production of the commentaries and therefore also for the transmission of this particular tradition of exegetical

---

who notes that Theodore was duplicitous, promising to destroy his *Commentary on the Psalms*, but in fact preserving it. See Van Hoof/Manafis/Van Nuffelen 2016, 518–519.

65 A close analogue for this are the four teachers ("rhetors") who were employed at Libanius' school in Antioch, mentioned in *Or.* 31 (Foerster 1906, 119–146). Additional assistant teachers are known from Libanius' correspondence, on which see Cribiore 2007, 33–37.

66 The earliest we hear of this idea is centuries later, in Barḥadbšabba, *Cause* (Scher 1908, 378).

67 Although, as for the biography of Diodore, we only have a few historical hints about his life (many of which are written a century or two after his death). Nevertheless, for a good account of his life, which makes use of the available sources, see Swete 1911.

knowledge. For the sake of demonstrating the plausibility of this reconstruction, I mention two less likely alternatives.

The first possible alternative is that a wealthy patron or patrons funded the production of Diodore's and Theodore's commentaries, for the sake of building up their own Christian library and for circulating these works among their peers. While the elite would undoubtedly spend huge amounts of money for books that might lend both erudition and prestige, it is hard to imagine that these grammatical commentaries would be among them: they are not high philosophy or rhetoric, nor are they even theological commentary.[68] They are also highly repetitive — which perhaps relates to their pedagogical context, in which the same students might not always have been present. Certainly biblical commentaries were funded by patrons with high social and intellectual standing. This occurs as early as the commentaries of Origen and, closer to Diodore's time, in the scholarly pursuits of Jerome. But these commentaries are often more erudite works. Within this close-knit school of Diodore, we have the example of Theodore's *Commentary on John*, which was probably his final work. This commentary appears to have been funded by an individual patron, to whom it is addressed.[69] Unlike his *Commentary on the Psalms* (and those on Paul and on the prophets), this commentary is highly theological. Other than paraphrase, we see in the *Commentary on John* few of the grammatical markers of his other commentaries. (Notably, in the single preface from these grammatical commentaries that survives — that of Diodore — the work is not addressed to a patron, but is intended to be useful for ecclesiastical or monastic communities who spend time praying or chanting the psalms.[70]) This *Commentary on John* was probably not produced in a school context. Indeed, the differences between this commentary and Theodore's (and Diodore's) other commentaries is illustrative: the differing funding models (patron-funded vs. [perhaps] diocesan-funded) and the different generic markers (theological vs. grammatical) point to different contexts of production. Therefore, while we have evidence of books which were produced for elite individuals, these grammatical commentaries are another type of literature altogether.

A non-diocesan or non-hierarchical monastic context is even less likely, given the nature of monasticism in Syria and Asia Minor in the fourth century. As far as we know, Syrian monasteries in the environs of Antioch were not yet

---

68 On the expense of books, see Bagnall 2009, 50–70.
69 Theodore of Mopsuestia, *Comm. Jo.* pr. (Vosté 1940, 3).
70 Diodore of Tarsus, *Comm. Ps.* pr.1 (Olivier 1980, 4).

the economic centres that they would become shortly thereafter.[71] Neither were monasteries yet the centres of scholarship and scribal production that they would become in later centuries in, for example, the monasteries of the Syriac world and of Constantinople, respectively.[72] Therefore it is unlikely that a monastery which was independent of the urban diocesan hierarchy would have had the resources, whether financial or institutional, for the production of books.

Roger Bagnall, who has written most extensively about the economics of book production and ownership in late antiquity, has commented that "Christian books had no role in the traditional Greek educational system of these centuries. Thus no copies would have been made for ownership by teachers [or] for use in schools...".[73] However, by the fourth century we do indeed see the emergence of Christian institutions of higher learning (e.g., those of Didymus and Diodore), and we have good reason to believe they were producing books.[74] These schools were not "traditional," but were new Christian schools modelled on the traditional Greek educational system. Within these schools — just as within the grammatical, philosophical, and rhetorical schools — commentaries were used and produced. Diodore's school is one for which we have evidence; centuries later we have evidence for Syrian schools which make use of Theodore's commentaries (in Syriac translation).[75] Undoubtedly, there were other school contexts, more and less formal, in which Antiochene exegesis, through the use of these and other commentaries, were reproduced and transmitted. While many of these contexts are lost, Diodore's school is one identifiable step — and one of the most imporant ones — in the transmission of this tradition of exegetical knowledge.

---

71 See Daniel Hull's work on the monasteries of the Limestone Massif: Hull 2006; 2008.
72 On Syrian monasticism at this time, see Patrich 1995, 22–28; Vööbus 1960, 61–69.
73 Bagnall 2009, 50. Though, as Bagnall notes later in the same book (60), we know little about the economic activity of churches or monasteries anywhere in the Mediterranean or Near East in the fourth century.
74 Julian's decree against the Christian teaching of pagan classics furnishes further proof of Christian schools in the middle of the fourth century, though of course not all of these went on to teach on the basis of Scripture.
75 Space does not permit me to go into detail on the use of *others'* commentaries in grammatical or philosophical instruction. However, on the use of Theodore's commentaries in the school of Nisibis, see Becker 2006b, 113–125, and Possekel 2020b.

5 Conclusions

This institutional context for the production of the commentaries of Diodore and his school, which I have outlined here, has significant implications for the history of exegetical methods. First, the commentaries of Diodore and Theodore present a limited picture of Antiochene exegesis: they are *only* grammatical commentaries. This is why we do not see much "higher" exegesis in them. When we consider that there was another step in "Antiochene" theological pedagogy, we find that higher christological intepretations are no less a part of the Antiochene exegetical tradition. Diodore's own statements about *theōria* confirm this: "For *historia* is not opposed to higher contemplation, but is found to be foundation and basis of higher concepts."[76] Theodoret's comments concerning Diodore's theological teaching confirm the same thing: higher interpretation is an integral part of the Antiochene tradition. Nevertheless, we would be remiss to deny the effect that the *particular* grammatical training of the school of Antioch exerts. While both Didymus and Diodore teach grammar, each makes use of the freedom allowed of the *grammatikos*,[77] and includes different grammatical comments. Diodore and Theodore are selective, and the focus of their grammatical teaching indeed "historical." Even when John Chrysostom or Theodoret interpret biblical texts christologically, the historical thrust of Antiochene interpretation does not disappear. The higher level of Antiochene education is built upon the foundation of Antiochene grammar in the school of Diodore.

Nevertheless, this essay has not been primarily about exegetical methods. Instead, against the background of a tradition of scholarship which has focused on intellectual "influence" and "methods," this essay has located in the school of Diodore a concrete context in which an Antiochene tradition of biblical interpretation was passed on. This is just one institutional context which allowed exegetical knowledge, in the Antiochene tradition, to be, first, produced, and then, transmitted. Although we do not know exactly the status that *inter alia* Eusebius of Emesa's work had in the school of Antioch, it is likely that his commentaries formed a part of the literary tradition that Diodore was seeking to pass on when he wrote in his *Commentary on the Psalms*, "Therefore, leaving those who desire to consider, as they wish, to interpret the psalm thus, I myself

---

[76] Diodore, *Comm. Ps.* pr. (Olivier 1980, 7): Οὐδὲ γὰρ ἐναντιοῦται ἡ ἱστορία τῇ ὑψηλοτέρᾳ θεωρίᾳ, τοὐναντίον δὲ κρηπὶς εὑρίσκεται καὶ ὑποβάθρα τῶν ὑψηλοτέρων νοημάτων.
[77] See, e.g., Bonner 1977, 52.

will interpret historically, *as I also received*."⁷⁸ Diodore was passing on the exegetical knowledge that he had received and which, in all likelihood, was delivered to him also in a pedagogical context which is now lost to us — as most ancient school contexts are. Nevertheless, like Diodore's school, the transmission and further production of exegetical knowledge did not take place primarily through individual readers, taking inspiration from the methods of previous writers, but in social-ecclesial contexts of reading and writing. These contexts differ in their formality or institutionality, but the production and transmission of this exegetical knowledge always had material and social components. We do not have one lone genius after another, inspired by one another in some long chain. Instead, contexts such as Diodore's school were responsible for the continuing transmission and production of knowledge.

Bibliography

Abramowski, R. (1931), "Untersuchungen zu Diodor von Tarsus", *Zeitschrift für die neutestamentliche Wissenschaft* 30, 234–262.
Amirav, H. (2001), "Exegetical Models and Chrysostomian Homiletics: The Example of Gen. 6.2", *Studia Patristica* 37, 311–318.
Amirav, H. (2003), *Rhetoric and Tradition: John Chrysostom on Noah and the Flood*, Leuven.
Bagnall, R. (2009), *Early Christian Books in Egypt*, Princeton.
Barnish, S. (1989), "The Work of Cassiodorus after His Conversion", *Latomus* 48, 57–87.
Baur, C. (1929–1930), *Der heilige Johannes Chrysostomus und seine Zeit*, 2 vols., Munich.
Bayliss, G. (2015), *The Vision of Didymus the Blind: A Fourth Century Virtue-Origenism*, Oxford.
Becker, A. (2006a), "The Dynamic Reception of Theodore of Mopsuestia in the Sixth Century: Greek, Syriac, and Latin", in: S. Johnson (ed.), *Greek Literature in Late Antiquity*, London, 41–60.
Becker, A. (2006b), *Fear of God and the Beginning of Wisdom: The School of Nisibis and the Development of Scholastic Culture in Late Antique Mesopotamia*, Philadelphia.
Becker, A. (2008), *Sources for the History of the School of Nisibis*, Liverpool.
Behr, J. (2011), *The Case Against Diodore and Theodore: Texts and Their Contexts*, Oxford.
Bonner, S. (1977), *Education in Ancient Rome: From the Elder Cato to the Younger Pliny*, London.
Brändle, R. (1999), *Johannes Chrysostomus: Bischof, Reformer, Märtyrer*, Stuttgart.
Bunge, G. (2018), "Évagre le Pontique fut-il un condisciple de saint Jean Chrysostome?", *Irénikon* 91, 163–183, 323–345.
Bürsgens, W. (2003), *Cassiodorus. Institutiones divinarum et saecularium litterarum*, 2 vols., Fontes Christiani 39.1, Freiburg.

---

78 Diodore, *Comm. Ps.* 5.pr (Olivier 1980, 28): Καταλείψας οὖν νοεῖν ὡς βούλονται τοῖς ἐπιθυμοῦσιν οὕτως ἑρμηνεύειν τὸν ψαλμόν, αὐτὸς τὴν καθ' ἱστορίαν, καὶ ὡς παρέλαβον, ἑρμηνείαν ποιήσομαι.

Chin, C.M. (2008), *Grammar and Christianity in the Late Roman World*, Philadelphia.
Cribiore, R. (1996), *Writing, Teachers, and Students in Greco-Roman Egypt*, Atlanta.
Cribiore, R. (2001), *Gymnastics of the Mind: Greek Education in Hellenistic and Roman Egypt*, Princeton.
Cribiore, R. (2007), *The School of Libanius in Late Antique Antioch*, Princeton.
Crook, J. (1995), *Legal Advocacy in the Roman World*, Ithaca, NY.
Edwards, R.G.T. (2021), "The Gospel of John and Antiochene Christology: The Diverging Paths of Theodore of Mopsuestia and John Chrysostom", *Scottish Journal of Theology* 74, 333–345.
Fairbairn, D. (2007), "Patristic Exegesis and Theology: The Cart and the Horse", *Westminster Journal of Theology* 69, 1–19.
Fiaccadori, G. (1985), "Cassiodorus and the School of Nisibis", *Dumbarton Oaks Papers* 39, 135–137.
Foerster, R. (1906), *Libanii Opera III: Orationes XXVI-L*, Leipzig.
Goodblatt, D. (1975), *Rabbinic Institutions in Sasanian Babylonia*, Leiden.
Halporn, J. (2004), *Cassiodorus: Institutions of Divine and Secular Learning and On the Soul*, Liverpool.
Han, J. (2021), "Mani's Metivta: Manichaean Pedagogy in its Late Antique Mesopotamian Context", *Harvard Theological Review* 114, 346–370.
Harries, J. (2016), "Legal Education and Training of Lawyers", in: P.J. Du Plessis/C. Ando/K. Tuori (eds.), *The Oxford Handbook of Roman Law and Society*, Oxford.
Henry, P./H.-R. Schwyzer (1964), *Plotini Opera I. Porphyrii vita Plotini. Enneades I-III*, Oxford.
Hezser, C. (1997), *The Social Structure of the Rabbinic Movement in Roman Palestine*, Tübingen.
Hill, R.C. (1998), *St. John Chrysostom: Commentary on the Psalms*, Brookline, MA.
Hill, R.C. (2005), *Reading the Old Testament in Antioch*, Leiden.
Hill, R.C. (2006), *Theodore of Mopsuestia: Commentary on Psalms 1–81*, Atlanta.
Hull, D. (2006), *The Archaeology of Monasticism: Landscape, Politics and Social Organisation in Late Antique Syria*, Ph.D. diss., University of York.
Hull, D. (2008), "A Spatial and Morphological Analysis of Monastic Sites in the Northern Limestone Massif, Syria", *Levant* 40, 89–113.
Johnson, W. (2009), "Constructing Elite Reading Communities in the High Empire", in: W. Johnson and H. Parker (eds.), *Ancient Literacies: The Culture of Reading in Greece and Rome*, Oxford, 320–330.
Johnson, W. (2010), *Readers and Reading Culture in the High Roman Empire: A Study of Elite Communities*, Oxford.
Kelly, J.N.D. (1995), *Golden Mouth: The Story of John Chrysostom — Ascetic, Preacher, Bishop*, Ithaca, NY.
Leconte, R. (1957), "L'Asceterium de Diodore", in: *Mélanges bibliques, rédigés en l'honneur de André Robert*, Paris.
Leith, D. (2009), "Question-Types in Medical Catechisms on Papyrus", in: L.C. Taub/A. Doody (eds.), *Authorial Voices in Greco-Roman Technical Writing*, Trier, 107–123.
Liebeschuetz, J.H.W.G. (2011), *Ambrose and John Chrysostom: Clerics between Desert and Empire*, Oxford.
Malavasi, G. (2015), "Diodore of Tarsus' Treatise Against the Manichaeans: A New Fragment", *Vigiliae Christianae* 69, 296–304.
Mariès, L. (1919), "Extraits du Commentaire de Diodore de Tarse sur les Psaumes", *Recherches de Science Religieuse* 9, 79–101.

Martens, P. (2012), "Origen against History? Reconsidering the Critique of Allegory", *Modern Theology* 28, 635–656.
Martens, P. (2017), *Adrian's Introduction to the Divine Scriptures: An Antiochene Handbook for Scriptural Interpretation*, Oxford.
Meyer, L. (1933), *Saint Jean Chrysostome: maître de perfection chrétienne*, Paris.
Mitchell, M. (2005), "Patristic Rhetoric on Allegory: Origen and Eustathius Put 1 Samuel 28 on Trial", *Journal of Religion* 85, 414–445.
Mitchell, M. (forthcoming), *John Chrysostom on Paul: Praises and Problem Passages*, Atlanta.
Most, G.W. (1999), "Preface", in: G.W. Most (ed.), *Commentaries – Kommentare*, Göttingen, vii–xv.
Münter, F. (1811), *De Schola Antiochena*, Copenhagen.
Nelson, A. (1995), *The Classroom of Didymus the Blind*, Ph.D. diss., University of Michigan.
Neuschäfer, B. (1987), *Origenes als Philologe*, Basel.
O'Donnell, J. (1979), *Cassiodorus*, Berkeley.
Olivier, J.-M. (1980), *Diodorus Tarsensis. Commentarii in Psalmos I: Commentarii in Psalmos I-L*, CCSG 6, Turnhout.
Patrich, J. (1995), *Sabas, Leader of Palestinian Monasticism: A Comparative Study in Eastern Monasticism, Fourth to Seventh Centuries*, Washington, DC.
Périchon, P./P. Maraval (2006), *Socrate de Constantinople. Histoire ecclésiastique, livres IV–VI*, SC 505, Paris.
Possekel, U. (2020a), "Transmitting Theodore to the Church of the East: The Contribution of Thomas of Edessa", *Journal of Ecclesiastical History* 71, 712–737.
Possekel, U. (2020b), "'Go and Set Up for Yourselves Beautiful Laws …'. The School of Nisibis and Institutional Autonomy in Late Antique Education", in: M. Perkams/A. Schilling (eds.), *Griechische Philosophie und Wissenschaft bei den Ostsyrern: Zum Gedenken an Mār Addai Scher (1867–1915)*, Berlin, 29–48.
Reggiani, N. (2020), "Digitizing Medical Papyri in Question-and-Answer Format", in: M. Meeusen (ed.), *Ancient Greek Medicine in Questions and Answers: Diagnostics, Didactics, Dialectics*, Leiden, 181–212.
Schäublin, C. (1974), *Untersuchungen zu Methode und Herkunft der antiochenischen Exegese*, Cologne.
Scher, A. (1908), "Mar Barḥadbšabba 'Arbaya, Évêque de Ḥalwan (Vie siècle). Cause de la fondation des écoles", in: R. Graffin/F. Nau (eds.), *Patrologia Orientalis* 4, Paris, 319–397.
Sharples, R. (1990), "The School of Alexander?", in: R. Sorabji (ed.), *Aristotle Transformed: The Ancient Commentators and the Influence*, Ithaca, NY, 83–111.
Sluiter, I. (1999), "Commentaries and the Didactic Tradition", in: G.W. Most (ed.), *Commentaries — Kommentare*, Göttingen, 173–205.
Stefaniw, B. (2019), *Christian Reading: Language, Ethics, and the Order of Things*, Oakland.
Swete, H.B. (1911), "Theodorus", in: H. Wace/W. Piercy (eds.), *A Dictionary of Early Christian Biography*, London.
Ter Haar Romeny, R.B. (1997), *A Syrian in Greek Dress: The Use of Greek, Hebrew, and Syriac Biblical Texts in Eusebius of Emesa's Commentary on Genesis*, Leuven.
Usener, H. (1892), "Ein altes Lehrgebäude der Philologie", in: *Sitzungsberichte der philosophisch-philologischen und der historischen Classe der k. b. Akademie der Wissenschaften zu München*, 582–648.
Van Hoof, L./P. Manafis/P. Van Nuffelen (2016), "Hesychius of Jerusalem, *Ecclesiastical History* (CPG 6582)", *Greek, Roman, and Byzantine Studies* 56, 504–527.

Vööbus, A. (1960), *History of Asceticism in the Syrian Orient, Volume 2: Early Monasticism in Mesopotamia and Syria*, Louvain.

Vosté, J.-M. (1940), *Theodori Mopsuesteni Commentarius in evangelium Iohanis apostoli*, CSCO 62, Leuven.

Young, F. (1989), "The Rhetorical Schools and their Influence on Patristic Exegesis", in: R. Williams (ed.), *The Making of Orthodoxy: Essays in Honour of Henry Chadwick*, Cambridge, 182–199.

List of Contributors

Monika Amsler (PhD, University of Zurich) is a historian of religion and currently a postdoctoral researcher at the Institute of History at the University of Bern, Switzerland. Her first book *The Talmud and Late Antique Book Culture* is forthcoming with Cambridge University Press. Other than education and book production, her research interests cover medicine, magic, and religion, that is, ancient world making more broadly.

Elizabeth Mattingly Conner is a Roman historian with an interest in late-antique aristocratic self-presentation and the transformations of Hellenism in the later Roman Greek East. Since 2015, she has worked as a lecturer and researcher at the University of Maryland, College Park. She also taught at the Eberhard Karls Universität, Tübingen (2017–2018). Her book manuscript, "Mapping a Late Antique Republic of Letters," investigates the role of classical culture as an implement of patronage, leadership, and intellectual sociability in the letters of under-studied Christian literati from the Greek East.

Jeremiah Coogan is Assistant Professor of New Testament at the Jesuit School of Theology of Santa Clara University in Berkeley, California. Coogan is a historian of early Christianity whose research focuses on Gospel reading, material texts, and late antiquity. His monograph *Eusebius the Evangelist* (Oxford University Press, 2022) analyses Eusebius of Caesarea's fourth-century reconfiguration of the New Testament Gospels as a window into broader questions of technology and textuality in early Christianity and the late ancient Mediterranean.

Robert Edwards (PhD, University of Notre Dame) is currently a Humboldt Research Fellow and Guest Researcher at the University of Göttingen, having studied previously in Canada and the USA. As a scholar of ancient Christianity, particularly in the Greek tradition, he has published broadly on early Christian history, theology, and exegesis. His first book, *Providence and Narrative in the Theology of John Chrysostom*, is forthcoming with Cambridge University Press.

Lillian I. Larsen did her doctoral work at Columbia University/Union Theological Seminary. She is presently a faculty member at the University of Redlands in Southern California. As Professor of Christianity and Crawford Chair of Religious Studies, she teaches courses in Christian Origins, Greek Language, Christian History and Comparative Religions. In complementary work, her research examines monastic sayings, stories, and material records, in light of ancient pedagogy. Published articles, a co-edited volume, *Monastic Education in Late Antiquity* (CUP 2108), and her current book project, 'On Learning a New Alphabet', have effectively re-scaffolded the missing chapter that is the history of monastic (and derivatively Christian), education.

Daniel Picus (PhD, Brown University) is a scholar of religion, and particularly rabbinic Judaism. He is assistant professor in the department of Global Humanities and Religions at Western Washington University, and has held postdoctoral fellowships at the University of Michigan and Carleton College. He writes on textuality and materiality in late antique religion, and is interested in knowledge that is transmitted in unexpected ways. He is also an associate editor of the Ancient Jew Review.

Nicola Reggiani is Research Fellow of Papyrology at the University of Parma. His main research interests currently focus on the materiality of the Greek papyri, the Greek medical papyri, and Digital Papyrology (digital encoding and digital critical edition of Greek documentary, literary, and paraliterary papyri). Among his most recent works: *Papirologia. La cultura scrittoria dell'Egitto greco-romano*, Parma 2019; *La papirologia digitale. Prospettiva storico-critica e sviluppi metodologici*, Parma 2019; *I papiri greco-egizi ed Erodoto. Per un percorso diacronico e interculturale*, Parma 2021.

Courtney Roby is Associate Professor in the Department of Classics at Cornell University. Her work focuses on the cognitive and literary aspects of ancient Greco-Roman texts on scientific and technical topics. Her books include *Technical Ekphrasis in Greek and Roman Science and Literature: The Written Machine Between Alexandria and Rome* (Cambridge University Press, 2016), and *The Mechanical Tradition of Hero of Alexandria: Strategies of Reading from Antiquity to the Early Modern Period* (Cambridge University Press, forthcoming).

Rebecca Stephens Falcasantos, Assistant Professor of Religion, Amherst College. Her research focuses on the intersection of religious practice, the formation of ritualized bodies, and contestations over cultural dominance in the late Roman east. She is the author of *Constantinople: Ritual, Violence, and Memory in the Making of a Christian Imperial Capital* (University of California Press, 2020), as well as articles on late antique pilgrimage, religiously motivated violence, and ritual habits. Her current project explores the work and reception of Socrates of Constantinople.

General Index

Aaron 39–40
Acerbi, Fabio 172
Adrian the Exegete 259
Aelian 23
Aeneas of Gaza 84, 99, 100
Aetius, doxographer 87
Aetius, medical writer 151
Aëtius, teacher of Eunomius 109
Agati, Maria Luisa 118
Agelius, Novatian bishop 125
Alamanni, military campaign 197
Alexander the Great 227
Alexander, bishop of Constantinople 110
Alexandria 83, 87, 100, 101, 110, 112, 114, 115, 122, 268
– bishops 117
– episcopacy of 109, 114, 121, 155
– iatrosophists 143
– medical school 8
– monasteries 99, 100
Alexandrian majuscule 145
Alexandrian philology 143
Alexandrian scholarship 143
Amirav, Hagit 259
Ammonius, philosopher 100, 101, 269
Amsler, Monika 20, 22
Anaximander 91
Antinoupolis 143–144, 145
Antioch 257, 258
– clergy 259
– school in 258
– Synod of 109, 121, 123
Antiochene school (exegetical) 259
Antiochenes 259
Antony 221, 223–224, 228, 229
Apollonius, mathematician 157
Aramaic 73, 192, 204
– literature 53
– pedagogy 32
– poetry 196
Archimedes 155, 157, 172, 173
– manuscript tradition 161
Arethas, patron 118
Arian ursurpations 109

Arianism 115, 122
Arianizers 18, 105, 107, 108, 110, 112, 114, 116–117, 125, 126
clergy 116
Arians 122
Ariminum, Synod of 109
Aristotle 94, 99, 100, 227
Arius 109, 113–114, 116, 117
Ark of the Covenant 37
Arsenius 221–24, 228, 229, 252
Artaxerxes, King 137
Asper, Markus 155
Athanasius 18, 107, 108, 109–110, 110, 112, 113, 115, 116, 122, 123, 124–125, 126, 127
Athenaeus 13, 201
Augustamnica I (Roman province) 86
Augustine 206
Aulus Gellius 196, 199, 205, 212
Ausonius 189, 196–198, 201, 205, 208
Auxanon, Novatian 125
Babylonia 45, 50, 203, 209
Babylonian Exile 34, 36
Babylonian Talmud 4, 8, 9, 12, 43, 45–51, 189–190
– Mishnah and 45
– numerical maxims 190–195
– tractates 14
Bagnall, Roger S. 155, 158, 164, 165, 171, 178, 182, 276
Baillet, Jules 163
Barnes, Timothy D. 112
Barry, Jennifer 114, 115
Baruch 34, 38
Basil of Caesarea 91, 225–226, 227, 228, 229, 231, 236, 243, 248, 249, 250
Bavli see Babylonian Talmud
Becker, Adam 258
Beni Hasan 235, 237, 240, 242
Berliner Schlüssel (Berlin Key) 1–2, 4
Berytus 100
Bethlehem 227
Biblioteca Medicea Laurenziana 18
Biedenkopf-Ziehner, Anneliese 234

bishops
- Nicene 117
Boethius 207
- Cassiodorus letter to 84–85
Book of Kings 265
Book of Maccabees 265
Burrus, Virginia 115
Caesarea Maritima
Carman, Christián C. 166
Carterius 258, 270
Cassiodorus 84–85, 257–258
Chin, Michael 2
China 181
Christianity Nicene 127
Christians 88
churches
- church of Dionysius 109, 110
- Constantinople 111
- Hagia Eirene 110, 123, 126
- Hagios Akakios 112
- Novatian 111
- Novatian Anastasia church 125
Cicero 12
Cleomedes 87, 91
Conner, Elizabeth M. 17–18, 22
Constans, emperor 124
Constantine sarcophagus of 112
Constantine 106, 114
Constantinople Arians 122
Constantinople 85, 110–111, 114, 115, 122, 126, 258
- church of Dionysius 109, 110
- episcopacy of 109, 113
- episcopacy of 113
- Hagia Eirene 126
- Hagia Eirene church 110, 123
- Hagios Akakios church 112
- Novatian Anastasia church 125
- Novatian churches 111
- Novations 128
- Pelargos, suburb 125
- Sicai, suburb 125
Constantius II, emperor 110, 122, 123, 126
Coogan, Jeremiah 4, 17, 22
Coptic 239, 240
Corcoran, Simon 162

Cosmas Indicopleustes 259
Council of Nicaea 108, 115, 116
Council of Sardica 124
Covid-19 pandemic 133
Cranz, Isabel 38
Crawford, Matthew 4
Cribiore, Raffaella 159, 249–250, 263, 267
critical theories 2
Crum, W.E. 244, 248
Ctesiphon (Mahoza) 209
Cuomo, Serafina 162, 163
Cyril of Jerusalem 125
David 265
Davis, Robert B. 159, 169, 171, 175, 176, 180–182
Deichgräber, Karl M. 140
Demiurge 85, 90, 98
Democritus 91
Dicaearchus 200
Dickey, Eleanor 63
Didymus the Blind 8, 161, 268, 277
- commentaries 21, 268, 269
- school of 276
Diocaesarea 109
Diodore of Tarsus 21, 257, 258, 259, 261, 262, 263–266, 267, 271–272, 277–278
- commentaries 21, 260, 261, 263, 267
- curriculum 267–268
- higher interpretation 272–273
- school 270–276, 277–278
Diodorus of Sicily 196
Diogenes 242
Dionysius, church of 109, 110
Dionysius of Halicarnassus 196
Dionysius, patron 118
Dionysodorus 172
Dorotheus, doctor and deacon 92–93
Edwards, Robert 21, 22
Egypt, excavations 209
Egypt 151, 223
- Greek medical papyri 133, 134
- monasticism 228
- monks 22, 101
Egyptian mathematical papyri 162
Eleusis of Cyzicus 125
Enaton 101

England 181
Epiphanius 67
– monastery of 231–33, 240, 241, 244–246, 247
episcopacy
– Alexandria 121
– Constantinople 113
epistemology 2–3, 85, 128
Erlwanger, Stanley H. 171,
Euclid 155, 157, 158, 159–161
Eunomians 109
Euripides 14, 88, 96, 196
Eusebius of Caesarea 2, 4, 17, 22, 57, 61, 67, 68–71, 71, 72, 73, 75, 76, 91, 110, 119, 123, 124, 126
Eusebius of Emesa 109, 259, 266, 269
commentaries 260, 277
Eusebius of Nicomedia 114, 122
Evagrius of Pontus 221–224 228, 229, 252, 272
Evelyn White, H.G. 244, 248
Exile in Babylon 34
Ezekiel 30, 30–31, 34–36, 42
Book of 29
fable 190
Falcasantos, Rebecca Stephens 12, 18, 22
Flavian, bishop 270
florilegia 101
Fowler, David 159, 185
Gabriel Qatraya 206
Galen 93–99, 99, 137, 144
Gallus 125
Gaul 122
Gaza 83, 84, 86, 87, 99
– monasteries 100
Geminus 91
Genette, Gérard 120, 134
Gennadius of Constantinople 259
Gentry, Peter 66
George of Cappadocia, Arian bishop of Alexandria 109–112, 112, 113, 114, 116, 122, 124, 126, 127
George-Macedonius cycle 118, 109–112, 123, 124
Gessner, Conrad 10–11
Gospels 2, 17, 22

graded numerical parallelism 191
Grafton, Anthony 64–65
Greek 72, 226, 239, 240, 267
Greek mathematical papyri 158
Greek medical papyri 133, 134, 151
Gregory of Nazianzus 157
Gregory, Arian bishop of Alexandria 109–110, 112, 114, 115, 121, 122, 126, 127
Gribetz, Sarit Kattan 36
Gundobad of Burgundy 84
Gurd, Sean 14
Hagia Eirene, church 110, 123, 126
Hagios Akakios, church 112
Hansen, Günther C. 119
Harland, Philip A. 203
Harlizius-Klück, Ellen 14
Harrison, Thomas 11
Hebrew (language) 72, 73, 189, 192, 265, 266
Hebrew Bible 29, 32
Heiberg, Johan L. 156, 161, 161–162, 173–174, 176
– *Stereometrica* recension 160
Hellenizers 117
"Helping Hand" 185
Henry, W.B. 140–141
Heracles 84
Hermogenes, general 110
Hermopolis 162, 163
Hero of Alexandria 155, 156, 157, 160, 161, 162, 168, 171–172, 173, 174
– metrological works 176
Herodotus Medicus 142
Herodus Atticus 200
Hexapla 63–67, 68, 69, 72, 75, 75–76
Hezekiah 265
higher interpretation 272–273
Hippocrates 133–134, 137, 144, 151
– corpus 146
– epistles 137–138
Homer 14, 244, 261, 263
Hosius 109
Howley, Joseph 61
Hultsch, Friedrich 156, 161
Hunt, Thomas 220, 252
Hutchins, Edwin 67
Iamblichus 208

iatrosophists 143
Imhausen, Annette 163–163
Instone-Brewer, David 203
Isaiah, ascetic 99, 100
Isaiah, Book of 29
Isidore of Pelusium 17, 18, 22, 83, 85–87, 87–91, 92–93, 93–99, 99, 101
– Letters 86–87
Isidorus of Miletus 162
Israel, people of 8
Italy 258
Jackson, Christa 166–168
Jacob, Christian 13
Jeremiah 34, 38
Jerome 67, 113, 225, 226–227, 227–228, 228, 229, 231, 233, 234, 235, 239, 241, 246, 248, 275
Jewish revolt in Diocaesarea 109
Jews 88, 117
Jocasta (character in Euripides)
Johannes the deacon 87
John and Barsanuphius 86
John Chrysostom 115, 225, 227–228, 228, 229, 231, 258–259, 262, 264, 269, 271, 272, 272–73, 277
– higher interpretation 272–273
John Rufus 99–100, 100
Johnson, William 260
Jones, Alexander 155, 158, 164, 165, 171, 178, 182
Josephus 265
Joshua b. Levi 4, 10
Julius Africanus 208
Julius, bishop of Rome 110, 122–123
Junillus Africanus 258, 259
Kennedy, George 250–251
kephalaia (headings) 18, 107, 128, 118, 119–120
Kings, Book of 265
Kiperwasser, Reuven 190
Klein, Gil 202
Klepsydrion 201
Knorr-Cetina, Karin 1
knowledge construction 185–186
knowledge transmission, gendered mode 36
Knust, Jennifer 2

Krajewski, Marcus 57–58, 76
Kudlien, Fridolf 151
Laeta, mother of Paula 226–227
– Jerome's letter to 229
Larsen, Lillian I. 11, 20–21, 21, 22
Latin 226
Latour, Bruno 1, 1–2
Lave, Jean 169, 183–184
Lehoux, Daryn 2
Leibniz, Gottfried Wilhelm 11
Lessing, Gotthold Ephraim 11
Levine, Lee I. 202
Libanius 271
Lieber, Laura 196
linguistic turn 2
literature, Tannaitic 73
Locher, Alfred 10
Lucian of Samosata 13
Lundon, John 149
Maccabees, Book of 265
Macedonius of Constantinople, bishop 18, 107, 109–116, 122, 123, 124–125, 126
Maiouma 99
Manichaeans 117
Mantinium 112
– Mantinium Novatians 125
Marathonius of Nicomedia 125
Marcellus 123, 124, 126
Marganne, Marie-Hélène 142
marginal notations 107, 119
Marrou, Henri-Irénée 20, 219, 219–221, 223–225, 228–231, 236, 238–239, 242, 245–253
Martens, Peter 259
Martial 198
material turn 2
mathematical papyri Egyptian 162
mathematical papyri Greek 158
maxims 189–190
– attributed (chreia) 189
– numerical 190–195
– reminiscence (apomnemoneuma) 189
– simple (gnomai) 189
Maximus, bishop
McNamee, Kathleen 136, 143, 145
mediaeval scholia

Meletius, bishop 270
Menander 242
Metrodorus 210
metrological works 155–159, 176
Milan, Synod of 109
mimesis 8
Miriam 39–40
Mishnah 50, 73
– Babylonian Talmud and 45
mnemotechnics numerical maxims 193
Modestus, prefect 183
monasteries
– Alexandria 99, 100
– Gaza 100
Monastery of Epiphanius 231–33, 240, 241, 244–46, 247
Monasticism, Egyptian monks 22
monks, Egyptian 22
Moses 39–41, 42, 206
Myers, Carol L. 37
Myers, Eric L. 37
Nakamori, Yoshiteru 11, 22
Nestorius 117
Netz, Reviel 166
New Historicism 2
New Testament manuscripts 2
Nicander 143, 147
Nicene bishops 117
Nicene Christianity 127
Nichols, Stephen 126
Nicomedia, Synod of 109
Nikomachos of Gerasa 207
Nilus of Ancyra 86
Nisibis 258
– school of 257–258
Novatian Anastasia church 125
Novatians 111–112, 113, 126, 128
– Constantinople 128
– Mantinium 125
numerical maxims
agglutination 192–193
– Babylonian Talmud and 190–195
– lists of 10 191, 192
– lists of 3 191
– lists of 4 191
– lists of 5 191, 191–192
– lists of 6 191, 192
– lists of 7 191, 192
– lists of 8 191, 192
– mnemotechnics and 193
– purpose 193–194
Olympiodorus of Alexandria (the Deacon) 259
Optatian 15
Oribasius 142, 151
Origen of Alexandria 17, 57, 61, 63–67, 68, 69, 70, 71, 72, 73, 75–76
– commentaries 275
– *Hexapla* 63–67, 68, 69, 72, 75, 75–76
ostraca 8, 15
Oxyrhynchus 137, 138, 158
P. Math. 19, 155, 158, 159, 163–165, 168, 170, 171, 173–179, 181–185
Pachomius 225, 228, 231, 239–240, 241–242, 242
Paeonius 85
paideia 32, 83, 87
Palestinian Talmud 195
– rabbis of 47, 61, 71–75
Palladius 115
papyrus 8, 15, 18
– Egyptian mathematical 162
– Greek medical 133, 134
– medical 19
Paralius, fellow student of Zacharias 101
Paralius, student of Zacharias
Pasternak, Ariel-Ram 190–191
Patrick 230, 231
Paul, Nicene bishop of Constantinople 110, 113, 122, 123, 124, 126
– expulsion 123
Paula 226–227, 241
Pelargos, suburb of Constantinople 125
Pelusium 86
Pentateuch 43, 44
– Pentateuch, on Torah scroll 72
Persia 137
– interior furnishing 203
Peter the Iberian 99, 100
Petronius 198
Philip, prefect 123
Philippopolis, Synod of 124
Philo of Alexandria 206, 263
Philoponos 207

Philostratus 200
Phoenicia 100
Photinus 126
Picus, Daniel 16–17, 22
Plato 88, 95, 97, 98, 99, 100, 159, 206
Pliny the Elder 10, 12
Plotinus 99, 100, 269
Poch, Apryl 166
Polybius 196
Polychronius of Apamea 259
Porphyry 269
Posidonius of Apamea 87
Procopius of Caesarea 84
Procopius of Gaza 84, 101
– commentary on Genesis 101
progymnasmata 189
proof in an inquiry (thesis) 190
Prosechius, letter recipient 95, 96
Psalms, Book of 265
Pseudo-Martyrius 115
Pseudo-Plutarch 91
Pumbedita, town 209
Pythagoras 206
Quintilian 21, 236, 242–243, 263, 265
Rabbi Aibo 44
Rabbi Elazar 211
Rabbi Ishmael 211
Rabbi Jose the Galilean 207
Rabbi Oshaya 52–53
Rabbi Yohanan 211
Rabbi Yose 40
rabbis of Palestinian Talmud 47, 61, 71–75
Rappe, Sara 251–252
Rav Hisda 47
Rav Pappa 211
Reay, Brendon 60
Reed, Annette 53
Reggiani, Nicola 18–19
Riggsby, Andrew 4, 23, 62, 66
Roberts, Michael 13
Roby, Courtney Ann 19–20, 22, 62
Roman Empire 2, 10, 31
Rosnick-Clement phenomenon 181
Rottländer, Rolf 10
Rufinus 112, 113
Sabinus, supporter of Macedonius 110

Sardica, Council of 124
Satan 116
Saturnalia, Roman festival 198
Schäublin, Christoph 261–262
Scheuermann, Amy 166, 166–168
Schironi, Francesca 66
scholia, mediaeval 144
scholia, see also marginal notations 128
scholia 128
schools
– Alexandria 8
– medical 8
– Nisibis 257–258
scroll Sotah 50
Seleucia, Synod of 109
Septuagint 37
Severus of Antioch 100
Sicai, suburb of Constantinople 125
Sirmium, Synod of 109, 123
Smyly, J. Gilbart 163
Smyrnaeus 91
Socrates 12, 95
Socrates of Constantinople 18, 22, 105, 105–119, 124–128, 258, 260
Solomon's Temple 37, 45
Sorabji, Richard 100, 101
Sotah ritual 36, 38
Sotah scroll 50
Sozomen 124, 258
Stefaniw, Blossom 268
Stephanus of Athens 146
Stereometrica, Heiberg recension 155, 156, 158, 160–162, 173, 175, 176, 177, 180, 183, 184, 186
subtitles 128
Suda 200
Sura, town 209
Symmachus 205, 265
Symmachus, recipient of Ausonius riddle 205
Symphosius 197–198, 199–200
Synesius of Cyrene 85
Synod
– Antioch 109, 121
– Antioch (seventh) 123
– Ariminum 109
– Milan 109

– Nicomedia 109
– Philippopolis 124
– Seleucia 109
– Sirmium 109, 123
Syriac (language) 265
Syrian Antioch See Antioch
tablets, wooden 8, 15
Taisbak, Christian M. 185
tannaim 42
Tannaitic literature 73
Tawatha 86
Temple 51
– Jerusalem 44
– Solomon 37, 45
Tent of Meeting
ter Haar Romeny, R. B. 266–67, 269
Tetrapla 65, 67
Thebes 231, 247
Theodore of Mopsuestia 257, 258–259, 260, 261, 263, 263–266, 267, 271, 272, 277
– commentaries 260, 263, 267
Theodoret of Cyrrhus 91, 258, 269, 262, 271–272, 277
Theognis of Nicaea 114
Theon 91
theories of thingness 2
Too, Yun Lee 251

Torah 6, 45–51
Towner, Wayne S. 190–91
Tragedians 263
Tuchman, Barbara 24
Ursacius 122, 126
Usener, Hermann 266
Valens 122, 126
Van Garderen, Delinda 166, 166–168, 168
Varro 23, 205–206
Vetranio 125
Vidas, Moulie 71–72
Vitrac, Bernard 156–157, 161, 172
Vitruvius 87
Wasserman, Mira Beth 13
Watts, Edward 100
Wellmon, Chad 60
Williams, Megan 64–65
Wimbush, Vincent 219, 251
Wolfenbüttel 11
Woolgar, Steve 1
Yona, Shamir 190–191
Young, Frances 261, 263, 265, 267
Zacharias Scholasticus 99, 100, 101
Zechariah 30, 30–31, 36–38
– scroll 43, 44, 45
– vision (of the scroll) 44

Index Locorum

Adrian the Exegete
Introduction to the
Divine Scriptures 259

Aelius Theon
3.96   189

Aeneas of Gaza
Letters
25   84
29   84
Theophrastus   100

Anonymous
Treatise on acute diseases   141

Apophthegmata Patrum   190

Apophthegmata Patrum (Alphabetic) 222
Arsenius 5   222
Arsenius 6   223, 235

Apophthegmata Patrum (Systematic) 222
7.27   224
10.5   222
10.20   224

Archimedes
Method   172, 173

Aristotle
Nicomachean Ethics
1161a30–b6   61

Arrian
Discourses of Epictetus   74

Athanasius
Apologia contra Arianos
3–20   112
Apologia de fuga sua
3   113
7   116
20   112
24   112
25   112
33   112
De synodes Arimini in Italia et
Seleuciae in Isauria
22–23   112
De synodis
26   124
Encyclical Letter to All Bishops 115
3.3   112
7   114
Historia Arianorum
7   113
11.1   112
Life of Antony   252
1   221, 223–224
55   224

Athenaeus
The Learned Banqueters   13

Augustine
De doctrina christiana
2.16.25   206

Aulus Gellius
Attic Nights   205
Praef. 10   212
3.10.1–17   206
18.2.1–6   199

Ausonius
Riddle of the
Number Three   189, 196–197, 205
prol.   197
4–6   197

Babylonian Talmud 8, 43, 45–51, 189–190

Berakhot   193
3a   191
7a   191
10a   191

10b	192	**Hagigah**	
43b	192	12a	192
44b	192	13a	192
51a	192	16a	192
57b	192		
12b	192	**Eruvin**	47
17b	212	14a	209
27a	192	17a	191
42a	191	21	47–48
44b	192–194	21a	45
50b	191	53a	54
51a	191, 192	87b	191
54b	191		
55a	20, 191, 192	**Pesahim**	
56b	192	42a	191
57b	192	49b	192
62a	191	51b	212
		54a	192
Shabbat	7	54b	192
23a	191	55a	212
34a	191	56a	192
75b	191	55b	192
66b	203	76b	192
77a	192	77b	192
81a	192	89b	210
87a	191	109a/b	209
109b–110b	9	111a	191
118b–119a	203	112a	192
119a	9	112b	191
127a	192	113a	191
129b	191	113a/b	201
129b	206	113b	192
151b	203	116b	191
156a	7–8	118a	192
156a–b	206		
156b	9	**Yoma**	
		9b	191
Ta'anit		18a	192
26a	192	21b	192
28b	192	22a/b	193
29b	212	23a	192
		69b	198
Mo'ed Qatan		83b	192
18a	191	84a	191
Megillah	191	**Sukkah**	
		29a	191

Betzah
3b	192
11b	191
15b	191
21b	191
23a	191
32b	192
39a	191

Rosh Hashanah
16b	191
18b	191

Yevamot
16a	191
62a	191
81b	192

Ketubot
10b	191
39a	191
42a	191
109a	192

Nedarim
	191, 192
39b	192

Nazir
	191, 192
8b	209
52a	192

Sotah
15a	192
25a	191
42b	191

Gittin
	45, 192
6b	191
28b	191
55a	203
60a	45, 45–46, 46–47
68b–69b	9
69b	209
70a	20, 191, 192, 192–193, 196, 203
70b	192

Qiddushin
82a	192

Bava Qamma
4a	191
4b	191
26a	191
26b	191
53b	191
55b	191
82a	20, 192
82b	192
83b	192
84a	191
85a	192
91a	192

Bava Metzia
	191
32b	212
84b	211
86a	198

Bava Batra
10a	192
145a	192
147a	191
164b	209

Sanhedrin
11b	191
37b	191
26a	198
64a	198
88a	191
96b	198

Makkot
19a	191
23a	191

Shevu'ot
8a	192

Avodah Zarah
	13
9b	210
17b	192

28a–29a	9	**Tamid**	191, 192
29a	192	31b	192
Horayot		**Niddah**	
13b	192, 198	8a	191
		16b	191
Zevahim		17a	191
2b	192	51a	191
46b	192		
64a	191	**Barḥadbšabba**	
72b	192	*Cause*	274
Menahot		**Basil of Caesarea**	
29a	191	*Homilies on the Hexaemeron*	
51b	192	9.1.480.10–16	91
71a	192	*Homilia in illud:*	
73b	192	*"Attende tibi ipsi"*	249
104a	192	*Longer Rule (Reg. Fus.)*	225–226, 229
		15	225–226, 236, 240, 243, 244, 246
Hullin			
104b.	192		
Bekhorot		**Bible**	
8b	198	**Hebrew Bible/Old Testament**	
54	193	Genesis	270
42a	193	1:1	51, 52
46a	203	1:1–5	64
46b–47a	203		
54b	193	Exodus	40, 41
60a	209	33	40
62a	193	33:17–23	39
70a	193	33:23	41
Arakhin		Leviticus	43
16a	192	5:1	43, 44
32b	192		
		Numbers	
Temurah		5	34, 36, 37, 38
28b	192	12:6	39
		12:6–8	39
Keritot	191, 192	12:8	40
16a	192		
26a	192	Deuteronomy	
		17	34
Me'ilah	191, 192	28	46
15b	191	27–28	38

Index Locorum

1 Kings	37	3:3	30, 31
		7:26	42, 48
Job	48	32:16	42, 48
11:9	48		
		Joel	
Psalms	43, 264, 270, 273	4:13	37
2	264		
3	264	**Zechariah**	37, 45, 49, 50, 54
31:11	192	5	33–34, 38, 43
34:2	264	5:1	16, 43
38:11	192	5:1–4	29, 36–38
77.23	90	5:2	44, 46, 49
91:5–6	213	5:3	30, 31, 44
92	42	5:3–4	37
92:4	42		
92:48	42	**Bible, New Testament**	
102:24	192	**Matthew**	
118:89	90	10:28	98
119:96	47–48		
		Luke	
Proverbs	43, 53	12:24	98
8	51		
8:22	52	**John**	
8:27	51	4:7	90
8:30	51	4:8	90
13:7	248		
13:13	248	**Jude**	
30:18–20	191	1:12–13	87
		13	87
Isaiah	29		
4:10	49	**Cassiodorus**	
6:5–7	36	*Institutiones*	
6:6	44	praef. 1	257
45:12	90	*Letters*	
		1.45	84–85
Jeremiah			
36	34	**Cicero**	
38:2–4	38	*De oratore*	
		2.354	12
Ezekiel	29, 34, 37, 41, 48, 49, 50, 54		
		Dicaearchus	
2:10	41, 42, 49	*On Musical Contests*	200
1	40		
2	34, 41, 43	**Didymus the Blind**	
2–3	33–34, 38, 39, 40	*Commentary on Ecclesiastes*	268
2:8–3:3	16, 29, 34–36	*Commentary on the Psalms*	268
3	40		

Diodore of Tarsus

Commentary on the Octateuch	262
Commentary on the Psalms	21, 262, 263–266, 272–273
pr.	277
pr.1	275
2.3	264
2.5	264
3.5	264
5.pr	277–278
5.11a	264
7.13–14a	264
9.1	272
21.21	265
32.4	266
34.2	264
37.18	264
118	272
15.11c	272
23.10b	272
25.1b	264
26.6a	265
26.12b	266
32.14a	264
34.3b	264
42.1b	264

Dionysodorus

On the torus [lost]	172

Epiphanius

On Weights and Measures (Mens.)

7 [Syr. 50c–d]	64

Panarion (Pan.)

64.1.1–2	65
64.3.4	67
64.3.5–7	64
64.3.6	64

Euclid

Elements	158, 159
I.47	160
III.1	160

Euripides

Alcestis	96
fragments	
853	196
906	196
907	196
Phoenician Women	
546	88

Eusebius of Caesarea

Chronography	68
Chronological Tables	17, 22, 68–69, 69, 70, 72, 75–76
Ecclesiastical History	118
6.16.1–4	64
6.16.2–3	64
6.18.1–2	67
6.18.2–4	65
6.22.1	62
6.23.1–2	67
6.36.1	67
7.32.14–19	62
Gospel canons	69–70, 72, 74–75, 75–76
Martyrs of Palestine	118
Onomasticon	68
Preparation for the Gospel	70
15	91
Psalms Pinax	68

Facundus of Hermiane

Pro defensione

3.6	273

Gabriel Qatraya

Commentary on the Liturgical Offices	206–207

Galen

On the Composition of Drugs according to Kind (Comp. med. gen.) 147

De placitis Platonis et Hippocratis

1.II	93, 94

The Faculties of the Soul Follow the Mixtures of the Body (QAM) 93, 94

774	94
775	95, 97
776	97

778	96	IV 1	144
774–775	95–95, 95	IV 4	144
811–812	98	IV 5	144
		V 43–68	139

Genesis Rabbah 52, 53
1:1 51, 52

Articulations (*Artic.*) 145
Epidemics (*Epid.*)
III 3, 16, 1–4   134
Female diseases (*Mul.*)   151

Gnomai of the Council of Nicaea 190

I 1, 8–14   138
II 200–201   151
Prognostic (*Progn.*)   141

Gregory of Nazianzus
De theologia
25   157

Hippocrates (pseudo)

Gregory of Nyssa
Life of Macrina
962D   225

Epistles	140
3	137–138
4	137–138
4a	137–138
5	137–138
6	137–138
6a	137–138

Hero of Alexandria

De mensuris	161
Geodaisia	156
Geometrica	156, 161
Metrica	156, 157, 159–160, 171, 172, 174, 184
II.12	171–172
II.13	172
II.14	173
II.15	172
Stereometrica	155, 156, 158–162, 173–177, 180, 183–184
2	160–161
2.28–44	176
2.28–45	173
2.37	174

Homer
Iliad
1.22   244
1.201   244

Iamblicus
Theologia Arithmetica
35.6ff   208

Isidore of Pelusium

Letters	85–86
2.273	91, 95
2.282	86
2.286	86
1435	87–90, 95
1475	92
1791	93–98

Herodotus Medicus
De remediis   142

Hippocrates

Regimen in Acute Diseases (*Acut.*)	24–27
Nutriment (*Alim.*)	140
Aphorisms (*Aph.*)	140, 144, 145
I 1–3	145
I 2	145
I 3	146
III 24	144
III 27	144

Jerome
Chronicon

324 (317f–i)	113
342 (317h–i)	113
359 (323h)	113

Commentary on Titus
3.9   64
Epistle to Laeta   226–227, 229

Epistles
43.1   67
102   64
107   225, 226, 227, 231
107.4   231, 233, 234, 235,
             240, 241
On Illustrious Men (Vir. ill.)
61.3   67
56   67
73   62
54   64
54   65

John Chrysostom
*Against Opponents
of the Monastic Life* 227, 229
III   225
III 11–13   228, 229
III 17–18.   227
Commentary on the Psalms 273
9.3   273

John Climacus
Ladder of Divine Ascent 224

John Rufus
Plerophories 100
13   100
14   100
57   100
38   100
77   100
78   100

Julius Africanus
Cesti
24–25   208

Justinian
Three Chapters 273

Leviticus Rabbah 43, 51
6:3   43–45

Libanius
Orations
31   274

Life of Patrick
II   230

Lucian of Samosata
On Salaried Posts
27   199
True Story 13

Macrobius,
Dream of Scipio 206
Saturnalia
VI.12   212

Manuscripts
Cairo Genizah   64, 193
Cambridge, University Library,
Taylor-Schechter 12.182   64
Codex Seragliensis G.I.1   173
Florence, Biblioteca Medicea
Laurenziana, Plutei 70.7   18, 105, 107,
                             117–119, 121,
                             127–28
Milan, MS Ambrosianus
B. 106. sup. (Rahlfs 113)   64
Milan, MS Ambrosianus
O. 39 sup.   64
Munich, [Hebr.] 95   192, 193, 194
Oxford, Bodleian Library,
Auct. D. 4. 1   68
Paris, Suppl. Gr. 446   145
Rome, Vat. Barb.
gr. 549 (Rahlfs 86)   64
Rome, Vat.
gr. 1747 (Rahlfs 271)   64

Martial
Epigrams
5.20   211–212
13, 14   198
14.8–9   10

Midrash Ma'asseh
Ḥuppat Eliyahu
(The Canopy of Elijah)   193
Midrash Shloshah ve-'arba'
(Midrash of 'Three and Four') 193
Pirqe Rabbenu Ha-Qaddosh

(Lectures of Our Holy Teacher) 193, 208

Mishnah
Eruvin
2:1	47
Sotah
2:3	74
2:3–4	50

Avot	190, 208

Me'ilah
4:2	191

Nicander
Theriaka	143, 147
344	143

Nichomachus
Introduction to Arithmetic	161

Oribasius
Medical Collections 151
V 30,6–7	142

Origen
Commentary on Matthew
15.14	64
Epistle to Julius Africanus
1–5	64
6–7	72
Epistle to Gregory
1	65
Hexapla	63–67, 68, 69, 72, 75, 75–76
Philocalia	89
26.8	89
19–20	90
26.8.9	89

Ostraca
AM 21 (C.O. 16)	235
Cairo 44674,118	248
O.BM. Inv 19082	232
O.BM. Inv 18816	232
O.BM. Inv 18798	232
O.BM. Inv 18972	232

O.Col. Inv. 766	249
O.MMA. 12.180.107	231–232
O.MMA. 14.1.139	244
O.MMA. 14.1.140	244
O.MMA. 14.1.188	232–233
O.MMA. 14.1.210	245
O.MMA. 14.1.549	214
O.MMA. 14.1.549	240

Pachomius
Praecepta	225, 228, 229, 236
138–139	231, 240
139	228, 240, 241–242, 244
140	228

Palatine (Greek) Anthology	210

Palestinian Talmud
Orlah
1:1, 60d	73

Pe'ah
7:5, 20b	73
7:6, 20	73

Palestinian Talmud 61, 71–75, 75–76, 195
Demai
3:4, 23c	73

Kil'ayim
1:1, 27a	74, 195

Ma'aserot
2:4, 49d	74

Megillah
1:8, 71d	72

Shabbat
12:5, 13d	73

Gittin
3:2, 44d	72
9:6, 50c	72

Bava Batra
10:1, 17c   72

Shevu'ot
9:9, 39a   73

Palladius
Dialogue on the life of John Chrysostom
9.196–205   115

Papyri
BM 10399	162
BM 10520	162
BM 10794	162Carlsberg
30	162
Griffith I E7	162
Heidelberg 663	162
Michigan Medical Codex	139, 147, 148, 150
P.Amh. Gr. I.3c (Rahlfs 912; LDAB 3475)	64
P.Ant. I 28	144
P.Ant. I 28	145
P.Ant. II 64	146
P.Ant. II 86, fr. A	139
P.Ant. III 125	147
P.Ant. III 126	150
P.Ant. III 126	151
P.Ant. III 183	144
P.Ant. III 183	146
P.Ant. III 184	143
P.Ant. III 186	147
P.Berl.Möller 13	148
P.Berol. 11632	61
P.Cair. [inv.] 10758	163
P.Cair. cat 19758	182
P.Cairo	162, 163
P.Corn. inv. 69	164
P.Dub. 1, 32	140
P.Eirene III 25, 3	142
P.Köln. I 19	145
P.Köln. I 19, 19	140
P.Köln. V 206r	147
P.Math.	19, 155, 158–159, 163–164, 168, 170–185
P.Mich. Inv. 926	238
P.Mich. Inv. 4966	163
P.Mich. XVII 758	150
P.Oxy. VIII 1088	149
P.Oxy. IX 1184	137–138, 139, 140
P.Oxy. LVI 3851	142
P.Oxy. LXXIV 4969	144
P.Oxy. LXXIV 4977	149, 149–150
P.Oxy. LXXX 5220 (1), 17	140
P.Oxy. LXXX 5221	138, 139
P.Oxy. LXXX 5223	141
P.Oxy. LXXX 5224	141
P.Oxy. LXXX 5233	141
P.Oxy. LXXX 5240 (1), 2	140–141
P.Oxy. LXXX 5247	146
P.Oxy. XIX 2221r	147
P.Ryl. I 56v	138
P.Ryl. III 531	151
P.Strasb. inv. 1187	140
P.Tebt. II 272v	142
PSI Congr.XXI 3v	149

Petronius
56.7–10   198

Philo
On Dreams
1.21   90
On Special Laws
4.18   206

Philostratus
Lives of the Sophists
2.10, 585–586   200

Plato
Laws
674a–b   98
810e–812a   243
Republic   159
Timaeus
28c   88

Pliny the Elder
Natural History   10, 12–13
35, 2.11   205

13.77–78	38	1.1.30–31	226
		1.1.30–35	226
Plutarch		1.1.31	236, 239
De liberis educandis		1.1.31–32	243
4C	243	1.1.34–35	239
		1.1.35	246
Porphyry		1.1.35–36	244
Life of Plotinus		1.1.36	243, 244
14.10–18	269	1.1.4	226

Procopius of Gaza
Commentary on Genesis 101

Rufinus
Apology
II, 8   227
Ecclesiastical History
10.28   113
Inquiry about the Monks of Egypt (Hist. Mon.)
332–333   227

Pseudo-Anatolius
De ratione paschali 62

Pseudo-Gregory
Oratio panegyrica
8   65

Pseudo Isocrates
Ad Demonicum
12   243

Scholia on Aristophanes
Wasps
1222   200

Sifre Numbers   39, 49
103:1   39–43, 50

Pseudo-Martyrius
Funeral Oration in Praise of John Chrysostom
93   115

Socrates of Constantinople
Ecclesiastical History   12, 16, 18, 105–107, 113, 258

Pseudo-Plutarch
Placita philosophorum   90, 91

1	108, 113, 127–128
1–3	119
1.6	114
1.4.6	113
1.6.31	114
1.8.28	113
1.9.28	113
1.38.8–9	114
2	105, 107, 108–120, 125
2.1	109, 112, 119
2.10	119, 121
2.11	109, 114, 121, 122
2.13	122
2.14	114
2.15	112, 114
2.16	114
2.17	112

Ptolemy
Geography
2.1.3   63
Handy Tables   62
Harmonica
III.3.64–71   23

Quintilian
Institutio Oratoria   225
1.1.1–37   226
1.1.25   231, 234, 235
1.1.26   231
1.1.27   226, 233
1.1.27–28   231
1.1.28   233

2.18	123	2.27.4–7	115
2.2	114	2.27–28	109, 118, 124
2.21	118, 123, 124	2.28.3–14	121
2.22	121	2.28.4–11	111
2.23	110, 121	2.28.10	125
2.27	110, 124	2.28.12	116
2.28	110, 112, 124, 125	2.28.21–22	125
2.30	109	2.29–20	109
2.31	109	2.31.3	115
2.32	109	2.33–34	109
2.37	109	2.35.4	114
2.38	109, 110, 111, 118, 124	2.36–37	109
2.4	70	2.38.5–9	111
2.40	121	2.38.9	125
2.42	112	2.38.11	113
2.10.2	121	2.38.29–32	112
2.10.21–22	122	2.38.40–42	112
2.10–11	112	2.38.40–43	114
2.10–21	109, 1182.11.3122	2.39.8	113
2.12.4	122	2.39–41	109
2.12.5	114	2.40.44–45	126
2.12–15	110	2.41.18–23	126
2.15.8	113, 123	2.45.9	125
2.16.13	123	3.2	112
2.16.3	123	3.10.11	113
2.16.6	123	3.25.19	113
2.17.3	123	3.38.5–43	115
2.17.9–10	113	4.12.41	113
2.17–21	110	4.22.1	113
2.18.3	124	4–7	119
2.18–20	109, 123	5. pref. 2–3	108
2.19.20–22	124	6.3.6–7	258
2.2.4	114	7	117
2.2.5	114	7.3	118
2.8	109	7.6	118
2.8.5	114	20.5	124
2.10	109	38	125
2.20.5	113		
2.20.8–9	124	**Sozomen**	
2.20.13	124	*Ecclesiastical History*	
2.21.3	121	3.11	124
2.21.7–12	121	4.17	124
2.23.49–58	122	8.2.5–6	258
2.25.4	114		
2.26.5	126	**Stephanus of Athens**	
2.27.1	110	*In Hippocratis Aphorismos* 146	
2.27.4	110		

Stobaeus
Eclogae physicae 90

Suda 91, 200

Suetonius
Vita divi Augusti
74 199

Symphosius
Aenigmata (*Riddles*) 197, 199–200

Synesius of Cyrene
To Paeonius concerning the gift of an astrolabe
4.1 85

Tablets
T.Mich. inv. 763 238
T.Mich. inv. N. 765 238, 239

Theodore of Mopsuestia
Commentary on John 275
pr. 275

Theodore of Mopsuestia
Commentary on the Psalms 263–266, 273
34.8a 265

34.13b 265
34.26b 264fr. 273

Theodoret of Cyrrhus
Curatio affectionum Graecarum
4.24 91
Ecclesiastical History
4.25.4 259, 271
5.39 259, 271

Thomas of Marga
Book of Governors
I 74.3–10 229
I 75.1–14 229

Varro
Hebdomades 205
On the Latin Language
10.22 23
On the Beginnings of Numbers 205

Zacharias Scholasticus
Ammonius 100
Life of Isaiah
8 99, 100
Life of Peter the Iberian
114 100
Life of Severus 100

www.ingramcontent.com/pod-product-compliance
Lightning Source LLC
Chambersburg PA
CBHW050515170426
43201CB00013B/1970